DATE DUE

DAGGERS AND JAVELINS

DAGGERS AND JAVELINS

Essays, 1974-1979

AMIRI BARAKA

QUILL
NEW YORK 1984

Library of Congress Catalog Card Number: 84-60088

ISBN: 0-688-03431-4
ISBN: 0-688-03432-2(pbk)

Printed in the United States of America

First Quill Edition

1 2 3 4 5 6 7 8 9 10

BOOK DESIGN BY ELLEN LO GIUDICE

"Afro American Literature and Class Struggle" was previously published in *Black American Literature Forum*, Spring 1980 issue, copyright © 1984 by Amiri Baraka.

"Ngugi and Modern African Writing" was previously published in *The Literary Review*.

"A Reply to Saunders Redding" was previously published in *Journal of American Studies*, Summer 1979 issue, copyright © 1984 by Amiri Baraka.

Grateful acknowledgment is made for permission to reprint the following:

"Black Liberation/Socialist Revolution," Revised, and "National Liberation Movements" from *Selected Plays and Prose of Amiri Baraka/LeRoi Jones;* copyright © 1979 by Amiri Baraka. By permission of William Morrow and Company, Inc.

The poem on page 189, "Lynch," taken from page 69 of *Patria o Muerte: The Great Zoo and Other Poems* by Nicolás Guillén; copyright © 1972 by Robert Marquez. Reprinted by permission of Monthly Review Press.

The poem on page 164, "White Man," taken from page 5 of *Good Morning Revolution*, published by Lawrence Hill & Company, 1973; copyright 1936 by Langston Hughes. Reprinted by permission of Harold Ober Associates Incorporated.

Vincent D. Smith, the noted painter, has exhibited internationally. He has been the recipient of many awards and grants. He has done mural commissions for the Board of Education and the Human Resources Administration and is in many private and public collections, including the Museum of Modern Art, Newark Museum, the Brooklyn Museum, and Chase Manhattan Bank.

Mr. Smith is listed in *Who's Who in American Art, 1978.*

for Amina
& the brothers & sisters
of CAP
& the comrades
of RCL (M-L-M)

Contents

Introduction

Some of these pieces are essays, others magazine articles; still others are speeches. There are a few which were originally notes for lectures at various universities, that I later expanded. Some of these pieces have never been published (some even after being commissioned); some others are reprints.

There is some variation in the topics, but there is a line of ideological consistency through most of them. The essays of the earliest part of this period are overwhelmingly political in the most overt sense. Although, of course, as I said, there is a line of political analysis and discussion that runs through all of them, regardless of the subject. But they can be roughly categorized as political–literary–general culture.

Among the overtly political essays, there is one focus on the international situation (ca. 1974–1979), particularly the revolutionary struggle of African, Asian, and Latin American people (the Third World) against world imperialism and specifically against the two superpowers, the U.S. and U.S.S.R. What was somewhat different during this period than today was that the thrust of revolution was clearly a main trend throughout the world. (See "Africa, Superpower Contention, and the Danger of World War," "The Third World and People's Struggles in the 'Advanced Countries,'" "A Trip to Tokyo," "National Liberation Movements," "Only Revolution Will Transform South Africa," "African Liberation Day 1977.") Though, even during those recent years, the trend of world war was clearly discernible. The Soviet Union was on the move and sliding into places where the U.S. was getting kicked out (it still is) and the contention between the U.S. and the U.S.S.R. was sharpening daily (particularly in the Third World).

There is also, naturally enough, a domestic focus among the political essays as well. "'Clout,'" a partial analysis of the black bourgeoisie in their attempts at economic development, was commissioned by *Black Enterprise Magazine*, but the publisher rejected the article even though I got paid! "Marxism and the Black Community," "Black Liberation/Socialist Revolution," "Black Liberation Today," "Ten Years Later," "The Significance of Black History Month," "Malcolm X and Paul Robeson," "Black Solidarity," are all focused not only on the struggles particular to the African American people inside the U.S., but of American working people generally. There is also a continuously sounded note of trying to introduce Marxism-Leninism into the Black Liberation Movement. A few of these appeared as articles in *Unity and Struggle*, which was the newspaper of the Revolutionary Communist League M-L-M,* of which I was a member. (RCL was a descendant of the old Congress of African People, originally a black cultural nationalist organization, of which I was chairman. CAP, in 1974, became a Marxist-Leninist organization and in 1975 changed its name to RCL. Hence some of the insistence on Marxist-Leninist stand and viewpoint are coming from a relatively recent Marxist, with all the fervor of a recent convert.)

One important point that is made in most of these political pieces focusing on the struggle inside the U.S. is the need for a revolutionary Marxist-Leninist party. This is a constant theme running throughout these essays, since it is my opinion (and that should be obvious from reading these works) that the Communist Party U.S.A. is a revisionist party which has turned its back on revolution and socialism. In fact, one important point I seek to make in many of these essays is that the central task of Marxist-Leninists and all progressive people in the U.S. is the building of a new multinational communist party. And this is as true today as it was between 1974 and 1979.

Quite a few of the political pieces were originally speeches and as such are heavily agitational: "The Third World and People's

---

*Marxist–Leninist–Mao Tse Tung thought.

Struggles in the 'Advanced Countries,'" which was made at an international conference in Tokyo on political repression in South Korea and the need ultimately to unify North and South Korea. "Black Liberation/Socialist Revolution"; "Black Liberation Today"; "Ten Years Later"; "National Liberation Movements"; "Only Revolution Will Transform South Africa"; "Your Future and America's Future," a speech at a New Jersey high school graduation; the speech at Wesleyan in support of the student movement aimed at getting large universities to divest themselves of their South African holdings. "African Liberation Day," given in Washington, D.C., after the 1977 African Liberation Support Committee march against dying colonialism in Africa.

"The Significance of Black History Month" was a speech written and given at various universities during Black History Month. One oft-repeated theme in the essays that focus on black liberation or black history is an attempt to bring some clarity around the Afro-American National Question. I attempt to explain in a variety of ways the historical reasons for the political and economic powerlessness of the African American people, analyzing the slave trade, slavery, the Civil War, the Reconstruction, and the origins of the African American Nation in the black belt of the U.S. South. Indeed, this is one of my key themes and it is sounded in many of the essays even if they are not mainly about politics. Even the literary pieces, like "The Revolutionary Tradition in Afro-American Literature," "Langston Hughes and the Harlem Renaissance," "Black Boy as Slave Narrative," the answer to Saunders Redding, "Afro-American Literature and Class Struggle," and even the "Notes on the History," etc., make direct reference to these ideas about the development of the Afro-American Nation and black people in the U.S. as an oppressed nationality with the right to national *self-determination* in the black-belt South where some 60% of them still live in their largest area of concentration in the U.S.!

The literary essays are also obviously political. "Not Just Survival," which is principally historical notes on Afro-American drama, seeks to analyze the historical development of that drama from a frankly political, viz., a Marxist-Leninist, perspective. "The Revolutionary Tradition in Afro-American Literature" and "Afro-American Literature and Class Struggle" are very similar pieces; in fact, the latter is but a further development of the former. In these the attempt to analyze the history of black literature in the U.S. from a

11

Marxist-Leninist perspective are the basis for a book I hope to do on that literature from that perspective.

The essays on Langston Hughes, Sembene Ousmane, Richard Wright, Nicolás Guillén, and Aimé Césaire were all developed as lectures in university courses I taught at Yale and George Washington, which I still use now at SUNY Stony Brook where I am Associate Professor of Africana Studies. It is obvious to me now that such essays as these focusing on the great Pan-African writers are badly needed, since not only are black writers ignored by the racist U.S. academic establishment, but certainly Marxist criticism is important to correct the largely bourgeois-oriented criticism and "analysis" of black literature that does exist.

The writers whose works these essays analyze are especially important to me, Hughes and Wright among the greatest of the African American writers; Ousmane, not only a great writer but the most important black filmmaker in the world! Césaire, one of the shapers of the Negritude movement, which is still one of the most influential black literary movements in the world today and directly inspired by the writings of people like Hughes and Claude McKay and the Harlem Renaissance. Guillén was also heavily influenced by Hughes and the Renaissance, and he is certainly one of the best-known writers in Spanish internationally (except for the U.S.) and a writer whose works were first translated by Hughes.

Ngugi Wa Thiongo, along with Ousmane, are two of the standard bearers in Africa of an aesthetically powerful, politically committed art. Certainly the essay on Ngugi's work is meant to counter the propaganda from the western bourgeois literary establishment that the only African writers of any consequence are dull imitations of dull English bourgeois writing.

As for the essays, articles, termed general culture, "Not Just Survival" could be included in that, since it is a look at black drama and the social and cultural context of its historical development. "Notes on the History of African/Afro-American Culture" is exactly what the title outlines. It is meant to be notes; in some aspects it is merely a gloss of Engels' *Origins of the Family, Private Property and the State*, stitched together with several other relevant readings on civilization and culture in general, e.g., Woodward's *The Origin of the Human Race* and many texts on African history and culture, e.g., Jackson's *Introduction to African Civilization*, DuBois' *The World and Africa*, plus a great deal of reliance on the grand teaching instrument, *The History of the Communist Party of the Soviet Union (Bolshevik)*.

These notes were for classroom lectures, particularly for a team-taught course at Yale on black culture. The other members of that "team" were William Ferris, now head of the Center for Southern Culture at the University of Mississippi; the musician and scholar, bassist Willie Ruff; and the well-known scholar on African art and culture Robert Thompson.

Also in the category of general culture would be the article "The Me Generation," commissioned by a publication of the English Department at George Washington University, but not published; "Reply to Saunders Redding's 'The Black Revolution in American Studies,'" which was commissioned for the *American Studies Quarterly*, also based at George Washington University where I taught for one year, between September 1978 and June 1979.

The article "Howdy Doody and the Mind Bandits!" was written for New York's *Village Voice* but also rejected. It too should be included in the category general culture, but it is meant as a closer and intensely political look at the U.S. culture manipulators and czars of popular and media culture today, or at least during the reign of Howdy Doody (Jimmy Carter).

Two other important points I think should be made. I mentioned the repeated reference in the international grouping to the Soviet Union as a superpower imperialist country. Together with the United States, the two superpowers, these are the main enemies of the world's peoples. The whole question of the emergence of the Soviet Union as a social imperialist power (socialism in words, imperialism in deeds) had become agonizingly clear during that period. It has become even clearer today with support of the Ethiopian junta, propping up the junior hegemonist Vietnamese to annex great parts of Southeast Asia including Kampuchea (Cambodia) and Laos and the recent invasion of Afghanistan. But there was a great deal of contention about the assertion of their being a social imperialist country in those days; I imagine there still is.

Part of this struggle over the identity of the Soviet Union took place between many of the relatively small and relatively young soi-disant Marxist-Leninist organizations that characterized the "Anti-revisionist Marxist-Leninist Movement," i.e., the young people, including myself and the organizations I was in, who declared themselves to be the vanguard of new party-building activities after the Communist Party U.S.A. declared its revisionism (1957), i.e., that socialism could be brought in the U.S. with elections. So that many of the names of these organizations appear in a few of the articles (Revolutionary Union/Revolutionary Communist Party; October League/Communist Party (Marxist-Leninist); Puerto Rican Revolutionary Workers Organization/Revolutionary Wing; Workers Viewpoint Organization/Communist Workers Party; Revolutionary Workers League; Resistencia/League for Proletarian Revolution; Congress of African People/Revolutionary Communist League, MLM; Communist League/Communist Labor Party; Black Workers Congress.

Almost all these organizations no longer exist (ca. 1982)! The Revolutionary Union became the Revolutionary Communist Party and has now split into the RCP and Revolutionary Workers Headquarters. The old October League became the Communist Party (Marxist-Leninist). It has all but folded and is about to be absorbed by RWH. PRRWO, RWL became the Revolutionary Wing and went up in a smoke of ultra-leftism. The various stripes of the split Black Workers Congress all disappeared except one splinter called MLOC which has since taken on the unlikely name Communist Party USA-ML. WVO became the Communist Workers Party, and it has been savagely assaulted by the U.S. state, which murdered five of its cadres at Greensboro, North Carolina, in 1979! RCL, my own organization, has since merged with the League of Revolutionary Struggle, which was formed from the merging of the old I Wor Kuen, a largely Asian organization, and August Twenty-ninth Movement, a largely Chicano organization. The Communist Labor Party goes on in its fanciful ways, first way left, then way right; it is now rubbing up against the still revisionist CPUSA. LPR no longer exists.

In a sense this disorder and splitting and failure sum up the current state of the anti-revisionist communist movement, indeed of the entire Left and anti-imperialist and progressive and national movements in general. It is a deeply right-wing period we find ourselves in today. Capitalist societies the world over lurch sharply toward the right, headed by Ronald Reagan in the U.S. U.S. imperialism, to fight its arch rival the Soviet Union, has grown now openly bellicose, and while once ashamed of its warmongering now overtly preaches it as the only method of saving the world (for its own exploitation)!

These essays now might seem to some, for these last reasons, unreasonably optimistic and revolutionary. Mao said, nothing moves in a straight line, certainly not revolutionary struggle. The twists and turns and agonizing resistance which change must struggle to overcome are the brutal facts of our epoch. It has become even clearer to me today that we have only two choices, socialism or fascism. These essays like the ones I am still writing today are dedicated to the people of the world and their eventual victory and the bringing of world socialism!

AMIRI BARAKA
Manhattan Community Correctional Facility
October 1982

Only those who can kill can preserve life;
only those who know hatred can have love;
only those who want to preserve life and have love can write
literature.

—Lu Hsun (1881–1936)

Africa, Superpower Contention, and the Danger of World War

In order to understand what is going on in Africa, and indeed with the liberation struggles there, and throughout the Third World, one needs to have some understanding of the international situation. The basis of this understanding must be first an understanding, as Lenin said, that "this is the epoch of imperialism and proletarian revolution," and from that we should know that this is "the epoch of the victory of socialism and communism." Leninism "exposed the contradictions in our great epoch—the contradictions between the working class and monopoly capital, the contradictions among the imperialist countries, the contradictions between the colonial and semicolonial peoples and imperialism, and the contradictions between the socialist countries, where the proletariat has triumphed, and the imperialist countries. Leninism has therefore become our banner of victory" *(Long Live Leninism,* pp. 523–28). It is these contradictions that describe the international situation and that we must understand correctly to analyze the many partial movements, forward and backward motions—in general, "the great disorder" throughout the world that our Chinese comrades speak of. These four contradictions that Lenin laid out continue to shape and characterize our world today.

Of these four fundamental contradictions of capitalism turned to imperialism—contradictions which imperialism takes to the extremes beyond which social revolution begins—the two sharpest are imperialism versus the Third World (the developing countries of Asia, Africa, and Latin America and other regions) and the contradiction between the imperialists themselves, the sharpest and most deadly being between the superpower imperialisms of the U.S.A. and the U.S.S.R., between United States imperialism and Soviet socialist imperialism, which is socialism in name but imperialism in practice.

These two sharpest of the four fundamental contradictions are developing hourly, daily. And we must understand that these two contradictions produce two clear trends in the world today. The first is the struggle between the Third World and imperialism, which is the force driving revolution around the world. It is the main contradiction, the principal contradiction in the world today, and therefore revolution is the principal, the main trend in the world today.*

The second is the contradiction and struggle between the two superpowers, which shows itself in innumerable conflicts, now in Portugal, now in the Middle East, now in Cyprus, now in Africa. This struggle will almost invariably lead to world war. "Their intensified global rivalry for spheres of influence and world hegemony is the cause of world intranquility. But no matter how desperately they may struggle, they will not escape their ultimate doom. The people are the masters of history. The future of the world belongs to them, and it is very bright" *(PR,* no. 20, May 14, 1976, p. 7).

But even though we say that the principal trend in the world today is revolution, and we must criticize ourselves for sometimes being unclear on that and making the two trends of war and revolution equal, we must still not make the idealist, metaphysical, and subjectivist error of saying that there are not two sharp trends, that not only is revolution the main trend but, as some mistaken comrades have implied, revolution is the *only* trend. Hsueh Li says,

> It is also necessary to adhere to the theory of two points in analysing the world situation. In his solemn statement "People of the World Unite and Defeat the U.S. Aggressors and All Their Running Dogs!" issued on May 20, 1970, Chairman Mao pointed out: "The danger of a new world war still exists, and the people of all countries must get prepared. But revolution is the main trend in the world today!" "The danger of a world war" and "revolution" are the two aspects of an

---

*This was true in the mid-seventies. By the middle eighties, however, it is the contention between the superpowers that seems principal—hence the growing danger of imperialist war!

"entity"—the world situation. What are the conditions regarding these two aspects? Chairman Mao pointed out: the former "still exists" and the latter is "the main trend."

He goes on to say,

> Countries want independence, nations want liberation and the people want revolution; this has become an irresistible trend of history which shows the main trend of development in the world situation today.

> The world is changing in a direction increasingly favorable to the people of all countries. This is one aspect, a principal aspect. But we must also see the other aspect—the aggressive nature of imperialism will not change. . . . Modern war is born of imperialism. Lenin said as long as imperialism exists, there will be no tranquility in the world. The danger of a new world war still exists. This is *another trend* in the development of today's world. It is dangerous if we see only the raging flames of the revolution without noticing the enemies sharpening their swords and think we can lower our vigilance because of the excellent situation.

> To uphold the theory of two points, it is imperative to oppose the theory of one point. The latter means idealist metaphysical methodology, it means thinking in terms of absolutes and a one-sided approach to problems. . . . ["The Theory of Two Points" in his *Study Philosophy*]

In fact the very sharpening of the struggles of the peoples and nations of the Third World, intensifying and carrying the driving force of revolutionary effort, is felt around the world and causes the very confrontations between the superpowers, relentlessly increasing the danger of war. In turn as these contradictions sharpen, all the fundamental contradictions in the world today are sharpened. The struggle by the Third World peoples against imperialism, particularly that of the superpowers, is gaining momentum, as the Third World scores one victory after another. The United States is in decline, exposed before the world as a bloody-beast imperialist. It has been driven out of Southeast Asia; its lackey colonial imperialists have been beaten and driven out of Africa. At the same time, hoping to capitalize on the weakened position and the objective decline of the United States, the Soviet social imperialists screaming "peace" and "detente" like deadly con men, intensify their contention with the U.S.A. by trying to slide in the back door, peddling their neocolonial wares as soon as the U.S.A. is kicked out of the front door.

This is very clear throughout the Third World, but it is also evident in Europe. Although the Soviet Union is wide-reaching in its hegemonist and imperialist aims, Europe and its developed industrial wealth is in most instances the focus of superpower contention.

"Increasing its military threat against Western Europe has always been the Soviet Union's chief method of seeking hegemony in that part of the world. For years the Soviet Union has deployed in Europe a conventional armed force far surpassing that of the West" *(PR,* no. 11, March 12, 1976). What Schlesinger and Reagan say, as odious as they are, is in part correct, that although the Soviet Union has a gross national product only half as large as the United States', it spends roughly the same amount of money on armaments. While the leaders maintain some aspect of socialist forms, the fact is that the restoration of capitalism in the Soviet Union, and the turning of the dictatorship of the proletariat into a dictatorship of the bourgeoisie, has brought a Hitler-type fascism domestically that enables the government to centralize the production process, to maintain the nation on a totally mobilized war economy, and to pursue its social imperialist international posture. The rise of revisionism in the U.S.S.R. was the rise of the bourgeoisie and the restoration of capitalism. Bureaucratic monopoly capitalism inside the country can only be manifested internationally as social imperialism.

> Compared with the capitalist imperialist countries, state monopoly capitalism in the Soviet Union is more monopolistic by nature, has a higher degree of concentration, and exercises tighter state control. A handful of Soviet bureaucrat-monopoly capitalists assumes complete control of the country's economy and home market, bleeding the Soviet working people white at a rate of exploitation doubling that in tsarist Russia. Hence, the various sharpening contradictions in the country. Domestic monopoly will of course grow into international monopoly. As Lenin put it, "The capitalists divide the world, not out of any particular malice, but because the degree of concentration which has been reached forces them to adopt this method in order to obtain profits" *(Imperialism, the Highest Stage of Capitalism).* To obtain maximum profits the Soviet bureaucrat-monopoly capitalist class sets out to step up aggression abroad, annex new territories, expand spheres of influence, make off with other countries' raw materials at low prices, dump commodities on foreign markets, export capital, and shift its burden of crises on to others. Thus Soviet social Imperialism has become one of the world's biggest exploiters. [*PR,* no. 5, March 30, 1976, p. 10]

The Soviet Union has now stationed 500,000 men more or less permanently in Eastern Europe to cement its hegemony. And in their armed forces generally the figures have risen from 3 million men in the 1960's to 4.2 million presently, with reserves of 25 million men (International Institute for Strategic Studies, London). They have raised the number of ICBM's from 75 in 1962 to 1,618 today. The number of submarines increased during the same period from 100 to 784. The proportion of military spending taken from the national income has risen from 13.1% in 1960 to 19.6% in 1974 and is still rising. In terms of comparison with the U.S.A.,

> as present military strength stands, both now match each other in nuclear weapons . . . although the Soviet Union still remains behind the United States in total naval craft tonnage, the former has outstripped the latter in the number of vessels, particularly submarines. Moscow has less long distance bombers . . . but more combat aircraft. Soviet ground forces are now better equipped with four times as many tanks as the United States. The Soviet Union has surpassed the United States by almost 100 percent in the numerical strength of the military forces. And though the United States is generally economically stronger than the U.S.S.R. the sly line of "detente" and "materialization" of detente where the United States gives the U.S.S.R. wheat, technological know how, and equipment is simply feeding the tiger that plans on devouring you. Engaged in unbridled aggression and expansion abroad in contending for world hegemony, Soviet social Imperialism inevitably will go to war. Above all, this is determined by its social system. [*PR,* no. 8, January 30, 1976]

Three-fourths of the Soviet Union's troops are deployed in Europe. And even though Brezhnev and his clique talk about European security and have sham conferences to obscure their real designs, this nonsense they talk about peace reminds one, if we look at history, of the same smokescreen put out by Hitler fascists shortly before their *Blitzkrieg* which almost annihilated Europe four decades ago. The Soviet Union is the most dangerous of the two superpowers precisely because the U.S.A. is exposed and in decline.* Moreover the Soviet Union is armed with the signboard it carries by which it tries to disguise itself as "socialist," when it is simply an imperialist aggressor.

---

*Still true strategically, though at present (1983) the U.S. under Reagan has become more aggressive. (A.B.)

Marxism-Leninism holds that war is the continuation of politics, a social phenomenon between two peaceful periods. For the most dangerous imperialist force of aggression, all the rhetoric about peace is only an instrument in its preparation for war and this has been proved time and again by the history of the twentieth century. Before overrunning the whole of Europe, Hitler too made a big fanfare about his 13-point "peace" proposal which included a "disarmament" program. Hitler chanted the lullaby that "Germany needs peace and desires peace," but before long Europe was ravaged by the gunfire of aggression and the European people had to pay for it in blood. If we do not forget the past, we can draw lessons from it. When we hear Brezhnev and his ilk again harping on the tune of "peace" and "disarmament" at the "25th Congress," it is of immediate and realistic significance for us to review the historical lessons of the 30's. [*PR*, no. 12, March 1976]

In light of this, the revelations of the Egyptian people recently have been very educational and enlightening to the people of the world in regard to the fake claims of the Soviet Union to socialism and its real designs of imperialist hegemony and expansion. The Egyptians mention the Soviet Union's con-man line of being the "natural ally" of the Third World countries, which momentarily tricked them. But then the reality of the Soviet intention was revealed. "The Soviet Union did give Egypt some arms, but not for nothing; it sold the arms and ammunition at high prices and with an exorbitant interest rate, and it controlled the right to use them." Interested only in its contention with United States imperialism in the Middle East, the Soviet Union withheld key parts of strategic weapons. Even during the war with the Israeli Zionists the Soviet social imperialists continued to withhold the key parts. They opened military bases on Egyptian soil, and even forbade Egyptians to enter them. They gave Egypt loans at rates more exorbitant than Western capitalists. The Soviet social imperialists would never teach the Egyptians how to operate the more advanced weapons so that Egypt had to rely on Soviet technicians. And in a fit of anger after being denounced by the Egyptians, the Soviets pulled these technicians off the weapon sites. And as far as the loans they made to Egypt, the Soviets continued to harangue and harass the Egyptians for repayment no matter what the situation and how pressed Egypt was. They even told the Indians not to sell the Egyptians spare parts, in true imperialist fashion giving orders to their sidekicks. No wonder the Egyptians abrogated the so-called treaty of friendship between Egypt and the U.S.S.R. Sadat summed up such "friendship" as the kind of friendship a cat professes for a mouse. The Egyptian people would have none of it, and so they demanded that the Soviets get their hat.

This is a revelation of special importance to the Third World peoples, and particularly at this time to Africa where under the same sham banner of "socialism" and the "natural ally" of the Third World, the Soviet Union has set up shop spectacularly in Africa, particularly blatantly in Angola, after agitating a civil war between the Angolan liberation organizations. They went so far as to threaten and intimidate the O.A.U to back their development of a new neo-colonialism in Africa. The Soviets set up and made possible the slaughter of hundreds of thousand of Africans by Africans (but even more so by Cuban mercenaries) in a short period, after taking a low profile in the Angola conflict between the Angolan liberation movements and Portuguese colonialism for fourteen years. Where were the tanks, MiGs, rockets, bombs, from the Soviet Union against the Portuguese? Why only after the three Angolan liberation movements had agreed amongst themselves to administer the postcolonial Angolan state did the great push by the Soviet Union begin? Because it recognized the weakness of the United States imperialist superpower, and saw the time as right to push its thrust for hegemony. One reason why we call the Soviet Union the most dangerous of the superpowers is because it is the newcomer at the imperialist banquet and it is wildly ambitious, even daring, in its quests for a bigger share of the international pirates' booty. And this is precisely the cause of imperialist war. It is why Lenin said the content of imperialist politics is war, because the imperial powers *must* struggle to try to redivide the world. In the epoch of imperialism the world has been totally divided amongst the imperialists and so they must fight world war for its redivision. It is also why Lenin said, in *Under False Flag,* "*Present-day democracy will remain true to itself only if it joins neither one nor the other of the imperialist bourgeoisie, only if it says that the two sides are equally bad, and if it wishes the defeat of the imperialist bourgeoisie in every country. Any other decision will in reality be national-liberal and have nothing in common with genuine internationalism*" (*CW*, vol. 21, p. 144). Thus we have the problem of so-called "pan-Africanists" covering over the danger of the Soviet social imperialists—who are the main danger of war,* the setters-up of a new

---

*By the mid-eighties, Reagan's aggressiveness has, at least temporarily, made U.S. imperialism more dangerous! (A.B.)

neocolonialism—by saying that the Soviet Union's use of the Cubans, tragically like Nixon's Vietnamization or Cambodianization of the war, as a mercenary force in Africa to carry out the Soviet expansionist designs, somehow accords with proletarian internationalism (which apparently they know nothing about, except how to say it). The export of revolution has nothing to do with Marxism-Leninism, but is an idealist sham that attempts to hide a burning question that has arisen throughout the communist movement as to which class is really in power in Cuba, and that has allowed the heroic Cuban people to be made the surrogates for social-imperialist outrage against the African people!

And as for lies that the Cubans were there to fight the South Africans, let us run down a quick chronology of events in Angola that will expose that piece of imperialism and imperialist lackey B.S. for what it is!

In January 1975 about the time of the signing of the Alvor agreement on the independence of Angola, over one hundred Soviet military advisers arrived in Angola. Large consignments of arms soon followed them in March of that year. In July, four months later, the Soviet Union singlehandedly stirred up a civil war in that country. In September large groups of Cuban troops were dumped in Caxito, Northern Angola.

From September 25 to October 23, 1975, Moscow sent five shiploads of weapons and over 2400 mercenaries into the country, and in the week ending October 18 more than 750 Cuban soldiers were transported into Angola. All these facts can be found in the official records. Moscow for all its subterfuges cannot dodge the following questions: Since South Africa intruded into the land of Angola on October 23, whom were you fighting previously? Were South African forces the target of your devastating blows in the Caxito area and on the northern front in Angola? Was it the South African racists that you describe as "the reactionary forces in Angola?" Are the thousands upon thousands of people you have killed with "powerful gunfire" South Africans? Indisputable facts show that there is no denying the Soviet aggression in Angola and Africa while its talk about opposition to South African's intrusion into Angola is a sham.

There is a further question: Why did the Soviet Union and its followers cling to their statement that it was only after October 23 that they dispatched troops into Angola? The simple answer is that they urgently needed to use the South African invasion as a pretext for the extension of their own interference in Angola. The Soviet Union surreptitiously dispatched mercenaries into Angola before October 23, and after South Africa's invasion it openly went into action on a big scale. But the unbridled Soviet actions in Angola even then were directed against the Angolans and not in the least against the South African troops. After suppressing one liberation organization in early February, 1976, in Northern Angola, the Soviet Union then directed its mercenaries to launch a massive attack on another liberation organization along the Benguela railway. By January, 26 1976, the South Africans' troops had withdrawn to the border area in Southern Angola. We would like to ask the new tsars: at what time did you launch an attack on the South African troops during their stay in Southern Angola? [*PR,* no. 15, April 9, 1976, pp. 10–11]

The answer is never!

Angola is not the only place where the Soviet Union is expanding in Africa, and this is becoming well known. More and more this grim truth is being exposed very widely. And as they expand, the conflict with the United States imperialists intensifies, occasioning the first trip by a United States Secretary of State to Africa in six years! Kissinger, complete with checkbook, roamed Africa trying to stimulate some romance for United States imperialism, at the same time uttering scare phrases at the Soviet Union and its Cuban mercenaries.

The Jimmy Carter Traveling Snakeoil Show did the Kissinger One-nighters one better by enlisting one of the black bourgeoisie's activists, ex–SCLC Dr. King staffer Andy Young, to speed around Africa popping the soul handshake on the Africans and the other forces in the Third World, but principally the Africans, showing the ultimate viciousness of bourgeois nationalism, and the oppression and exploitation such nationalism can be used to obscure. But Andrew Young's line on Cuban troops in Angola is the same as Stokely Carmichael's and many of the pan-Africanists who can now be seen as social democrats and national liberals trying to clean up Soviet social imperialism. The Carmichael AAPRP principles of unity for their demonstration of African Liberation Day include a call for unity with the Soviet Union as "a socialist country." What madness. The Nazis called themselves national socialists. We must understand that an incorrect political line, like bourgeois pan-Africanism, will lead to backward, reactionary positions like becoming the Soviet Union's Andy Young.

The examples of Zaire and Ethiopia should help even further to

25

clarify the Soviet Union's real role in the Third World, and especially now in Africa. They are the tiger storming the back door, as the United States goes deeper into a decline that even the great liberalfascist Jesus Carter cannot abate. The Soviet Union has backed the Kataganese gendarmes to invade Zaire, the same bloody mercenaries that murdered Lumumba at Moise Tshombe's bidding. It is the hungry ambitious new imperialism, Soviet social imperialism, trying to roll through Africa, and in doing so, the Soviets' contention with the United States mounts by the hour. But we should also see that many of the halfstepping, petit bourgeois and national bourgeois leaders in Africa and the Third World, such as the Ethiopian junta, who must now utter some doubletalk about socialism so as to try to fool the revolutionary masses, will move to Soviet social imperialism. Since the Soviets also babble their revisionist garbage and hide behind the signboard of socialism, tyrants like the Ethiopian junta can now claim to have kicked out imperialism and to be building socialism. But in reality they will become the lackeys of the Soviet social imperialists, and try to strengthen their tottering capitalist regimes, while vainly trying to suppress the genuine revolutionaries and Marxist-Leninists.

And the Soviets stepping up their offensive, eyeing Africa like a big steak, outflank United States imperialism, and ol' Andy, by sending not one but two badwill ambassadors, Fidel Castro in one direction and the Soviet president, Podgorny, in the other, both carrying the mail for the more youthful imperialism. They are pressing for "progressive" compromise in Zimbabwe, Namibia, and Azania, while the United States openly backs the racist regimes. The Soviets want to suck these soon-to-be-liberated territories into their orbit, or to promote a no-war, no-peace agony such as goes on in the Middle East, with the blatant Soviet sellout of the Palestinian people's struggle. The Soviets' moves for compromises in these struggles fits in exactly with the halfstepping various national bourgeoisies and their various sham versions of socialism.

But in such conflict rise the very elements necessary for a new world war, which could have its initiation almost anywhere in the globe, even though the main contention is Europe. To try to thwart the drive of revolution emanating from the Third World, and the growing importance the countries of the Third World are exercising over world affairs, superpower contention will intensify and become more deadly in the Third World, and certainly in Africa. While the

United States waves money, and utters scare phrases, the Soviet Union, screaming "socialism" and "natural ally," offers aid to get rid of United States imperialism (if it doesn't interfere with its "materialization of detente") but only to replace United States imperialism with its own Moscow-grown brand of imperialism, hegemonism, and a new neocolonialism. Just as the United States "opposed" colonialism in the 1950's when it was trying to replace British and French colonialism, so that Rock Hudson and Sidney Poitier in *Something of Value* would focus on exposing the evils of British colonialism. But look at Kenya now, a United States imperialist preserve with a neo-colonial comprador elite that must be crushed in the struggle to liberate Kenya and bring democracy and socialism.

In America, the successful struggles of the Third World, making revolution an irresistible trend in the world today, carry over inside this fortress of imperialism by intensifying the contradiction between labor and capital. Cutting away the superprofits that imperialism has scooped out of the Third World with the sharp edge of revolutionary struggle against imperialism contracts the material base of opportunism inside the United States. It shrinks the superbooty used to pass out reforms and the illusion of progress to the working class; it shrinks the material base of racism and national chauvinism among white workers so much that the bourgeoisie has to re-introduce busing and pull the Ku Klux Klan out of mothballs with bloody spectacles like Boston and Louisville and even Queens to keep black and white workers at each other's throats rather than at the ruling class's. With the contention between the U.S.A. and U.S.S.R. escalating every day the bourgeoisie must spend more and more on war-making preparations, and the monies they would spend on social programs, more reforms, and illusions of progress and democracy are cut back. And the mounting motion of cutbacks, layoffs, and unemployment makes the United States multinational working class and other elements of the population more and more fed up with monopoly capitalism and national oppression, and subjectively more and more revolutionary-minded, and objectively more united with the revolutionary struggles of the peoples and nations of the Third World against imperialism. "In the United States, the war machine is also running at high speed. During the present economic crisis, only the war industry is flourishing both in production and marketing. A number of institutions are studying when and where war will break out, its scale, its level, how it will be fought and how it will end" *(PR,* no. 2, January 9, 1976, p. 18). This is why an important task of Marxist-Leninists is to fight against superpower preparations for war, and combine that with propaganda and agitation against budget cuts, layoffs, and other attempts to put the weight of imperialist decline on the back of the working class.

The central task of Marxist-Leninists inside this country is to build a revolutionary Marxist-Leninist communist party, based on Marxism–Leninism–Mao Tse Tung thought, an antirevisionist vanguard party, to lead the working class in the destruction of the United States bourgeois state apparatus, and the transformation of the means of production from privately owned and profit oriented to publicly owned, state property under the revolutionary dictatorship of the proletariat. To do this Marxist-Leninists must not only unite ideologically and politically but also win the advanced workers and advanced elements of United States society to the side of communism. Since the tragic fall to revisionism of the CPUSA, party building has been a central task of all genuine Marxist-Leninists in the U.S.A., and this is true now more than ever as all the fundamental contradictions in the world increase, especially the tide of revolution and the danger of war. Whether revolution will prevent the war, or whether an imperialist war will bring on revolution, we must build a party to make such a revolution, and only with such a party can we lead the masses in turning imperialist war into the death song of United States imperialism. With the danger of war comes also the rise of fascism. Because it is only by means of a sharp and deadly move to the far right, a dictatorship by the most reactionary, chauvinist, and imperialist sector of finance capital, to paraphrase Dimitrov, that the bourgeoisie could mobilize to make war on the highly centralized and already mobilized Soviet social imperialists. The United States bourgeoisie certainly must be aware of this, though there are tactical differences in the ruling class as to how to approach this factor, but the differences are secondary ultimately to the working class because whatever sector of the bourgeoisie wins out, it will still mean oppression and exploitation for the working class. As for the danger of war, if we do not prepare, as the Chinese say, we will suffer. And the only preparation for revolution, which is the irresistible trend in the world today, or for the growing danger of world war, is a revolutionary Marxist-Leninist communist party.

What's the answer? Revolution! Why is that? It's the only solution!

People of the world unite to defeat the two superpowers: United States imperialism, and Soviet social imperialism.

In the U.S.A., Marxist-Leninists unite—win the advanced to communism!

Build a revolutionary Marxist-Leninist communist party based on Marxism–Leninism–Mao Tse Tung thought!

Not Just Survival:
Revolution
(Some Historical Notes
on Afro-American Drama)*

We are meeting to discuss a complex theme, "Beyond Survival: Two Centuries of Black Literature, 1776–1976." What the theme's framers had in mind is not completely clear, but they have provided at least a place to begin talking. To talk about black literature, and its survival, or its dealing with themes of survival, we have to begin by talking about black life, of which the literature is only a reflection. If we are materialists we understand that matter or material life or social life is primary, and that ideas are secondary, a reflection of that material life. We then have to look at the material base, the economic base, which is the shaper of that social life, that which is the basis for the material life, in order to understand what black life has been, what it is, what black literature has been and what it is, and lastly what they will be.

To understand the literature, we have to understand the life; to understand the development of ideas, we have to understand the development of life. Such a theme as survival poses first the question, survival from what as what? And it seems clear that all the forms of survival mentioned, "personal, economic, the survival of art forms, of needed institutions and organizations, the purpose of survival, and the need not only to survive but to prevail," cannot be cast in the abstract but must be dealt with as concrete issues of real life, otherwise we are wasting each other's time.

To understand black life in the United States, we must first un-

*Speech delivered at a Howard University Writers' Conference, April 1976.

derstand its social origins: that black people were introduced into the United States via the European slave trade, and that this slave trade is primarily accountable for the emergence of Britain and the U.S.A. as world powers, and for the accumulation of wealth and development of capitalism that ultimately led to imperialism. The Industrial Revolution in Great Britain was impossible without the trade in African slaves, and the so-called Triangular Trade between Great Britain, Africa, and the New World is actually the beginnings of world trade. In *Capital*, Marx explains, "Without slavery you have no cotton; without cotton you have no modern industry. It is slavery that has given the colonies their value; it is the colonies that have created world trade, and it is world trade that is the precondition of large-scale industry."

The U.S.A. is a society, as indeed is the entire modern capital-ist-imperialist industrial world, built on the African slave trade, on the subjugation of blacks and the continued exploitation and oppression of blacks (as well as the entire working class). Every aspect of United States society then, if probed, reveals the enslavement of the African and the Afro-American, historically and chronologically: as newly imported chattel, as slaves in a patriarchal society, or as slaves of a feudal economy, slaves with the added horrors of capitalism imposed on that slavery, freed black peasants, an Afro-American nation, and part of the multinational working class exploited as workers in relationship to capital but also as part of an oppressed black nation whose landbase is the black-belt South, and who exist everywhere else in the United States as an oppressed nationality struggling for democratic rights. Black people in the U.S.A. suffer from a dual oppression then, not only as part of a multinational working class exploited by capitalism (the private ownership of the means of production) but also as an oppressed Afro-American nation, struggling against imperialism for liberation and self-determination. There is no question of survival that can be put that is separate from these facts. Our personal and economic survival, the survival of art forms, of needed institutions and organizations, all must be directed to, and these questions in fact issue from, the circumstance of our double oppression as workers of an oppressed nationality. For black women, and women of other oppressed nationalities in the United States, there is finally a triple oppression, not only class and national oppression, but also oppression because of their sex. But all these forms of oppression and exploitation rest ultimately on the material base of monopoly capitalism, the fact that the land, the factories, the mineral wealth and machines—the means of producing wealth in this society—are owned privately by a handful of superbillionaire capitalists, while the masses of us own nothing but our ability to work for these vultures or starve to death!

Looking at black life in America, one sees immediately oppression, exploitation, and injustice, unless one is an oppressor, exploiter, or thrives or thinks he thrives on injustice. But one must also see the resistance to these things from slave trade, to slave ship, to slavery, to national oppression. The slave revolts, whether on the African coast, in the slave ship, on the plantation, or in the modern cities, are a constant feature of American life. The Black Liberation Movement, the generalized struggle of the Afro-American people in various class strata, organizations, and movements against our national oppression and exploitation, is a movement that has had many "tortuous twists and turns," developing in whatever objective situation that existed throughout American history. It reflected the consciousness of black people in the United States environment, how they adapted to it, and how they tried to transform it. But it corresponds to objective conditions as well as being a subjective thrust of the black masses in motion.

For instance, speaking about black drama, we see that the whole development of an Afro-American art is linked directly to the development of the people. Drama, because it is formally social, involving groups to perform and intended for groups to be appreciated, had specific problems of development that music, poetry, writing, graphics, did not have. African ritual, celebrations and funerals, fertility and puberty rites, harvest and yam festivals, coronations of kings and queens, pageants of the gods, and spirits' lives invoked for support or destruction, all these were transported to the United States via the slave ship. But the slavers and plantation owners learned, and the rebellions against United States slave life confirmed, that elimination of African culture helped make the slave system more secure. So the occasions of many of the rituals were removed by slavery, and black slaves were forbidden their invocations and evocations; their gods were humiliated. In fact the reality of black slavery was the ultimate humiliation for the African gods. The metaphysical-feudal basis of African life was not, of course, totally obliterated; there are African "survivals" even today. But they often took other forms. The slavers in the U.S.A., to continue their racist justification for slavery, said that slaves would receive their freedom once they embraced the Christian god, but the slavers had to drop this line in a few years because Africans quickly found a concrete use for their Christian indoctrination. They formally embraced Christianity, though many times the content of their worship remained African animism. In Catholic countries the Orisha and the saints are intermixed in convenient syncretism.

This earliest slavery included both black slaves and white indentured servants, locked in servitude. There were no white servants staging plays either, no white servant literature. The English bourgeoisie was trying to break through with apologies for rising capitalism, but to do that in a real way they would have had to show that it was tied inextricably to the slave trade and that the incipient Industrial Revolution that made England and later the United States the most powerful countries in the world was tied directly to the enslaving of Africans.

In the early colonial United States there was almost no dramatic literature of any kind to speak of because of the domination of Calvinist Puritanism and its metaphysical belittling of human life on earth (which is a perfect cover for any ruling class: while the people's faces are turned toward the hereafter the rulers gorge themselves, undercover, on the now). Formal American literary drama of any kind did not develop until after the middle of the eighteenth century. And in England the Puritans closed the theaters in 1642 because they said plays were licentious and turned men from "business and godliness." Moreover in the American colonies there were no large cities to support theatrical entertainment. And when it did come it was Elizabethan and Restoration dramas or American versions of same. "But drama did not gain acceptance until after the American revolution, and did not become a real form of American literary art until the twentieth century" *(American Poetry and Prose,* Foerster, et al., pp. 9–10). Church sermons, and these ministers' dialogues and histories, were the real literature of early America. And the first real literature of the Afro-American generally existed in these same forms. A real American drama does not exist until Eugene O'Neill, and importantly it was O'Neill who also first put forward something approximating black life in reality from the American stage. That is, it took until the twentieth century for United States drama to break out of the colonial relationship it had with England and Europe. Note also that this is the period when the

United States moves fully onto the scene as a powerful imperialist nation. With the rise of its productive forces, its expanding capitalism had leaped outside its national boundaries by the end of the 1890's, engaging in its first imperialist war (the Spanish-American War to conquer Cuba, Puerto Rico, and the Philippines). This war provided the tragic occasion for petit bourgeois intellectuals to wonder at the passing of American innocence (competitive vigorous capitalism), and witnessed the rise of the United States as a world force of undeniable and still to be fully experienced negativity.

The black drama of the earliest experience of Africans brought to America, and the emerging Afro-Americans, is in their religious rituals, and the chief form of black literature that was not formal song was the sermon. And though the black evangelical and wholly metaphysical and Calvinist-animist preachers obviously abounded in the United States, the most dramatic literature coming from the pulpits was the sermon of liberation, of redemption on the earth by the people themselves. And these sermons differed profoundly from the work of, say, Jupiter Hammon, who thought that "slavery was an endurable and perhaps justifiable institution" because it prepared blacks for divine submission. The sermons of the late eighteenth century and early nineteenth century and on differed also from the formal literary imitativeness of a Phillis Wheatley, who like Hammon was a privileged house slave pushed forward by whites because their themes upheld slave society. Wheatley for instance in her "On Being Brought from Africa to America" begins: "Twas mercy brought me from my pagan land,/Taught my benighted soul to understand./That there's a God, that there's a Savior too." She goes on: "Some view our sable race with scornful eye,/'Their colour is a diabolic die.'/Remember, Christians, Negroes, black as Cain,/May be refined and join the angelic strain." This is the party line of the church serving the interests of the merchants, the superstructure serving the economic base. There is not a word of the horrors of slave trade, a race ripped away from its roots, traditions, spilling its blood, as 100 million beings are transported into slavery. No, we were being saved, by being allowed to be Christians, and in exchange for this wondrous gift we were permitted to contribute our unpaid labor for the whole of our lives until we died or were killed.

The late-eighteenth- and early-nineteenth-century thrust of liberation verse from the pulpits by black orators coincides with a new development in American life. After the Revolutionary War, the war that liberated the United States colonies from England, it was generally assumed that slavery would be ended, that gradually it would disappear largely because it was not profitable. One notable play that appeared in the eighteenth century in the United States that took up an American theme, *The Fall of British Tyranny*, speaks to the role of blacks in the American Revolutionary War and the key role the slaves played. At first being refused entrance into the colonial army they and the Indians fought with the British and the tide roared in the Britain's favor. The British royal government of New York and Virginia called for blacks to join the British, offering them freedom and equality, and the slaves flocked to do this. But later, George Washington and company, understanding the foolishness of their policy, recruited 5,000 blacks into the war on the American side. After the war the promises of freedom were broken, but many blacks still were able to run away, heading west.

In the early nineteenth century slavery, which seemed to be dying, was turned all the way around by the emergence of cotton as an international cash crop. This was made possible by the invention of the cotton gin, and it is then that to the already existing lifetime feudal slavery of blacks were now added the horrors of capitalism. Slave laws were intensified, and even the civil rights of the black freemen were restricted, and the right to vote taken away from them. Cotton became king, as Karl Marx says:

> As soon as people, whose production still moves within the lower forms of slave-labour, corvee-labour, &c., are drawn into the whirlpool of an international market dominated by the capitalistic mode of production, the sale of their products for export becoming their principal interest, the civilized horrors of over-work are grafted on the barbaric horrors of slavery, serfdom, &c. Hence the negro labourer of the Southern States of the American Union preserved something of a patriarchal [or feudal] character, so long as production was chiefly directed to immediate local consumption. But in proportion, as the export of cotton became of vital interest to these states, the over-working of the negro and sometimes the using of his life in seven years of labour became a factor in a calculated and calculating system. It was no longer a question of obtaining from him a certain quantity of useful products. It was now a question of production of surplus value itself. [*Capital*, Vol. 1, p. 226]

So it is during this period of the early nineteenth century that you find not only the pre–Civil War revolutionary black nationalist

David Walker and Henry Highland Garnet, Harriet Tubman, and also C. H. Langston and Frederick Douglass, William Wells Brown (who wrote the first play attributed to a black, as formal drama, in the United States along with the first novel, *Clotel*), but also you have Gabriel Prosser, Nat Turner, and Denmark Vesey, who were not only speakers and activists but who organized armed struggle against slavery. And there will be a time soon when those writers who are truly committed to the liberation of the black nation and to revolution in the United States must also, like David Walker, write a prose or drama or poetry so opposed to this very system that people are arrested if they but possess it.

It is during this period on the other hand that minstrelsy emerges as well. The Jim Crow song and shuffle routine of white people like T. D. Rice began also in the early nineteenth century, in the 1820's. It seems obvious that this, like the early inception of racism, was to justify the most horrible period of slavery, since the capitalist imposition on feudal slavery had reduced the working life span of the fully matured slave-worker to seven years. So the need arose to make ridiculous, to distort, and to show as a clown and lowly animal type the black slaves that developing capitalism was exploiting, oppressing, and murdering. The minstrelsy was derived in imitation of the plantation entertainments of the slaves, distorted to ridicule black life itself. Ironically, the slave entertainments which were more dramatic, full of song, and more lifelike, and therefore more interesting than dead American imitations of Shakespeare and Restoration comedy, were to a certain extent satirical takeoffs on the whole of plantation life, including the life of the slave-owning class and their curious mores.

In the northern United States, in New York City, James Hewlett and Ira Aldridge opened the African Grove Theatre in 1821. But again the emergence as a popular American form of white actors in burnt cork ridiculing blacks was called for by developments in the economic base, again it is the superstructure serving the economic base. A ruling-class art arose to justify its domination and exploitation of a subordinate class. And this minstrelsy represented blacks the same way English drama treated the stage Irishman. (Ironically, when we look at English drama or drama written in English after the eighteenth century, the great dramatists and writers in English, in that part of the world, are unalterably Irish: Shaw, O'Casey, Yeats, Synge, Wilde, Joyce, Beckett. And Shaw was a reformist or Fabian socialist, while some of O'Casey's plays still cannot be played every-where because of, as one book says, his "alien beliefs," i.e., com-munism.)

It should also be remembered that the next re-emergence of minstrelsy came after the Civil War; more precisely it shot up after the destruction of the Reconstruction governments. When, after the South had been defeated in the Civil War, which was at once the second phase of the American bourgeois democratic revolution and at the same time the dominance of one social system over another, i.e., the domination of Northern industrial capitalists over Southern slavocrats. The Wall Street monopolists who had now benefited by combining industrial capital with bank capital to form financial capi-tal could fully dominate the American economy as American society moved from early competitive capitalism to monopoly capitalism and imperialism. The Northern monopolists needed the blacks during the early days after the Civil War to secure the land and stabilize the Southern governments because the ex-slaves were obviously the most loyal antislave elements in the South, best suited to set up the occupation governments. And these Reconstruction governments were more democratic than those that preceded them or came after them, even for poor whites. "The Negro governments in the South accomplished much of positive good. We may recognize three things which Negro rule gave the South: 1. Democratic government 2. Free public schools 3. New social legislation" *(Black Reconstruction in America*, p. 19). "They opened up the ballot box and jury box to thousands of white men who had been debarred from them by a lack of earthly possessions. They introduced home rule into the South. They abolished the whipping post, the branding iron, the stocks and other barbarous forms of punishment . . ." (Judge Albion W. Tour-gee). But once these governments had stabilized the South, the Northerners, having turned the Southern planter class into a landless comprador class wholly tied to Northern industrial capitalism through Wall Street banks, then allowed these compradors to lead a counter-revolution to topple the Reconstruction governments, take all power from the blacks, retake the land, and try to plunge the blacks back into a new slavery. This was heralded and set up by the Hayes-Tilden Compromise (1876), which pulled Northern troops out of the South and turned over the governments of the Southern states to the Southern ex-planters. And as part of this "redemption of the South," so called, Black Codes were enacted which increased

37

segregation, creating the separate and unequal system, removing all black representation from the Southern legislatures. In fact there was no black, Southern congressman after 1901 until Andrew Young (1974). And from 1891 to 1945 only one black congressman in Congress at any time. From 1901 to 1929 there were no representatives at all. Blanche K. Bruce and Hiram Revels were the only two black senators before Brooke, and Bruce's term ended in 1881. In 1969, with six congressmen, there were two less than in 1878. Half of those today have been elected since 1971.

The rising black nation, an Afro-American nation, evolved through slavery and came into being after the destruction of these Reconstruction governments and all democracy for Afro-Americans especially under the racist terrorism that characterized the national oppression of blacks in the black belt of the South, the national homeland of the Afro-American nation in the U.S.A. It was a national oppression rendered by imperialism upon a people who over the years had come to fit Stalin's scientific description of a nation as "a historically constituted, stable community of people, formed on the basis of a common language, territory, economic life, and psychological make-up manifested in a common culture." And the rise of the black bourgeoisie, which signified the class development that indicates the developed common economic life of a nation (since a nation is also a historical category), is accompanied by the appearance of spokesmen for that class again justifying the interests, the economic base, of that class. Both Booker T. Washington and W.E.B. DuBois were spokesmen for the black bourgeoisie, but Washington spoke for the compradors or those wholly representative of imperialism, while DuBois was the spokesman at that time, objectively, for the national bourgeoisie, that sector of the black bourgeoisie that had some antagonistic contradictions with imperialism, ultimately in a struggle for control of the black market. The national bourgeoisie arose initially at the end of the nineteenth century, the 1880's, in such endeavors as undertaking establishments, catering services, savings and loans, and insurance, serving a black market that the big capitalists because of discrimination and segregation would not serve. The national wing of the black bourgeoisie was at first a leader of the Black Liberation Movement, the so-called freedom movement (until the Depression wiped out large sections of it), and it enabled a black petit bourgeois leadership to emerge whose voice was Marcus Garvey, who in a combination of inspiration when he spoke of the need for racial pride and sovereignty for blacks, but of idealism and reaction when he spoke of Afro-Americans returning to Africa or when he supported capitalism and opposed communism, led the largest black movement before the Nation of Islam.

Booker T. Washington, who put forth a black conservatism, was sponsored by Carnegie and big business, and his sermons were reflected in some aspects of the black submissionist literature of Charles Chesnutt and Paul Laurence Dunbar. Washington was the last comprador who really assumed major leadership in the Black Liberation Movement, until with the decline of the Communist Party U.S.A. into revisionism in the late forties, the party began to push for "moderate" and even some comprador elements of the Black Liberation Movement as movement leadership.

DuBois was an activist, historian, economist, novelist, poet, and playwright, as well as founder of a drama company, the Krigwa Players, which performed black plays. DuBois advocated "a drama written by Negroes, produced by Negroes and supported by Negroes," a true national theater, which performed works by Willis Richardson (the first black who had a play performed on Broadway, *The Chip Woman's Fortune)* and poet Georgia Douglas Johnson. The theater group was organized in connection with *The Crisis* magazine, the organ of the NAACP which DuBois was affiliated with for a time, after it had been propped up by the big bourgeoisie (Du Pont, Firestone, McCormick) to replace the earlier, more militant Niagra Movement of DuBois and Monroe Trotter.

The national wing of the black bourgeoisie screamed against our national oppression; they were even progressive enough, as articulated by DuBois, to recognize the international oppression of black people and push Pan-Africanism as early as 1900. But unlike some pre–Civil War black revolutionary nationalists like C. H. Langston, who saw freedom and nationality linked to possession of land in the United States, they never conceived of calling for the self-determination of the black nation in the black belt, that is, of calling for a total war against imperialism to liberate the black nation, though DuBois became more and more a strident anti-imperialist and even joined the Communist Party near the end of his life, perhaps as a symbolic gesture. Ironically it would be only an anti-imperialist revolution that could secure for the national black capitalists theoretical control over the Afro-American market, but in reality such a revolution would be, in the United States, a socialist revolution, and it would have to combine all the nationalities led by the multinational working class. That is, the destruction of imperialism in the United States would not be a revolution to secure the black market for the black national bourgeoisie; on the contrary, the proletariat, including the proletariat of the black nation who would be a principal force in such a revolution, led by its revolutionary Marxist-Leninist Communist Party, would be struggling not for black capitalist hegemony over a black market but for socialism, the public ownership, as state property, of the means of production, and the dictatorship of the proletariat.

The dramatic outburst of the 1920's was a part of the total creative outburst of Afro-America, and of America as a whole. The whole of America had moved into the twentieth century, confirmed by the participation of the Spanish-American War and World War I as full membership, and as one of the most powerful, in the imperialist group of nations. The demands of monopoly capitalism in the last part of the nineteenth century and the early part of the twentieth, the cut-off of foreign migration by World War I, and crop failures caused by the boll weevil, along with the racist terror of national oppression in the black-belt South, led many black people to migrate to the North and some to the West. The period of the twenties is partially described by writer-aesthete Alain Locke in this way: "Here in Manhattan [1925] is not merely the largest Negro community in the world, but the first concentration in history of so many diverse elements of Negro life. It has attracted the African, the West Indian, the Negro American; has brought together the Negro of the North and Negro of the South, the man from the city and the man from the town and village; the peasant, the student, the business man, the professional man, artist, poet, musician, adventurer and worker, preacher and criminal, exploiter and social outcast. . . . Harlem has the same role to play for the Negro as Dublin has had for the New Ireland or Prague for the New Czechoslovakia."

But Locke, a petit bourgeois intellectual, an apologist for bourgeois aesthetics, translated through black forms to some degree, could also put down the political or, as he called it, the "race work" aspect of the new outpouring of creativity from black artists coming into Harlem. He did not see the fact of the nationalist political ferment of Ireland and Czechoslovakia as one of the principal reasons that radical nationalist art of those places flourished. Locke saw the

Harlem Renaissance as part of the avant-garde development of Western culture in general more than he saw, or at least supported, the direct political aspect of much of what was being created.

Locke speaks disparagingly of really outspoken nationalist drama: "Especially with the few Negro playwrights has the propaganda motive worked havoc. In addition to the handicap of being out of actual touch with the theatre, they have had the dramatic motive deflected at its source. Race drama has appeared to them a matter of race vindication, and pathetically they have pushed forward their moralistic allegories or melodramatic protests as dramatic correlatives and antidotes for race prejudice." Locke goes on to say in the same essay ("The Drama of Negro Life" in *Black Expression*, Addison Gayle, ed., pp. 123–24, 127), "The finest function, then, of race drama would be to supply an imaginative channel of escape and spiritual release, and by some process of emotional re-enforcement to cover life with the illusion of happiness and spiritual freedom"—a pure bourgeois line. Art is not a weapon of the dominated people, the dominated class, to strengthen the attack of the people on their oppressors, but is an escapist aesthetic pacifier to cool them out and take their minds off their struggle.

The emergence of the Harlem Renaissance is the true emergence of a full-up national literature, the reflection of the Afro-American nation in its development and oppression, the oppressed black nationality arriving in the urban centers merging a peasant background with a growing proletarian present.

Black theater went to Broadway, not only Willis Richardson, but also the cleaned-up minstrelsy of Chocolate Dandies, Shuffle Along, and a stream of musical stars who went from minstrelsy, like vaudeville, to Broadway: Bert williams, Florence Mills, Sissle and Blake, Miller and Lyle, Bill "Bojangles" Robinson. Even though they had to submit most times to racist contexts, like their predecessors the Congo Melodists, Ethiopian Serenaders, Georgia Minstrels, and Dunbar's Clorindy and Jes Lak White Folks, they were not the same total distortion and ridicule of blacks like that the white minstrels were. When black musicals of the twenties were designed primarily for blacks, they were the basis for real stirring American musical comedy, since black music ran big until the Depression wiped away that Broadway concession.

O'Neill's works (and Ridgely Torrence's before him), beginning in 1920 with *The Emperor Jones* produced in Greenwich Village with the great black actor Charles Gilpin, and O'Neill's other plays with blacks, *The Moon of the Caribbees, The Iceman Cometh, The Dreamy Kid,* and *All God's Chillun Got Wings,* were positive, to a degree, because they put black characters on stage in roles other than straight-out minstrels. Actors like Gilpin and Paul Robeson were able to give serious peformances, though any analysis of the characters in these plays will reveal an ultimate shallowness. O'Neill was trying nevertheless to create an American theater, as were American playwrights Elmer Rice and Philip Barry.

Black drama groups spread, like the Gilpin Players in Cleveland, DuBois's Krigwa Players, Langston Hughes's Suitcase Theater in New York. Still, in 1927, only half of the plays contributed to Alain Locke's *Plays of Negro Life* were written by blacks. But men like Willis Richardson, Frank Wilson, Jean Toomer, and Wallace Thurman were writing plays, and in 1933 Hall Johnson opened another play, *Little Chillun,* on Broadway. But until that time, the best-known works in the American theater about blacks were written by O'Neill, Ridgely Torrence, and Paul Green, all white.

The giant of this period, and indeed of black drama and black literature in general, is Langston Hughes. His play *Mulatto,* with its theme of illegal, integrated sexual relationships and the conflict between a mulatto son and his white father, was a vehicle for exposing the racist terror of national oppression and chauvinist sexual exploitation. It caused a great deal of controversy, but ran for two years. It still holds the record for the longest-running serious black play to appear on Broadway. Hughes is the black playwright with the dubious distinction of having the most plays appear on Broadway, at this writing four, but at the same time he wrote militant plays—some openly proletarian dramas. And his works like *Troubled Island, Scottsboro Limited, Angela Herndon Jones, Don't You Want to Be Free,* are neglected by black theater groups just because Hughes's more militant works are kept away from a general audience today. Hughes's poems, like those found in the collection *Good Morning, Revolution,* are also kept well covered by the bourgeoisie. Poems such as "Goodbye Christ," "Letter to Academy," "White Man," "Revolution," "The Same," "The English," "Johannesburg of Mind," "Black Workers," "Cubes," "Black Seed," "White Shadows," "Envoy to Africa," "Memo to Non-White Peoples," "To Certain Negro Leaders," "Sunset in Dixie," "Rising Water," "Advertisement for Waldorf-Astoria," "Gangsters," "Poem to a Dead

Soldier," "To the Little Fort of San Rosella on the Ocean Front to Havana," "Merry Christmas," "Broadcast on Ethiopia," "Air Raid over Harlem," "To Certain Brothers," "How Thin a Blanket," "Tired," "God to Hungry Child," "A Christian Country," "Madrid 1937," "Air Raid Barcelona," "Moonlight in Valencia— Civil War," "Tomorrow's Seed," "Hero—International Brigade," "Roar China," "Park Bench," "Cane," "Christ in Alabama," and "Lenin," among many others, pushed today, would awake a whole other generation to the strength of Langston Hughes's work, especially in the period of the late twenties and thirties into the forties. It is significant that Hughes, who maintained his connection to Harlem black experience all of his life, was turned around from his most militant and revolutionary writing, his involvement with Marxism-Leninism, by the defection of the Communist Party U.S.A. to reformism, as were many other black intellectuals during the period, including men like Richard Wright and Claude McKay, and many others who were affected like people all over the world by the momentous transformation of the Russian Revolution in 1917.

But by the late 1940's the CPUSA had moved inexorably toward reformism and by 1957 had become an openly revisionist organization. Most black and other serious revolutionaries left the party in droves. The Communist Party U.S.A. finally reached such a nadir of contemptibility that in the sixties they actually were running a line that the nationalism of Malcolm X was like the nationalism of the Ku Klux Klan and that Malcolm was a police agent, which is why he opposed the comprador antics of Roy Wilkins.

The proletarian drama and black radical drama of the twenties often merged in places like Hughes's Suitcase Theater in Harlem, and even the Federal Theater Project. (See *Free, Adult, and Uncensored: The Living History of the FTP*, by John O'Connor and Lorraine Brown.) The latter was brought to an end when the bourgeoisie grew apprehensive about its left-of-center orientation. The Lafayette Theater, at that time the headquarters for the Federal Theater Project in Harlem, had a black drama company headed up by John Houseman with Orson Welles as director, and with actors like Rex Ingram and Canada Lee. Also places like the Suitcase Theater and Negro Peoples Theater did plays with militant consciousness like Hughes's *Don't You Want to Be Free*, Odets's *Waiting for Lefty*, and plays on the Scottsboro case, like *They Shall Not Die*, and plays of union struggles on the docks like *Stevedore*. Mike Gold's *Hoboken*

Blues ends with a black character, Sam, saying, "But folks, why can't there be a place for the poor man, Black and White, where birds sing sweet and every house is full of music, and there's sunflowers around the factory door? Where no one is hungry, where no one is lynched, where there's no money and bosses and men are brothers." Serious plays about black life by black radical playwrights, however, received no consideration at all, on stage or in Hollywood, though the FTP did a few, but left lots more unproducd. The whole upsurge of black radical plays and proletarian drama in the thirties was intensified by the Depression and the cruel fate that millions saw awaited them under monopoly capitalism. Also the leadership of the Communist Party of the period was inspirational, in that they had convinced a great sector of the intellectuals to believe in and work for proletarian revolution, a task the new revolutionary Communist Party we must build in the future must also take up.

The Black Arts Movement of the 1960's was a reflection of the Black Liberation Movement of the sixties, a further intensification of the struggle against black national oppression but full of a great many contradictions and contrasting aspects. In one aspect the Black Liberation Movement reacted against its domination by the black national bourgeoisie represented by Martin Luther King. The concrete reason that the black bourgeoisie got hold of the leadership of the Black Liberation Movement, again, can only be traced to the traitorous revisionism of the Communist Party U.S.A., and their general support for the black bourgeoisie. One of the reasons why Malcolm X seemed literally to burst through so forcefully into the leadership of the Black Liberation Movement during the sixties was that his articulation of the line that black people were a black nation with the right of self-determination, self-respect, and self-defense signified the re-emergence of the black working class into significant leadership of the Black Liberation Movement. And even though the civil rights movement was a mass movement, led by the national wing of the black bourgeoisie, and supported ultimately, in some aspects, by the big bourgeoisie themselves (witness the march on Washington, which Malcolm called "a black bourgeois status symbol"), still in the future it will become more and more obvious that the most farsighted and influential leader of his time was Malcolm X.

In the same way that Malcolm X had to rebel against the bourgeois-controlled civil rights political line, the Black Arts Movement

saw itself reacting against the bourgeois integrationism of the compradors, and against the nonviolent we-shall-overcome-ism of the national bourgeoisie and its petit bourgeois intellectual spokesmen and
-women. The idea of integrating into the filth of American life as co-
exploiters seemed ludicrous at best, and traitorous looked at evenly.
Finally it is the line of the black bourgeoisie, and petit bourgeois
bureaucratic elite, to be in charge of the black sector of the American exploitation machine. But that is what we reacted against,
learning from Malcolm X and the brutal practice of struggle for self-
determination and democratic rights in America. Again the traitorous
profile of the Communist Party U.S.A. must be seen as one reason
for the mistakes of the Black Liberation Movement. The communists made it seem as if white chauvinism spread itself throughout all
classes and sectors of white people, because their line of bourgeois
integration and opposition to black self-determination is just national
chauvinism. (The oppressed black nation in the black-belt South has
the right to self-determination up to and including secession. I am a
Marxist-Leninist, whose ideology is Marxism–Leninism–Mao Tse
Tung thought, and I favor the voluntary union of all nationalities.
But only the self-determination of the Afro-American nation can as-
sure that black people determine what their relationship will be with
even the proletarian U.S.A. The Communist Party U.S.A. denied
and denies this, and in denying this they cut the Black Liberation
Movement adrift and left it in the hands of the black bourgeoisie
and petit bourgeois idealists and cultural nationalists.)

The leftist theater in the fifties and sixties hardly existed, under
the twin hammers of McCarthyism and revisionism. The bourgeois
artists of the Village and Lower East Side of the late fifties usually
reflected the class stand and attitude of the petite bourgeoisie talking about art for the sake of art, talking about not getting involved
with politics, glamorizing counter-revolution, justifying collaboration
with the bourgeoisie. We reacted to all this as patriots and petit
bourgeois radicals but also we reacted to the bourgeoisie's con-
ception of art. We thought it was merely white art, the lives and
ideas of white people, but it was really the bourgeoisie whose lives
and ideas are opposed to the whole working class, the white sector
of the working class included. Though, as pointed out in the magazine *Albania Today*, "the policy of racism helps the business and
monopoly circles to exercise, alongside the exploitation of white
workers, a still more savage exploitation of the so-called colored

45

workers making them the object of double exploitation." But the righteous anger of Malcolm and the black masses' struggle against racism and black national oppression was turned by petit bourgeois idealism into defeatist reactionary cultural nationalism, of which I, myself, was one of the best-known pushers and projectors. The earlier lines of an essay of mine, "The Revolutionary Theater," stated, "It is a social theater, but all theater is social theater. But we will change the drawing rooms into places where real things can be said about a real world, or into smoky rooms where the destruction of Washington can be plotted. The Revolutionary Theater must function like an incendiary pencil planted in Curtis LeMay's cap. So that when the final curtain goes down brains are spattered over the seats and floor, and bleeding nuns must wire SOS's to Belgians with gold teeth." Thereby indicating, as it attacked white businessmen and the whiteman's theater, that I was still basically anti-imperialist. But later Malcolm's teaching on the need for Afro-Americans to be proud of and understand their African heritage, and support African liberation struggles against imperialism, was turned by reactionary cultural nationalism into bourgeois nationalism, into idealism, and romanticism, and chauvinism which has as its political content collaboration with the bourgeoisie against the workers of other nationalities. We were not guided by revolutionary science, Marxism–Leninism–Mao Tse Tung thought; we rejected it under the influence of cultural nationalism as an invalid "white thing." We attacked all whites because we felt it was they who were responsible for our torment and the torment of our people, saying proudly it is based on observable phenomena; we are empiricists; this is not a theory. And that was the main problem, that it was based on narrow experience, without benefit of the summed-up experience of the working class in the struggle for power all over the world, i.e., Marxism–Leninism–Mao Tse Tung thought.

The eclecticism and idealism and metaphysics of the Black Arts Movement was a reflection of the eclecticism and idealism and metaphysics that characterized the Black Liberation Movement in the 1960's. We spoke out against "white art," as we called it, because we understood instinctively that cultural aggression is one of the main weapons of imperialism, but influenced by the nationalist doctrine of Kawaida, we developed an incorrect idea of what culture was and began to see it as a static unchanging phenomenon, not as it really is, the constantly changing expression of the political and economic life of the people. The opposition to "dead white art" as we called it was positive insofar as it opposed cultural aggression and bourgeois ideology, but negative in that it saw no difference between Gorky or O'Casey and Tennessee Williams and Kipling.

Where earlier we had lamented "that the two groups, black and white workers, could not find some egalitarian revolution for mutually attainable goals" *(Home,* p. 191), and in our concept of the nation spoke of "seizing land and nationalizing property and resources" *(Home,* p. 247), it is a core of anti-imperialism that is turned completely around by reactionary cultural nationalism, even to the point of negatively redefining Malcolm's teaching of the black nation, and under cultural nationalism seeing not revolution freeing this nation but bourgeois reformism and electoral politics doing so. The makers of the Black Arts Movement, including the seminal Black Arts Repertory Theater, talked about black revolutionary art and put it in the streets of Harlem in 1965, when we were driven by Malcolm's murder to declare war openly on black people's enemies. We all thought that we were putting art to the service of the black nation. That we were warriors pure and simple trying to burn the whiteman's playhouse down, but our petit bourgeois class base, the lack of a revolutionary Marxist-Leninist party, the lack of real study, and domination by the reactionary lines of cultural nationalism of one form or another turned us around. But we were clear that we wanted to use our art as a weapon of struggle—myself and Charles and William Patterson, Cornelius Suares, Yusef Iman, Steve Young, Joe Overstreet, John Moore, Clarence Franklin, Clarence Reed, the other artists that worked with us, Larry Neal, Askia Muhammad Toure, Sonia Sanchez, and Sun Ra, Barbara Teer, Milford Graves, those that took up the challenge on the West Coast like Ed Bullins, Marvin X, Black Arts West, and in the Midwest like Ron Milner and later Woodie King, and the hundreds of black arts theaters that opened throughout the country. All of us wanted to use our art as a weapon of liberation, but in the main we fell into the error of cultural nationalism and many of us have yet to recover.

In 1967 we were doing benefits for the Panthers, but the clash between cultural nationalism and people who held they were revolutionary nationalists jumped off as early as spring '67, when Eldridge Cleaver got the Panthers to throw all the artists, most of whom were pushing an informal cultural nationalism, out of the Black House in San Francisco. And the breach began that was to come to bloody culmination in the death of Bunchy Carter and John Huggins in Los Angeles, which split the movement into two warring ideologies led by the Panthers and the US Organization. (Again, one splitting into two, wherein the contradictions inside a thing can even split that thing in two, since we know if we hold to the science of dialectical materialism that development is caused by the confrontation and collision of opposites.) The US Organization and cultural nationalist reactionary line that all whites were the enemy, and the imposition of a precapitalist continental "African culture" on Afro-Americans as a method of building revolutionary struggle, was a glaring misdirection in the Black Liberation Movement. But the Panthers' turning the correct line that black people have the right to armed self-defense into a *gun cult*, thereby allowing the state to come down on them and slaughter many of them, and the romantic and reactionary notion that it was the lumpenproletariat, the pimps, prostitutes, dope pushers, who would be the social force of revolution in the United States, rather than the multinational working class, were glaring and dangerous errors the Panthers made. But in the end, the movement has developed past both those incorrect lines, gaining clarity by the errors of both, as more and more serious revolutionaries discover the science of revolution, Marxism–Leninism–Mao Tse Tung thought, and begin to understand that without the destruction of monopoly capitalism, which is the cause and continuer of black exploitation and national oppression, there will be no black liberation. Some people who struggled against racism claim they cannot understand how it is that capitalism is the enemy. In too many cases some of these people merely wanted to get into the system, to find their starring or costarring role in it; they did not want to smash it. And I think this conference would do well if it passed a resolution openly condemning Nikki Giovanni's casual support of Gerald Ford.

For playwrights and all artists it is important to understand that basically all drama or poetry or art is saying something about reality. It reflects the sayer's place in the production process, his or her material life and values. As a form, it reflects the material life and values of the society in which it exists, and in which the sayer, the artist, exists. The various trick definitions of art and its uses, whatever they are, no matter how "deep," profound, obtuse, obvious, irrational, etc., reflect exactly a specific group of people and a specific production and social relationship of that group to the society and to the world in which they live.

For instance, the bourgeois-sanctioned middle-class poetry and drama which is most important to the American academy is a reflection of American middle-class life and interests—petit bourgeois and bourgeois social and production relations. And in many cases, after some conflict about national oppression, the black and white sectors of the American "official intelligentsia" curve into a single curve, a dipthongated yet whole strata of material life and values which support and are the class interests of an American petite bourgeoisie. Our material life and values are not as monied as the whites', but we are an oppressed nation and our bourgeoisie and petit bourgeois intelligentsia are smaller and shakier than the main United States variety, but they all we got. The interests, values, and consciousness issue from a material base absolutely supportive of, finally an extension of, the material base, interests, values, and consciousness of the American ruling class. And art is apologia for one particular class or another and that class's views, needs, and visions.

To paraphrase Mao Tse Tung from *The Yenan Forum on Art and Literature,* which we all must read and become familiar with, poetry, drama, art reveal the class stand and attitude of the writer, reveal the audience to whom the writer and artist address themselves; it also reveals what work they have been active in and what studies they are involved in. There is no art that is above the views and needs or ideology of one particular class or another, although the rulers pretend that art is classless and beyond political definition, but such a line is itself a bourgeois ideology of art for art's sake. That is why we must aim at an art that serves the great majority of people, a theater that serves the working masses of people. That is why we must make an art that praises what helps the people and puts down mercilessly what oppresses or exploits them. That is why we should try to make a poetry, an art, a drama, that speaks to, after first learning from, those same dynamic working masses. We learn from the omni-eyed, multinational mass, the scattered, raw, unsystematized, and even refined, and we reorganize, re-intensify, dynamize, make gigantic, and give back what we learned. We deal with reality, "to get truth from facts" as Mao says, and with the class stand, attitude, and strength of the inspired worker give it back to inspire, educate, mobilize, persuade, involve, the people. We want to raise the level of the people, but to do that we must start where they are which is on a much higher level than the majority of intellectuals and artists. We also want to popularize, the make popular, to make a popular mass art, to take the popular and combine it with the advanced, not to compromise but to synthesize, to raise and to popularize.

The question of the audience is key, is central to the work. "For whom" is the problem as Mao Tse Tung sounded it. For whom does one write, to whom is it directed? That is the key to the class stand and attitude of the work. That answers the question of whether or not the art serves the people or serves their exploiters. The work and study should be work, active work, toward making revolution, toward seeing the masses of people in this society first build a revolutionary vanguard party, a new Communist Party, an antirevisionist party, a party guided by the science of Marxism–Leninism–Mao Tse Tung thought, and then led by that party smash the bourgeois state machine, seize state power, and turn the means of producing wealth, the land, factories, machines, mineral wealth, from private property owned by a handful of superbillionaire vampires to state-owned public property under the dictatorship of the proletariat. That is the work we are putting forth. Our study, as artists, should be of revolution as well as art, but revolution first and foremost. We should study the world based on the science of Marxism–Leninism–Mao Tse Tung thought, because this will clarify and change our class stand from petit bourgeois to proletarian, from a sideline watcher of the struggle to a remolded worldview of the working class and the revolutionary.

For whom do we write: for the people, for the revolutionaries, but also for the generations to come reared under the dictatorship of the proletariat, socialism, and eventually communism. Yes, our art must be a weapon of revolutionary struggle; otherwise it is a teacup in Rocky's summer palace, a distraction, an ornament the imperialists wear to make a gesture toward humanity.

Many of us feel since we are "anti-establishment" that that makes us heroes. Nonsense. Most such anti-establishmentarianism is just petit bourgeois anarchism and failure to take up the responsibility intellectuals had better understand they have to actually help make life better for all of us. The unclarity, romanticism, and pessimism, the little tearful odes to weakness we write, are things the people don't need. They need odes of strength, attack pieces. Art describing reality and methods of changing it. Objectivity, clarity, information, science, as well as love and concern. We should be reading discovering the world through the classics, Marx, Engels, Lenin, Stalin, Mao Tse Tung, working it in day-to-day in hard struggle against the enemies of humanity. Otherwise, what are we writing about in our last play? We need a drama that directly describes the situation of the people and tells us how we change it, that shows us our lives and gives us the responsibility for mobilizing ourselves around life and revolution rather than drifting impotently in support of death and bourgeois rule. This is difficult because many playwrights, poets, artists in the United States are petit bourgeois, a class which because of its place in the production process between the working class and the bourgeoisie continuously vacillates, revolving like tops between bourgeois interests and consciousness and the interests and consciousness of the oppressed masses. The struggle to change that consciousness where it does not vacillate is a revolutionary struggle and it can only be achieved by struggling to change external reality!

Because the Black Arts Movement was ultimately dominated by bourgeois nationalism, cultural nationalism, it was easy for many of its spokesmen to move easily into straight-out bourgeois expression. And then the bourgeoisie co-opted what it did not have to destroy. It paid out a few bucks and opened black and Negro theaters, skin-houses, itself to put out confused, submissive, bourgeois plays. It put out just enough exploitative films to let a few black actors work, many of whom used to sound off about black arts but who now found themselves in *Nigger Charlie* or *Blacula* or *On the Rocks* or *The Jeffersons,* TV soap operas, cop dramas, and whose justification for their prostitution must be spendable if not fascinating. The bourgeoisie encouraged reactionary, even antiblack, so-called black arts, and gave Pulitzer Prizes and grants and fellowships and residencies to push anything that spoke openly or complexly against revolution. Many of the people who opposed black arts, the bourgeoisie put in charge of it, or legitimatized and made the greatest practitioners of the arts. One such playwright even put out that to struggle against our domination and oppression was a white thing, a "charliesickness," and ended his prize-winning drama in drag after having murdered the militant black gangster, moaning that now that we had killed our resistance to oppression, a new life would begin for us. He was given the Pulitzer Prize for this debacle. It is proof that whenever we really begin to talk about liberation the ruling class will reintroduce minstrelsy and pay well for it. The spate of exploitation films speak directly to this return of minstrelsy.

We cannot speak merely of survival. We are over 25 million in this country and we have survived. We cannot put out the bourgeois collaboration political line that somehow we can survive and co-exist within the capitalist system, without having to destroy it, that we can build revolutionary institutions that exist comfortably within monopoly capitalism, growing capitalism into some romantic, primitive communalism. That is idealism and metaphysics, bourgeois ideology, and it must be opposed. We must speak not of survival but revolution, socialist revolution, and what does not contribute to that revolution will not survive, but will be lost with the other detritus of bourgeois society, whether it is colored black or white. We should at least be clear by now that skin color is no indicator of political line.

As Marxist-Leninists, we hold that the central task that confronts us today is the building of the revolutionary Marxist-Leninist Communist Party I spoke of. And essentially that task must be carried out by uniting communism. Because it is only led by such a party that the people of the United States can end their oppression and achieve socialism.

We must build our revolutionary party before the ruling class moves to fascism, and artist and intellectuals must contribute to the building of this party, or objectively they will be working against it and therefore supporting bourgeois rule, the exploitation of the working masses, and black national oppression. In New York City we have formed an Anti-imperialist Cultural Union of artists and writers to serve the people, and we must harness our efforts to party building in this critical period. As part of the motion to unite Marxist-Leninists and win the advanced to communism it is important for revolutionary people within the Black Liberation Movement to bring Marxism–Leninism–Mao Tse Tung thought to the forces of black liberation, particularly the advanced workers, to unite the struggle of black liberation with the struggles of the whole working class and oppressed nationalities, to unite the Black Liberation Movement with the struggle of the whole people towards democracy, revolution, the dictatorship of the proletariat, socialism, and the eventual emergence of communism.

Long live revolutionary artists and writers!

People of the world unite against United States imperialism and Soviet Social Imperialism!

Marxist-Leninists unite, win the advanced to communism!

Liberation of the black nation!

Socialist revolution!

Victory to all oppressed people!

The Third World and People's Struggles in the "Advanced Countries" *

First I should like to bring greetings from the heroic and struggling working class and oppressed nationalities of the U.S.A., as well as the Revolutionary Communist League (M-L-M). We wish to express deep feelings of solidarity with the worldwide struggle against imperialism, in all its forms, colonialism, neocolonialism, superpower hegemonism, zionism, and specifically we wish to declare our revolutionary solidarity with the fighting people of South Korea in their ultimately triumphant struggle against United States imperialism and the fascism of their lackeys, the Park Chung Hee clique.

There is intense turmoil in the world today, which is positive because it is caused by the intense and victorious struggles of peoples all over the world to liberate themselves. As our Chinese comrades have said, "Countries want independence, nations want liberation, the people want revolution"—this is an irresistible tide sweeping the world today. The fundamental contradictions of capitalism turned into imperialism, which Lenin laid out sixty years ago, are clearly in evidence today: (1) between labor and capital in the Western capitalist countries; (2) between imperialism and the peoples and nations of the Third World (which is the developing countries of Asia, Africa, and Latin America and other regions); (3) between imperialism and imperialism, the sharpest of this kind of contradiction today being between the two superpower imperial-

*Text of a speech partially made at a conference on the unity and independence of South Korea in 1976.

isms, the U.S.A. and the U.S.S.R.; (4) between imperialism and the socialist countries.

Of these four fundamental contradictions the sharpest are those between imperialism and the Third World, and between imperialism and imperialism. This fact gives rise to two rapidly rising trends, one of revolution, whose motor is the struggle between imperialism and the Third World, and the other is the struggle between the two superpowers, the U.S.A. and the U.S.S.R., for domination of the world, and this contradiction gives rise to the increasing trend toward world war. But clearly, revolution is the main trend in the world today, an irresistible tide sweeping the people to victory, democracy, and ultimately to socialism throughout the world.

The peoples of the Third World are the main force combating imperialism, colonialism, neocolonialism, superpower hegemonism, zionism, and fascism, but the force of their struggle is felt by all the people of the world who are in turn part of that revolutionary tide. For instance, in the capitalist countries, the normal cycle of economic crisis, which used to be between eight and ten years, has been speeded up to around three years, and where there used to be significant periods of relative stability in the capitalist economies, now no such stable periods exist. And this is in part because of the revolutionary blows struck by the peoples of the Third World fighting their way free of imperialism therefore causing the imperialists' source of raw materials, markets, and places to export capital to shrink and contract. Because the superprofits that imperialism had ripped out of the Third World are being cut back by revolution, now the imperialists have to try to shift the weight of their crisis onto the backs of the working people right inside the imperialist countries themselves. In the U.S.A., for instance, the bourgeoisie has been forced to lay people off their jobs wholesale, cut back in social services and reforms, close schools, cut budgets for people's institutions, at the same time prices continue to skyrocket. This causes the people inside the U.S.A. objectively and subjectively to come to more revolutionary positions, intensifying the struggle that they are waging along with the rest of the people in the world against imperialism, especially against the two superpowers.

Revolution is the main trend in the world, but there is another trend, which is also sharpening, caused by the contention for world domination of the two superpowers, and that is the trend toward world war. The content of imperialist politics is war. Lenin said,

"Imperialism is a system of war. . . . An essential feature of imperialism is the rivalry between several great powers in the striving for hegemony." And "world domination is to put it briefly the substance of imperialist policy" *(Imperialism, the Highest Stage of Capitalism).* And just as this kind of imperialist contention led to World Wars I and II, it will lead to World War III. World War II enabled United States imperialism to become the most powerful in the world, "plundering other peoples economically . . . with its tentacles stretched around the world . . . featuring a big stick policy of undisguised armed interference in the internal affairs of other countries" *(On Studying World History,* p. 7).

But in the post-war period "the unprecedented upsurge in the revolution of the Asian, African, and Latin American peoples, the drastic decline of world capitalism, the sharpening of different contradictions in and outside, amid growing contradictions among the imperialist countries—all these very soon sent United States imperialism tumbling from the peak of its strength" (ibid.).

The decline of United States imperialism has been marked very clearly by its series of defeats at the hands of the surging revolutionary tide of people around the world, especially the Third World. Twenty-six years ago United States imperialism attacked the Korean people, launching an open war of aggression against Korea as well as occupying Taiwan, which is a part of China, by force. Three years later the U.S.A. was defeated in Korea; this signaled the beginning of United States imperialism's open decline, which has continued and sharpened with the humiliating and crushing defeats in Southeast Asia. Vietnam and Cambodia not only demonstrated that it is the people who are strong and not imperialism, but also exposed United States imperialism's staggering, blundering retreat in the face of the terrible wrath of the revolutionary peoples. Defeats for its lackeys in Africa, specifically the death of Portuguese colonialism in Guinea-Bissau, Mozambique, and Angola, are merely further indications of the imminent death of imperialism.

But where imperialism generally is suffering defeat after defeat, with United States imperialism in sharp decline, the Soviet social imperialists are the aggressive newcomers to the world imperialists' banquet, just as Germany, the U.S.A., and Japan have been before it. This means that the U.S.S.R. is the starved and ravenous imperialism, lusting after the other imperialists' booty and "wildly ambitious," and the danger of world war comes principally from them, because they are willing to take more chances, trying to cash in on the U.S.A.'s rapid decline. It is for this reason that the Soviet social imperialists are everywhere, especially in the Third World where United States imperialism has suffered defeat after defeat. The Soviets are trying to sneak in the back door, as our Chinese comrades have put it, while the heroic revolutionary people of the Third World are putting the United States out the front door. This intensifies the contention between these two superpowers as they plunge deeper and deeper each day into an insane arms race, talking nonsense about disarmament all the time. The U.S.S.R. especially goes around the world talking about "detente," hiding its imperialist designs under the disguise that it is a socialist country, when in reality capitalism has been restored in the Soviet Union for twenty years or more. Angola is a clear example of how the people of the Third World drive United States imperialism and its lackeys out the front door. But the Angolan people's true independence is still in question because of the hegemonistic actions of the Soviet Union and its mercenaries. Even though the Soviet Union styles itself as socialist to hide its real imperialist features, the Third World peoples especially, and even many of the developed countries of the Second World, are now openly beginning to oppose the Soviet Union's attempts at hegemony and interference in their internal affairs. The Egyptian people's abrogation of their friendship treaty with the Soviet Union is one clear example, and the Japanese people's struggle to get back their northern islands from the new czars is another example.

While the danger of war increases, revolution, as I said, is the principal, the main trend in the world today. And the revolutionary tide is shaking all imperialism, intensifying the general economic crisis of imperialism throughout the world. The revolution not only rips away more and more of the superprofit stolen from the peoples of the Third World, but also the superpowers must spend more and more on weapons with which to fight the world war for which they are feverishly arming. This crisis and preparation for world war has also forced the two superpowers to become more open and more bold in their contention for new markets, new sources of raw materials, new places to invest capital. It has particularly made United States imperialism even more strident in protecting its dwindling holdings. This can be seen for instance in the U.S.A.'s open support for the most degenerate fascist and neocolonial governments in the world, especially in the Third World where these kinds of ultra-repressive governments are instituted by imperialism to try to stop the tide of revolution. South Africa and Zimbabwe are examples, and clearly Korea is one, where United States imperialism openly, before the world, supports the brutal fascist Park Chung Hee clique.

The Korean people have been trying peacefully to reunite their country. The Korean people have again and again demanded the withdrawal of United States troops from South Korea, "but United States aggression and intervention are the biggest obstacles to the independent and peaceful reunification of Korea." The Park Chung Hee clique could not possibly exist a day longer without the open support of United States imperialism. The Korean people would rise up and smash the fascist Park regime, which is unpopular with the great majority of Korean people of all classes. The suppression of the South Korean people is carried out directly with sophisticated armaments supplied by the U.S.A.

Last year at the United Nations, a resolution was adopted calling for the dissolution of the so-called "U.N. Command," which is really a cover for the direct intervention of United States imperialism into Korean affairs and the direct stationing of United States on Korean soil. In answer to the demand of the Korean people, the people of Asia, and the great majority of the pepole of the world that the so-called "U.N. Command" be dissolved and that the United States withdraw all its troops from South Korea, the U.S.A. talked rashly, like a true international pirate, saying it would meet any attempt to unify Korea with force, even nuclear force. And while talking endlessly about democracy, the United States in countries like South Africa, Zimbabwe, and Korea supports the most antidemocratic, racist, and fascist regimes that exist, pumping aid money into these repressive governments, money which is really the tax dollars of the American people used against their will to support imperialism.

But the people of Korea, like the people of Zimbabwe and Azania, will not suffer such oppression quietly. Where there is oppression there is resistance. The Park clique grows more and more isolated as the people's opposition to its fascism forces it to become even more and more repressive. Its kidnapping and arrests of Kim Dae Jung, and particularly Kim Chi Ha, exposed its ugliness on a still broader scale, and the United States imperialists are having a harder and harder time pretending that Park is anything but the fascist he is. Support for the Korean people's struggles is mounting even inside the fortress of imperialism itself. Just as the people's heroic blows against the white racist government of South Africa, which is also backed by United States imperialism, is forcing the U.S.A. to try to pretend that it is not the chief backer of that fascism.

Inside the U.S.A. itself, the working class and oppressed nationalities are intensifying their struggle against monopoly capitalism and the bourgeoisie, and since the degeneration of the old CPUSA the building of a new Marxist-Leninist communist party has been the central task of all Marxist-Leninists and advanced forces in the country. The building of such a party is part of the irresistible tide of revolution which is sweeping the world. Just as the eventual liberation of South Korea from the Park clique's fascism and the reunification of the country is also part of that revolutionary tide and will happen no matter what machinations and opposition United States imperialism and its lackeys might mount.

But in the capitalist countries generally, and in the U.S.A. specifically, the general crisis of imperialism, the dying postures of monopoly capitalism on its death bed, is everywhere evident. And the "great disorder" that marks the world wracks the bourgeois United States rulers. Amidst growing strikes and mass struggles of the people against the bourgeoisie's attempt to put the weight of the crisis onto the people, inflation and recession exist at the same time. The exposure of Watergate corruption, the daily defeats of imperialism around the world, especially in the Third World, a growing united front by peoples of the Second and Third Worlds against the superpowers, the exposure of the international corruption of the United States bourgeoisie with incidents such as the Lockheed bribery scandal in Japan, all these are calamities for the American bourgeoisie but give great impetus to the people's struggles inside the U.S.A. And even though the struggles have not been proceeding with the general ferocity of the struggles of the sixties, when the struggles of the Afro-American people and the antiwar movement, specifically, created armed rebellions throughout the country, indications are everywhere that such intensity will reoccur, but at an even higher level.

What is developing swiftly in the U.S.A., and with growing influence on the masses, is the movement to build a new Marxist-Leninist communist party, an antirevisionist communist movement, which can lead the working class and oppressed masses in making socialist revolution. This movement is proceeding as the spontaneous workers' movement intensifies. Especially inspiring is that many elements which developed in the national struggles of the 1960's, the Black Liberation Movement, the Chicano and Puerto Rican and Asian Liberation Movements, are now taking up the study of the science of Marx–Lenin–Mao Tse Tung (M-L-M) and are actively working to build a new antirevisionist communist party. This means that as party building develops the United States working class and oppressed people will be able to give even more support and be in even more unity with revolutionary struggles around the world, particularly the Third World. The building of such a party in the U.S.A. is part of the irresistible tide of revolution in the world today. Just as the people's struggle in Japan against monopoly capitalism and for socialism and just as the heroic struggles of the Korean people to unify their country and smash the fascism of the Park Chung Hee clique are all part of this heroic unstoppable torrent of revolution. We would be idealists to think this revolutionary process proceeds in straight lines, that there are no twists and turns, setbacks and reverses, but at the same time, if we are revolutionaries we know, to paraphrase Comrade Mao Tse Tung, that the people and they alone are the true makers of history—the American people, the Japanese people, the Korean people, the people of Asia, Africa, Latin America, the people of the world, ultimately triumphant, smashing capitalism and building socialism!!

People of the world defeat United States imperialism and Soviet social imperialism!!

United States imperialism out of South Korea!
Smash fascism, democracy for South Korea!
Support the reunification of Korea!
Taiwan is part of China!!
Victory to all oppressed people!!!

A Trip to Tokyo:
Emergency International
Conference on Korea*

This was my first trip to Japan. I remember there was even a debate before I left (not a sharp one) wherein some people wanted to place Japan in the Third World, and where others wanted to characterize Japan as belonging to the Second World. The difference is significant. Third World countries are the developing countries, for the most part made up of countries in Asia, Africa, and Latin America. "Developing" countries is the key to the definition. It is not an ethnic definition, although many people think that only the countries of Asia, Africa and Latin America (the so-called colored peoples) are Third World. But these countries are mostly in the Third World because they are the colonies, the semicolonies, the countries most sharply exploited by imperialism. They are "developing" only by means of their struggle against imperialism. Imperialism, by and large, is the reason for their "underdevelopment," not innate ethnic inferiority as racism, the ideology developed for the slave trade by developing capitalism, would try to pretend. Northern Ireland, where British imperialism has been exploiting and oppressing the Irish people for well over a hundred years, should be classified as Third World, and also Albania.

Second World countries, in contrast, are countries that are developed capitalist countries or the revisionist countries of Eastern Europe. Our arrival in Japan would immediately cut the heart out of

---

*Written for Japanese *Playboy*, but rejected.

the debate about whether Japan was in the Second or Third World. Japan is a developed, highly developed, capitalist country, an imperialist country as a matter of fact, itself exploiting weaker countries all over the world, by ripping off raw materials, exporting capital, imposing hegemony. But at the same time, even though Japan and some of the other Second World countries are imperialists, still they are smaller imperialists than the two superpowers. And because of this they are prey themselves to those two superpowers, the U.S.A. and the U.S.S.R. It is also because of the contradictions between the Second World countries, who themselves are interfered with and whose sovereignty itself is often compromised by the superpowers, that the world strategy for revolution is the united front against the superpowers—unite the many to defeat the few—the great masses of people and nations in the world in opposition to the two bloody imperialist superpowers! And in this respect, even Japan has a role to play at defeating these international brigands. But Third World country, no indeed. Japan is in quite a few ways even more highly developed than the United States, and certainly cleaner and safer.

I came to Japan to participate in the Emergency International Conference on Korea, to express the solidarity not only of the Afro-American people, but of United States communists and the great majority of workers and oppressed nationalities in the United States. Solidarity in the fight against the Park Chung Hee fascist clique, which is openly supported by United States imperialism. The United States supports reactionary fascist governments all over the world, especially the Third World, because the tide of revolution is rising so strongly that the only defense the international imperialists have is straight-out repression and bloodletting without even the facade and illusion of "democracy" the big capitalist countries give. (It is fantastic, for instance, to witness the United States and Israel put down Idi Amin, when they are the very bastards who put him in power, by providing the muscle for Amin's coup against Milton Obote's weak but verbally radical petit bourgeois nationalist government!)

Going to the conference, we had to pretend we were tourists (that was the advice we were given) to make certain that the Japanese would give us a visa, to make sure there was no other interference. And while these kinds of precautions are good, all progressive, radical, revolutionary, socialist people should constantly be aware that just as we know from the science of dialectical material-

61

ism that internal contradictions are the cause of all development, so we must always look to the internal makeup of our own organizations for the source of most obstructions, misdirections, etc. At the Emergency Conference there were some people who were opposed to the political line of my contribution to the conference (see "The Third World and People's Struggles in the 'Advanced Countries'"). It was, admittedly, a contribution conceived in light of the ideology and political line of Marxism–Leninism–Mao Tse Tung thought, the science of revolution.

And some of the participants of the conference, while correct that it will take a very broad "united front against fascism," of different classes, organizations, interests, etc., use Park Chung Hee's strident and bloody "anticommunism" cries to try to keep communists out of the united front. But it is my view that only a united front against fascism that is led by the working class by means of its party, a Marxist-Leninist vanguard party, can end fascism and bring democracy, and see as well to the continuation of the construction of socialism.

Park Chung Hee is striking out in all directions, his government an open fascist dictatorship (i.e., rule by the most chauvinist, terroristic, imperialistic sector of finance capital) because he has no choice. The only method of keeping capitalism in Korea is through fascist repression. It cannot be maintained by any liberal facade, because it is cut and dried that the Korean people's needs cannot be met under capitalism, so now the resort to open terror to put down resistance. All capitalism rules by means of bourgeois dictatorship, but in the advanced capitalist countries like the U.S.A. and Japan, there is bourgeois democracy, which means there is, beside the stick, the carrot, and the illusion of majority rule. But in reality all capitalist states are governed by a small handful of supervampire capitalists who own the means of production, i.e., the land, the factories, oil wells, mines, transportation, communications, storehouses; and the great majority of people in these societies, the working class, the proletariat, must sell their labor power, their ability to work, to these vampires, because they own nothing else.

Park Chung Hee is forced to oppress and exploit even the national bourgeoisie of South Korea, the native bourgeoisie, who are patriotic because they can only develop as capitalists once the fascist Park Chung Hee clique, which represents United States imperialism and is a comprador class, wholly serving imperialism, is smashed.

Petit bourgeois democrats, national bourgeois Catholics, other Christian groups, Buddhist groups, all stripes of radicals, even anarchists, pacifists, as well as civil servants, all sectors of the peasantry, the urban petite bourgeoisie, and naturally the proletariat, all oppose the fascist Park regime, but it must be the proletariat, the working class, which leads this broad antifascist united front, because it is only with such leadership that that united front can proceed all the way over to socialism and carry the revolution through to the end!

Some forces in the front are opposed to even the mention of socialism. Some of the important sponsors of the conference were very grateful to steer the conference generally around the question of socialism, or the dictatorship of the proletariat. This is natural, because many of the participants only want South Korea to proceed to the stage of bourgeois democracy, such as is found in the United States or Japan. And in this united front against fascism we must respect all members of the front, in a united war against the fascist Park Chung Hee, but at the same time, Marxist-Leninists cannot be excluded, because it is the working people, in alliance with all the democratic classes, who must lead.

In my speech I tried to lay out exactly what I saw as the situation in which Korean events take place. And I sent a copy of the speech to Japanese *Playboy* to publish it so that Japanese readers would have benefit of this point of view. But they turned it down. There was an extra edge of controversy provided by the speech, since it proceeded from the straightforward views of Marxism–Leninism–Mao Tse Tung thought.

There were two areas that gave rise to sharp controversy in the address I gave at the conference. First, announcing that I was at the conference representing a communist organization (the Revolutionary Communist League M-L-M) must have been news even to those in the steering committee whom I had talked to the most when they visited the United States, because when they met me I was chairman of the Congress of African People. But a series of meetings and discussions were under way, even during that period, to consolidate around a name change. These discussions were secret, and so there is no way the conference organizers would have known.

The second area of controversy arose because of the international analysis I delivered, which clearly characterized the Soviet Union as a superpower, an imperialist country, in which capitalism has been restored, which is domestically a social-fascist country, and internationally a social-imperialist one. I used "social" as prefix before fascist and imperialist, because the U.S.S.R. styles itself "socialist," but that is merely the signboard it uses to press for hegemony around the world. I mentioned Angola as a place where this was clear: not only the contention and struggle between the two superpower imperialists, U.S.A. and U.S.S.R., but also the Soviet Union's continued imposition of its neoimperialism and neocolonialism on Angola, even tragically utilizing the Cuban people as its mercenaries.

The fact of Soviet imperialism is a tender spot with many liberals, especially those who have always been a little "left leaning" but who have never been serious enough to become actual Marxist-Leninists. It is also a tender spot to people who are receiving or are the would-be recipients of aid from the superpower styling itself "socialist." I had a long interesting conversation with one comrade, a magazine editor, who initially refused to understand what we meant when we pointed out that the Soviet Union was the most dangerous now of the two superpowers. Most dangerous because it is the "lean and hungry" imperialist, the newcomer to the international banquet of exploitation, willing to risk more serious confrontation to get its "share" of the world ripoff booty. The United States on the other hand is the old, exposed imperialist, known the world over as a bloody exploiter. Where it, in the forties and fifties, used to wave the signboard "democracy" to get over as it replaced British and French imperialism in Africa, Asia, and Latin America, now it is exposed by its long and bloody practice, and the Soviet Union is moving in on it, with the signboard of "socialism" used as its cover story.

The very day we had our conversation, with the magazine editor protesting that we could not stop opposing United States hegemony in Japan (and I in full agreement with him), there was a picture of Brezhnev and the Japanese Economic Minister concluding a fifteen-year "trade pact" worth three billion dollars! I had mentioned the Japanese opposition to the Soviet Union's continued possession of Japan's northern islands. The motion is that as the people, of the Third World especially, are kicking United States imperialism out the front door, the Soviets try to come in the back door. And in Japan it is exactly this motion which is taking place. Sure the United States is in Japan like the United States is in South Korea, but reality is in *motion*, it is not static and metaphysical. The slogans of our

Australian comrades whose position has some parallels to the Japanese people ought to be understood: "Yankees out, don't let the Russians in!" This slogan, and the drive led by the Communist Party of Australia (Marxist-Leninist), is the key to the dialectical materialist stand, viewpoint, and method of approaching reality. And this was the content of a long and fruitful discussion between the journalist and myself. Getting down to the basics of dialectics, seeing all things and processes *in motion*. The United States is in steep decline; the humiliating defeats in Southeast Asia should have made that clear for the world to see. That is why the Soviets felt they could risk so much in Angola, because they were clearly aware of the United States reeling and rocking back on its heels, and the Soviets took advantage of it as they will try to do all over the world. But incidents like the heroic Egyptian people abrogating the so-called Friendship Treaty they had with the U.S.S.R., because of Soviet interference, meddling, bad faith, and attempted hegemony, should make it clear that people will not long stand for imperialism from any quarter, and people are now getting busy opposing imperialism from the U.S.S.R. like they oppose United States imperialism.

I had to withdraw from the conference because some people among its organizers felt that any mention of communism would jeopardize South Korean people still in the country, like Kim Dae Jung and Kim Chi Ha. Because the fascist Park clique is always labeling people, from devout Catholics to the patriotic national bourgeoisie, as "communists," so that they can imprison, torture, and kill them. But people must understand this is the cat's-paw of United States imperialism; Park Chung Hee could not last one day in South Korea without the open military and economic support of United States imperialism. And it is precisely because the United States is in decline, is literally being tossed out on its ear, for instance in Asia, that it is willing to openly back a critter as loathsome on the surface as Park Chung Hee, even against the protests of the local bourgeoisie, the churches, and any other liberal and democratic sectors. The death threat that hangs over the head of poet Kim Chi Ha, who is critical of the regime but clearly not a communist, has mobilized even nonpolitical types throughout the world to protest against the regime's excesses and its very existence. The Congress of African People led a multinational demonstration in New York City last year at the South Korean Information Office demanding the halting of all United States aid to the South Korean fascists and protesting the imprisonment and death sentence given to Kim Chi Ha. Even the conservative P.E.N., an international literary association, sponsored a demonstration against Kim Chi Ha's death sentence.

My "withdrawal" from the conference allowed time for the Afro-Asian Writers Association to set up a great many interviews and dialogues with literary figures in Japan, which I found extremely stimulating and enlightening. There was a dialogue with Makota Oda for the *Asahi Newspaper* in which Mr. Oda, one of the conference's organizers, tried to liken my position (from his viewpoint as a national-liberal, i.e., a combination of nationalism and liberalism) to Kissinger's, not understanding that all imperialism must be combated. He was trying to palm Japan off as a "small country" and part of the Third World, whereas Japan in reality is a highly developed Second World country, itself an imperialist country.

Another dialogue was a panel discussion with Noma, the novelist; Ngugi wa Thiongo, the Kenyan essayist and novelist; Saib, an Algerian poet; Oda; and myself. In this discussion, sharp lines were drawn about the role of the writer, with the dominant stance being that the writer must serve the people, that the writer's art must be a part of the arsenal with which the people make revolution. We pointed out how the writer must have the class stand, viewpoint, and method of the proletariat if he is actually to serve the people rather than their enemies, the bourgeoisie. Oda and Noma made qualifications of this, Oda speaking out against what he thought of as "socialist realism" in art, and Noma spoke of the difference between the language of the people and the language of the writer. Sharp discussion flew back and forth upon these points, with both Mr. Ngugi and I opposing this line by upholding that it is the writer's task, if he is a revolutionary, to speak as clearly, simply, and directly in his art as he can. To uphold bourgeois art is to uphold the bourgeoisie. Oda asked me if it was hard to make a revolutionary art, referring to my book of poetry *Hard Facts*, which had just come out. The answer must be obvious, of course. We are surrounded on all sides by bourgeois ideology of what art is, what life is, etc. Thus our revolutionary creation is made as an act of struggle against the corrupt bourgeois ideology and practice that is powerful all around us.

During one day over one hundred right-wing pro-Park demonstrators tried to push their way into the hall where the conference was going on. The young Koreans, the most energetic and sincere participants in the conference, easily repulsed them, and maintained a courteous vigilance throughout our stay in Japan. I was even given a book that turned my attention to those days of April, 1960, when young students initiated a national demonstration that brought another United States backed tyrant, Syngman Rhee, down—sixteen years ago! Yet some of these young people were only sixteen now, and they had to link up with the great working class, in alliance with the masses of peasants, and in a united front with all the antifascist, democratic classes, to bring another tyrant down, but this time, led by the revolutionary working class, they had to carry the revolution through to its completion, socialism.

No one mentioned the north or the great Marxist-Leninist Kim Il Sung throughout the part of the conference I was in. There were conversations that made me know that this was done quite purposely. There were papers circulated saying, "The north represents equality, the south freedom. . . . The unity of north and south would be a combination of these to raise both to a higher level." The goals of democracy and unity in Korea will be reached, but the Korean people will understand that there is no freedom without equality, and they will understand that when capitalists speak of "freedom" they mean the freedom to exploit the people. As Park Chung Hee is free to exploit the people now, under the protection of United States imperialism, free until the people of South Korea rise up and smash him, and the compradors who condemn the South Koreans to slavery! The mighty symbol of the north is a powerful image that the imperialists must always seek to oppose. The image of the powerful Peoples' Republic of North Korea is one the United States imperialists and their lackeys, led by Park Chung Hee, constantly try to hold up as the bogeys which make suspension of all democratic rights necessary in South Korea, in order to hold the state in preparation for some imminent "attack" from the north. This is the lie upon which the United States based its most recent provocation. Kissinger and Co. timed this provocation about "cutting down a tree" at the DMZ (!) "coincidentally" *at the same time the nonaligned nations were meeting in Columbo, and immediately after the conference in Tokyo,* again to throw out distortions about North Korea, to justify their continued presence in South Korea, despite the United Nations' ruling that the so-called "UN Command," which is largely the United States military presence in South Korea, be recalled. As long ago as 1972, North and South Korea met and issued a joint statement calling for peaceful reunification, without reliance on outside force. But Park Chung Hee only gave this declaration lip service, and has opposed it consistently, and now openly. The fake United States–initiated provocation over the tree incident again gave the U.S.A. and Park the cover they needed to maintain a United States presence and the division of the two Koreas, one a progressive socialist state, the other a fascist dictatorship under the absolute domination of United States imperialism.

Just as the nonaligned nations condemned the United States presence in South Korea, and Park Chung Hee's fascism, so the anti-Park cries are being raised around the world, as well as demands that the United States get out of South Korea. Even inside the U.S.A. itself, the fortress of imperialism, there is a strong sense of solidarity rising with the South Korean people, against fascism and for democracy and unity. During my visit to Japan, I tried to give this sense to the many Japanese intellectuals and artists I talked to, also to point out that the main trend of revolution which rages around the world can be felt even inside the U.S.A., as the United States and other capitalist countries are caught in the intensifying pressures of a worldwide imperialist economic crisis, and the American people become objectively and subjectively moved to more revolutionary positions, protesting against so-called "budget cuts," layoffs, cutbacks, rising unemployment, Watergate corruption, the rising dangers of fascism, and the continued superexploitation of oppressed nationalities and women.

In the last days of the conference, as it went on and I talked to different individuals and groups in Tokyo, I was taken to breakfasts, luncheons, and dinners all to talk and exchange ideas. Despite the presence of some petit bourgeois idealism and individualism, there was a rising feeling of solidarity from the working people and youth in and around the conference, and from the working people of Japan, going about their day-to-day business in struggle against the Japanese bourgeoisie, complete with their feudalistic prop "Emperor" Hirohito, who sits in the middle of Tokyo like Central Park as a shrine to uphold all the remnants of feudalism still useful to Japanese capitalism. I got the feeling of solidarity with those working people, with all the people struggling for democracy, and ultimately for socialism. Tanaka was indicted the day I left, in a striking parallel to Watergate, revealing essentially how connected are the international bourgeoisie and their lackeys—they are stumbling all over the world. And Japan and the United States have many parallels, highly industrialized capitalist imperialist states, with high levels of opportunism and reformism, with revisionist "communist parties," conciliating with monopoly capitalism, and with new communist movements struggling to come strongly into focus with new antirevisionist (antireformist) Marxist-Leninist parties. I met some friends, some new comrades, exchanged much information, discussed and argued, and the last night toasted to the international solidarity of and ultimate victory of the people!

"Clout":
What It Is?*

The word clout itself, in its unique American context and con-notation, means impact, i.e., "pull" or influence. It is a word connected with "mainstream" American politics and business. It sig-nifies the ability to get things done, to work one's will, for whatever purpose. What really is meant is *power!*

What is interesting, in asking what it is here in this particular magazine, is the siphoning-off of the real force and scaling down of the real import of the question, compared to its actual existence, very clear in the 1960's, in the *demand* black people made for power—*black power!* Today basically the same question, no longer bold and revolutionary, can be "politely," albeit journalistically and rhetorically, posed, with all scariness (i.e., threat to the capitalist, white-supremacist power structure) removed like a spayed tom.

What was made clear in the turbulent sixties was the fact that black people had no power. This was the forcefulness of Malcolm X's message, which used the reaction of the "powers that be" to the civil-rights movement to teach by negative example this illuminating factor of black life in the U.S.A. Counterposed to Martin Luther King's idealistic, metaphysical line and leadership of the mass civil-rights movement, which objectively articulated the interests of the black national bourgeoisie, Malcolm X developed his slashing com-mentary on this society, a commentary that clearly voiced the feel-ings of the black masses.

---

*Commissioned in 1977 by *Black Enterprise Magazine*, but rejected, although paid for!

The question of power, and how it is dealt with, is the central question one confronts when describing United States society, or describing who is asking that question and where they are in that society. The question reveals the two fundamental sides or aspects of the black national question and the Black Liberation Movement. Dr. King talked of civil rights, what basically are the democratic rights due to any citizen of a particular society. Malcolm raised, with stunning clarity, the obvious (except for years of brainwashing) fact, that if we had to raise the cry of civil rights, i.e., democratic rights, then we must not be citizens in the first place! What we saw as the contradiction between what Dr. King was saying and what Malcolm X was saying was that each was articulating the views and needs of a particular class within the Afro-American nation and oppressed nationality: Martin L. King, the black national bourgeoisie and petite bourgeoisie; Malcolm X, the black sector of the working class.

Black people in the United States suffer from national oppression, regardless of class, although obviously there is a difference between the degree of national oppression that is directly visited upon black workers in the central cities or small farmers or migratory workers or sharecroppers or unemployed workers, as contrasted to the degree of national oppression directly experienced by a black media executive or owner of a food-processing business. The fact that the masses of blacks suffer this national oppression means that they are twice oppressed: by class as workers in relationship to capitalism, and by their nationality. Black women are triply oppressed, when we add to these other two scourges the weight of sexual oppression.

In United States society, the struggle between labor and capital, between the workers and the bourgeoisie, is the principal contradiction, the principal struggle, and the principal question. This is the motive force driving history forward. The struggle for black liberation is part and parcel of this struggle, a component part of what will be proletarian revolution. In the United States context the fact of the black national question, and the Black Liberation Movement it engenders, serves to heat up even more intensely the entire conflict between the owners and the workers.

When we can understand the basic class nature of American society, a capitalist society in which a handful (0.6%) of superrich vampires own the land, factories, mines, transportation, machines,

communications, waterways, then we will understand that the ultimate "clout," i.e., *power*, is in the hands of this grim minority. The
owners of the means of production, to whom the rest of us must sell
our labor power, our ability to work, or starve, have *all* the clout!
That is what the struggle is about in the first place.

In the civil-rights movement, the national wing of the black
bourgeoisie could seem to speak for a broad sector of the black
masses, because even the black bourgeoisie were restricted by the
lack of democratic rights which deeply repressed the black masses.
The removal of the most blatant apartheid restrictions of national
oppression (in the black-belt South particularly) was necessary for
the black bourgeoisie and petite bourgeoisie as well. Equal access to
public facilities, voting rights, the slight relaxation of certain exclusive segregating business practices, e.g., loans and insurance to
black business, were clearly needed by upper- and middle-class
blacks under the conditions of national oppression. Joseph Stalin described these conditions in *Marxism and the National-Colonial Question*
as "the system of exploitation and robbery of oppressed peoples, the
measures of forcible restriction of the rights of oppressed nationalities, resorted to by imperialist circles. These, taken together,
represent the policy generally known as a policy of national oppression." But the civil-rights movement's leadership, the black bourgeoisie and petite bourgeoisie, only needed that movement to
succeed to a certain extent; a much lesser extent than the black
masses needed, since the tokens given by the civil-rights movement
were usually given to the black bourgeoisie and middle class. The
March on Washington was finally orchestrated by John Kennedy,
i.e., the United States bourgeoisie. Malcolm X called it (listen to the
record *The Wisdom of Malcolm X)* "a black bourgeois status symbol,"
and went on to say how it would do nothing for the masses of working-class blacks, nor would the passing of the civil-rights bill.
Malcolm's working-class line has proven clearly correct. The entire
civil-rights movement, for the most part, extended only some cosmetic change to the United States system, altering the most visible
parallels between United States capitalism and racism and, say,
South African capitalism and racism. The United States "modernized" its imperialism and racism, and that is essentially the struggle
the American bourgeoisie is having with the South African and Rho-
desian rulers now, that they are too backward with their shit: "Like
straight-out colonialism, ugg! man, that went out with neocolonial-

ism" (you can hear Henry the K huffing and puffing at Vorster and Ian Smith now).

The black national bourgeoisie is more militant than the compradors (i.e., those who are wholly servants of imperialism, in this case, big white capital), because the national sector of the black bourgeoisie is still fighting for control of the black market (Afro-Sheen vs. Vaseline—ten rounds to a knockout . . . and the winner's got your head!). But black capitalism cannot ever fully develop because the black nation (whose land is the black-belt South, even though a significant part of its bourgeoisie is located in the North, as well as its ghetto market) is oppressed and exploited by United States imperialism. In order for the black national sector of the bourgeoisie to take over control of their own market (black people!) they would have to fight an anti-imperialist struggle in the same way the people and nations of the Third World are doing. But then, the cutting irony of this situation is that such an anti-imperialist revolutionary struggle would be led almost invariably by the working class in the first place, by means of a revolutionary party, and the goal of such a revolution (even though in the Third World these new democratic revolutions, as Mao Tse Tung termed them, might include the national sector of the bourgeoisie in a united front to smash imperialism, foreign domination) would certainly not be the deliverance of the black masses into the domination of a black bourgeoisie to replace the domination of the imperialists (big white bourgeoisie, in this case)! Ultimately the goal of such a revolution would be socialism.

It is this market-dominance aspect of the struggle however that equipped the black bourgeoisie early in the Black Liberation Movement, after the Civil War up to the early part of the twentieth century, to lead that movement. But its political and economic flabbiness, its dualistic vacillating ideology, sent the leadership of the Black Liberation Movement to the petit bourgeois pan-Africanists in the 1920's (Garveyism) and allowed in the 1930's even working-class leadership to emerge. What delivered the leadership of the black masses back to the bourgeoisie was the self-destruction of the Communist Party U.S.A. because of its final domination by reformism and revisionism (linking it then and since to the revisionist "Communist" Party of the Soviet Union). It was this basic degeneration through opportunism of the once strong CPUSA, in the 1940's, that allowed it openly to turn its back on the black people's struggle—

dropping its support for self-determination for the Afro-American nation—leaving blacks and indeed the entire multinational working class without revolutionary leadership. And this grim state of affairs has existed *formally* since 1957 (since the sell-out Sixteenth Congress of the CPUSA).

In its degeneration, the CPUSA even began to push black comprador bourgeois spokesmen as the leadership of the Black Liberation Movement and said of Malcolm X that he "was a police agent" and that "the nationalism of Malcolm X is the same as the nationalism of the Ku Klux Klan," very revolutionary, in fact about as revolutionary as the United States bourgeoisie.

The civil-rights movement did provide the black bourgeoisie and petite bourgeoisie with more "clout." The great majority of political muscle the black upper and middle class have, as minuscule as it is, has come as a result of the civil-rights struggle, but more importantly, this "clout" has come finally as a result of the violent mass-rebellion movement in the 1960's, which moved the Black Liberation Movement past where the black national bourgeoisie was prepared to take it, although the most progressive sector of the middle class identified very closely with the rebellions. But these rebellions were carried out by the *working-class* blacks and not the *lumpen,* i.e., the pimps, prostitutes, junkies, and winos as Elder Cleaver and his petit bourgeois, Bakunist anarchism, masquerading as Marxism, erroneously and unfortunately put out.

The voting rights act was finally so important to the black bourgeoisie and petite bourgeoisie, because they would be the ones to run for office and be elected, or given some select post (like Carter's appointees) because of the "impact" that the black vote might have. But essentially what is being created with this largely false "clout" the black bourgeoisie and petite bourgeoisie have achieved as a result of the black mass struggle, is a kind of neocolonialism, although the black nation in the United States is *not* a colony but an oppressed nation, fighting for the right of self-determination, i.e., political control over the black-belt South as well as democratic rights for black people throughout the rest of the United States. But it is neocolonialism in the sense that United States imperialism has modernized its oppression and exploitation so that it uses "black faces in high places" to run the same monopoly capitalist game that white faces did.

We can demonstrate how it is that the mass movement of black

74

people has made the only "clout" that blacks have, but that this is used by the U.S. bourgeoisie to set up a black petite bourgeoisie elite superficially to "manage" black affairs (the real management remaining where it always did, with the big bourgeoisie). We need only cite the following statistics: "From 1891 to 1945, there was only one black representative at any time in Congress at all. From 1901 until 1929, there were no blacks in Congress at all! The first black congressman from the south since 1901 was elected in 1974! . . . until six years ago there were only six black members of Congress and one senator to represent over 20,000,000 people. Most of the present black members of congress have been elected since 1969, half since 1971!" *(Afro-American National Question,* Box 663, Newark, NJ 07101).

To go further and show the utter lack of "clout" this "clout" represents, that is to say its tininess, we have only to point out that "the total number of black elected officials in the United States is 3,503 (1974). This total, according to the Joint Center for Political Studies, represents a 196% increase in the number since 1969 [the effect of the rebellions]. . . . However black people who are 11% of the United States population continue to account for less than one percent of the more than 500,000 elected officials in the United States" *(Afro-American National Question).* The largest number of black elected officials (in 1969 there were six black congressmen, two less than in 1875) was right after the Civil War, as the Reconstruction governments were developed, supported initially by the victorious Northern industrial capitalists to keep the defeated Southern slavocrats in line, but ultimately betrayed with the Hayes-Tilden compromise (1876), which removed Federal troops from the South, and delivered black people back into neoslavery via Klan terrorism, black codes, rigid discrimination and segregation, and robbery of the land which could be the only basis for black integration into a democratic U.S.A. That promise of Reconstruction was ended with the so-called "redemption of the South," and the destruction of the Reconstruction governments. The only black senators *ever* before Brooke (who came in 1967, rebellion at its highest) were 1869–1871, Hiram Revels, and 1875–1881, Blanche K. Bruce. *There have never been any other black senators!!*

So much for black political "clout" within the bourgeois system. What "representation" there is exists to *control* blacks, not to carry out their wishes, and these representatives are members of the petit bourgeois elite whose basic interests are serving that class's needs (and only as a function of being the servants of the big United States bourgeoisie), not the black masses! The wall-to-wall bureaucrats in Newark, as one microcosm for instance, its mayor, police director, city council president, superintendent of schools, are there without a doubt because of the mass struggles of blacks, but they are there to serve capitalism, not blacks; they are there to cool out the Black Liberation Movement (which got them there in the first place), not give it correct leadership. And finally they have allegiance to their class of blacks, the bureaucratic petit bourgeois elite, and the big bourgeoisie, not to the black masses!

In class society, a particular class has influence, within that society, according to the degree of its ownership of the means of production, its place in the social organization of production and society, the amount of wealth its members get in that society, and their method of obtaining that wealth. In fact it is the similarity or dissimilarity of these relationships, with relationship to the means of production being the most important, that are the demarcations and parameters—distinguishing traits—of the different classes. The bourgeoisie obviously has the most clout in United States society (the Du Ponts, Mellons, Rockefellers, Fords, Morgans, etc.); this is the corporate class. It is their lieutenants who run the country for them (the Carters, Kissingers, Fords, heads of the corporations and runners of the state apparatus); they also have enormous influence. Together they make up around one and one-half percent of the total population, and this is where the ultimate "clout" is.

The middle class, the petite bourgeoisie, are largely the functionaries or "interpreters" of the bourgeoisie, and their "clout" is drawn from this relationship. (This is the upper strata of the petite bourgeoisie; the lower strata is much closer to the proletariat and has little of this bourgeois-derived "clout.") The masses, the working class, and oppressed nationalities, have "clout" only insofar as they organize, mount mass movements, and take direct action to carry out their ends and meet their needs. And ultimately this impact that the working class must make on society is totally to transform it, so that instead of a small handful of vultures controlling society, the ownership of the land, mineral wealth, factories, machines, transportation, communication is seized by the workers themselves. And this can only be done by first building a revolutionary Marxist-Leninist party, and then carrying through with an armed socialist revolution.

There is no "clout," or stated nakedly, there is no power to be obtained under capitalism for the black masses, 96% of whom are in the working class. The black sector of the working class is part of the whole multinational working class in the U.S.A., and ultimately it shares the same heroic destiny despite racism and the fact that at the present time blacks inhabit an almost separate, and surely marginal, labor market from the rest of the working class. But this is the way capitalism uses the oppressed nationalities to depress the whole labor market, and keep all the workers' wages lower, chained to the superexploitation of the blacks and other oppressed nationalities, and especially chained to the imperialist exploitation of the Afro-American Nation in the black-belt South.

Necessarily, the black petite bourgeoisie and bourgeoisie are marginal classes as well in the sense of their relationship to the United States petite bourgeoisie and bourgeoisie, "restricted to the leftovers of the dominant white ruling class; they are a class of small entrepreneurs" (Haywood, *Negro Liberation*, p. 195). The "clout" that the black bourgeoisie and middle class have in American society is laughable, as laughable as black capitalism. Consider this if you doubt: black business in the U.S. represents about 2.7% (1972) of all business! The gross receipts of black business compared to the gross receipts of all business in the United States (excluding corporations, because the majority of black businesses are sole proprietorships, not corporations) is 1.7%! And when you throw in the corporations, the black percentage compared with the overall U.S. total is about 0.6%! Ninety-five percent of all black business (in 1969) employed less than ten people, and by 1972 the average number of employees employed by black business was six. The majority of the black business people are not even members of the bourgeoisie, but the petite bourgeoisie, because they hire no employees at all. Also, most black business is not in industry. "In 1972, black-owned firms remained highly concentrated in . . . retail trade and selected services. These firms accounted for 65% of all black-owned firms, about the same proportion which existed in 1969. The category 'selected services' includes hotels and other lodging places, personal services, business services, automotive repairs, garages, etc." *(The Social and Economic Status of the Black Population in the United States, 1974).* All the black businesses in the United States taken collectively are just chump change, compared with the $28.3 billion in world sales of General Motors, the $18.7 of Exxon, the $16.7 of Ford, the $9.4 of General

Electric, etc. In 1972, the gross receipts of black-owned business (in the ten largest major industries) was $4,791,507,000, or just about as large as Westinghouse, which is $4.6 billion, all by itself!

"With its growth stunted by monopoly capitalism the efforts of Negro business enterprises had been shunted off to nonindustrial pursuits, such as small-scale banking, insurance, real estate, retail merchandising, and the like. The market of the Negro business man has been limited almost exclusively to the segregated community. Even in this narrow field, big white capital takes the lion's share" (Haywood, *Negro Liberation*, p. 195). Black business is for the most part limited to a part of the black community. "The result is that the Negro businessman, and to a large degree the Negro professional, finds himself caught in an inescapable contradiction. On the one hand he has what might be called a 'vested interest' in Jim Crow, upon which he is economically dependent for his market. At the same time, Jim Crow is the chief obstacle to his social development. The result is a split social personality" (ibid.).

Also, and very significant, while the majority of black business has been developed and exists off capital developed in the black community, thus indicating a bourgeoisie that is national in character (only about one-third of the black businesses are comprador, i.e., developed initially by "white capital"), still, in the last few years, the rise of the comprador has been dramatic, indicating that one of the results of the civil-rights movement has been to allow the big capitalists to penetrate even more effectively the black bourgeoisie's market, the black community.

DATE FOUNDED	PERCENT OF LARGEST BLACK BUSINESSES WITH A COMPRADOR CHARACTER
Up to 1959	17.4
1960's	26.5
1970's	46.4

From a document of the African Liberation Support Committee, 1973.

Many of the so-called "black" businesses opened as a result of the rebellions were in fact initiated with the capital of the big bourgeoisie, especially the flashy auto dealerships, liquor dealerships, franchise ownerships, etc. Despite the fakery of the ruling class in trying to make it seem that blacks had been integrated into United States imperialism, in fact, proportionally, as far as wage differential, there is even more disparity than thirty years ago! In 1971 there was a $3,700 gap between black and white families, measured against only a $2,700 gap in 1947, and by 1973 it had grown to $5,326. And the same is true even for the black petite bourgeoisie: a black college graduate after 4 years of college could still only make an average annual wage of $8,669 as opposed to the $8,829 a white high-school graduate could expect. As a matter of fact only 54% of black students even finish high school, right now. During the hot sixties the percent of black salaries to all salaries in the United States rose from 57.8% in 1966 to 61.3% in 1970, but by 1973 it was down to 57.7% again. We are saying that anything resembling "clout" within the bourgeois society is an illusion for working people in general, and certainly the black masses. (And as for people who would say, well the unions represent "clout" for the general working masses, that is the tragic joke of our time. For the most part the unions are run by trade-union bureaucrats like Meany, Abel, Woodcock, Fitzsimmons, etc., who represent directly the interests and policies of the bourgeoisie, and that's all!)

But even with more black politicians, and a bigger and richer black bourgeoisie, the black masses would have no power, no "clout." The question only has meaning in the mainstream of American business and politics, and only for the bourgeoisie and the petite bourgeoisie. The "clout" of the black upper and middle classes, as we have shown, is satire. The civil-rights movement did not complete the aborted democratic revolution that the Civil War was supposed to bring about, and the rebellious sixties could go no further than rebellion, because the Black Liberation Movement was a spontaneous mass movement without the leadership of a revolutionary Marxist-Leninist communist party. Even the Urban League has pointed out that over 25% of the black working force is unemployed, and one-third of all black people still have incomes below the official poverty guidelines. This does not show power, but the lack of it.

There are a few more bloods "by the door" as window dressing for an illusory democracy, and certainly the peanut vendor, also known as Smilin' Jack or Howdy Doody, the incoming "presidenk," will definitely trot out a few more middle-class black lightning rods to try to keep tricking people that something is happening that's not. It is true that people like Andy Young, who will now become the best-known "Andy" since Charles Correll and Freeman Gosden stopped their television series, will be used in ways that are more ingenious than older tokens. With his track record of SCLC activism and as chief aide for Martin Luther King, during the Selma, Birmingham, etc., wars, who also, it's said coincidentally, has had the daughter and son of one of Azania's (South Africa's) most respected liberation leaders, Maguliso Subukwe, living in his house for some time, Young will be used to try to dazzle and trick the peoples of the Third World, not just domestic blacks. So tokenism is becoming more ambitious. Patricia Harris, board member of Scott Paper and other huge corporations, becomes Secretary of HUD, but none of it represents "clout" for blacks in the least. Unless what is meant by "clout" is where one middle-class Negro can get a reservation at the inaugural ball for some more middle-class blacks . . . and ain't much happenin there either!

The question of power (which is what the use of the term "clout" cannot obscure) for the majority of black people, and the working people in capitalist U.S.A., can only be answered on a class basis, that is, as a result of the mobilization of the entire class of bourgeoisie. The "clout" we speak of is not a few favors that indicate a prestigious social mobility in the existing system. The "clout" we speak of is the power to control our lives, which can only be gained by completely transforming the present decadent, oppressive society. In order for black people to have any real power, any real control over their lives, capitalism must be eliminated and this can be done only in concert with the rest of the working people in the state. First by building a vanguard Marxist-Leninist party, and the building of such a party is the central task of all revolutionaries at this point in our history; then by mobilizing the great masses of working people, led by such a party and guided by the science of Marxism–Leninism–Mao Tse Tung thought, to wage armed struggle, and smash capitalism and this bourgeois dictatorship, and replace it with socialism and the dictatorship of the proletariat. To transform the now privately owned means of production, to publicly owned state property under the absolute control of the majority, the working class. This is the only real *clout* there is!

Marxism and the Black Community

From the outset, revolutionary Marxism as it developed in the United States was obstructed by opportunism, racism, and chauvinism. This is because initially the United States was a slave society, or had within its borders, along with a developing capitalism based on free labor, a slavocracy, based on the slave trade, the development of which was responsible for the development of capitalism itself, the expansion of Europe into the New World, the initiation of world trade, and the emergence of the U.S.A. as a world power. The racism developed with the slave trade, as its justification, and the nation built on the slave trade, the U.S.A., internalized this aspect of capitalist ideology into the superstructure of American society very early.

Since the fall to revisionism of the CPUSA, party building has been the central task of genuine Marxist-Leninists and advanced forces in the U.S.A. The inconsistent and erroneous positions of many organizations and formations around the Afro-American national question have been a continuing obstruction to the formation of a new Leninist party. And black activists must understand that it is this party that will lead the whole of the multinational working class to revolution, as well as lead in the liberation of the black nation in the black-belt South. Groups like RCP* and OL† hold posi-

---

*Revolutionary Communist Party.
†October League; later became Communist Party (Marxist-Leninist).

tions along white chauvinist lines on the Afro-American national question, where they on the one hand pretend to recognize the right of self-determination of the black-belt nation, but on the other hand deny that that nation has the right to secede, if that is what the masses want, and set up an independent state. They claim that they do not want to uphold petit bourgeois separatist lines on the national question, but what they are upholding is a bourgeois national chauvinist line. What they should do is start upholding the Leninist Comintern line! Without the right to secession, the right of self-determination is idle talk, and to try to deny this right, while the Afro-American nation suffers under imperialism, is straight out chauvinism. The out-and-out liquidationists, like the revisionist *Guardian*, merely uphold the old Lovestoneite line, which is absolutely in support of the United States imperialist domination of the black nation. Organizations like RWL* continue to say nothing about the Afro-American national question except that they have no position, which is peculiar since they have positions on just about everything else. It also brings into question the basis for the unity of RWL and PRRWO† as the so-called "revolutionary wing," since the PRRWO is supposed to uphold the self-determination of the Afro-American nation.

These organizations, with their opportunist practices, obstruct the building of a new communist party, yet they all claim to recognize party building as the central task. The OL and RU'S‡ right opportunism, which is the main danger in the communist and workers' movement and in which they tail the mass movement, and PR-RWO and RWL's left opportunism, which isolates them from the mass movement, both objectively oppose party building.

We are now in the second stage of party building, the preparty period, the stage at which political line is the key link. And where the chief method of arriving at the correct political line is through practice in the mass movement and ideological struggle between Marxist-Leninists and the other advanced groups. By political line we mean in a very general sense the application of the theories of Marxism–Leninism–Mao Tse Tung thought as the only science of revolution, as opposed to the eclecticism and spontaneity of national

*Revolutionary Workers League—no longer exists.
†Puerto Rican Revolutionary Workers Organization—no longer exists.
‡Revolutionary Union; later became Revolutionary Communist Party.

and student movements during the late sixties and the seventies. In the second and present stage of the party-building process the political line is a key link, because now we must see if our grasp of Marxism–Leninism–Mao Tse Tung thought adheres to the objective reality of making revolution in the U.S.A. And it is only the struggle over a political line which will confirm that we have not only affirmed Marxism–Leninism–Mao Tse Tung thought, but that our actual practice is characterized by the stand, worldview, and method of the proletariat, and of dialectical and historical materialism, which is the basic philosophy of communism.

Ideological struggle over political line is the chief method by which we carry out our two main tasks at this stage of the party-building process, namely, "Marxist-Leninists unite—win the advanced to communism." This means that Marxist-Leninists must move to unite with each other, but only on a method based on communist principles. The ideological struggle over political line will unite the genuine Marxist-Leninists and differentiate them (that is, demarcate them) from the sham Marxists or opportunists. This ideological struggle over a political line (i.e., how do we apply M-L-M to the multiplicity of questions in the U.S.A.: the trade union question; the Afro-American, Chicano, and various other national questions; the woman question) must represent not merely formulations but the actual struggle to apply Marxism–Leninism–Mao Tse Tung thought to the day-do-day struggle in the U.S.A. This ideological struggle over political line must be carried out not only between Marxist-Leninists but also in front of and with the participation of the advanced workers, i.e., those workers, to paraphrase Lenin, who are class conscious, politically active, can win the confidence and trust of the masses, educate and organize the proletariat, studying and actively seeking answers to questions thrown up by the movement and society, consciously accept socialism, and will become communists based on their contact with Marxism–Leninism–Mao Tse Tung thought and their active study to turn themselves into communists.

In carrying out these two tasks, it is our view that while these two tasks must be carried out simultaneously, of all the contradictions of party building the principal contradiction is between Marxist-Leninist unity versus Marxist-Leninist disunity, with Marxist-Leninist disunity being the principal aspect of the contradiction. This disunity objectively holds the entire revolutionary development back. Marxist-Leninist unity is therefore principal in the entity "Marxist-Leninists unite—win the advanced to communism," because it is the act of uniting Marxist-Leninists that will also win the advanced to communism, since the act of uniting can only be accomplished as an outcome of an ideological struggle over political line while at work in the mass movement, which will separate the genuine form from the sham and simultaneously win the advanced to the correct line.

The fundamental principle in building a communist party is the principle of fusion, i.e., the bringing together of the communist movement with the spontaneous working-class movement. The masses struggle every day against capitalism with strikes, demonstrations in the streets, and boycotts, but that struggle is spontaneous, it rises and falls in waves, like the spontaneous struggles waged by the Black Liberation Movement in the 1960's. But Marxism–Leninism–Mao Tse Tung thought does not come from spontaneous movement but from science, and although the working class gravitates toward socialism, this positive gravitation is offset by the imposition of bourgeois ideology twenty-four hours a day on the workers by the ruling class. Therefore it is the role of the revolutionaries to bring science to the working class, and, as the degree of this fusion increases, build a Marxist-Leninist communist party.

Left opportunists hold that party building is the *only* task, but this is incorrect and leads practically to the isolation of the communists from the working-class movement. Our central task, our most important task in this prepary period is party building, because without the vanguard communist party socialist revolution is impossible. Party building is linked to two other strategic tasks, the building of an anti-imperialist united front to bring all sections of the population to revolutionary positions, and finally armed struggle to smash the bourgeois state and usher in the dictatorship of the proletariat. During the present period, party building is principal and it is chiefly stressed, but even now some of our tasks relate to other strategic tasks for socialist revolution, and party building is integrally bound up with both the united front and armed struggle.

The chief obstruction to party building is right opportunism and revisionism. Revisionism, which is the use of Marxist-Leninist terminology to put forward reformism and collaboration with imperialism, has as its main source the CPSU, which has restored capitalism in the U.S.S.R., and the CPUSA, the fifth column in this country for the social imperialist Soviet Union. In the anti-revisionist communist movement, right opportunism is chiefly pushed by the RCP and the October League; the former has already declared itself a bogus nonparty based on opportunism and trailing the mass movement and economism, and the latter, the OL, is primping and priming itself to do the same thing any minute, declaring itself a party when it has not even put together a program or united Marxist-Leninists and the advanced based on the struggle over political line. The struggle over political line is key, because it is necessary to take these various critical political lines and eventually put together a *program* that is minimum and maximum goals, and to devise strategy and tactics to carry out these tasks. It is the program which is the basis for calling a party congress and around which a legitimate Marxist-Leninist communist party can be built.

There is also a left deviation which uses super-revolutionary phrases to hide its essential opportunism, its dogmatism and empiricism. Dogmatism is starting from quotes and unrelated phrases taken from Marxist-Leninist classics but missing the essence of Marxism-Leninism, while empiricism is the opposite of dogmatism, but equally dangerous. It is following one's narrow experience and belittling revolutionary theory. The dogmatists and empiricists are joined together in a little antiparty clique known as the "Revolutionary Wing," consisting of PRRWO, dogmatist leader, and RWL, empiricist follower. For them party building is the *only* task, revolution is the *only* trend. They are opposed to all work within mass spontaneous working-class movements. They disconnect theory and practice, putting forth only propaganda, discounting the fact that propaganda, which is the general in-depth explanation of capitalism and socialism and revolution, is educational material aimed not only at the advanced workers but also at other elements of society. The wing disconnects this propaganda, which is our chief form of practical activity in this period, from agitation, which is focusing on specific issues affecting the working class and participating in those struggles, giving communist leadership to the extent that that is possible. Propaganda without agitation is sterile. Agitation without propaganda bows to spontaneity. In order to build our revolutionary vanguard party, we must expose and isolate both the right opportunists and the left opportunists of RCP and OL on one hand and PRRWO and RWL on the other. But the main danger is from the right, because in form and essence it is an open collaboration with the bourgeoisie.

The process of party building in the U.S.A. is part of the main trend of revolution which is sweeping the world, particularly the Third World. In fact the struggles of the Third World—Asia, Africa, and Latin America and other developing countries—against imperialism is the motor driving revolution around the world, the principal contradiction in the world today. Revolution is the main trend in the world today. "Countries want independence, nations want liberation, the people want revolution." Chairman Mao said that revolution is "the irrestible tide sweeping the world." The world is in great disorder, Chairman Mao said, but it is a good thing for the people; it means the old systems are falling apart, being destroyed by the force of revolution around the world. Although revolution is the main trend caused by the sharp contradiction of imperialism versus the Third World, there is another sharp contradiction of imperialism, one of the four fundamental contradictions of imperialism in the world today, and this contradiction among imperialism itself is sharpest between the two superpower imperialisms, United States and Soviet Union. This contradiction, the contention for world domination between the two superpowers, causes the trend of world war to rise as well. So that the factors for both revolution and war are rising, but clearly revolution is the main trend. We, nevertheless, must prepare for war or, as the Chinese say, we will suffer. But the major preparation for war or revolution is the building of a multinational vanguard communist party. But either revolution will stop the war or will bring revolution. And the most dangerous source of war is the social imperialist Soviet Union, which under the signboard of socialism has restored capitalism and practices imperialism and under the trick talk of "detente" is steadily preparing for world war.

As we said, the central task of revolutionaries and advanced forces in the U.S.A. today is party building, the building of a Marxist-Leninist communist party. Any political line that opposes directly or objectively the building of such a party is a bourgeois line opposed to the basic needs of the masses of people in the world, and such a line must be defeated. Lenin said that to speak of defeating imperialism without waging a relentless struggle against opportunism is a sham. The narrow nationalism which some black activists use as the reason why a multinational party cannot be built in the U.S.A. (as I said before) is just a highly processed kind of opportunism and only a communist party can wage real struggle against this opportunism. To oppose the multinational communist party is objectively to support national chauvinism and to support the bourgeoisie. Those who claim to be interested in the liberation of the black nation or in securing equal rights for black people all over the United States must be in support of the building of a vanguard communist party, because it is only with a socialist revolution that the black nation can be liberated. Otherwise, the masses of people in the United States, the multinational working class, will never be liberated. The black liberation movement must be fused with the struggle to bring proletarian revolution to the United States, to the struggle of the entire working class for revolution. This is the only way to smash capitalism and bring about the dictatorship of the proletariat, socialism, and the eventual emergence of communism.

People of the world unite to defeat the superpowers, United States and Soviet Social imperialism!

Marxist-Leninists unite: win the advanced to communism!

Build a Marxist-Leninist communist party in the U.S.A.!

Liberation for the black nation; victory to all oppressed people!!!

Black Liberation/
Socialist Revolution

The slave trade, which brought masses of Africans to the New World, marks the expansion of capitalism; it is also the beginning of world trade. The so-called triangular trade that DuBois spoke of— with slaves being brought by New England traders to the West Indies and the Southern colonies, exchanged for raw materials (e.g., cotton and tobacco, molasses) which went to England and Europe with manufactured items going to Africa to be used in trade for more slaves—this was the beginning of world trade as we know it today. And it was slaves that were the foundation of this world trade, as Karl Marx pointed out; it was slaves and world trade that made the New World important.

Millions of slaves perished during the slave trade, but this lucrative slavery business went on forming the basis for the so-called primitive accumulation of capital that made the later expansion of capitalism, including the industrial revolution, possible. There is no industrial capitalist Europe nor prosperous American colonies without the trade in African slaves.

Throughout United States history these slaves and ex-slaves have played an extremely important role in the shaping of American society, especially in the country's democratic revolutions: the Revolutionary War, which made the United States an independent developing capitalist state; the Civil War, which saw the Northern bankers and industrial capitalists defeat the Southern slavocrats for total domination of the nation; and we can include the civil-rights movement and rebellions of the 1960's as still another phase in the

U.S.A.'s democratic revolutions. In the first of these, the American Revolutionary War, black slaves and Indians at first put in with the British because they were promised freedom. When the thirteen colonies came around to seeing the doom this spelled for them, they then took up the same convenient tack of promising freedom, because at that time it was thought that slavery would just fade away since there was dwindling profit in it. But after the Revolutionary War, the cotton gin was invented, and cotton became an important international commodity, so that onto the burden of the previous patriarchal or feudalistic-type slavery was added the murderous weight of newly expanded capitalism. It was during this period in the early nineteenth century that slavery in the black belt became so notoriously brutal that the average slave had a twenty-five-year "death expectancy," which the slaver-capitalists had calculated exactly so as to get the most production for their money.

The Revolutionary War against Great Britain did not solve the slavery question, and the celebrated documents of beginning bourgeois democracy—the Declaration of Independence and the Constitution—do not even directly address the issue of slavery except to support it. When cotton became an international commodity, bringing in millions of dollars, the slavers introduced even harsher measures and even took "democratic rights" away from some of the freed slaves. For these reasons this was the period of the most intense slave rebellions, beginning with Gabriel Prosser, Denmark Vesey, and Nat Turner and Harriet Tubman's Underground Railway, later John Brown's assault on slavery.

The same pattern characterized the Civil War: the North finally was backed into using blacks to fight, because the South was winning. The North, using slaves and Northern blacks, was able to put 186,000 additional fighters into the field. At the end of the Civil War, again there was a chance for black people to become integrated into a democratic U.S.A., but that was not the intention of the ruling class. After the Northern industrialists defeated the Southern slavocrats, spearheaded by masses of working people in the North who saw slavery as a direct threat to their lives and black slaves who took up arms to ensure their own freedom, there were Reconstruction governments set up in the South. These Reconstruction governments, many of them with blacks in key and critical governing roles, brought a measure of democracy to the South, insured the enforcement of the Thirteenth, Fourteenth, and Fifteenth Amendments, which actually brought education and the vote to many poor whites as well as blacks. These Reconstruction governments were necessary at first so that the big Northern capitalists could thoroughly put down the defeated Southerners. And who was more loyal than the blacks to the Federal government which had just freed them? But once having achieved stability, the Northern bourgeoisie in the notorious Hayes-Tilden compromise of 1876 removed Federal troops from the South, and delivered the governments of the Southern states back to the defeated Southerners, who were now a comprador class for the Northern banks and industrial capitalists. Through armed counterrevolution and terror the revived Southerners destroyed the Reconstruction governments and plunged black people back into near slavery, with black codes, segregation, Jim Crow laws, KKK terror, all bought, paid for, and directed by Northern bankers and industrialists on Wall Street. And to this day the Southern bourgeoisie and managerial class are still tied directly to Wall Street.

With the destruction of the Reconstruction governments, and the imposition of rigid segregation and discrimination, all conditions now had come together for the emergence of an Afro-American nation* in the black-belt South. The black belt is an area stretching from Delaware to Texas, some 1,600 miles long and 300 deep: it could be called the cotton belt, where blacks existed for many years as slaves delivering up a cotton crop for international distribution, speaking an Afro-American dialect of American English, participating in a common economic life expressed by the development of all the classes

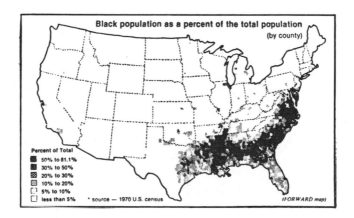

Black population as a percent of the total population
(by county)

Percent of Total
■ 50% to 81.1%
■ 30% to 50%
▨ 20% to 30%
▨ 10% to 20%
▢ 5% to 10%
☐ less than 5%   * source — 1970 U.S. census   (FORWARD map)

found in a modern nation. They were at first a largely peasant people, and a petite bourgeoisie developed even during slavery among the freed slaves. The bourgeoisie emerged, after the destruction of the Reconstruction governments, serving a segregated black market, beginning with catering, funeral service, savings and loan associations, and insurance. The existence of an Afro-American culture is by now well-known.

It is essential that we understand very clearly the relationship between the Afro-American nation in the black belt in which the majority of black people still live, and the black oppressed nationality scattered in twenty-six cities across the United States multinational state. The fundamental democratic demand of the Afro-American people must be *self-determination for the Afro-American nation in the black-belt South!!* Liberation for the black nation! This is the only guarantee of equality, the only guarantee that the demand revolution.

It is essential that we understand very clearly the relationship between the Afro-American nation in the black belt in which the majority of black people still live, and the black oppressed nationality scattered in twenty-six cities across the United States multinational state. The fundamental democratic demand of the Afro-American people must be *self-determination for the Afro-American nation in the black-belt South!!* Liberation for the black nation! This is the only guarantee of equality, the only guarantee that the demand for equal rights and democratic rights for the black oppressed nationality scattered throughout the United States will be satisfied. But there is no equality without power. Only a naïve or a brainwashed American believes otherwise. Malcolm told us that without political power there can be no social equality. Black power is still a correct cry! Black unity is still a correct cry! But black power can only come through revolution, a revolution that destroys the basis for the oppression of the black nation which is United States imperialism, white racist capitalism. And black unity, a black united front, must be formed on the basis of revolutionary principles and struggle. This struggle will be first between the different classes in the black nation so that the direction of that united front is according to the needs of the black majority, that is, the black working class, and then the struggle will be against the black nation's enemies. The black nation and oppressed nationality are composed of all the classes in a modern nation. Black workers (assembly-line workers, equipment operators, coal miners, steel and iron workers, service workers), they compose some 90–96 percent of the black nation and oppressed nationality. There is a black petite bourgeoisie, the teachers, preachers, doctors, lawyers, social workers, which is about 3–4 percent of the black nation, a small minority. There is also a class of small farmers, peasants—who used to be the majority of the black nation prior to the migrations out of the black belt in the early part of the twentieth century. There is finally a tiny fragment, called the lumpen, the pimps, prostitutes, dopefiends, muggers, who are already broken by capitalism, which is what their name means. Obviously black unity must be based on the needs of the black majority, the working class, which is not only the largest class in the black nation and oppressed nationality, but also the most revolutionary.

Self-determination for the Afro-American nation is the basic demand of the black liberation movement: *the political control of the South!* Also throughout the U.S.A. in the ghetto reproduction of the black belt, where the black oppressed nationality lives, political control over those areas is simply the democratic rights or equal rights of the Afro-American people. But the right to decide what will be the relationship between the Afro-American people and any United States, even a socialist one, is a fundamental democratic demand which cannot be belittled in the slighest way.

The newly emergent black bourgeoisie, for a time, were the leaders of the black liberation movement, what was called the freedom struggle. But the peculiar economic and political flabbiness of the black bourgeoisie made it lose leadership of the freedom movement in the twenties, when after the sharpest economic crisis in monopoly capitalism, one-half of all black business closed. So that the struggle between the comprador sector of the black bourgeoisie, represented by Booker T. Washington and the national sector represented by W.E.B. DuBois during the nineties, was replaced later by the debate between DuBois and Marcus Garvey, who represented the impoverished sector of the petite bourgeoisie, the lawyers without clients, doctors without patients, small businessmen, who seized leadership over a great mass of black people, predominantly the newly displaced Southern peasants just arriving into the North in the twenties. The idealism and utopianism of this petite bourgeoisie, with their nationalism and "back-to-Africa-ism," was positive only insofar as it expressed the idea of race pride, solidarity between Africans and Afro-Americans, and the need for black sovereignty, but in most other respects it was wanting. It revealed clearly that the black bourgeoisie had forfeited leadership of the Black Liberation Movement.

By the 1930's, a working-class leadership had arisen, given impetus by the militant work and correct lines of the Communist Party U.S.A. by 1928 a great many blacks had been recruited into the party. The 1928 Comintern and CPUSA position on the Afro-American national question reaffirmed the Leninist position that black people constitute a nation in the black belt of the South with the right of self-determination up to and including secession! The struggles to build the unions, the Scottsboro boys' fight, the founding of the militant Sharecroppers' Union in the South were all part of the revolutionary work that the CPUSA performed. This was also the deepest incursion of Marxism-Leninism among the black masses. But by the 1940's the opportunist leadership of the CPUSA represented by Earl Browder and others had used the Second World War and the correct united-front tactic put forward by the Comintern to legitimatize their desired collaboration with the United States bourgeoisie. They put out theories of American exceptionalism: that somehow United States capitalism was different from all the rest of capitalism, that it did not adhere to universal laws governing the development of capitalism. Browder said that American capitalism was still a young progressive competitive capitalism, that it had not yet turned into its opposite, imperialism. Therefore, the traitor Browder babbled that since American capitalism was an exception one could collaborate with it, and that American capitalism would help the United States working class. But this was, and is, pure bullshit—pure traitorous bullshit!

Capitalism is the enemy of working people everywhere, and in its present monopoly stage, called imperialism, it is a menace to the majority of peoples on the planet. Capitalism is an economic system, a mode of production characterized by private ownership of the means of production, the land, factories, mineral wealth, transportation, communication, waterways, etc. This means of production is owned privately by a single class in capitalist society, called the capitalist class or the bourgeoisie. The principal contradiction in this bourgeois society, and the United States is the leading bourgeois society in the world, is the contradiction between the private ownership of the means of producing wealth, against the public character of the production process itself. That is, it takes millions of people to produce the wealth, laboring long hours in factories, mines, on docks, in shops, yet the class that makes gigantic wealth from this labor is the bourgeoisie, who do no work at all. All the wealth that the workers produce that they do not get is called *surplus value*, and this is the secret of capitalism that Karl Marx discovered. One hundred workers in 1 hour put together 100 automobiles from which a gross profit of $500,000 can be realized. The workers are paid for that hour $10 each, times 100 is $1,000. Subtract that $1,000 from $500,000 and you begin to understand what surplus value is, and you also understand why capitalism must be destroyed and why working people will always be relegated to the bottom of the heap as long as the fruit of their labor is appropriated by the 0.6 percent who constitute the bourgeoisie!

Imperialism is capitalism in its monopoly stage, when it has left the boundaries of one country, having used up and controlled the raw materials and capital inside its own boundaries. It then begins to look for new sources of raw materials, new markets for its goods, new places to export its surplus capital (capital is wealth used to exploit labor). And to do this it must scramble around the world, overturning governments, setting up colonies and neocolonies, supporting tyrants.

When the leadership of the CPUSA came out saying United States imperialism was an exception they were merely laying the stage for their own liquidation, following the, by that time, bankrupt Communist Party of the Soviet Union into the tragic traitor path of revisionism. The once proud party of the Soviet Union turned revisionist after the death of Stalin, as the result of a political coup led by Nikita Khrushchev, who was an agent of the old and new bourgeoisie within the Communist Party of the Soviet Union. The CPUSA, with its own opportunist leadership, and history of critical struggle against opportunism and chauvinism, now degenerated completely into revisionism. Revisionism is the use of Marxist-Leninist phrases and terminology to cover reformism and collaboration with the bourgeoisie. The CPUSA abandoned the militant Sharecroppers' Union in the black belt, and then reversed itself on the Afro-American national question, eliminating the call for self-determination for the Afro-American nation in the black-belt South. By 1957, the CPUSA was a completely consolidated revisionist clique, a pack of new liberals who one day will probably run their lies of "peaceful transition to socialism" from the official buildings in Washington, D.C., trying to save capitalism.

The effect on the Black Liberation Movement and on the working-class struggles and struggles of other oppressed nationalities was grave. Without a revolutionary Marxist-Leninist party to give leadership, the various mass struggles remain spontaneous, rising and falling in waves. The BLM is a particularly classic example of this. First the CPUSA began to support the comprador sector of the black bourgeoisie as the leadership of the Black Liberation Movement, the Wilkinses, Whitney Youngs, and the like. Martin Luther King emerged as spokesman for the black bourgeoisie's national sector, the sector that still has some militance, in that it objectively is in contradiction with the big bourgeoisie over its market, black people. The national sector of the black bourgeoisie wants control over its market, but this is impossible because the Afro-American nation is oppressed by imperialism, and to gain control over that black market, the black bourgeoisie would have to fight an anti-imperialist war of liberation against foreign domination. The bitter irony of this for them, however, is that any such war would invariably be led by the black working class, which might include them as part of a united front, but would never let them lead. And the goal of such a liberation struggle would be new democracy or people's democracy, and then upward to socialism. It certainly would not have as its aim the delivery of the black masses into the hands of a black bourgeoisie in place of the imperialists. Because of the traitorous actions of the CPUSA the leadership of the BLM was delivered back into the hands of the black bourgeoisie. This was the era of the civil-rights movement, a mass movement for democratic rights led by the national sector of the black bourgeoisie and petite bourgeoisie. The contrast with the black bourgeoisie position and the position of the actual masses of working people is the contrast between Dr. King's political line and the line articulated by Malcolm X, who was a spokesman for the black sector of the working class. Without a doubt Malcolm X was the most influential black leader of his time, and historically will be judged to be the most significant leader of the entire period.

It was Malcolm, who in the face of the line of "we shall overcome" and "turn the other cheek," which were the metaphysical watchwords of the black bourgeois leadership, put forward the line that black people had the right to *self-determination, self-respect, and self-defense.* He said that if we had to struggle for civil rights, which are merely the democratic rights of any citizen of a society, then we must not be citizens in the first place. Malcolm made us aware of our connection with Africa, both historically and politically. It was Malcolm X who said that the March on Washington was "a black bourgeois status symbol," which would solve nothing!

Malcolm X influenced a whole generation of black people and people of other nationalities as well. And his expulsion by the Nation of Islam for remarks he made about the Kennedy assassination was merely one splitting into two, showing that the revolutionary nationalism of Malcolm X could not exist within the cultural and religious nationalist and black capitalist framework of Elijah Muhammad's Nation of Islam.

The line of self-defense was picked up by people like Robert Williams in North Carolina, who comprador Wilkins also fired for "firing up" some Klansmen in Monroe, North Carolina. Also the Deacons for Self-defense in Bogalusa and the Black Panther Party in California were deeply influenced by Malcolm as well as Stokely Carmichael and Rap Brown of SNCC. Carmichael's cry of "black power" was merely putting forward Malcolm's line of black nationalism, and Huey Newton's militant leadership and Bobby Seale and the Panthers marching into the California legislature with arms were simply carrying out in practice Malcolm's message to the grassroots of armed self-defense.

As a result of Malcolm's great leadership, the BLM moved very quickly from an idealist-led mass movement with metaphysical goals to a revolutionary mass movement, culminating in the mass rebellions in the late sixties carried out predominantly by black working-class people. The motion from Dr. King's "we shall overcome" to Rap Brown's revolutionary cry "if America don't come round, America need to be burnt to the ground" is not possible without Malcolm X's revolutionary leadership and example!

But the lack of a revolutionary Marxist-Leninist party remained a tragic vacuum dooming the Black Liberation Movement and the other workers' movements to spontaneity. It should be clear that the reason the black rebellions of the 1960's could not become revolution is that there was no Marxist-Leninist leadership in the form of a revolutionary party. And renegades like the CPUSA played the bourgeoisie's game by constantly denouncing leaders like Malcolm, calling him "a police agent," and "the same as the Ku Klux Klan." If they were examples of Marxists, of communists, then we wanted nothing to do with them. But they weren't. It should have been obvious they were simply misguided petit bourgeois reformists and white chauvinists to boot.

Malcolm X's assassination left a vacuum in the Black Liberation Movement, one made even more glaring and tragic by the principal vacuum left by the absence of a genuine communist party in the U.S.A. For one thing, petit bourgeois leadership moved into this vacuum, and leading forces in the Black Liberation Movement made tragic errors. The cultural nationalism that simply ascribed black oppression to all white people was finally simply the ideology of the small merchants protecting their tiny market, a bourgeois philosophy that objectively served the bourgeois ruling class by dividing the working class. Chauvinism has the same political base as opportunism, collaboration with the bourgeoisie, even going so far as to work with the bourgeoisie against the workers of other nations. The economic base of opportunism is the superprofits ripped out of the Third World by imperialism that allows it to bribe a small section of the working class and petite bourgeoisie, the so-called labor aristocrats.

Nationalism, like everything else, must be looked at dialectically. It has two aspects, a revolutionary nationalism, which is positive, and the negative side, which is reactionary or narrow nationalism. Revolutionary nationalism is the resistance by the oppressed nation to that oppression; it is resistance to imperialism, the will to self-determination. It is the key element motivating the people and nations of the Third World as they wage their just revolutionary struggles against imperialism all over the world. The struggle between the Third World and imperialism is the sharpest contradiction in the world today, and the motor driving revolution around the world!

Black people are a nation in the black-belt South, and an oppressed nationality throughout the rest of the United States. It is absolutely natural that they should be animated by the fiercest of revolutionary nationalism. Reactionary nationalism, in contrast, which preaches exclusiveness, isolation, the superiority of onè nationality over the other, is an exact replica of white chauvinism reversed. Reactionary nationalism is metaphysical, and like one variation of it, cultural nationalism, uses culture in a static, unchanging way. Reactionary nationalism is also the cover which the bourgeoisie of a nation try to get over, so that we get black capitalism preached to us by certain Negroes as more positive than white capitalism. As if black exploitation was sweeter than white or black bullets could not kill black people like white ones. (Ask Africans and West Indians; they'll tell you!)

The absence of a vanguard party, and the practice of the revisionists and chauvinists who masqueraded as communists, such as the CPUSA, was also another catalyst for the bourgeois cultural nationalism that developed in a large sector of the Black Liberation Movement. The organization I was a member of at that time, the Congress of African People, has engaged in self-criticism for being involved with this bourgeois ideology, and some time ago removed itself from the ranks of cultural nationalists to embrace Marxism—Leninism—Maoism.

The other major trend of the BLM during the sixties was represented by the Black Panther Party, which initially forcefully carried out Malcolm's correct line of armed self-defense: the right to bear arms in the defense of our lives, in contrast to turn the other cheek—and let it get blown away too! But without Marxist-Leninist guidance this line was perverted into a kind of gun cult, which quickly brought the brutal forces of the bourgeois state down on the Panthers in bloody repression. Also, under the sinister influence of the Bakuninist-anarchist ideology spread by Elder Eldridge Cleaver, which masqueraded as Marxism, the Panthers pushed the incorrect line that the revolutionary class base that would lead socialist revolution was the lumpen, i.e., the pimps, hustlers, dopepushers, and prostitutes; thus romanticizing an inconsistent, sometimes dangerous, class already destroyed by capitalism. But the revolutionary social force of proletarian revolution is the working class, the masses of workers, who armed with the science of revolution, Marxism—Leninism—Mao Tse Tung thought, by means of a revolutionary vanguard party, will smash capitalism, establish the dictatorship of the proletariat, and build socialism.

The Black Liberation Movement includes a number of tendencies and organizations and classes all struggling in some way, to some degree, against national oppression and for democracy. There are black capitalists such as the Nation of Islam who consider themselves part of it. There are right-wing nationalists such as CORE, which recently advocated sending black Vietnam veterans to Angola in a scheme that seemed to have leaped directly from the State Department's feverish brow. There are cultural nationalists, who are also part of the broad and contradictory Black Liberation Movement, some of whom are still including health tips, such as chewing your grains 1,000 times, as methods of liberation. There are Pan-Africanists (black Zionists) who still think we must return to Africa to find our home. While we must realize the historical and political significance of our relationship to Africa, we must abandon the idealism and confusion that does not allow us to see that our principal struggle is for the land we have lived on for almost four centuries, for the liberation of the black nation in the black-belt South and the black oppressed nationality throughout the rest of this country. The broad masses of black people who are struggling day after day against the robbery and exploitation and limitation of democratic rights that characterizes national oppression realize it. And this national oppression comes with the added horrors of racism, the monster created by capitalism and its slave ships.

We must understand that there will be no black liberation until the system of monopoly capitalism is destroyed, that this is the economic base and root of our oppression. Finally only those aspects of the Black Liberation Movement which oppose imperialism and fight for consistent democracy can really be considerd as revolutionary; the rest must be exposed as reactionary and as aides to our oppressors.

We must also be very clear by now that skin color is no indicator of one's political line, and that black liberation, the self-determination of the Afro-American nation and the liberation of the black oppressed nationality, will only come through armed, violent revolution, but a revolution made in concert with the entire multinational working class. In order for such a revolution to become a reality, the masses of working people must be led by a Marxist-Leninist communist party, the party Lenin described as the party of a new type, a party of the working class, a party composed of the advanced sector of the working class, advanced because they are armed with the science of revolution. This is why the central task of all revolutionaries in the U.S.A. today must be the building of such a Marxist-Leninist party, because without such a party we are at the mercy of monopoly capitalism and its bloody bourgeois rulers.

In the United States today there is a severe economic crises, despite the constant yammer of the bourgeoisie's paid liars who tell us different, who try to conjure up once a week a new "upturn." Depressions are cyclical occurrence in capitalism becauses of the anarchistic production of commodities for profit rather than for people's needs. Periodically markets are flooded because the impoverished masses simply cannot absorb the torrent of unnecessary commodities. Workers are then laid off, while sometimes prices rise at the same time, because the capitalists try to make the same profit off a lower volume of sales. And the largely paper money of the decadent society no longer represents actual labor, but instead printers' ink and bourgeois desperation, and so we have inflation.

To the wave of this economic crisis which grips the entire capitalist world is added the powerful force of the peoples and nations of the Third World, Africa, Asia, and Latin America and other regions, which are the chief fighters against imperialism, colonialism, neocolonialism, Zionism, and superpower bullying and control—called hegemonims. As the revolutionary forces drive United States imperialism out of Asia and Africa and Latin America, the economic crisis grows even more intense, because the captive markets and sources of cheap raw materials and labor that the imperialists counted on to make superprofits are forcibly ripped away from them. And the exploitation of workers inside the United States must also intensify, or the bourgeoisie cuts back and lays off.

At the root of a great deal of the tension and disorder in the world today is superpower contention. The struggle between the U.S.A., and the U.S.S.R. for control of the world. Since the Vietnamese War, the United States has been in open decline, clearly on the defensive, trying desperately to hold on to its ill-gotten gains, while the lean and hungry superpower, the newcomer to the banquet of imperialism, the Soviet Union, has become the more aggressive superpower, and the main danger of war. The reason for this is that the United States is still economically stronger than the Soviet Union, and in order to contend with the United States, as Lenin pointed out in his book *Imperialism, the Highest Stage of Capitalism*, they must wildly seek to expand, which is what imperialism must do to live. Imperialism must seek new sources of raw materials, new markets for its goods, new places to invest capital, new spheres of interest—it must seek new places to dominate, to assert its hegemonism, or it will perish. In the era of imperialism the whole world has already been divided up, so that there are no new places to discover; there is only contention, and finally war, to see who will dominate what exists. In the Middle East, Africa, Southeast Asia, the superpower contention is sharpest, yet its focus is Europe, with its wealth and strategic political location: Because of their economic system the Soviet Union is the most dangerous source of war.* They are a cap-

---

*1976.

italist country—capitalism was restored in the early 1960's, after the death of Stalin—and internationally they are an imperialist country. Their gross national product is half that of the United States, yet they have already surpassed the United States in conventional weapons, and spend more on war preparations than the United States. Hence, with a war economy, like Hitler's "Guns Before Butter" program before World War II, Soviet socialist imperialism is desperate for colonies, as its wild antics in Angola, Zaire, Ethiopia, Somalia, Egypt, and the Sudan show. Eventually this superpower contention will lead to World War III, but revolution is the main trend in the world, and either revolution will prevent war, or war will lead to revolution.

Even though revolution is the main trend in the world today, the factors for both war and revolution are rising. And the people must prepare for this imperialist war despite the fraudulent line of "detente" which one superpower throws around and the other conjures with. The politics of imperialism is war, and the people must prepare for such a war, or suffer. The only preparation for such a war, just as the only preparation for revolution, is the building of a vanguard Marxist-Leninist communist party, to smash capitalism and transform the privately owned means of production, the land, factories, mineral wealth, mines, transportation, into publicly owned state property under the revolutionary dictatorship of the proletariat.

Black liberation will come only through revolution and it is part and parcel of proletarian revolution. Socialist revolution can only come led by a party which combines the entire multinational working class guided by Marxism–Leninism–Mao Tse Tung thought. Stooge Jimmy Carter's eighty-eight teeth, his colored stooges, women stooges, trade-union bureaucrat stooges, will change nothing in this society but the accent in which the lies will be told. There will never be the change we seek under capitalism; only revolution and socialism can bring a truly just and equitable society.

Marxist-Leninists unite—win the advanced to communism!!
Build a revolutionary Marxist-Leninist party in the U.S.A.!!
Black liberation—socialist revolution!!

Black Liberation
Today

Since the 1950's the BLM, then entering its civil-rights phase, has undergone many dramatic changes, transformations, and developments. On the other hand, the civil-rights movement was a mass movement but led by the black national bourgeoisie, with a political line most objectively represented by Martin Luther King. We call it the national bourgeoisie because we refer to that sector of the Afro-American bourgeoisie that has some objective antagonistic contradictions with imperialism. It is that sector of the black bourgeoisie that is in reality struggling for control of the black market, which they can never get because the imperialists will not give up control of this market without revolution. But when there is revolution it will not be a revolution that will put the black bourgeoisie into hegemony over the black nation in the black-belt South, or the black oppressed nationality that is spread throughout the rest of the U.S.A.

It was the national wing that could articulate some struggle against black national oppression, against our oppression as a black nation, but because of its class interests could never carry the struggle beyond the civil-rights phase. The extension of democratic rights that marked "equal access," voting rights, and slight economic liberalism that black capitalism was supposed to signify only totally benefited a small sector of the black population, the black bourgeoisie and petite bourgeoisie, the upper class and middle class. Although there were some cosmetic changes offered to the black working class and small farmer, these were for the most part illusions, and by now, with the rising tide of economic crisis throughout the capitalist world, these illusions are being rapidly destroyed. The election of Jimmy Carter notwithstanding.

On the other hand, the comprador wing, that part of the black bourgeoisie that directly represents imperialism, articulated by the leadership of the NAACP and Urban League, could never really lead the Black Liberation Movement since the time of Booker T. Washington, although the bankrupt Communist Party U.S.A., which had by the fifties turned totally revisionist, cutting out proletarian revolution and the dictatorship of the proletariat from its sham version of "Marxism," pushed the compradors, led by Roy Wilkins, as the leadership of the BLM. In their slimy revisionist illogic they now said that bourgeois integration was the road to socialism. And while we favor the voluntary union of all nationalities in common struggle against monopoly capitalism and imperialism, the bourgeoisie's fabric of delusion and illusion have nothing to do with the communist goal of unification of the whole multinational working class. The CPUSA went so far as to characterize the great working-class black revolutionary Malcolm X as "a police agent," and said that "the nationalism of Malcolm X was the same as the nationalism of the Ku Klux Klan."

Why was this? Because once the CPUSA turned its back on Marxism-Leninism, it reversed its line on the black nation. It no longer viewed black people in the black belt of the U.S.A. as an oppressed nation, which they are, with the right of self-determination ("up to and including secession"), whose struggle for liberation is part and parcel of the overall struggle of the whole working class and oppressed nationalities for democracy and socialist revolution. The CPUSA began to say that black people in the U.S.A. had already achieved self-determination, and that we had opted for integration into America under imperialism. Truly a traitorous and chauvinist statement! As if the black masses are voluntarily being oppressed!

An incorrect position on the Afro-American national question and hence failure to support black self-determination in the black belt has plagued so-called socialists in the United States, undermined by opportunism and its "finished form," chauvinism. Failure to understand the specific scientific basis for the Afro-American nation's existence has led to the right-opportunist (Lovestoneite) liquidation of the question, claiming that the black nation has been totally absorbed within the United States imperialist structure, which is word-for-word support of the bourgeoisie and its policy of national oppression of the Afro-American people. Failure to understand this key question is a consistent democratic demand for a nation, scientifically defined as a "historically constituted community of people, formed on the basis of a common territory, common language, common economic life, with a common psychological makeup, manifest as a common culture," has also led some people to make such errors as claiming that black people were a nation wherever they were in the U.S.A., and also to uphold other petit bourgeois, nationalist deviations such as cultural autonomy, i.e., seeking cultural separation of nationalities, rather than political autonomy for oppressed nations—the right to self-determination.

Malcolm X's development and articulation of the ideas that black people were a black nation with the rights of self-determination, self-respect, and self-defense signaled the reemergence of the black working class into a leadership position in the Black Liberation Movement. And although the mass civil-rights movement was led by the black national bourgeoisie, in the future it will be understood that the most significant and farsighted leader of the Black Liberation Movement during the sixties and throughout the whole period was Malcolm X. Even though there were a host of movements, organizations, different class strata, and interests being sounded all as part of the overall Black Liberation Movement, once Malcolm X came forward, although he came out of the religious and cultural nationalist framework of the Nation of Islam, he took a consistent and developing revolutionary black nationalist and clearly anti-imperialist position. The dramatic split between Malcolm X and the Nation of Islam came shortly after John Kennedy was assassinated by the CIA, and Malcolm called it "chickens coming home to roost." He was fired from the Nation of Islam, as fast as Robert Williams was fired from the Monroe County NAACP earlier for publicly stating black people "must meet violence with violence" when "nonviolence" was the battle cry of the black bourgeoisie. These kinds of splits showed the development of the BLM, away from the leadership and control by the black bourgeoisie, and back toward the leadership by the working class, who are the most militant fighters for democracy and ultimately for socialism.

Malcolm knew that black liberation was a political struggle, not a religious struggle. He knew it was an anti-imperialist struggle, not a struggle for black capitalism. Malcolm knew it was an international struggle, and he sounded the call for the struggle of Third World people versus imperialism, which is still one of the sharpest struggles in the world and the motor for revolution around the world. As a result of Malcolm's political line, the student movement, characterized by SNCC, which had been influenced by the black bourgeois line of nonviolence and bourgeois assimilation, began to turn around under the leadership of Stokely Carmichael and Rap Brown. Stokely Carmichael was identified with the cry "black power," which was a further thrust of the black nationalism that Malcolm talked about. And Rap Brown was identified with the national eruption of black rebellions from Harlem to Watts, to Newark and Detroit, which showed the truly revolutionary nature of the BLM!

The calls and movements for self-defense identified with Robert Williams, the Black Panthers, the Deacons from Louisiana, all were indebted to the political line of Malcolm X, representing the articulation and reemergence of the black working class into leadership. Africanism and Pan-Africanism were also inspired by Malcolm's call for black people in the United States to recognize our African origins, as part of the struggle against the cultural aggression that is part of imperialist oppression. But also Malcolm was pointing out the need for unity by the Third World against imperialism, which Chairman Mao Tse Tung still calls for, even today.

The splits in the Black Liberation Movement bear out the fact that one splits into two, that the contradictions inside a thing, the confrontation of opposites that is the dialectical definition of development, can also make a thing split in half, into two opposites. The Malcolm X–Nation of Islam split, the Robert Williams–NAACP split, the SNCC-Panther split, the Panther–"US" organization split, the Congress of African People–"US" organization split, all revealed the truth of one splitting into two. The Black Liberation Movement, as its name suggests, was and is a broad front of various organizations, class strata, and interests, generally united against black national oppression. But on how (or if) that national oppression is to be ended forever these groups diverge.

The Black Panthers for instance made significant contributions to the struggle for black liberation. They raised to a higher level Malcolm's line on self-defense. By carrying guns into the California legislature in 1967 they established in the consciousness of Afro-Americans from coast to coast that we had the right to armed self-defense, and that we did not have merely to turn our cheeks as our little children got blown up in churches or as we ourselves were beaten in the street. The Panthers also introduced talk of Marxism-

Leninism into the Black Liberation Movement again, but not for the first time, since the African Blood Brotherhood of the early twenties actually put forward scientific socialism as the only ideology to liberate black people. (See *Black Bolshevik*, by Harry Haywood, Liberator Press, 1977.) Also during the thirties Marxism-Leninism made a distinct impression on the *BLM* when the CPUSA was at the peak of its revolutionary militancy and taking the correct line on the Afro-American national question, but that was reversed with the traitorous actions of the CPUSA when they turned revisionist and reformist.

In fact, it cannot be overstated that the fall to revisionism of the CPUSA left the spontaneous struggle of the many disoriented and without scientific leadership. It must be seen as the principal condition of the erroneous and harmful domination of bourgeois nationalism and cultural nationalism in many parts of the BLM. Malcolm X's assassination completed the vacuum, destroying the truly revolutionary and working-class leadership of the BLM, leaving it to be directed more and more by petit bourgeois trends.

But the Panthers' error was, first, that they turned the correct cry of self-defense into a "gun cult," and, second, that they incorrectly identified the lumpenproletariat, the pimps, hustlers, and prostitutes, as the social force that would make revolution in the U.S.A., when in reality it is the working class, the black working class in unity with the other sectors of the working class, the other nationalities, who led by a vanguard Marxist-Leninist party will make socialist revolution. The notorious split between the Panthers and the "US" organization was of course largely the work of police agents and the FBI, who now openly admit it. But the "US" organization and its spearhead of Africanism that others raised to a higher level of militant Pan-Africanism, in support of the African liberation movements, also made critical errors. For instance, seeing whites as the enemy rather than the system of monopoly capitalism as the true adversary, and thinking that imposing some neotraditional "African culture" on blacks in the United States would produce a revolutionary movement. These are errors of bourgeois nationalism and petit bourgeois idealism, of which I and the organization I belong to, CAP, were also guilty, and for which we must still make extensive self-criticism.

The fact that there was an "US"-Panther split, and for several years intense polemics between the two general ideological tendencies inside the BLM, covered the fact that within the cultural nationalist movement there was also a split. And the militant Pan-African movement that was characterized by organizations like YOBU, CAP, borrowed from both wings of the split movement of the late 1960's and culminated in the development of two broad liberation fronts: the National Black Assembly, which first met in Gary, Indiana, in 1972, and the African Liberation Support Committee, which brought together 50,000 people all over the U.S.A. to march against colonialism and imperialism in Africa. As many of us, who were cultural nationalists to one extent or another, came closer and closer to the real African liberation movement, as we witnessed our brothers and sisters in Guinea-Bissau, Mozambique, Angola, Namibia, Azania, fighting against imperialism, it became clearer to us that African liberation was primarily against imperialism, and that imperialism itself was the enemy. And as the neocolonial African rulers of several nations, and neocolonial leaders in the West Indies, and finally our own developing petit bourgeois, bureaucratic elite inside the United States emerged, by the middle seventies, it was clear that imperialism could also rule through native agents, as Cabral pointed out. We found out further by the time of the 6PAC (1974) that the most progressive governments of Africa had also recognized that neocolonialism was a critical enemy of liberation in Africa, and also stated openly that revolutionary Pan-Africanism had to be a worldwide struggle by African people against imperialism and for socialism!

There are many other contrasting aspects to the whole Black Liberation Movement as a broad and somewhat contradictory front against black national oppression. We have black capitalists who consider themselves part of it, the Nation of Islam for instance. There are also right-wing nationalists such as CORE, which recently advocated sending black Vietnam veterans to Angola in a scheme that seemed to have popped directly out of the CIA's feverish brow. There are cultural nationalists, some of whom are still including health tips for chewing your grains 100 times as a method of liberation. There are utopian Pan-Africanists who still think we must return to Africa to find our home, although when we understand our African history and heritage, we also understand that we have been here four centuries and that there is an oppressed black nation in the South that will be liberated, along with all the rest of the black oppressed nationality throughout the United States. There are also the broad masses of black people who are struggling day after day against the robbery and exploitation and limitation of democratic

107

rights that characterizes national oppression, with the added horrors of racism. It is our view, as Marxist-Leninists whose ideology is Marxism–Leninism–Mao Tse Tung thought, that there will be no black liberation until the system of monopoly capitalism, the economic base and root cause of our oppression, is destroyed. And that finally only those aspects of the Black Liberation Movement which oppose imperialism and fight for consistent democracy can really be considered as revolutionary, and the rest must be exposed as reactionary and as aides to our oppressors.

We are very clear now that skin color is no indicator of one's political line, and what is more that our liberation will come only through socialist revolution, and socialist revolution can only be made by uniting the multinational working class behind a revolutionary Marxist-Leninist antirevisionist communist party, what Lenin called the party of a new type, so as to distinguish it from the old social democratic, electoral-dominated parties. This party would be an advanced sector, an advanced detachment of the working class, advanced because it possessed the science of revolution. Such a party could lead the working masses in revolutionary people's war against the bourgeoisie and their lackeys. Such a party would be the highest form of organization in the working class, a party characterized by discipline, unity, that would not merely tail behind the masses but would be the general staff of the class to lead it in the struggle for power, to lead it in revolution, to lead it in the destruction of the bourgeois state machine and the seizure of state power. A party itself that would be the instrument through which the dictatorship of the proletariat would be instituted and the proletarian or workers' state created!

To understand how this will be done it is necessary to understand something about the nature of the world today. As our Chinese comrades say, "The world's in great disorder," meaning that all over the world the old order is being contested and overthrown, this is a good thing for the people. It means imperialism, which is the present ruler of much of the world, the monopoly, parasitic, moribund, or dying stage of capitalism, is truly on its death bed. That the four fundamental contradictions in the world today have all gone to the point beyond which socialist revolution begins—between labor and capital in the western capitalist countries; between imperialism and the Third World; between imperialism and imperialism, the sharpest of which is that between the U.S.A. and the U.S.S.R.; and between imperialism and socialist countries. These four fundamental contradictions are all sharpening, but the sharpest are the antagonistic struggle between imperialism and the peoples and nations of the Third World—Africa, Asia, and Latin America—which is the driving force of revolutionary struggle around the world, and also the contradiction between the two superpower imperialisms, the U.S.A. and the U.S.S.R. This struggle between the superpowers as they contend all over the world—in Portugal, the Middle East, Southeast Asia, Europe, and now in Africa/Angola—will invariably lead to war—either conventional or nuclear war. The struggle of the Third World's peoples against imperialism and the struggle between the U.S.A. and U.S.S.R. social imperialism forces more and more cutbacks, layoffs, and budget cuts inside the U.S.A. as the world market of imperialism steadily contracts. More and more of the existing wealth of the superpowers must be spent arming for world war so that many of the reforms and concessions given to workers inside the U.S.A. must be pulled back, and the whole working class grows more and more fed up with this unworkable system, becomes subjectively more revolutionary and more objectively in unity with the oppressed peoples around the world.

We must build our revolutionary party before the ruling class moves toward fascism, because only revolution, socialist revolution, can stop the world war, but on the other hand the people led by a Marxist-Leninist vanguard party will turn any imperialist war into revolution.

It is the central and critical task of all Marxist-Leninists to unite ideologically and politically and to win the advanced workers to Marxism–Leninism–Mao Tse Tung thought, in order to build the vanguard communist party necessary for revolution. It is the critical task of revolutionaries within the Black Liberation Movement to bring Marxism–Leninism–Mao Tse Tung thought, the science of revolution, to the forces of black liberation, particularly the working masses. It is our goal to unite the struggle for black liberation with the struggles of the whole working class and oppressed nationalities, to unite the Black Liberation Movement with the struggle of the whole people towards democracy, revolution, the dictatorship of the proletariat, socialism, and the eventual emergence of communism.

Marxist-Leninists unite, win the advanced to communism!
Build a revolutionary vanguard Marxist-Leninist communist party!
Liberation for the black nation!
Socialist revolution!
Victory to all oppressed people!!!

Ten Years Later: Newark/Detroit

Ten years ago (1967) small wars, rebellions, broke out in Detroit and Newark. Along with Watts, which took place two years earlier in 1965, these were the fiercest and bloodiest of the modern black rebellions. During this period, the mid-sixties, rebellions took place in over 100 major American cities. And they were not carried out, as the newspapers and media would have us believe, by pimps and prostitutes. Even the Civil Rights Commission report on the rebellions confirms that these armed uprisings were carried out by the black working class. By black workers rising up against their double oppression by monopoly capitalism.

Ten years ago in the turbulent sixties, these rebellions flared up violently throughout this whole society. Yet the causes of these rebellions are still part of American Society. Also those rebellions, while raising the Black Liberation Movement to a new high in militance, did not turn into revolution. Some facts for those who doubt the fierceness and militance of those rebellions: in Watts in 1965, 35 people died, and property damage was estimated at two million dollars. In Newark and Detroit, 2 years later: 26 died in Newark, 1,500 were injured, over 1,000 were arrested; in Detroit, 2 weeks later, 40 died, at least 2,000 were injured, and 5,000 left homeless. It was necessary to call up 4,700 Federal paratroopers, the 82nd Airborne, along with 8,000 National Guardsmen. When the bourgeois media speaks of "riots" they do so to denigrate, put down, the social focus and militancy of these uprisings. These were rebellions made against an oppressive social system, not drunken college students whoopin' it up at Georgia Tech!

But we have to understand just what made these rebellions, why they rose when they did, why they abated, and why things seemed to have cooled down. First, the rebellions mark the end of the civil-rights period; they are the qualitative change, the sudden leap which comes as a result of continuous quantitative buildup. Marxism teaches us that quantity changes into quality. The decade of civil-rights preaching, praying, singing, in the face of the mad-dog racist agents of United States capitalism, had given rise to a totally different kind (quality) of expression.

Malcolm X had been the harbinger, the predictor, of this change, as he time and again characterized the contradiction, the opposition, the black masses had to the ideological and political line of the national black bourgeois leadership of the civil-rights movement, embodied most completely by Martin Luther King. The black bourgeois and petit bourgeois leadership's ideological and political line was metaphysical and idealistic, as well as being essentially reformist. Many of the civil-rights demonstrations, especially the earliest, emphasized submissive Christian philosophy and rituals. Nevertheless, it was the masses' struggle against national oppression and for democratic rights, which this bourgeois leadership leaped to the front of, that made the civil-rights movement powerful. And the only reason the black bourgeoisie regained its leadership over the civil-rights phase of the Black Liberation Movement was because the working-class leadership that emerged in the 1930's was related to the then revolutionary Communist Party U.S.A., which by the 1940's had degenerated and by the late fifties was an openly reformist tool of the bourgeoisie, which it still is today. In the forties the CPUSA withdrew its slogan "Self-determination for the Afro-American nation in the black-belt South," and began to follow the chauvinist line that had circulated in the party for years that said that the Afro-American people had already won self-determination and opted for integration into the imperialist U.S.A.! And besides, according to the traitorous pig Earl Browder, who was chairman of the CPUSA and personally led the party into revisionism, "United States capitalism was young and progressive anyway and the working class should regard it as their ally." These traitors to working people then threw away Marxism-Leninism by pushing the bourgeois line that socialism should come peacefully. The peaceful, parliamentary transition to socialism, they still call it. And it is still a lie even as it drools out of the mouths of revisionists like Angela Davis and Gus Hall and Brezhnev today.

The fact that the leadership of the BLM fell back into the hands of the black bourgeoisie must be laid at the feet of the revisionist CPUSA, which backed the comprador black bourgeoisie, like Roy Wilkins, as the leadership of the BLM, and babbled backwardly that integration was the road to socialism. Not revolution but integration was the line. But discrimination, segregation, the pincers of national oppression, are caused by capitalism, and they cannot be destroyed until monopoly capitalism is destroyed. And monopoly capitalism cannot be destroyed peacefully. This was the truth of the rebellions. Only violence, armed struggle, can change capitalist society to socialist society; not turn the other cheek, or nonviolent "revolution," or we-shall-overcome by kneeling and praying as the police dogs attack, and the racists shoot us down. Malcolm X's line of self-determination, self-respect, self-defense, summed up the black working people's feelings in opposition to the black bourgeoisie's submission to exploitation/oppression by monopoly capitalist/racist United States society.

The "peaceful transition to socialism" the revisionists dished up and the black bourgeoisie's "nonviolent revolution" are reformist lines and simply metaphysics, idealism, and reformism running amuck. They are linked, and in a capitalist society so violent that in only five years it had assassinated both the working-class and black-bourgeois spokesmen for the Black Liberation Movement, as well as two bourgeois spokesmen as well: Malcolm X, Dr. King, John and Bobby Kennedy. This is a society so hellbent on destroying itself that in the decade since the major rebellions, all of its presidents have met with violent, unsatisfactory, or disgraceful ends right out in public. Neither Kennedy, nor Johnson, nor Nixon returned from public life to a private life full of adulation. They were killed or hounded out of office by the contradictions of swiftly declining United States capitalism.

The civil-rights movement was fomented and rose up initially in the black-belt South, the land base of the Afro-American nation. This was predictable because the black belt is the oppressed black nation victimized by United States imperialism in much the same way as the nations and peoples of the Third World, the so-called undeveloped countries of Asia, Africa, and Latin America and other regions, have been victimized. It was in the deep South that black people grew into a nation. The Black Liberation Movement after the destruction of the Reconstruction became in essence a struggle for self-determination in the black belt, for liberation of the Afro-

American nation, as well as a struggle for democratic rights for the blacks outside of the black nation itself. Both these struggles could only have meaning by directly challenging the monopoly capitalist rulers of United States society, and struggling to destroy them.

The black bourgeoisie could only take the civil-rights movement so far. As far as they needed it to go, to enable them to be more powerful capitalists and more thorough exploiters of the market: black people. And even this was not done. But the struggle against United States imperialism allowed a broad liberation front to form, which included working people, the student movement, nationalists both backward and revolutionary, the petite bourgeoisie and the national bourgeoisie. This is what should happen, but the leadership of such a broad unity must be in the hands of the working class, the proletariat, otherwise it will get stalled, sidetracked, or turned around. The 1960's showed us this very clearly.

In the northern cities however, more industrialized, where there was more of a concentration of the black proletariat and working people, the black bourgeoisie's metaphysical and idealist line was more quickly overcome by the people's outrage, led by heroic patriots like Malcolm X. Even though the ruling class's tools like the CPUSA put forth their reactionary chauvinist slime, condemning Malcolm as the same kind of nationalist as the KKK! The chauvinists never understand that revolutionary nationalism, which constitutes opposition to national oppression, is not the same nationalism as the oppressor's. And even though he came out of the bourgeois religious and cultural nationalist Nation of Islam, Malcolm X was a revolutionary nationalist patriot and anti-imperialist fighter. The fact that Elijah Muhammad had to expel him demonstrates that reactionary nationalism and revolutionary nationalism could no longer coexist in the same organization. The Nation of Islam's completely religious and black capitalist presence today points out these facts very plainly!

Malcolm's line of self-determination, self-respect, and self-defense was taken up by the most advanced sector of the black masses, and soon even organizations initially influenced by the black bourgeoisie like SNCC and CORE, both at first essentially petit bourgeoise integrationist organizations, became more nationalistic. SNCC had a fighting anti-imperialist kernel to it because they were students, and leadership like Carmichael's and later, more militantly, Rap Brown's, could pick up Malcolm's line, and take it to the black youth. Organizations like the Black Panther Party could also rise, picking up Malcolm's line of self-defense. Cultural nationalists like the "US" organization of Maulana Karenga also borrowed from Malcolm X, as did everyone else, in a truly eclectic fashion, to push their own concepts of "blackness." But two factors distorted the essentially correct line put out by Malcolm that he was refining and developing every day. First and principally, there was no Marxist–Leninist communist party in the U.S.A., guided by Marxism–Leninism–Mao Tse Tung thought. This, despite Malcolm's great and positive influence, meant that the Black Liberation Movement, and the workers' movement in general, was abandoned to spontaneity. It was not guided by science, and the only science of revolution is M-L-M. Malcolm X himself was drawn more and more in his anti-imperialist struggles toward socialism but he was not a socialist, although he condemned capitalism fiercely: "Wherever you find a capitalist you find a bloodsucker!" And he recognized, as he said in one of his lectures, that the whites he knew who most conspicuously fought against racism were all socialists. Also during his lecture at Oxford, which Gil Noble broadcast over ABC in 1977, in answer to a question about revolution Malcolm said, "When black people rise up to fight for their freedom in America, the majority of white people will join them!" He said this just two months before he was assassinated. And that is essentially why he was assassinated, because cut loose from the cultural and religious nationalism of the Nation of Islam, Malcolm's search for revolutionary truth was bound to lead to a philosophy more revolutionary than revolutionary nationalism and anti-imperialism. Such a philosophy is Marxism–Leninism–Mao Tse Tung thought! Malcolm's assassination was the second factor that led to the distortion of his line.

Various eclectic lines and organizations rise up sharply after Malcolm's death like blind men describing the elephant, all with a piece of the truth. The Panthers, largely under the anarchist and opportunist Eldridge Cleaver, perverted Malcolm's correct teaching on armed self-defense into a suicidal gun cult, and now today put forth largely the same kind of reformist programs they correctly criticized the cultural nationalist organizations like "US" and the CAP, which I belonged to, for putting out. SNCC disintegrated because of attacks on its leadership and the inability of the organization to move past the student phase. The student struggle later on was taken up by SOBU (Student Organization for Black Unity), which changed to YOBU (Youth Organization for Black Unity), which later still in the mid-seventies, together with other organizations like Malcolm X Liberation University, became Marxist-Leninists after going through the passage of Pan-Africanism and Carmichael-inspired Nkrumahism, so called.

The cultural nationalists went deeper and deeper into idealism and metaphysics, and along with that, reformism, and became essentially non-Christian metaphysicians or sometimes merely "blacker," i.e., more militant, Christian metaphysicians.

Pan-Africanism began to come into its own by the seventies and put forth the line that all black people all over the world had to unite to liberate Africa, a line to which Stokely Carmichael still holds. The danger of this line, which some of the Pan-Africanists like CAP never held, is that it says that black people should not struggle in the U.S.A., that the struggle is only in Africa. A line more helpful to United States imperialism has not been found in the black community except out-and-out open bourgeois lines. By the mid-seventies the most advanced sectors of the Pan-Africanist movement had completely broken with bourgeois nationalism and its so-called international application, Pan-Africanism, and moved to Marxism-Leninism. The fact that the AAPRP under Carmichael and some other opportunists was able to mount a march in Washington on African Liberation Day in 1977 and claim to have "founded" ALD is proof that the struggle against this reactionary nationalism is far from over.

The bourgeois and petit bourgeois leadership of the civil-rights movement has by now openly sided with the big capitalists of United States imperialism. This runs from ex-SNCC field workers who are now city councilmen and heads of boards of education in major cities like Washington, D.C., to Andy Young, one of the chief attractions in the Jimmy Carter Snake Oil and Revival Show, whose job it is now to dupe the masses into thinking United States imperialism's policy of oppression and exploitation of the Third World, especially Africa, has changed. When, of course, it has not changed at all! But because the United States imperialists are locked in dangerous confrontation and contention with the other superpower, Soviet social imperialism, the United States must now throw out a competing line to counteract the Soviets' slimy lie that they are socialist and the "natural ally of national liberation movements."

The United States imperialists, as Mao said in 1967, are still sitting on a domestic volcano, not only from the principal contradiction, labor versus capital, the bourgeoisie versus the proletariat inside the United States, but also from national movements and national struggles, such as the Black Liberation Movement and struggles by other oppressed nationalities, such as the Puerto Ricans, Chicanos, Asians, Indians, which all serve to intensify the contradictions inside this fortress of imperialism. The Puerto Rican rebellion in 1977 or the masses' reaction to the lights-out in New York City are just two examples of struggle. Internationally, the oppressed nations and peoples of the Third World have been kicking United States imperialism's behind hard and regular, and actually sent it into a decline. Defeats in Korea, Cambodia, Vietnam, Africa, have taken a deep toll of United States imperialism, and the defeat in Vietnam left it in open reeling decline. This means the superprofits it scooped out of the Third World are being ripped away, reducing and contracting the material base of opportunism here in the U.S.A. This means they have less and less superprofits to bribe and trick the people in the U.S.A. with.

At the same time, the steadily rising contention between the United States and Soviet social imperialism means that the United States must plow more and more of its national product into weaponry and cut back its illusory social programs. The Soviets have already surpassed the United States militarily, and that social imperialist–social fascist clique stands ready to launch a third world war!! The Soviet social imperialists are the most dangerous source of war in the world today, and the most dangerous threat to the independence of the Third World, cloaked as they are under the banner of "socialism." War is visibly on the horizon as the imperialists can resolve their contention through no other means but war. Modern war is based on imperialism, and the content of imperialist politics is war. But even though the factors for both war and revolution are rising, events all over the world, particularly the Third World, convince us that, despite superpower contention and their push toward inevitable war to control the world, revolution is the main trend in the world today. And the people of the Third World, Asia, Africa, and Latin America, are the fiercest and indeed the main strugglers against imperialism, colonialism, Zionism, and superpower hegemonism and domination. These are obvious facts that investigation of the world situation will readily produce. In Rhodesia, South-West Africa, South Africa, Ethiopia, Eritrea, the revolutionaries press on hour after hour to destroy imperialism in Africa. Superpower contention and intervention such as in Angola and Zaire (both times through its Cuban mercenaries) has only served to sharpen the struggle by the revolutionaries as in the case of Angola, or it has served to awaken people to the essentially vile profile of Soviet social imperialism.

The building of a revolutionary Marxist-Leninist communist party based on M-L-M in the U.S.A. is the central task, the main work, of revolutionaries today. It is part of the main trend of the revolution which is sweeping the world as an irresistible tide. Despite the bribery of some of the sixties leadership of the BLM or others' inability to abandon incorrect lines, especially bourgeois and cultural nationalist lines, the situation inside this country deteriorates from minute to minute! The same year as the Newark and Detroit rebellions, both Carl Stokes and Richard Hatcher were elected as black mayors of major cities. And the Coleman Youngs and Kenneth Gibsons that came soon after were all designed to de-ignite the BLM. But the reality of raising a petit bourgeois bureaucrat class to administer the inner cities was that this was the barest illusion. Of 500,000 elected officials in the United States, there are 3,979 black ones, or less than 1 percent.

Black capitalism was another illusion put forth after the rebellions to offer black people a nonexistent entrance into capitalism. Black business represents 2.7 percent of all business! The major black industries collectively in 1972 totaled $4.7 billion. But Westinghouse made $4.6 billion by itself—one United States giant corporation and not even one of the real giants! There was only a $2,700 gap between the income of the average white family and the average black family in 1947; in 1971 it was $3,700; but in 1973 it had grown to $5,326. As Lenin pointed out, under imperialism the working masses are ground even further and further down. Ten years after the rebellions the *Peking Review* points out that ten years ago the unemployment rate among young people was 12.2 percent; now it is 19.9 percent. Among young blacks it was 15.8 percent in 1955, 30.2 percent in 1973, and 40 percent in April 1977. Especially mentioned by *Peking Review* was Detroit, "where most of the 1.4 million people are black and the unemployment rate among black youth increased from 50 to 75 percent!" These kinds of trends exist throughout the capitalist world. But these figures show that concretely the situation has gotten worse. There is no more progress under capitalism, only degeneration, which is why the people must smash it.

We must learn from the rebellions. Learn from the sixties, emotionalism and patriotism are not enough. Some of the nationalists and Pan-Africanists of the sixties followed their idealism to its dead end. Some run mines and plantations in mother Africa in direct partnership with the national bourgeoisie. And as the two superpowers are run up out of Africa, and the principal contradiction becomes the people's own domestic bourgeoisie, these bourgeois nationalists will be the object of the wrath of their own people. Just as the bourgeois collaborators in the U.S.A. are being more and more exposed—the McKissicks, Innises, Cleavers, Carmichaels—all are objectively putting themselves in opposition to the people, while ten years ago these same men were thought to be progressive, even revolutionary. But the level of struggle has continued to rise. In the early seventies some of the national movement organizations actually began to take up and affirm M-L-M as the only revolutionary theory and to oppose and condemn eclecticism. In the last couple of years the fact has become clearer to more and more revolutionaries that party building, is our central task, and the struggle over political line, which is the concrete application of the theories of M-L-M to the concrete situation of making revolution in the U.S.A., has emerged as the key cog in the mechanism driving our struggle forward. We have moved to the second stage of the pre-party party-building period. By 1974 the most advanced elements of the Pan-Africanist movement had moved to M-L-M, undertaken self-criticism, and begun rectification to completely rid themselves of the errors and bourgeois ideology of their nationalist Pan-Africanist phrase, as they took up the struggle to build a genuine communist party in the U.S.A.

Our simultaneous tasks: "Marxist-Leninists unite—win the advanced to communism!" "Marxist-Leninists unite" is principal because it is the catalyst that increases the number of advanced forces who can be won over to M-L-M. In the 1960's, rebellion did not become revolution because there was no genuine communist party, but such rebellions will come again, even more intense and violent than the sixties, because all the contradictions in capitalism have intensified and become even more antagonistic. A few days before the lights went out in New York City the bourgeoisie was patting itself and its petit bourgeois bureaucrats on the back for cooling out the national movements. Then wham the lights go out, and there is more breaking and entering than during the sixties!

But this spontaneous struggle is not enough. Capitalism must be destroyed, and socialism built, under the dictatorship of the proletariat, the absolute domination by the workers. This can only be done by the masses, under the leadership of a genuine communist party. It can only be done through revolution, not reforms. The building of a revolutionary Marxist-Leninist communist party is the biggest step forward toward revolution we can take—and we must take it. There have been quite a few incorrect or sham party-building attempts since the degeneration of the CPUSA: groups like the POC (Provisional Organizing Committee), which turned splittist, and the PLP (Progressive Labor Party), which declared itself *the* party after early contributions like struggling against the U.S.S.R.'s revisionism and reprinting the works of Stalin. They finally sided with Liu Shao Chi against Chairman Mao and condemned all nationalism as simply nationalism, a Trot-like line, and they quickly degenerated. Another group was the NLC (National Liaison Committee) under the hegemony of the RU (Revolutionary Union), then making a contribution by introducing M-L-M to national movements such as the Young Lords, now the Puerto Rican Revolutionary Workers Organization, and the Black Workers Congress, later split into the Revolutionary Workers Congress, the MLOC (Marxist-Leninist Organizing Committee), and the Revolutionary Bloc and Workers Congress. And the IWK (I Wor Kuen) was a part of the NLC as well. Finally this broke up because a struggle had to be waged against RU, now "RCP" (Revolutionary Communist Party), for its national chauvinism in regard to the Afro-American national question and for its practice of tailing the mass movement, and the economist errors this produced and still produces.

The NCC (National Coordinating Committee) under the CL's (Communist League) tutelage, also with PRRWO and LPR (League for Proletarian Revolution), broke up because of CL's, later CLP's (Communist Labor Party), Trotskyite line, especially their attack on the People's Republic of China on May Day, 1974.

Since that time the "RCP" and CLP have both declared themselves to be parties, as well as the October League, which is now the "CP (M-L)" (Communist Party [Marxist–Leninist]). These are all opportunist groupings that are in direct opposition to a party of the proletariat. Other organizations like WVO (Workers Viewpoint Organization) and the "left" opportunist Dangerous Duo PRRWO and RWL (Revolutionary Workers League) stand on the sidelines and are threatening to call themselves *the* party as well. A heap of petit bourgeois nonparties, but no party of a new type in the U.S.A. today!

The subjectivist, petit bourgeois element still dominates the antirevisionist communist movement, which is the main reason we have no genuine Marxist-Leninist communist party. But we do have the appropriate objective conditions, such as the intensifying class struggle inside the U.S.A., the fact of an economic crisis that has worsened in the decade since the rebellions, the U.S.A.'s international position, which is desperation in decline. As the *Australian Communist* pointed out, United States imperialism "strives desperately to hang on to what it has and to extend where it can. Everywhere it runs into the slogan of Yankee Go Home." These factors are positive for the building of a revolutionary Marxist-Leninist communist party, guided by M-L-M, to end the suffering of the people, the exploitation of the workers, the oppression of nationalities and women, by destroying capitalism, instituting the dictatorship of the proletariat, and building socialism. But the subjective factor prevents this in the U.S.A. Marxist-Leninists are not united. The multitude of advanced workers in the key industries throughout this country have not been won to communism. Fusion between the spontaneous workers' movement and M-L-M is low. Yet the subjectivist, petit bourgeois socialists in their predictable frenzy, as Lenin characterized it, declare themselves, yes, *declare themselves*, right and left, forward but mostly backward, *the party*. In Britain there is a similar situation, where "the few hundred Marxist-Leninists . . . are divided into a dozen different organizations"—preventing the mobilizing of all positive factors. The reason says the Communist Federation of Britain in a recent *Peking Review* is, as Mao said, "some people act as though the fewer the people, the smaller the circle, the better. Those who have this 'small circle' mentality resist the idea of bringing all positive factors into play, of uniting with everyone that can be united with, and of doing everything possible to turn negative factors into positive ones." Party building can proceed only if the subjectivism and small-group mentality that goes with it are defeated. The article concludes by pointing out something else that Mao said, that in order to build the unity of Marxist-Leninists, which is the principal factor necessary to winning the advanced to communism, we must "do more self-criticism and seek common ground on major questions while reserving differences on minor questions."

Genuine Marxist-Leninist organizations should not think that the party we seek can spring full blown out of one organization's brow like the mythological Athena from the brow of Zeus. Such parties will be equally mythological. "Marxist-Leninists unite—win the advanced to communism" is the only correct method, and this will be carried out by grasping the key link, the ideological struggle over political line waged in the midst of taking part in the mass movement, the actual application of the theories of M-L-M to the concrete conditions for making a revolution in the U.S.A. This struggle for the correct political line will divide the genuine from the sham, the communists from the petit bourgeois subjectivists, who as Mao said are king of the mountain just as monkeys are in the absence of the tigers. The tigers are the proletariat! We can have no party without three critical factors: (1) the union of genuine Marxist-Leninists in the U.S.A.; (2) the existence of advanced workers in key industries who have been won to communism across the U.S.A.; (3) a party program, around which to unite principally, which has been constructed through the ideological and political struggle before the masses, with mass participation, while deeply involved in mass struggle. To have any of those three factors missing is not to have *the* party, the party of the proletariat, the party of a new type that Lenin spoke of, but to have a petit bourgeois social club, good for nothing—good-for-nothing parties, Lenin called them. And we have and apparently will continue to have many of these.

Ten years after the rebellions, our work is clear and cut out for us. Our central task is to build a revolutionary Marxist-Leninist communist party based on M-L-M. There will be more rebellions, fiercer, bloodier, drawing in even broader sectors of the people. But without the leadership of a genuine communist party, they will subside as they did ten years ago, and a few bureaucrats like the Ken Gibsons and Coleman Youngs can get over by showing how well they can cool us out. By now it must be clear that simply putting black faces in high places does nothing, that the entire system of monopoly capitalism—don't care who's fronting it off—must be smashed. And the Youngs, Gibsons, Andy Youngs, Maynard Jacksons, the black caucuses, if they oppose the uprising, the rebellion, of the people, if they oppose the motion of history, like their bourgeois masters, they will indeed disappear, along with capitalism!

Long live the rebellion of the people against monopoly capitalism and national oppression!

Marxist-Leninists unite—win the advanced to communism!!!

Build a revolutionary Marxist-Leninist communist party in the U.S.A.!!!

National Liberation
Movements

There are four fundamental contradictions in the world today, contradictions of capitalism turned to imperialism! These were first clearly pointed out by Lenin in *Imperialism, the Highest Stage of Capitalism*. Stalin reiterates these in his seminal work *The Foundations of Leninism*. Lenin pointed out that imperialism, which is moribund or dying capitalism, "carries the contradictions of capitalism to their last bounds, to the extreme limit beyond which revolution begins." The first contradiction, in the Western industrial countries, is that of labor vs. capital. "Imperialism brings the workers to revolution." Under imperialism, trade unions, cooperatives, parliamentary parties, and parliamentary methods have all been proven totally inadequate.

The second of these contradictions is between the financial groups and imperialist powers themselves: imperialism vs. imperialism. It is these intra-imperialist struggles that invariably lead to imperialist war, such as World War I and World War II. The imperialists contend for new sources of raw materials, new markets, new spheres of influence, new places to export capital; they struggle to redivide the world, and this struggle leads to war. In the present era the sharpest of these struggles is the constant contention between the two superpowers, the U.S.A. and U.S.S.R., between United States imperialism and Soviet social imperialism, which is socialism in words but imperialism in deeds.

The third contradiction is the sharpest one in the world today, imperialism vs. the peoples and nations of the Third World (the colonies and semicolonies of Asia, Africa, Latin America, and other regions). It is these struggles that fan the flame of revolution around the world. They are the motive force of revolution, and the people and nations of the Third World are the chief strugglers against imperialism, colonialism, racism, Zionism, neocolonialism, and superpower domination, called hegemonism.

The fourth contradiction is between imperialism and socialism. It is the confrontation between that which is dying and going out of existence, imperialism and monopoly capitalism, and that which is coming into being and therefore invincible, socialism.

These contradictions produce two clear and strong trends in the world today. The contradiction between the imperialists themselves produces the trend towards imperialist war. And it is sharpening daily, hourly, as the two superpowers contend all over the world for domination of the world, which neither will get. Despite hollow cries of "detente" which one superpower uses to lull people into a false sense of security, or "human rights" which the other uses, while both these international bandits go through the charade of attending yet another security conference or peace conference, they are both arming to the teeth and preparing for a new world war. A new world war is already visible on the horizon, and people of the world must prepare or suffer. The superpowers contend in Southeast Asia, the Middle East, Latin America, and now with deepening and clearly warlike intensity in Africa, although the focus of their contention remains Europe, which they both deem a political and economic prize.

But although the danger of war is increasing visibly, revolution is still the main trend in the world today. The contradiction between imperialism and the peoples and nations of the Third World is the sharpest of the four fundamental contradictions of capitalism/imperialism. "The days are gone when imperialism and social imperialism could do as they wished. Countries want independence, nations want liberation, and the people want revolution—this has become the irresistible tide of history." It is out of the struggles of the peoples of the Third World versus imperialism that the national liberation movements arose and why they continue to grow in effectiveness and world recognition. The expansion of capitalism worldwide as imperialism is in the main to seek out superprofits. To do this the imperialists must superexploit the peoples and nations of the Third World, and because wherever there is oppression there is resistance, Third World reaction is doubly intense. "In exploiting these countries imperialism is compelled to build there railways, factories and mills, industrial and commercial centres. The appearance of a class of proletarians, the emergence of a native intelligentsia, the awakening of national consciousness, the growth of the liberation movement—such are the inevitable results" of imperialism. "The growth of the revolutionary movement in all colonies that are dependent countries without exception clearly testifies to this fact. This circumstance is of importance for the proletariat inasmuch as it saps radically the position of capitalism by converting the colonies and dependent countries from reserves of imperialism into reserves of proletarian revolution." This is how Stalin put it in *Foundations of Leninism*.

But further, Lenin goes on to point out "that under imperialism wars cannot be averted, and that a coalition between the proletarian revolution in Europe and the colonial revolution in the East in a united world front of revolution against the world front of imperialism is inevitable." Imperialism is a world system, and it brings about conditions for revolution on a worldwide basis, but most intensely in the colonies and semicolonies. Imperialist war can be stopped only by revolution, and even when the imperialists mount their world war, revolutionaries will turn such a war into revolution. But comrades who belittle the national liberation struggles, the national revolutions in the Third World, saying that world war can be stopped only by revolutions in the two superpower states, the U.S.A. and the U.S.S.R., miss the points made by Lenin in his great work on imperialism. Moreover, Stalin says, in *The Foundations of Leninism*,

> formerly it was the accepted thing to speak of the proletarian revolution in one or another developed country as of a separate and self-sufficient entity opposing a separate national front of capital as its antipode. Now, this point of view is no longer adequate. Now we must speak of the world proletarian revolution; for the separate national fronts of capital have become links in a single chain called the world front of imperialism, which must be opposed by a common front of the revolutionary movement in all countries. . . . formerly the proletarian revolution was regarded exclusively as the result of the internal development of a given country. Now this point of view is no longer adequate. Now the proletarian revolution must be regarded primarily as the result of the development of the contradictions within the world system of imperialism, as the result of the breaking of the chain of the world imperialist front in one country or another. [p. 29]

There are liberation struggles against imperialism all over the globe. And their overwhelming success year after year steadily weakens and debilitates imperialism. The liberation movements in Southeast Asia, principally in Vietnam, Cambodia, and Laos, drove the United States imperialists into open decline. The spectacle of billions of dollars and hundreds of thousands of troops the United States sank into the Southeast Asian debacle and defeat was much like the wolf and the tarbaby: the harder he punched the more pitifully mired in the tar he became, and finally he died there trying to punch. The Southeast Asian struggle also raised the level of revolutionary consciousness of the people of the United States as well, causing a series of domestic crises for the United States bourgeoisie which ended with the Watergate ritual sacrifice, implying that the country's Vietnam policy was the concoction of Richard Nixon's sick mind alone, whereas it was the general policy of the United States bourgeoisie, from the "liberal" Kennedy to the repressive Nixon.

The Korean War started the United States' long decline, and the only answer its leaders have to the massive liberation movements worldwide against imperialism is to fight them in the open as in Southeast Asia, which has proved totally bankrupt, or to prop up fascist gangsters such as Park Chung Hee in South Korea, where United States imperialism opposes democracy and unity for the Korean peninsula, or in cases like Thailand, where as the government moved further away from the United States orbit it staged coups and murdered communists, national revolutionaries, and even petit bourgeois democrats. In Africa the United States policy of backing repressive colonial governments was clearly exposed with its backing of the Portuguese fascists in Guinea-Bissau and Mozambique and Angola, who were defeated utterly by the African masses. United States imperialists continue to support racist illegal regimes such as these in Zimbabwe, Namibia, and Azania, though with the coming of the Jimmy Carter Snake Oil and Holiness Show, the United States bourgeoisie is trying to change its image in the Third World by bringing in one of the black bourgeoisie's political cadres, Andy Young, to go around the Third World, Africa principally, throwing the soul handshake on the Africans, pretending the United States is no longer the chief supporter of Rhodesia's, South Africa's, and South-West Africa's fascist, racist regimes.

United States imperialism has been exposed worldwide as a bloody beast imperialist, and the national liberation movements have caused it to back up around the world. And that is the reason why Soviet social imperialism is so dangerous, because it is still somewhat disguised. Covering its naked expansionist moves in Africa by calling itself "socialist" and "natural ally of the liberation movements." As the people of the Third World through their liberation movements kick U.S. imperialism out the front door, Soviet social imperialism tries to creep in the back door and set up the same imperialist shop, under a new-style neocolonialism. Consider, for example, the Soviet actions in Angola, where it sent its Cuban mercenaries in to singlehandedly start a civil war between the three liberation movements in Angola, all of whom had contributed to the defeat of Portuguese colonialism. These three liberation organizations, FNLA, MPLA, and UNITA, had already signed two agreements, one in Alvor, Portugal, the other in Nakuru, Kenya, that they would set up a government of national unity combining all three organizations, now that the Portuguese were defeated. But the Soviet Union capitalized on the weakness of the other superpower, and the existence of old feuds between the three movements, to back one of the movements, term the others reactionary, and using the South Africans as a surface cover story sent thousands of Cuban mercenaries into Angola, plus modern weapons and heavy armaments never sent during the struggle against Portuguese colonialism. In the year or so that the Soviet Union and its mercenaries were in Angola they killed over 150,000 Africans, Angolans—more than the Portuguese in 17 years of national war. And the Cubans continue in Angola as an occupying force of mercenaries in the pay of Soviet imperialists.

In Zaire the Soviets used the Katanganese gendarmes, Moise Tshombe's old enforcers, to invade Zaire in shameless fashion in a further attempt at expanding Soviet control in Africa. These were the same Katanganese mercenaries who helped kill Patrice Lumumba, and they are now being used by the Soviet social imperialists for the same sorts of purposes, the attack by imperialism.

Soviet social imperialism has gotten so funky in Africa that both the Egyptians and recently the Sudanese have had to send them packing, denouncing them for interfering in their countries and trying to practice their domination and hegemony. And in countries where national liberation struggles are raging like Zimbabwe and Azania, advanced forces there are very hip to the bloody expansionism and hegemonistic practice of the Soviet Union, even as they wage war on tottering racist regimes bound to United States imperialism hand and foot. In Azania, for instance, where rebellions and armed offensives against the racists are growing in their consistency and intensity as in Soweto and Capetown, leading national liberation organizations like PAC (Pan-African Congress) have openly denounced the machinations of Soviet social imperialism behind the scenes, its actually collaborating with the Vorster regime through its puppets like the so-called Communist Party of South Africa, which until a minute ago was preaching "peaceful transition" in South Africa! Meanwhile Moscow ceaselessly makes a big noise about "supporting" Zimbabwe's armed struggle and opposing the Smith racist regime. But the African countries and people know well enough that this so-called support simply means using military aid as a lever to project its influence into a future liberated and independent Zimbabwe. Its "opposition" simply means replacing racism there with its own neocolonialism. In Zimbabwe the liberation movements practicing a higher level of unity, and persisting in armed struggle, have caused the racist Smith regime to shake visibly, and their American and British backers to call for Smith to effect some settlement immediately. They try to lull the movement to sleep by babbling about the need for negotiations, but negotiations, as the advanced forces understand, must be based on armed struggle. The liberation movement there is using dual revolutionary tactics, talking negotiation but continuing to fight, against the racists' use of counter-revolutionary dual tactics, talk of negotiations but continuing to attack, even carrying criminal assaults into Mozambique and Zambia. The imperialists meanwhile try to raise the reactionary Idi Amin to prominence with daily reports of his lunacy, to make it seem that the problem with Africa is Amin and clownish Africans rather than imperialism. They expose Amin, who they put in in the first place; why not expose Vorster and Smith? But this diversion like the Andy Young number are tricks the people see through readily, because the people do not stop the armed struggle, which is the only method of liberation.

Many liberation movements which wanted to take a noncommittal or even soft position on Soviet social imperialism last year have had to learn the hard way that the Third World's most dangerous enemy is Soviet socialist imperialism, because it is hidden but no less imperialist than that of the United States. In Ethiopia, for instance, where the United States was openly backing the feudal-bourgeois military junta, a bloody pack of oppressors having the

127

nerve to call themselves socialist pretend to kick out imperialism and thus legitimatize their claim to be called socialists by closing up United States agencies, while simultaneously embracing the infamous imperialists from the Soviet Union. This is a wedding made in blood, both having the same relationship to socialism—social fascists.

This means the social imperialists will also be helping the Ethiopian junta attack the Eritrean national liberation movement, which is struggling for Eritrean self-determination in Ethiopia. It shows clearly that only a high level of unity, self-reliance, and armed struggle can resolve the national liberation struggles, not dependence on any so-called "natural allies," who want to practice an "avant-garde" imperialism.

In the Palestinian struggle, the liberation movement, though making steady progress against the illegal, Zionist racist regime calling itself Israel, nevertheless is being constantly obstructed from pursuing the most direct course of struggle against the Zionists because of United States–Soviet collusion. Israel has become one of South Africa's staunchest allies and is another of the United States imperialists' antifreedom projects. But the Soviet Union, again under the guise of aid, has consistently kept the Palestinians in a no war/no peace condition, and as the Egyptians exposed so clearly when they terminated their friendship pact with the Soviets, the U.S.S.R. will not give the Arabs the weapons they need, as the United States does for Israel. And the U.S.S.R. will not even show the Arabs how to operate the more advanced weapons, an old colonialist trick. The Soviets are even going along with the imperialist game of offering the Palestinians a little strip of land on the west bank of the Jordan River to pretend they are getting their land, "a national home" they call it, and Soviet Social imperialism is urging the PLO to settle for this.

It is the superpowers' contention which is at the base of the disorder and intranquility in the world today. But as our Chinese comrades say, "No matter how desperately they may struggle, they will not escape their ultimate doom. The people are the masters of history. The future of the world belongs to them, and it is very bright" (PR, no. 20, 14 May 1976, p. 7). Mao said, "The world is changing in a direction increasingly favorable to the people of all countries. This is one aspect, a principal aspect. But we must also see the other aspect—the aggressive nature of imperialism will not change. . . . modern war is born of imperialism Lenin said. As long as imperialism exists, there will be no tranquility in the world. The danger of a new world war still exists. This is another trend in the development of today's world." We must be very careful to see both trends in the world, and our tactics must change if the trends themselves change. The superpowers are opposing and interfering with national liberation movements, as they must. One openly siding with colonialism and racism, although trying to hide it now more and more; the other superpower calling itself socialist, undermining revolution wherever and whenever it can. Its open line of peaceful transition to socialism is public knowledge; how then can it support armed revolution in people's democratic struggles?

In the countries fighting by means of liberation movements against imperialism, there are two stages of revolution. First is the stage of democratic revolution, against absolutism, colonialism, foreign domination, feudalism, and in such struggles a broad liberation front of all the classes opposed to imperialism can be united to make democratic revolution. But as Lenin pointed out in his great work *Two Tactics of Social Democracy in the Democratic Revolution*, and later Mao Tse Tung in this work on *New Democracy*, it was no longer necessary to stop at the stage of democratic revolution, as the countries of Western Europe and the United States, which became bourgeois dictatorships, had done. Lenin pointed out, and the Russian Revolution, and Chinese Revolution, and democratic revolutions in the Third World in the main have confirmed it, that if the democratic revolution is led by the proletariat, then at the stage of democratic revolution there is no bourgeois dictatorship, because the proletariat will lead uninterruptedly to the next stage of revolution, socialist revolution. And this process is going on all over the Third World.

The liberation movement in Puerto Rico, on the doorstep of the U.S.A., against United States imperialism is heightening, and the bourgeoisie's talk of statehood is a last-ditch diversion trying to stave off the inevitable, the liberation of the Puerto Rican people from United States colonial rule. To exploit this state of affairs, in which the people are driving United States imperialism into the sea, Soviet social imperialism is sneaking around trying to penetrate the national liberation movement through the resurgent Puerto Rican Socialist Party, which has become the open puppet of the bankrupt CPUSA. We must support the Puerto Rican liberation movement against both superpowers, and while *struggling principally against United States imperialism* we must not close our eyes to the dangers of Soviet social imperialism. Moreover, the Puerto Rican people in the United States are an oppressed national minority, part of the multinational United States proletariat.

In the U.S.A., an advanced imperialist country, there is a need for only one-stage revolution. And even in the black-belt South, the land base of the Afro-American nation, a black united front for self-determination must eventually join with the multinational proletariat to destroy the white racist monopoly capitalist class. However, in the U.S.A., we lack a genuine communist party, to lead the masses of us in revolutionary struggle—a revolutionary Marxist-Leninist communist party, based on Marxism–Leninism–Mao Tse Tung thought. We have had no such party in the U.S.A. since the tragic degeneration in the late 1950's and fall into revisionism of the CPUSA, which is now the "left wing of the Democratic Party." Because of this, party building is the central task of all revolutionaries in the United States. Party building is part of the revolutionary main trend of revolution which is coursing through the world today. Such a party must be built if we are to make a socialist revolution in this country, smashing capitalism and building socialism under the dictatorship of the proletariat. Such a party is also the people's only defense against imperialist war.

As the liberation movements of the Third World drive imperialism out the front door, the normal internal economic crisis of monopoly capitalism intensifies, since now the superprofits gouged out of the Third World are cut back by revolution, and there is less booty to use to spread opportunism inside the fortress of imperialism itself. The bourgeoisie must shift its economic crisis onto the backs of its own people. Its budget cuts, layoffs, phasing-out of social welfare programs and ghetto coolout programs, all contribute to the steadily rising tide of revolutionary consciousness inside the United States. The struggle to build a new communist party in the U.S.A. is part of the world front of revolution aimed at smashing the world front of imperialism. But in the United States today there are many sham party-building travesties going on that serve only to confuse the masses, though advanced forces learn even from these petit bourgeois fantasies what the party of the proletariat must *not* be as well as what it must be. The so-called Communist Labor Party, the so-called Revolutionary Communist Party, and just recently OL's newly formed Communist Party M-L are all examples of petit bourgeois frenzy and impatience but not examples of the party of a new type that Lenin spoke of. These sectarian little groups have neither unified Marxist-Leninists nor won the advanced to communism, so that advanced workers form the greatest part of their parties in key industries all over this country. And their programs have more to do with reform than revolution. And in the wings others, such as the bankrupt so-called Revolutionary Wing of PRRWO and RWL wait to stumble into the public eye with their latest mistake, which they will call the United States Bolshevik Party and which will also not be *the* party. And now WVO threatens to make the same mistake—although we hope they do not.

But whatever these groups do, they cannot stop the ultimate formation of a revolutionary Marxist-Leninist communist party, based on M-L-M, which will destroy declining United States capitalism from within, just as liberation movements all over the world are mashing it harder against the wall every day, and bringing revolution in the U.S.A. closer by the minute. Unlike backward elements like Stokely Carmichael's AAPRP, which thinks that revolution can *only* be made in Africa, thereby protecting the United States bourgeoisie as cleverly as Andy Young, we know that revolution can and will be made in the United States, and by the multinational proletariat. Our cry:

Victory for the national liberation movements against imperialism is a victory for the United States proletariat and oppressed nationalities!

People of the world unite to crush the superpowers: United States and Soviet social imperialism!

Marxist-Leninists unite—win the advanced to communism!

In the U.S.A. build a revolutionary Marxist-Leninist communist party based on M-L-M!

Only Revolution Will Transform South Africa

In South Africa, real name Azania, or in Rhodesia, real name Zimbabwe, or South-West Africa, real name Namibia, the fundamental question, the fundamental struggle, is against imperialism and its racist colonial structure in all these countries of southern Africa.

The illegal racist governments of these countries exist only because of imperialism, and will fall only because imperialism will have been driven out by the enraged people of those countries.

In Zimbabwe, the racists led by Ian Smith are backed against the wall with nowhere to turn. They talk negotiation, but all the time they go on killing. All the time they maintain a dehumanizing colonial system, not with words but with bloody bayonets and barbed wire. Their desperation has reached such extremes that they are now enacting a minstrel show called "Real Negotiations Are Proceeding"—going through a dumbshow of supposed dialogue on the transfer to majority rule with traitorous Negro capitulationists and stooges who are not only denounced by the African majority but also dismissed even by *The New York Times*, so weak are their disguises as African patriots. And even in this ugly charade there are obstructions, because Ian Smith simply cannot adjust to the cold (for him) realities of the last part of the twentieth century: that colonialism is dead, and the corpse so rotten it cannot even be painted up to look like it's alive.

The Patriotic Front composed of ZANU and ZAPU continues its war of liberation, and despite the diseased doubletalk that Smith and his lackeys embarrass us with, the people of Zimbabwe are aiming to win their liberation through unity, self-reliance, and armed struggle.

In Namibia, the racist South Africans have been repeatedly exposed before the world because of their illegal and bloody presence in that country. The U.N. has repeatedly demanded that South Africa leave Namibia, but the South Africans persist in their illegal presence and repression and have recently sought to raise up some so-called "tribal chiefs" as alternatives to SWAPO, which is the legitimate revolutionary group leading the Namibian people to liberation. But this South African sham, like the minstrel show in Zimbabwe, is doomed before it even begins and will fool only people committed to colonialism and neocolonialism. The African majority will persist in building greater unity and self-reliance, and continuing the armed liberation struggle to the end.

In South Africa itself, Vorster, the leader of the racists, has taken a totally intransigent position based not only on the metaphysics of white supremacy—i.e., they think that the black masses will never be able to drive them out—but also on their knowledge that South Africa is important to the general survival of imperialism! They know that were South Africa to be liberated by the black majority Great Britain itself would burst open in revolutionary ferment like an overripe tomato (somewhat like Portugal), and the United States economy, already reeling from its repeated losses all over the Third World, would rush toward irreversible crisis.

The United States imperialists feel that *neocolonialism* can save the day for Western imperialism all over southern Africa, and that is their contradiction with the Ian Smiths and Johannes Vorsters. The United States imperialists feel that they could continue to rule through "native agents," as Cabral described them. The Carters, Vances, Brzezinskis, like the Kissingers before them, feel that if they could just come up with the right set of Negroes, some African Andy Youngs and Tom Bradleys and Kenneth Gibsons on the continent, that their fortunes could be saved. The Smiths and the Vorsters are already anachronisms as far as United States imperialist policy is concerned, and they will either have to shape up and get them some colored boys and girls to front off for imperialism, transform colonialism into neocolonialism, or 007 will dispatch them into a pit. The problem for the United States imperialist is this: if the true revolutionaries in southern Africa continue to strengthen their forces and mobilize the broad masses not just against colonialism but imperialism and capitalism itself, the national liberation struggles, once victorious, will continue the social revolution beyond formal independence and commit their countries to the total elimination of dependence on imperialism, the elimination of capitalism itself, and the building of scientific socialism.

The genuine forces of African revolution face not one superpower, however, in their struggle for liberation, but both the giant, powerful, repressive imperialist powers. Both the United States superpower and the social imperialist Soviet Union (socialist in words, but imperialist in deeds) contend over the African continent. Actually everywhere in the world these two superpowers contend for domination and hegemony, and the focus of their struggle is economically rich, politically critical Europe, but not only would political dominance of Africa mean Europe's southern flanks could be pressured, but also Africa would be controlled, which of course is rich in raw materials, markets, places to invest capital, and is a key area in the world to try to mount spheres of influence.

The U.S.A. since the Vietnam War has been in open, marked decline. United States imperialism's defeat in Vietnam, followed by a defeat in Cambodia, and its defeats in Mozambique, Guinea-Bissau, Angola, have sent it reeling on the defensive. The revolutionary struggles waged by the people of the United States against the Vietnam War, against black national oppression, and for democratic rights, and the general overall struggle of the working class against the United States ruling class, combined with the devastating shocks of its defeat in Southeast Asia, have put the United States imperialists in a position where they must frantically struggle to hold on to their bloody possessions. While the new imperialist U.S.S.R., which is the lean and hungry newcomer to the imperialist banquet, is aggressive, willing to take chances, and has already launched into adventurist imperialist expeditions in Angola, Zaire, and now Ethiopia. The United States has been exposed throughout the world as a bloodybeast imperialist, after its doubletalk in the 1940's and 1950's about democracy. The U.S.S.R. with its misleading signboard of "socialism" is able to get some mileage at the people's expense until its mask is totally ripped away and all its ugly imperialist features are wholly exposed! Meanwhile they try to sneak in the backdoor as United States imperialism is being driven out the front door.

But these two superpowers contend and sometimes collude in

Africa, just as they do all over the world. And it is they who are the principal enemies of the world's peoples, just as the people in Ethiopia are finding out now, as they wage their war of liberation against the ruling military junta. It is imperialism and social imperialism which are the main enemies. In South Africa, the racist Vorster government could not last out the year if it were not for United States imperialism. There is no way the racists could withstand the armed might of the African masses without United States imperialism, and even with it, colonialism will still be crushed.

The struggle inside the U.S.A. to help with the liberation of southern Africa must focus primarily on the role of the superpowers; we must strive to be an active part of the revolutionary world united front against the superpowers, made up of the overwhelming majority of people in the world.

The presence of American corporations in South Africa is not arbitrary or accidental; they are, as the corporate form of imperialist penetration and control, the public face of imperialist rule. The military might of South Africa, including its stated ability soon to develop nuclear weapons, is a planned characteristic of this racist settler colony. It is not some weird accident that amazes the rulers of the United States; they are specifically responsible for this armed might. As for the racist apartheid system, the United States clamors loudly for South Africa to end this inhumanity, but only to protect imperialism. Apartheid, wherein 4.5 million whites rule 19 million blacks, inhabit 87 percent of the land, and control 75 percent of the national income, is a system which at one time offered imperialism its maximum protection. But now imperialism rules best through a black elite as the most modern form of exploitation and oppression, and the United States rulers know that apartheid even opposes the raising and putting forward of such a bankrupt black elite.

The movement to get universities to divest themselves of their corporate stock in South Africa is a correct movement, and one method whereby continuous pressure and struggle can be mounted against the racist colonial governments of southern Africa. But we do not expect the universities to cooperate without a major disruptive struggle. Certainly the cry of "United States corporations out of South Africa!" is a correct slogan, but we should also understand that only revolution will ultimately drive them out, as they are *the reasons, the cause,* of the present rule of imperialism in South Africa, not casually incidental to it.

135

We have said that revolution is the main trend in the world to-day, and this is true, but at the same time we should understand that with the sharp contention between the United States and the Soviet Union for raw materials, markets, places to invest capital, and spheres of influence there is also a real possibility for an imperialist war to happen in the not-too-distant future. Notwithstanding doubletalk about detente and strategic arms limitations talks, the only industry in the United States running continuously at top capacity is the military industry, and although the Russians have a gross national product that is only one-half the size of the American GNP, they are producing weapons at about the same rate. The United States in its decline, and faced with the need steadily to arm for war, has been putting the weight for these setbacks onto the backs of its people, with layoffs, cutbacks, especially in the social programs, and rising unemployment. The United States imperialists will not face the possibility of losing South Africa to the African masses without a long, drawn-out, and increasingly bloody struggle. This means that we must intensify our struggle here inside the U.S.A. against the racist settler colonies and raise up to a higher pitch the struggle, inside this fortress of imperialism, against imperialism and the rule of monopoly capitalism here in the factories and fields and streets of the U.S.A.

People of the world unite to defeat the two superpowers: United States imperialism and Soviet social imperialism!

Death to apartheid!

Death to colonialism!!

The Revolutionary
Tradition in
Afro-American
Literature

Speaking about the general ghettoized condition of Afro-American literature within the framework of so-called American literature, Bruce Franklin, a professor at the Newark branch of Rutgers University, had this to say in the *Minnesota Review:*

> If we wish to continue to use the term "American Literature," we must either admit that we mean white American literature or construe it to include the literature of several peoples, including the Afro-American nation. The latter course leads to a fundamental redefinition of American literature, its history, and the criteria appropriate to each and every American literary work. For the viewpoint of oppressed people can then no longer be excluded from the criticism and teaching of American literature. . . . The most distinctive feature of United States history is Afro-American slavery and its consequences. This truth is at the heart of our political, economic, and social experience as a nation state. It is also at the heart of our *cultural* experience, and therefore the slave narrative, like Afro-American culture in general, is not peripheral but central to American culture.

These words are so important because Franklin calls attention to not only the fact that what is called American literature is basically the literature of certain white men, but he also points out the importance to American culture and life itself of Afro-American life and culture in this country. But if we look at the standard history of American literature—Franklin points to the *Literary History of the United States* by Spiller, Thorp, Johnson, Canby, Ludwig, and Gibson, a college standard, in its 4th revised edition in 1974—we find, in its 1,555 pages of small print, 4 black writers, Chesnutt, Dunbar, Hughes, and Wright, and in the section on literature produced by the South during the Civil War they devote 3 chapters and discuss such literary giants as Hugh Legaré, William Wirt, and George Fitzhugh, author of *Cannibals All! or Slaves Without Masters*. There is no mention of the slave narrative or slave poetry. There is no mention of William Wells Brown, the nineteenth-century black novelist and playwright. They do not even mention Frederick Douglass!! So we must face the essential national chauvinism of what is taught as American literature, even the "white part" of it, so that in many instances the anthologies and survey courses that we learn literature from are the choice of or have been influenced to a great extent by some of the most reactionary elements in American society. We have been raised up in literature too often on right-wing anthologies and the standards of right-wing critics, pushing conservative and reactionary literature, playing down progressive and revolutionary forces, and almost outright excluding oppressed nationalities and minorities and women.

It was the rebellions of the sixties, explosions in 110 U.S. cities, that created the few Black Studies and Afro-American Studies departments that exist today. At the same time, these uprisings created the agonizingly small space that Afro-American literature takes up in the canon of academic and commercial written culture. A few authors got "walk-on" roles, to paraphrase Franklin again.

First we must understand the basic distortion that is given to all American literary history and official reflections of American life and culture. This is obviously because the literary establishment, and the academic establishment, far from being independent, represent in the main the ideas and worldview of the rulers of this country. These ideas, and the institutions from which they are mashed on us, constitute merely the *superstructure* of this society, a superstructure that reflects the economic foundations upon which it is built, the material base for United States life and culture, monopoly capitalism. So that in the main what is taught and pushed as great literature, or great art, philosophy, etc., are mainly ideas and concepts that can help maintain the status quo, which includes not only the exploitation of the majority by a capitalist elite, but also national oppression, racism, the oppression of women, and the extension of United States imperialism all over the world.

Afro-American literature as it has come into view, fragmented by chauvinism and distorted by the same reactionary forces that have distorted American literature itself, has indeed been laid out in the same confusing and oblique fashion. A method intended to hide more than it reveals, a method that wants to show that at best Afro-American literature is a mediocre, and conservative, reflection of the mediocre and conservative portrait that is given of all American literature.

In Afro-American literature for instance we have been taught that its beginnings rest with the writings of people like Phillis Wheatley and Jupiter Hammon. Ms. Wheatley writing in the eighteenth century is simply an imitator of Alexander Pope. It was against the law for black slaves to learn to read or write, so Ms. Wheatley's writings could only come under the "Gee whiz, it's alive" category of Dr. Frankenstein checking out his new monster! Also Wheatley's writing abounds with sentiments like "Twas mercy brought me from my pagan land," evincing gratitude at slavery—that the European slave trade had actually helped the Africans by exposing them to great European culture: which be the monster remarking how wise how omniscient be her creator!

Hammon is, if possible, even worse. In his stiff doggerel are such great ideas as slavery was good for us Africans because it taught us humility—so when we get to heaven we'll know how to act around God. Pretty far out! (Both were privileged Northern house servants reflecting both their privilege and their removal and isolation from the masses of African/Afro-American slaves.)

But these two are pushed as Afro-American literature simply as a method of showing off trained whatnots demonstrating the glory of the trainer. But this is not the beginnings of Afro-American literature as a genre.

The black people of this country were brought here in slavery chains on the ships of rising European capitalism. It is impossible to separate the rise of capitalism, the industrial revolution, the emergence of England and later America as world powers, from the trade in Africans. And from their initial presence as commodities initiating world trade through the triangular trade route of slaves to the New World, raw materials to England, and manufactured goods to Africa for the African feudal ruling class who had sold the other Africans into slavery, black life has contributed to and animated Anglo-American life and culture. But a formal, artifact-documented presence could easily be denied slaves. African culture was banned by the slave masters as *subversive*. Christianity was used first as a measure of civilization (if you weren't a Christian you weren't civilized—the papal bull states, it's cool to enslave non-Christians) but later it was used as a pacifier and agency for social control (its present function). The development of a *specifically* Afro-American culture must wait for the emergence of the Afro-American people, the particular nationality composed of Africans transformed by the fact and processes of slavery into an American people of African descent.

The most practical artifacts of that culture are the tools and environment of day-to-day living. In these practical pursuits are found the earliest Afro-American art—artifactual reflections of the life of that people. Music, because it is most abstract and could not therefore be so severely limited and checked by slave culture, must be the earliest of the "non-practical" arts to emerge (although a work song is to help one work!): the work song, chants, hollers, the spiritual, eventually the blues.

Afro-American literature rises as a reflection of the self-conscious self-expression of the Afro-American people, but to be an Afro-American literature, truly, it must reflect, in the main, the ideological and socio-cultural portrait of that people! The Wheatleys and Hammons reflect the ideology of Charlie McCarthy in relationship to Edgar Bergen. (Is that before anybody's time?)

The celebration of servitude is not the ideological reflection of the Afro-American masses, but of their tormentors.

In the slave narratives, the works of Frederick Douglass, Henry Bibb, Moses Roper, Linda Brent, William Wells Brown, the Krafts, Henry "Box" Brown, and others, Solomon Northrup, James Pennington, etc., are found the beginnings of a genuine Afro-American written literature. Here are the stirring narratives of slave America, the exploits and heroism of resistance and escape, the ongoing struggle and determination of that people to be free. Beside this body of strong, dramatic, incisive, democratic literature where is the literature of the slavemasters and -mistresses? Find it and compare it with the slave narratives and say which has a clearer, more honest, and ultimately more artistically powerful perception of American reality! (Yes, there are William Gilmore Simms, John Pendleton Kennedy, Augustus B. Longstreet, and George Washington Harris, touted as outstanding writers of the white, slave South. But their writing is unreadable, even though overt racists like Allen Tate and the Southern Agrarians prated about the slave South as a "gracious culture despite its defects." Those defects consisted in the main of millions of black slaves, whose life expectancy at maturity by the beginning of the nineteenth century in the deep South was seven years. One of the main arguments, as Bruce Franklin points out in *The Victim as Criminal and Artist,* for black slavery was that the blacks could do the manual labor "for which they were best suited . . . leaving their owners free to create a fine, elegant, and lasting culture" (p. 28). But check it out. At best such artistic efforts representing this so-called lasting culture are embarrassing satires, the efforts of the Southern Agrarians to represent them as something else notwithstanding.

The slave narratives are portraits of a people in motion, and they come into being as creations of the economic, social, and political life of the United States. The early part of the nineteenth century was marked by an intensification of slavery and by the taking away of the limited civil rights of free blacks as well. This was because slavery did not die out toward the end of the eighteenth century as was predicted. With the creation of the cotton gin, to the feudalistic or patriarchal slavery imposed on blacks was now added capitalist exploitation. Karl Marx points out in *Capital* that once cotton became an international commodity, no longer used only in United States domestic markets, blacks were not only tied for life to domestic slavery, but now had added to their inhuman burden the horrors of having to produce *surplus value,* as a kind of slave and proletarian in combination. The seven-year life expectancy came about "down river" in the black-belt cotton region because the slavemasters discovered that working slaves to death and then replacing them was more profitable than letting them live to grow old, less productive but still eating, wearing clothes, and taking up space!

This period of intense repression is when Afro-American literature emerges. It is also the period when the resistance of the Afro-American people intensifies. It is now that Gabriel Prosser, Denmark Vesey, Nat Turner, lead their uprisings and rebellions, and Harriet Tubman develops the underground railway.

At the approach of the Civil War, there is also another strong movement in Afro-American literature, the pre–Civil War revolutionary black nationalists: David Walker, the activists Henry Highland Garnet, Charles Lenox Remond, C. H. Langston, as well as William Wells Brown, an escaped slave who became the first black playwright and novelist. It is a literature sparked by protest, an anti-slavery literature, a fighting oral literature, that even when it was written was meant to be proclaimed from the lecterns and pulpits of the North and circulated secretly to inspire the black slaves in the South. These were black abolitionists, damning slavery in no uncertain terms, proclaiming death to slavery, and calling for rebellion from the slaves. This was not upper-class white abolitionism, morally outraged but politically liberal. (The most genuine of the white abolitionists was John Brown—he knew what to do about slavery, wage armed struggle against it!) These were black revolutionists, some like Langston even calling for black people to seize the land they toiled upon because it was only that land that provided a practical basis for the survival and development of the Afro-American people!

Usually in discussing Afro-American literature, teachers of literature combine the Wheatleys and Hammons with perhaps Douglass's narrative, and maybe Brown's novel, *Clotel.* The other slave narratives and the pre–Civil War black revolutionary nationalists are largely ignored or their importance diminished. Charles Chesnutt, who lamented that quality black folks had to be lumped together with the ignorant black masses, is pushed as a kind of father of black literature. Next, Paul Laurence Dunbar and James Weldon Johnson are raised to the top rank, but an analysis of the content of these men's works is made vague or one-sided. We are not aware perhaps that for all the positive elements of Dunbar's work, his use of dialect, which is positive insofar as it is the language of the black masses, is negative in the way that Dunbar frequently uses it only in the context of parties, eating, and other "coonery." Most of Dunbar's "serious" poetry is not in dialect.

Dunbar was deeply conservative, and his short story "The Patience of Gideon" shows a young slave, Gideon, who is put in charge of the plantation as the massa goes off to fight the Civil War. Gideon stays despite the masses of slaves running away as soon as massa leaves. Even Gideon's wife-to-be pleads with him to leave, but he will not. He has made a promise to massa, and so even his woman leaves him, alone with his promise to the slavemaster.

Johnson's quandary was how to create a "high art" out of Afro-American materials, not completely understanding that "high art" is by definition slavemaster, bourgeois art and that what was and is needed by all artists, or by those artists who intend for their works to serve the exploited and oppressed majority in this country, is that they be artistically powerful and politically revolutionary!

Johnson's *Autobiography of an Ex–Colored Man* tells of that quandary in social terms, with his protagonist existing in a never-never land between black and white and finally deciding because he is shamed and humiliated and horrified by the lynching of a black man that he cannot be a member of a race so disgraced. He disappears among the whites, forsaking art for commerce, pursuing the white lady of his heart!

The real giant of this period, the transitional figure, the connector between nineteenth-century Reconstruction and the new literary giants of the twentieth century and the Harlem Renaissance, is W.E.B. DuBois. His *Souls Of Black Folk*, which issued an ideological challenge to the capitulationist philosophy of Booker T. Washington, is the intellectual and spiritual forerunner of the writings of the Renaissance. DuBois's *Black Reconstruction* remains the most important work on the Reconstruction period done by an American. He was a social scientist, historian, as well as novelist, poet, and political activist. He founded black theatrical troupes like Krigwa Players, organized international conferences of black activists as leader of the Pan-Africanist movement, led social movements in the United States like the Niagara Movement and the NAACP, was a fighting literary editor, and his works of historical and sociological analysis are among the greatest written by an American. He studied and wrote about all aspects of black life and its connection with Africa and the slave trade. He was a socialist by 1910, and at the end of his life, inspired by and inspiring the African independence movements, residing in Nkrumah's Ghana, he became a communist. It is not possible to understand the history of ideas in the United States without reading DuBois. Not to know his work is not to have a whole picture of Afro-American literature, sociology, history, and struggle and is to have a distorted view of American life in general.

Langston Hughes's manifesto, "The Negro Artist and the Racial Mountain" (1926), is not possible without DuBois and his total rejection of American racial paternalism and cultural aggression. The Harlem Renaissance is simply the flowering of a twentieth-century Afro-American intelligentsia reflecting the motion of black people in America. It reflects a peasant people in motion out of the South toward the urban North to serve as cheap labor (a developing proletariat) for the developing United States imperialism cut off from its

European immigrants by the coming of World War I. It is a literature of the new city dwellers having left their rural pasts. It is a literature of revolt, it is anti-imperialist, and fights the cultural aggression that imperialism visits upon its colonial and nationally oppressed conquests—first by reflecting and proclaiming the beauty and strengths of the oppressed people themselves. By showing the lives of the people themselves in all its rawness, deprivation and ugliness. By showing them to themselves. It is a revolutionary nationalist literature at its strongest, especially the works of Claude McKay and Langston Hughes. It reflects the entrance into the twentieth century of Afro-American people and the U.S. in general. It is the sensibility of the Afro-American Nation that developed after the destruction of the Reconstruction governments (and the period of Reconstruction was the most democratic period in U.S. life)—the sensibility that survived the dark repression of the 1880's and 1890's, when the northern industrial capitalists no longer needed blacks to stabilize the south while the Wall Street conquerors stripped the southern plantation aristocrats of economic and political independence, so now the northern capitalists sold blacks back into near slavery with the Hayes-Tilden Compromise of 1876, to crush black political life with the Ku Klux Klan lynching, the black codes, segregation, and outright fascism!

The Harlem Renaissance influenced black culture worldwide, but it all reflected the fact that all over the world, oppressed nations and colonial peoples were intensifying their struggle against imperialism. In Haiti, where the U.S. invaded in 1915, there was the *Indigisme* movement; in Puerto Rico it was called *Negrissmo;* in Paris, Senghor, Cesaire, and Damas called it *Negritude* and cited McKay and Hughes as their chief influences!

One aspect of the Harlem Renaissance in the "Roaring 20's" as part of "the Jazz Age" was the stirring anti-imperialism—another part (showing how the bourgeoisie tries to transform everything to its own use) was the cult of exoticism the commercializers and, often pathological, bourgeois "patrons" of the "New Negro" made of this cultural outpouring. This was the period, Hughes said, when "the Negro was in vogue."

But by the beginning of the thirties, after the crash of 1929 and the great depression—only one of many cyclical recessions, the bust part of the boom-bust cycle pointing toward the eventual destruction of capitalism—the exotic part of the Renaissance was over. The philanthropists turned to other pursuits and, just as in factories where blacks are the last hired and the first fired, the literary flowering as manifested by American publishers came to an end!

In the depression thirties the revolutionary ideas of the Russian Bolsheviks, of Marx, Engels, Lenin, and Stalin, had enormous influence on United States intellectuals. It was apparent that capitalism could not solve the problems of the exploited majority, let alone of black people, and that the United States bourgeoisie was unfit to rule society. Black writers also show this influence, mostly as it was transmitted by the *then* revolutionary Communist Party USA. The works of Hughes and McKay especially show this influence, and even though Hughes later copped out before the inquisitors of the HUAC, a collection of his thirties writings, *Good Morning, Revolution,* is must reading to get at his really powerful works.

Richard Wright was one of the most publicized and skilled black writers of the 1930's and 1940's. His early works, *Uncle Tom's Children, Native Son, Black Boy,* including the long-suppressed section of this book called *American Hunger,* are among the most powerful works written by any American writer of the period. Wright was, even more than Hughes, influenced by Marxist-Leninist ideology, though Wright's individualism and idealism finally sabotaged him. He joined the CPUSA when he got to Chicago. (He came in from the John Reed Club, an anti-imperialist writers' organization. And if one believes *American Hunger,* the careerist aspects of this move, getting his early works published by the communists, etc., are not insubstantial.) Wright had just come from Memphis when he joined and he remained a member of the CPUSA until 1944. It was at this point ironically that the CP, burdened by opportunist reactionary leadership, sold out the Black Liberation Movement by liquidating the correct revolutionary slogans "Liberation for the black nation! Self-determination for the Afro-American nation in the black-belt South!" The CP even liquidated itself, temporarily becoming the Communist Political Association, "a nonparty movement following the ideals of Washington, Jefferson, Lincoln and Tom Paine." But Wright's individualism and petit bourgeois vacillation had begun to isolate him from the party years before, though the errors and opportunism of CP leadership must be pointed out.

Many of the left, anti-imperialist, revolutionary, Marxist, and even pro-Soviet ideas that grew to such prominence in the thirties were sustained into the forties because the United States by then had joined a united front with the Soviet Union against fascism. But by the fifties United States world dominance (which was enhanced by the fact of its emerging unscathed from World War II) dictated that it launch a cold war against the Soviet Union to try to dominate a world market. World War II had allowed the insurgent colonial peoples to grow even stronger as the imperialists fought each other, and in 1949 the Chinese communists declared the People's Republic of China. This occasioned an attempted blockade and isolation of China as well by the United States and resulted in the Korean "police action." This was accompanied by intense ideological repression inside the U.S.A. itself, as McCarthyism emerged: the modern capitalist inquisition to purge all left and Marxist and anti-imperialist influences from American intellectual life!

Hughes copped out before HUAC, said he would not do it again, and told James Eastland that all United States citizens had equality. A tragedy! Wright fled to France and became an existentialist. Another event with tragic overtones. DuBois was indicted as an agent of a foreign power and went abroad for an extended period. Robeson was persecuted and driven to his death as Jackie Robinson testified against him at HUAC. Powerful writers like Theodore Ward were covered with mountains of obscurity.

With the defection of the CPUSA to reformism, culminating in its 1957 pronouncement that it was now seeking socialism via the ballot in a "peaceful transition to socialism" and that the road to socialism was integration not revolution, the late 1940's and the 1950's were marked by a "reevaluation" of Wright's works. Both James Baldwin and Ralph Ellison spuriously condemned protest literature, and the general tone put out by well-published "spokespersons for black people" was that it was time to transcend the "limitations" of race and that Afro-American writing should disappear into the mainstream like *Lost Boundaries*. Baldwin of course later refutes his own arguments by becoming a civil-rights spokesman and activist, and by the sixties with *Blues for Mr. Charlie* he had even begun to question the nonviolent, passive pseudo-revolution put forward by the black bourgeoisie through its most articulate spokesman, Dr. Martin Luther King. And this is exactly the point in time when Ralph Ellison is put forward by the bourgeoisie as the most notable Afro-American writer!

Ralph Ellison's *Invisible Man* was the classic work of the fifties in restating and shifting the direction of Afro-American literature. The work puts down both nationalism and Marxism, and opts for *individualism*. This ideological content couched in the purrs of an obviously elegant technique was important in trying to steer Afro-American literature away from protest, away from the revolutionary concerns of the 1930's and early 1940's, and this primarily is the reason this work and its author are so valued by the literary and academic establishments in this country. Both Ellison and Baldwin wrote essays dismissing or finding flaws in Wright's ultimate concern in his best work.

But the fifties civil-rights movement was also superseded by the people's rapid intensification of the struggle in the sixties, and black literature like everything else was quick to show this. Malcolm X emerged to oppose the black bourgeois line of nonviolent passive resistance, which duplicates the reformist anti-Marxists of the CPUSA in their "nonviolent transition to socialism." Where the black bourgeoisie had dominated the Black Liberation Movement in the fifties with the aid of the CPUSA and the big capitalists themselves, in the sixties Malcolm X came forward articulating the political line of the black majority, self-determination, self-respect, and self-defense, and struggled out in the open against the civil-rights line of the black bourgeoisie, who could see black people beaten and spit on and bombed in churches, and whose only retaliation would be to kneel in the dust and pray.

Just as Malcolm's influence turned the entire civil-rights movement around, e.g., the student movement, which was SNCC, to the militance of Stokely Carmichael and Rap Brown, so the whole movement changed radically. The black bourgeoisie were no longer in control of the movement, and from civil rights we were talking next about self-defense, and then after Rap Brown about rebellion, to revolution itself.

All these moves were reflected by black literature, and they are fundamentally movements and thrusts by the people themselves, that the literature bears witness to and is a reflector of. The Black Arts Movement of the sixties basically wanted to reflect the rise of the militancy of the black masses as represented by Malcolm X. Its political line, at its most positive, was that literature must be a weapon of revolutionary struggle, that it must serve the black revolution. And its writers, Askia Muhammad Toure, Larry Neal, Clarence Reed, Don Lee, Sonia Sanchez, Carolyn Rodgers, Welton Smith, Marvin X, Henry Dumas, Gaston Neal, Clarence Franklin,

Ben Caldwell, Ed Bullins, Ron Milner, Mari Evans, etc., its pub-lications, its community black arts theaters, its manifestos and activ-ism, were meant as real manifestations of black culture—black art as a weapon of liberation.

On the negative side, the Black Arts Movement, without the guidance of a scientific revolutionary organization, a Marxist-Lenin-ist communist party, was like the BLM itself, left with spontaneity. It became embroiled in cultural nationalism, bourgeois nationalism, substituting mistrust and hatred of white people for scientific analy-sis of the real enemies of black people, until by the middle seventies a dead end had been reached that could only be surmounted by a complete change of worldview, ideology.

It is my view that this is exactly what is going on today in many places in the country. Afro-American literature is going through the quantitative changes necessary to make its qualitative leap back into the revolutionary positivism of the 1930's and the positive aspect of the black arts 1960's. For certain, the literature will always be a reflection of what the people themselves are, as well as a projection of what they struggle to become. The Afro-American nation is an oppressed nation, and its people, whether in the black-belt land base of that nation or as an oppressed nationality spread out around the rest of the nation-state, still face a revolutionary struggle. That nation is still oppressed by imperialism, and its liberation and self-determination can only be gained through revolution. The next wave of Afro-American literature, of a genuine people's literature, will dramatically record this.

Langston Hughes
and the
Harlem Renaissance

Pre-Renaissance Models

DuBois is a central figure in black struggle and black literature documenting that struggle. The period of Reconstruction, its destruction, and the deep reaction that followed is best summed up in its entirety, lyrically and objectively, by W.E.B. DuBois. He is a giant. He fought against national oppression and black and white reaction. He fought white folks, Booker T., and the idealism and narrow nationalism of Marcus Garvey. He was most of his life a revolutionary nationalist, one of the prime movers, before Garvey, of a progressive Pan-Africanism, a struggler whose political consciousness developed and broadened his whole life, a prolific, creative, and extremely important political writer and sociologist. The Harlem Renaissance seems impossible without *The Souls of Black Folk*, which sets the tone for the Renaissance in its most famous essay opposing the capitulationist line of Booker T. Washington. He improves upon this collection just as the Renaissance is moving into full swing with *Dark Water* (1920), in which he made a clear break with black capitalism as the hope for black people. He developed into a consistent outspoken anti-imperialist, known internationally and received in Moscow and China and Africa and Europe. DuBois was, by the end of his life, a communist. His life spanned the period from just after the Civil War to the red-hot acceleration of national liberation movements in the Third World and the BLM in the U.S.A. in the 1960's.

It is DuBois who is the link between the pre–Civil War revolutionary black nationalists and their fiery expressive writings and the flowering of the Harlem Renaissance. Dunbar, in contrast, too often represents an aspect of ideological reaction. His use of dialect was in many cases just like that of white chauvinists in that it denigrated and belittled. James Weldon Johnson is more progressive in some ways, in the spirit of "Black and Unknown Bards." Certainly his book *Black Manhattan* is a too-little-read classic of black life in the Apple and its history into the twenties. But *Autobiography of an Ex–Colored Man*, although finally condemning the negative self-hatred caused by national oppression and racism ("my birthright for a mess of pottage"), condemns it with the wave of a hand while expressing the consciousness of that flawed sensibility more than the transcendence of it. The NAACP, which Johnson headed in New York City, was and is the tool of the assimilationist black bourgeoisie and the outright compradors. It was created by Carnegie and the rest to coopt and displace DuBois and Trotter's more militant Niagara Movement.

The Renaissance itself can only be understood by looking at its real origins in society, its real material basis; it does not exist otherwise. Human life and its products are not an abstraction, except for those who intentionally obscure (the bourgeoisie) or the confused. The Renaissance was also identified specifically as the Harlem Renaissance, because that was the location of the most concentrated instance of its flowering and because it was the capital of black migration after Chicago. But this was not the only place of this efflorescence, only the largest example of a whole trend and development. What was being reflected in part was the movement of blacks from South to North, from country to city, from peasant to worker, the trek past the reactionary period of post-Reconstruction to a new "reconstruction."

Beginnings of the Renaissance

The Harlem Renaissance is one beginning of Afro-American modernism: the experience and retelling of America entering into the twentieth century. Uncle Sam was no longer a raw yokel farmboy, as his getup suggested, but was now big, muscular, influential, no longer a naïf and junior partner but, with the Spanish-American War and World War I behind him, a full-up imperialist power on the way to the big time. The first real American drama came to fruition in the same period—the plays of Eugene O'Neill (along with Barry,

Rice, Howard). And it is important that it was O'Neill who first put something nearly approximating black life in reality on the big-time American stage. That is, it took until the twentieth century for American drama and literature fully to break out of its colonial relationship with England and Europe. The exiles in Paris, Pound, Stein, Hemingway, Fitzgerald, Eliot in England, announced their American modernism from Europe. The truly modern William Carlos Williams and Afro-American writers, like Hughes and McKay, bohemianized their way through Europe for briefer periods, maybe because their money was never strong enough, but the true announcement of their American modernism was made from these shores.

Renaissance, of course, means rebirth. It is rebirth in modern America, the country blues turned city blues—in fact turned eventually into a big blue orchestra (or a "jungle band"). It is the transformation from the small New Orleans ensembles and the Chicago versions of them to the big Fletcher Henderson–born, Ellington-bred, blued expression of, as European critics said of Ellington, "the sophisticated citydweller." The blues itself made the trip from the black heartland to maybe the Lincoln Theater across Lenox Avenue, where one of the Smiths, Bessie, Clara, or Mamie, would combine the sticks with the stone, in such a mixture they called it "classic."

It was the growth of the whole society, and the growth of black people within that society—having struggled loose from slavery, and grasped at Reconstruction, and resisted and outlasted the period of reaction at the end of the nineteenth century. The Afro-American comes into the twentieth century drawn north by the imperialists readying for World War I and seeking cheap labor; running from the Klan, the boll weevils, the scene of the crime; going north, to promise.

The Renaissance is what the flight that *Black Boy* fleshed out gives rise to (although Wright himself was of a later, even more political generation, when the promise of the twenties gave way to the depression realities of the thirties). The Renaissance is what the bloods had to say once they stopped. They wanted to tell it all, and they had a lot to say.

The twentieth century opened up the world to the United States and the United States to the world. Both the Spanish-American War and World War I saw the United States send troops abroad, black

151

troops grudgingly among them. Although some thought that in these wars blacks could prove their "worthiness" to be United States citizens. Johnson in *Black Manhattan* talks about San Juan Hill, not in Cuba but on New York's West Side. It was called that because many of the blacks who "showed out" in the Spanish-American War came from that area, an area settled in the interim when the black community was shifting from way downtown to the Harlem area. The area was later called Hell's Kitchen and was the birthplace, by the way, of Thelonious Monk.

Black soldiers saw the world and brought it back. Intense race riots attested to this fact especially around the time of World War I and especially between white civilians and black soldiers. The outside exposure confirming in the modern Afro-American consciousness more exactly what the United States was. Racial stereotypes were simple lies told by the white rulers to keep black people down, more and more blacks understood, and this became the conventional wisdom. One might be quiet in the face of them to keep from getting shot or fired, but they were lies, and the people who subscribed to them were racists and fools. Around World War II the same kinds of struggles broke out, and for the same reasons. The old place blacks were supposed to stay in in America had grown too small. (But it *always* was!)

In one sense the Renaissance wants to take the broad deep experience of being black in America and consciously make literature and art. But also it wants to continue the tradition of the pre–Civil War revolutionary black nationalists, and the transition figure, DuBois. There have always been three distinct traditional "ideologies" among Afro-American people in relationship to this country: (1) split, (2) stay and submit, (3) stay and fight. The most important of the Renaissance writers talked of staying and fighting, although the other two lines are expressed as well. But Hughes, McKay, Sterling Brown, clearly said fight, and in the works of the other major figures in the Renaissance, the positive aspect is always an assertion that the Afro-American people are here, they are struggling, they will survive.

We have to see the Harlem Renaissance as the recognition of development and change in the national Afro-American community—from the black nation itself in the South to the new communities impacted and forming every day from migrations of black peasants northward. The Renaissance is a combination of the raw peasant, before that slave, grasp of reality and the working people's and urban people's broadening of that reality toward an understanding of black people in America and of America itself in a more all-around way.

Jazz is an American music. The blues is particularly an Afro-American expression, closer to the specific cultural and historical development of the Afro-American nation and its multiple tributaries. The blues impulse absorbs the whole American experience, and it is jazz: broadened instrumentally, harmonically, to take in a wider experience.

The Harlem Renaissance raises up Afro-American literature as an American literature. At its strongest it is a worker-peasant–oriented socially conscious art. At its weakest it is merely a reflection of a new middle-class mincing along with the trendy currents of petit bourgeois "modernism." Or it is not even that, but the reactionary or antiquated whims of the aesthete separated from the struggle of a whole people in the real world.

The Harlem Renaissance is both the flowering of a national literature, Afro-American literature, to its modern, mature voice and the development of that literature, the expression of the people, to a point where it could speak more certainly about the whole of society.

Langston Hughes's manifesto, "The Black Writer and the Racial Mountain," sums up to a great extent the philosophical underpinning of the Renaissance. There is a deep pride, a strength in blackness, a cry of independence from not only whites but also blacks—in the true manner of the petit bourgeois rebel, rebelling against *everything*. Two aspects of the Renaissance are expressed. The black consciousness, the sense of the people, of struggle, is everywhere, and so is the other aspect, the breaking with tradition, both the oppressive tradition of submission to national oppression and even with the traditional image of what black people thought of themselves. The second aspect, independence of white or black stereotypes (or pleas for "dignity" at the expense of reality), was turned by reactionaries into noninvolvement with the life of the people. In some cases this was turned incredibly enough into outright opposition to the people, as for instance George Schuyler, who developed into a ridiculous right-wing Negro writing in support of Portuguese colonialism in the *Pittsburgh Courier*.

These two aspects of the Renaissance could be represented under the negative pole of submission by the conservatism of a Dunbar and the *assimilationism* of a Johnson; under the positive pole by the *revolutionary nationalism* of a DuBois. Brilliant writers like Toomer, though he touched black beauty and grace in *Cane,* would submit to the assimilationist, invisible-man syndrome. And because the toll of life and consciousness is so high under the oppressive American social system, which heaps the double yoke of national oppression as well as capitalist exploitation on black writers, even positive writers, who began with revolutionary nationalism—read race pride—such as Langston Hughes and Claude McKay could get turned around under the pressure of beast-America.

For McKay, his strong angry works, such as "If We Must Die," were so forcefully evocative of all men's struggles that ol' Churchill plagiarized it in his "blood, sweat, and tears" rhetoric. But McKay finally turned away from social struggle, and disillusioned by what he thought to be the flaws in the international revolutionary movement embraced Catholicism, retreated into metaphysics.

Langston Hughes, when all is said and done, and one day when literary criticism reflects the needs of the majority in society, will emerge as simply the most impressive, the strongest, the most consistent over long periods of all the writers in the Harlem Renaissance. Hughes was a poet, first and foremost; and a biographer, playwright, short-story writer, nonfiction writer, and writer of juvenile books, as well as a journalist. Beginning with *The Weary Blues* in 1926, Hughes published fifteen books of verse, including *Fine Clothes to the Jew, The Dream Keeper, Shakespeare in Harlem, Scottsboro Limited, Fields of Wonder, One-Way Ticket, Montage of a Dream Deferred, Ask Your Mama, The Panther and the Lash.* He also published in hundreds of little magazines and pamphlets, some of which are not completely documented. The best collection of his work is the book *Good Morning, Revolution* edited by Faith Berry, in which are collected many of his best and most conscious poetry, essays, and short stories.

Hughes also wrote at least seven full-length plays and quite a few shorter ones. He, to this day, still has the dubious distinction of being the black playwright having the most plays on Broadway, four. His first Broadway play, *Mulatto,* with its theme of so-called miscegenation, and the conflict between a mulatto son and his white father, was a vehicle for exposing the racist terror of national oppression and chauvinist sexual exploitation. It caused a great deal of controversy and ran for two years.

Other significant dramatic works of Hughes were *Troubled Island*, about Haiti and the Haitian revolution, and *The Sun Do Move*, which is an extended and more complete version of his earlier *Don't You Want to Be Free*, which is a general pageant of black history, giving us the origins of black national oppression. Hughes also wrote musicals and comedies. He founded three different black theater companies: the Suitcase Theater in Harlem; the Negro Art Theater or New Negro Theater in Los Angeles; the Skyloft Players in Chicago. He even wrote a play about the Scottsboro boys, called *Scottsboro Limited*, but that was not as likely to find its way to the Broadway stage as his *Tambourines to Glory*, a religious morality musical, or *Simply Heavenly*, his light-comedy musical. But we must be quick to add that both *Heavenly* and *Tambourines* are much more interesting than the standard Broadway fare.

Hughes wrote at least six novels: four *Simple* series; his earliest novel, *Not Without Laughter*, which describes his early life; and the novel version of *Tambourines to Glory*. He published three books of short stories: *The Ways of White Folks* (1934), *Trying to Laugh to Keep from Crying* (1952), and *Something in Common* (1963).

He published two extremely interesting autobiographies, *The Big Sea* in 1940 and *I Wonder as I Wander* in 1956. Hughes also did a great deal of really excellent work for young people, books that should be used in elementary schools: for instance, *Famous American Negroes* (1954), *Famous Negro Music Makers* (1955), *Famous Negro Heroes of America* (1958), *The First Book of Negroes*, *The First Book of Rhythms*, *The First Book of Jazz*, *The First Book of the West Indies*, *The First Book of Africa*.

He also write popular, sometimes illustrated, histories that are invaluable: *A Pictorial History of the Negro in America* (which he did with Milton Meltzer), *Fight for Freedom: The Story of the NAACP*, *Black Magic: A Pictorial History of the Negro in American Entertainment*.

He was also an excellent translator, translating Jacques Romain, Nicolás Guillén, García Lorca, Gabriela Mistral, David Diop, Leon Damas, Jean-Joseph Ravearivelo—translating from French and Spanish. Hughes's collaboration with photographer Roy DeCarava, *Sweet Flypaper of Life*, is a classic and is actually a little-explored genre, the book of photographs with a story line. Langston Hughes also edited a great many anthologies, about nine in all, including *The Poetry of the Negro, 1746–1949* (with Arna Bontemps), *Poems from Black Africa*, *New Negro Poets USA*, *The Best Short Stories by Negro Writers*, and also with Bontemps, *The Book of Negro Folklore*.

Hughes wrote opera librettos, lyrics for over forty copyrighted songs, and radio plays, including two with Paul Robeson. He even wrote at least one screenplay, *Way Down South* (1942), collaborating with Clarence Muse, and one television script, *The Travelin' Twenties*, for Harry Belafonte (in 1966). Hughes made several records of his poetry, and wrote an extraordinary number of articles, essays, and columns for newspapers.

Langston wrote for a living through much of his life, which accounts for the wealth of work, the diversity. It also accounts for the superficiality of some of the work. But Hughes was also no self-cultivating, egotistical solipsist. His work was from his beginnings focused squarely on the lives and struggles of black people. His works are clearly meant to inform, to educate, to inspire black people.

The Harlem Renaissance had declared, we are a new generation sick to death of the old traditions of white domination or black submission. Men like Alain Locke, who did collect the new works, still wanted to use black art to explain mostly to whites that black people were actually intelligent, so intelligent, as a matter of fact, that this generation does not even have to worry about talking exclusively about the problem of black oppression. It can get off into "art." Yet in the strongest art that emerged from the Harlem Renaissance, it is the focus on the lives and struggle of the people that has made that art strongest.

Another aspect of the Harlem Renaissance was a focus on the beginnings of black people in a heroic and positive sense, the evocation of Africa, rather than shame about Africa as a reflection of the lies developed by imperialists to justify the slave trade. Racist ideology was developed as a result of the economic subjugation of Africans in the European slave trade. At first it was because we had no souls; later it was we had no culture, or history. The writers of the Harlem Renaissance, as had the revolutionary nationalists before the Civil War, again raised up Africa as positive, as a legitimate source. Even Johnson, in *Autobiography of an Ex–Colored Man*, sets up a dialogue with a traditional Southern aristocrat racist in which the exploits of the African people are laid out to refute the distortions of imperialism.

Hughes's earliest published work, "The Negro Speaks of Rivers," written when he was still in his very early twenties, remains one of the most beautiful poems in the language. Many of his work of this period very consciously seek to make a link with black history, and by so doing with Africa. Although acknowledging that it is far away, still Hughes and the most progressive black writers of the period saw Africa as the source of black history and black life. Just as in the European Renaissance the history and culture of ancient Greece and Rome was evoked and studied, what was wanted in the Harlem Renaissance was the image of a nonslave, preslave period of strength and beauty for black people, in order to hook up the new progressive spirit emerging after World War I among black people with a historical justification and legitimatization of it.

This is also the period of Garvey and his "Back to Africa" Movement: a movement essentially made up of black peasants newly arrived in the North and led by the impoverished sector of the black petite bourgeoisie—down-at-the-heels professionals, small shopkeepers, that sector of the middle class closest to the workers. And again it was DuBois, just as he had opposed Booker T. Washington and delivered polemics against Washington's reactionary line, who came forward again to oppose the idealism of Marcus Garvey. But the whole attention to Africa came out of the social movement of the people.

The black bourgeoisie had lost its leadership of the black masses by the 1920's. The crisis of 1920–27 wiped out from one-half to two-thirds of all black businesses, and that leadership had shifted to the petite bourgeoisie in the person of Garvey. This is also why the so-called "genteel tradition" could be opposed. This tradition tried to project the image of the Negro as exemplary within the tradition of conventional—read nineteenth-century prewar Protestant—ethic. The obvious contradiction in this was that this ethic was based economically and socially on black slavery and humiliation. The focus on morality and uplift and faith in a progress linking this morality and aspiration to a learned—read European, not even white American—culture would not hold by the twentieth century for whites nor blacks. The entrance of the United States into the world as a rising global power saw to this. It was the confrontation with black identity that was most clearly established by the Renaissance. This is the weight of the early Hughes poems for instance, of the *Home to Harlem* of McKay, that they bring blacks out *as blacks*, as Afro-Americans whose lives are black lives, who are not bound by the nineteenth-century Protestant ethic but who are actually victims of it. And they do not react quietly or stoically Uncle Tom–style to this victimization; they oppose it and even strike out against it.

DuBois early in the twentieth century still reflected some of the so-called genteel tradition, because he articulated the position of the national wing of the black bourgeoisie (in opposition to the compradors)—the wing whose contradiction with imperialism was antagonistic, that sector which led the black freedom movement at the end of the nineteenth century and the beginning of the twentieth. It was this aspect of DuBois that cause,d him to oppose some of the Harlem Renaissance material that showed "low types" and was not focused on "morality and uplift," etc. But DuBois's ultimate concern was on the real uplift and aspiration of black people, and by the time the *New Negro* anthology was published in 1925, DuBois wrote an essay called "The Negro Mind Reaches Out," which begins to lay out how the black struggle is linked to the struggle of labor versus capital.

The Harlem Renaissance wanted to show a whole reality, naked and stewing. It wanted to be governed by its own reality. Negatively, people like Alain Locke imposed the ludicrous bourgeois idea of "being racial solely for the purpose of art," as if national oppression were not real, but merely a creator of artifacts. Locke said also that blacks were "forced radicals," and implied that the masses would be superconservative if it were not for the accident of national oppression and racism. Of course he was mouthing the plight of the black bourgeoisie and petite bourgeoisie, who experienced the national oppression and cried out against it too, but who did not experience the basic class oppression of the workers, black or white. The system of minority rule, capitalist exploitation, was more OK with them, because they were not on the bottom.

Hughes's importance, and the strength of his work, lies exactly in the fact that he reflects in his best work the lives and concerns of the black majority. (Read "My People" and "Dream Variations.")

His characters are not passing into the white world like the character of James Weldon Johnson, who gives up black culture—his music—so that he does not have "to wear inferiority on his forehead," as he puts it. Hughes celebrated black culture. His drawing of black speech, the Afro-American dialect, is much more certain than Dunbar's, and the use of black speech does not make him focus on childish concerns as Dunbar too often did. Hughes's mulatto suffers the same origins as Johnson's ex–colored man but he attacks and kills his white father for disowning him and victimizing his mother.

Hughes was born in one of the territories, Missouri; Joplin, Missouri. The territories were what Texas, Oklahoma, Missouri, were called before statehood. These were the areas where many blacks came after leaving the deep South, Kansas City being the major center of that area. Hughes's father and mother are described as educated people. His grandmother's first husband, Sheridan Leary, had actually been with John Brown at Harpers Ferry, where he lost his life fighting against slavery. Hughes's parents separated early in his life, and from that time he had a hard way to go economically, as his mother had trouble finding a decent job. But his father went to Mexico and became a well-to-do businessman.

Hughes was given an intense education in matters of race from his grandmother, who raised him on the Bible and *The Crisis* magazine and "long beautiful stories about people who wanted to make the Negroes free." His grandmother also taught him the rich world of books. He moved around constantly in his youth, going to elementary school in Lincoln, Illinois, where he began to write poetry. In fact his white classmates voted him the class poet because, as Hughes said, all Negroes have rhythm. He went to high school in Cleveland, Ohio, and there came up under literary influences other than Paul Dunbar, who was his first model. He read Sandburg, Amy Lowell, Vachel Lindsay, Edgar Lee Masters, all of whom were trying to write an indigenous American poetry. Hughes said he began then writing poems like Sandburg, whose loose modernism was sufficient to draw poems out of Hughes which he describes as being "about love, about the steel mills where his stepfather worked, the slums where he lived, and the brown girls from the South, prancing up and down Central Avenue [Cleveland] on a spring day."

After high school, Hughes went to Mexico because his father was living there and promised to send him to college. The elder Hughes kept his promise but sent Hughes to Columbia to study mining engineering, something he had no interest in at all. This is how he got to Harlem however, and when he dropped out of school after one year, his relationship with his father ended.

Hughes held down all kinds of jobs in New York, working on a farm in Staten Island, delivery boy, mess boy on African-bound freighters, which is how he got to Europe and Asia. He was a laundry worker, assistant researcher, busboy. And it was while working as a busboy at Wardman Park Hotel that he met the poet Vachel Lindsay and left some of his poetry on Lindsay's tray, so he might read it. Lindsay read the poetry and liked it and talked to the newspapers about the Negro busboy poet. After this, Hughes's work began to receive more recognition. His poem "Weary Blues" won first prize in *Opportunity* magazine's poetry contest. Carl Van Vechten helped Hughes get a volume of poetry published entitled *The Weary Blues*. In 1925–26 he received a scholarship and entered Lincoln University in Pennsylvania. He was now publishing individual poems in places like *Vanity Fair*, the *New Republic*. He also continued to win awards. While still a Lincoln student, Hughes published his second volume of poetry and his first novel, *Not Without Laughter*. It was in 1926, at the age of twenty-four, that Hughes published the much-quoted "The Negro Artist and the Racial Mountain," which served as kind of manifesto of the Harlem Renaissance.

Throughout his life, Hughes was always a conscious literary worker, a willing man of letters. He was always willing to support younger writers in his later years, and he was always quick to hold up others' works and tout them wholeheartedly. At the heart of Langston Hughes's work was a genuine love and commitment to black people. He was a classic "race man." And as such he is connected to the Walkers, Garnets, Langstons, Remonds, and the other pre–Civil War revolutionary black nationalists, via W.E.B. DuBois (all of whose life was spent as a willing "ox" for the race). Ironically this is the very reason that Hughes is denigrated and underrated by bourgeois literary critics, whose judgments necessarily include national chauvinism and racism, which constitute capitalist society's relationship to black people in general. As Bruce Franklin says in a recent essay in the *Minnesota Review*, "What the academic establishment presents as American literature is still basically the literature of certain white people. . . . I do not mean to suggest that Black literature was excluded from the canon of American literature because of the skin color of its authors. If those professors editing anthologies surveying the literary history, and teaching the courses, could have found some Blacks who wrote like the white men they admired they would have been only too pleased to include them in their pantheon. These gentlemen are pained and shocked to hear themselves accused of racism, because they are merely applying the same criteria to Black literature as they do to all literature. That is precisely the point, for the criteria they apply are determined by their own nation and class, and Afro-American literature conforms to criteria determined by a different nation and a different class.

"If we wish to continue to use the term American literature we must either admit that we mean white American literature or construe it to include the literature of several peoples, including the Afro-American nation." The fact that Hughes was aggressively focused on Black life and speech in his work whether accusingly or humorously or sadly or ecstatically so meant that his work would always be judged by bourgeois critics of whatever skin color as lightweight. As "Folksy." But Hughes always imbued his folk materials, his blues poems, his ballads and songs and peasant-in-the-city plaints with the sophistication of conscious art. Hughes himself wrote so much that he tended also to publish anything, and at times he is somewhat uneven, but the general level of his work is high, it needs simply to be understood as Black poetry, blues poetry, jazz poetry, revolutionary nationalist poetry.

Another reason for Hughes's low rating, paradoxically, is because it seems in Hughes's own selection of his works, especially in the 50's and on, that his work does not progress. The entire work of the 30's is dropped out of any selection, even those he makes. The collection *Good Morning, Revolution* is especially valuable for this reason, because it is the uncollected writings of social protest that Hughes himself suppressed. Like DuBois who began as a revolutionary nationalist, Hughes's works also begin there but in the 30's undergo a profound change. A change from the somewhat narrow insistence on the strength and color and beauty of black life. He moved naturally into the celebration of the majority of people's struggles for liberation in general. In the late twenties and early thirties the strength of the Communist Party USA, which was emerging under the pressures of the depression, and the continuing national oppression of Afro-American people drew Hughes toward Marxism, as it did a great many other intellectuals black and white. His trip to Russia further influenced him in the belief that Marxism had certainly created a society that was leaps ahead of capitalist U.S.A., and his works of the period reflect this, and are among the strongest and most militant poems in the language. They are filled with the spirit of struggle and dauntlessness. They are still full of commitment for the black struggle, but now openly linking that struggle with the struggle of working people everywhere, against an oppressor that Hughes identifies not just as white but as a "C-A-P-I-T-A-L-I-S-T."

White Man

Sure, I know you.
You're a White Man.
I'm a Negro.
You take all the best jobs
And leave us the garbage cans to empty and
The halls to clean.
You have a good time in a big house at
Palm Beach
And rent us the back alleys
And the dirty slums.
You enjoy Rome—
And take Ethiopia.
White Man! White Man!
Let Louis Armstrong play it—
And you copyright it
And make the money.
You're the smart guy, White Man!
You got everything!
But now,
I hear your name ain't really White Man!
I hear it's something
Marx wrote down
Fifty years ago—
That rich people don't like to spell.
Is that true, White Man?
Is your name in a book
Called The Communist Manifesto?
Is your name spelled
C-A-P-I-T-A-L-I-S-T?
Are you always a White Man?
Huh?

Hughes published these poems and essays and plays in a number of magazines and pamphlets. One of his most interesting plays, *Scottsboro Limited*, takes up the struggle of the Scottsboro boys, eight black Southern youths sentenced to the electric chair for *not* raping two white women. The case was a cause célèbre; Langston Hughes even went into death row reading his poetry for the Scottsboro boys.

The Scottsboro case was one of the most impressive pieces of work that the CPUSA took up in the period when it attracted thousands of blacks into the party in one year. It fought to establish unions and to get blacks in the unions when they were still excluded. It built the militant sharecroppers' unions to fight the oppression that came with sharecropping and peonage in the black belt. It also took the Leninist position of supporting the self-determination of the Afro-American nation in the black-belt South. Many of the genuinely revolutionary nationalists were taken up by the party during this period.

The period of the beginning of the Harlem Renaissance also saw an increase in black workers' leadership, especially in relationship to the strike movement. And though the Garvey nationalists fought pitched battles with the communists and Garvey was anticommunist, there was a left wing that came out of the Garvey movement called the African Blood Brotherhood with its organ *The Crusader* that put forward a socialist line and even called for a black nation in the South. The leaders of the movement were later absorbed into the Communist Party. But by the thirties the Garvey movement was destroyed by the state and the depression.

In the 1930's the black working class assumed leadership of the Black Liberation Movement, and it was this swell of black working-class leadership largely through the Communist Party USA that gave a giant impetus to the attraction of black intellectuals to Marxism. Even during this period of maximum revolutionary impact of the CPUSA there were still intense struggles inside the party against opportunism, white chauvinism, American exceptionalism. And during the rise of fascism in the middle and late thirties the opportunist leadership of the party, represented by Earl Browder, used the correct united-front tactic, in which revolutionary people made a united front temporarily with the nonfascist bourgeoisie against German, Italian, and Japanese fascism, to secure a collaborationist relationship with the capitalists that they never changed. In a few years, the party abandoned the sharecroppers' unions, liquidated struggle against the union bureaucrats in the AFL and CIO, and finally dropped their slogan supporting self-determination for the black-belt South. Browder's speech "Terehan," in which he says that communism is twentieth-century Americanism and that the workers and capitalists in America can work together because America is an exception and American capitalism is still a young progressive capital-

ism, signaled the end of the Communist Party and its absolute
sellout of black people. By 1944 the party itself had disbanded and
become the Communist Political Association "founded on the ideals
of Washington, Paine, Lincoln, etc." This is a period of extreme
disillusion among black and white intellectuals, a period of shock for
working people in general. Although the party was re-formed, it was
in name only, because by 1957 in its Sixteenth Congress it dupli-
cated the fall of the Communist Party of the Soviet Union into revisionism—using Marxist terminology to push reformism—and
codified its Khruschevite opportunism as "peaceful transition to socialism," to confirm a debilitation from which it never recovered.

The death of the CPUSA, finally, in the fifties, set a lot of revolutionary people, especially intellectuals, adrift. In the fifties, also,
the rise of McCarthyism helped cut many people totally away from
any relationship to struggle, just as it was designed to do (as the
U.S. imperialists now came again into open confrontation with the
Soviet Union). And from the late forties on Hughes began recanting
his earlier Marxist-oriented works, making statements that he was
"misunderstood" when he wrote these and frankly withdrawing all
these kinds of works from publication. Questioned by the House
Un-American Activities Committee he completed his withdrawal,
saying to the committee, "Here, all of us are part of democracy."
Hughes's lectures were being picketed by the Un-Americans, and
he was blacklisted for a time. But by withdrawing certain of his
works, and recanting the thirties, he managed to survive the fifties
and continue publishing, even reaching Broadway again. This is in
contrast to Wright, who simply went into exile, or Robeson, for instance, who was hounded to death.

Hughes continued to publish some interesting work, but his
focus returns to the pre-1930's celebration of black life for its color,
strength, and beauty. Though as the Black Liberation Movement
took on its more militant shape in the 1960's, this change also was
reflected in Hughes's work, like *The Panther and the Lash*. But he
never openly embraced scientific socialism again. The *Simple* books,
and columns, and plays are exactly that, Simple, not because they
focus on black life, but because they focus on the top of it, the
surface of it, and come up with pseudo-folk answers that Hughes's
genuine attention to the folk, to the black masses, had supplied in
reality some years before. But he chose consciously to back off and
survive. There is no doubt much of his later work suffers from this

flattening of consciousness, this conscious taking up of the *Simple* persona, the hyper-"folksy" at the expense of advanced consciousness.

Art must fight for the progress of society; it must identify with the most advanced forces in society and reflect their struggle to perfect humanity consciously. To back away from this commitment is to commit oneself to the maintenance of the backward and the reactionary. This latter is a commitment the largely commercial, bourgeois literary world demands, more so today than ever before. Langston Hughes sacrificed himself on that altar; others are sacrificed against their wills. But Hughes remains a great Afro-American writer, and his work must be culled and edited with a great deal of care and attention to the exact content and socio-historic basis of its creation, then the greatness of Hughes will emerge. He, Richard Wright, and W.E.B. DuBois are perhaps the most eminent of the Afro-American authors. And as Bruce Franklin points out, "The most distinctive feature of United States history is Afro-American slavery and its consequences. This truth is at the heart of our political, economic, and social experience as a nation state. It is also at the heart of our *cultural* experience, and therefore the slave narrative, like Afro-American culture in general, is not peripheral but central to American culture" *(Minnesota Review,* Fall 1975, p. 56).

Sembene Ousmane's *Mandabi*

Sembene Ousmane is a Senegalese novelist, short-story writer, and, most importantly, a film maker. In fact, he is the best-known black film director there is, internationally. But he began as a writer. Left Senegal and went to France—worked on the docks of Marseilles—which might be the reason he has said that the most influential book on his earlier life was Claude McKay's *Banjo,* which focuses on black seamen and particularly the lives of West Indian and African sailors shipping in and out of Marseilles. (His first novel, *Le Docker Noir,* focuses on the same kind of setting and characters.)

In Paris, etc., Ousmane had many of the same influences as the older generation of blacks shaped by French imperialism—and his work has always, in one aspect, cast a steady, clearly critical, eye on French colonialism and bourgeois French culture, but also on the distortions that colonialism has worked on its victims.

Ousmane has also focused relentlessly, though with genuine compassion, on the chaos that colonialism has made of traditional African societies and the neo-colonial travesty the African bourgeoisie has made in Africa. These are themes that recur again and again in contemporary West Indian and African literature because this is the real-life context of modern West Indian and African life.

Ousmane's breakthrough into film is so critical because, in the main, black writers of whatever stature have not been able to utilize films because this medium is so important and powerful the bourgeoisie makes it very exclusive! Ousmane, trying to learn film-making, had, of course, to leave Africa. He went to Paris and was still largely frustrated. But he did begin his studies there, but finally his real development and study of film-making came only after he went to Moscow to study, under Mark Donskoi.

Mandabi (The Money Order) is one of Ousmane's most popular films. A few others, *Tauw, Xala, Black Girl, Emitai,* have been shown in the States. In my opinion *Emitai* is the most powerful.* (And more film festivals must be put together by conscious political types to get a real look at the international black and Third World and revolutionary films.)

Mandabi is one of Ousmane's fundamental themes—and in truth, as I mentioned before, a basic tone running through major African and West Indian literature—the effects of colonialism, the post-colonial African society. Neo-colonialism—the conflict of cultures, ideologies—the old and the new. And the painful, tragic, though often funny, struggle that is going on right now to get past this, to eliminate it.

What's more there is continuous *irony*, e.g., the *old*—the traditional—is not seen by African writers necessarily as *the good*. What was ugly was imperialism, colonialism, racism. But Ousmane's focus on Islam is not very sweet either and he does this often in writing about the Francophone peoples of West Africa who actually have been twice brain-blown. Islam came to sub-Saharan Africa through violent expansionism; it was brought with the point of a sword. (See the recent Sembene Ousmane film *Ceddo,* for which he was booted out of Senegal, for misspelling the word, Senghor babbled.) Ditto French culture—and submerged beneath French culture and Islamic culture are, in Senegal, for instance the Wolof culture and people, the people of Mali, the peoples from the ancient cultures of Songhay, Mali, etc.

In Ngugi's Kenya there is always the conflict between the Christian and the traditional animist religions—class conflict, cultural conflict, political conflict, which the religious conflict signifies. In Senegal, Ousmane shows us the similarity—the Islam imposed upon the Wolof animist, the French Christian on top of that—and the same kinds of conflicts are played out. A good indication of the kinds of class and political conflicts the religious and cultural layering characterizes is to be found in the present edition's glossary. The glossary calls a Griot a low-caste praise singer. This shows the class

---

*Written before seeing *Ceddo*.

domination of the Islamic, with its Muezzins, over the older African traditional animist religion whose historian-story-teller-poet-singers are called Griots.

The Mbaye's and the distant cousin with the white wife are held in even higher esteem—because they have assimilated the newest and most powerful invader—the French.

The plot of *Mandabi* is simple. Dieng gets a money order from a nephew in Toubab land (France). He tries to cash it and *cannot.* Simply because, at base, he doesn't understand how the shit works! He is not familiar with the new rituals of power and so he forfeits. The shibboleths and sayings of Islam are hopeless in the chaotic neo-colonial setting.

Dieng dresses exquisitely, keeps two wives (which was actually the province of the rich). He tries to pattern himself after a well-to-do Islamic patriarch and holy man, but in reality he is an unemployed worker, fired for striking, in a country of the perenially unemployed. Thus, Dieng lives in two or three worlds (Wolof, Islam, French), a neo-colonial pastiche, in which he has actually assumed a kind of desired identity for prestige when the prestige of that identity has vanished.

Sembene always mentions when characters speak French. Most times all characters speak Wolof or some other African language or dialect. Mety, Dieng's oldest wife, says *merde* a few times. The characters curse, give directions and pretense in French.

"The intense heat mingled with the suffocating smell of exhaust fumes that fouled the air. The square swarmed cripples, lepers and ragged children, all of them lost in that ocean. Drinking water overflowed from one basin into the cleaner one beneath it. Carts grated on their axles, cars and motor-cycles made a deafening din. A cunning old beggar held out his hand with its five fingers wasted by leprosy to the occupants of cars brought to a stop by the traffic lights. A blind woman, the mother of a little girl, lay stretched out in the road itself, calling in a barely audible falsetto voice."

This is a classic portrait of neo-colonial Africa. Here, it is Senghor's Senegal, Dakar, the beneficiary of so-called "African Socialism." Ousmane's pen and camera are chilling in their exactness.

Dieng is tied to the old tradition (the newer old tradition) which made mock of the older tradition, just as French imperialist culture makes mock of Islam. Dieng is naïve. He is burdened with illusions. *He does not know how to act.* (As my grandmother used to warn us!) He does not really know the code words and passwords of modern society though he is a prisoner and victim of it. His friend says to him at one point, "You know nothing of life today," which sums it up.

Ousmane speaks in *Mandabi* and in his other works about the role of women in the polygamous Islamic, West African tradition and their historic stereotype of docility, submission, obedience—the evils of this—their struggle against it—their behavior a great deal of the time in obvious contradiction to it. But in all of his works Ousmane shows the women writhing under this exploitation ("Her Three Days," "Bilal's Fourth Wife") and not just polygamy but the whole oppressive position in feudal and neo-feudal society. Again and again he takes up the women's cause and shows them fighting back or merely refusing to submit. (In *Emitai* two sisters come to get their brother to make him come home. They come, in the traditional submit posture, hands folded across their chests, but they still grab him and drag him off. Mety, Dieng's wife, is *practically* outspoken though formally (traditionally) submissive. The women in *Emitai* defy the French when the men will not . . . etc.)

Ousmane implies that it is the *religion* itself that teaches submission (and indeed it does, speaking always about submitting to the will of Allah/Yallah), so that even faced with unrelenting mad bureaucracy, confusion, lies, pettiness, assault, robbery—Dieng tends to think Allahuakbar—or Inshallah. (Reminds you of Tutuola in *Palm Wine Drinkard.*)

Ousmane pictures the overall society as incredibly corrupt, bureaucratic, exploitive, oppressive. (Like Tutola's monsters; but it is not Yoruban animist forces but forces of society—real beasts and monsters, witches and devils—that Dieng meets.) Money and contacts are necessary to make it not Allah and five *salats* a day, or Olorun for that matter. *Emitai* shows this and goes further, showing how as the old traditional society is threatened by invading French colonial troops the elders want to make sacrifices to their old gods, whose powerlessness to stop the invaders is obvious!

In delineating and showing the *force* and place of the conflicting cultures, the French imperialist culture is shown as it is, dominant. Ironically, to the people, the neo-colonial society seems even more corrupt than the straight-out colonialism, for one reason because they probably expected more.

The distant cousin with the white wife who, Dieng's sister says, has forgotten us. He prospers. He has assimilated the modern, the newest dominance. He knows how to act. The old kinship ties, which are screamed about throughout—the religious ties—he has "transcended" long ago. He even makes some small gesture to acknowledge these but his wife opposes this (as the modern state does): "They only want to get money." Which is a profound truth. The masses drown in the hopeless chaotic neocolonial society, tied too often to traditional ways of coping with society which no longer have relevance.

Borrowing is a way of life (just as in the neo-colonial state house), self-reliance a mode of revolutionary thought! The cutting-away of the negative aspects of the old and newer old traditions and the elimination of imperialism and its stepchild neo-colonialism. The corruption, bribes, and accompanying paranoia and blackmail can be summed up like this:

"'You did give it to him?' asked the other.

"'He wants too much.'

"'Everyone has his price. The main thing is to get what you want.'

"'Where is the country going to? Every time you want something, you have to pay.'

"'Speak softly,' advised the younger man, looking round at the other passengers.

"Dieng had missed nothing of their conversation. He was sure the old man had just had to bribe someone to obtain a service."

The thought is hammered at again and again. Honesty is a crime in this country. But old "home ties," old ties, are burlesque in the modern juggernaut. The very fact that Dieng has been sent money and cannot get it. It is a gift he cannot possess. He does not understand. He has no identity card—he doesn't therefore really exist. No birth certificate.

The final rip-off done to Dieng is by "the New Africa Generation" as Ousmane describes them, "men who combined Cartesian logic with the influence of Islam and the atrophied energy of the Negro." This one, Mbaye, had two wives, one Muslim and one Christian (with a "Brigitte Bardot wig") as well as a Peugeot 403. "He had reached the top."

Mbaye pulls a simple con-game on Dieng, claiming he has had the money stolen from him (and this, in effect, verifies Mety's dream and the tale she tells Dieng of him being robbed. And this comes true, in a way that is realest in that society).

Mbaye knows, is a product of, the new society. He is its creature. He gets the old man (the unemployed worker with two wives and nine children) to give him power of attorney, after Dieng's tearful letters to his nephew in which he assumes a patriarchal role, warning him of the dangers of being in Toubab land and needing *gree gree* (charms) against the evils, when in fact it is Dieng who really needs them. And not against the Toubab but his successor. In a story called "A Matter of Conscience" Ousmane has a black worker say, "These types have nothing in common with us! They're black outside—but inside they're just like the colonialists."

Mbaye says, after the rip-off, almost like one of the neo-colonial governments, "You don't seem to believe me, uncle. Still, I am telling you the truth, the absolute truth. I swear it by the name of Yallah. At the end of the month, I will pay you back. I am the victim of my kindness."

Dieng, finally dumbfounded by occurrences—what he would call the will of Yallah—fate—sits on a step with 50 kilos of rice and 5,000 francs Mbaye leaves him, in deep debt and utter despair. "He could find nothing to say."

But finally after telling his tale he does sum it up: ". . . it is only cheating and lies that are true. Honesty is a crime nowadays." And willing to lie down in his despair to "put on the skin of the hyena" he is stopped by the postman, who says:

"Tomorrow we will change all that."

"Who is we?"

"You."

"Me?"

"Yes, you, Ibrahima Dieng."

"Me?"

It is the measure of Sembene Ousmane's work that even amidst the pessimism and despair that he shows that neo-colonialism promotes, he will not accept the static, the unchanging, the metaphysical. He is calling for the collective struggle that is the necessary element of change, understanding change is the real nature of reality. And that one day, just as the colonialists were kicked out, so too will their black proxies, and that one day indeed the workers and peasants will rule Africa in reality!

Black Boy as Slave Narrative, *Black Boy* as Anti-imperialist Narrative

Richard Wright's *Black Boy* fits the characterization slave narrative, but it demonstrates in many ways the motion of history. Chattel slavery was supposedly ended in 1863, with the Emancipation Proclamation, and its finish confirmed in 1865 when the Civil War ended with the Northern industrial capitalists victorious over the Southern slavocrats. But in the early 1900's—the period just before the First World War through the middle of the 1920's, the period *Black Boy* covers, telling of Wright's earliest life and consciousness—it is apparent from a reading of *Black Boy* that chattel slavery, if it has disappeared, has been replaced by a bondage that is almost as complete.

Black Boy talks about this bondage, and the system and land in which it originates. The feelings one comes away from this tale with are not too different from our reactions to the slave narrative; they are simply raised, intensified, because finally Wright does not ask merely for entrance into a nonslave world, which in this case would be a world free of national oppression for the Afro-American people. He does not ask merely for the confirmation that such a system of national oppression represented by the life of a young black man in the South is thoroughly unjust; he tries to show us a young life that at its most aware is conceived in conscious psychological rebellion against this oppression—a rebellion that parallels other slave narratives in that its culminating act is flight, and that is conceived not only as an act of rebellion, but also as the narrative of an Afro-American life, the growth from youth to young adulthood, from unconsciousness and ignorance to partial knowledge. It is a tale of conflict and confrontation with the world of black oppression. It is a furthering, a later chapter, of the earlier slave narratives, and as such, it is not only revealing about the life and struggles of black people in the United States, particularly in the South, which is the homeland of the Afro-American people in this country, but also it is a heated, passionate, burningly critical portrait of United States society as well: its history, its development, and something of its future.

Wright was born in Mississippi, on a plantation in Natchez, in 1908. The beginning of the twentieth century and the end of the nineteenth century was perhaps a low point for blacks in the United States, short of old chattel slavery itself, because just forty years before, black people had been freed from chattel slavery by the Civil War—a war fought by white workers threatened by slavery in the North, and black slaves, who had escaped from slave bondage, sometimes burning the plantations behind them, but who were still excluded from the Civil War until Lincoln and the chiefs of the Northern industrial bourgeoisie perceived that they were losing the war, and in one swoop put 200,000 armed blacks in the war against the Southern slavocrats, 200,000 soldiers who were willing to fight to the death against slavery.

After the Civil War, the Northern capitalists having made it possible for themselves to have domination over the entire economy, and with that, the political life of the country, set up Reconstruction governments in which blacks played important parts. They also allowed the Thirteenth, Fourteenth, and Fifteenth Amendments to be passed. These are the classic planks of bourgeois democracy: making slavery illegal, guaranteeing the right to due process, and ensuring suffrage, the right to vote. But the reason these were passed was finally to secure the domination of the Northern industrialists. The entire Civil War had been fought between the two social systems, because the slave system impeded the development of modern capitalism. It was neither as efficient nor as profitable as the so-called free labor system, which meant wage slavery. The Reconstruction governments did bring democracy to the South for poor whites as well as blacks, even though they were actually occupation governments, secured by Northern troops. Once the industrial and banking bourgeoisie obtained absolute control over the entire life of the country, they made a deal to restore the Southern planter class to power. Under the domination of Northern bankers and industrialists—the entire South was now controlled directly from Wall Street, seventy percent of the land for instance was owned by Northern banks—the ex-slavocrats had become a *comprador* class, tied to the Northern banks. Once the power of the industrialists and bankers was secured, they committed the so-called Hayes-Tilden Compromise of 1876, and put the South back into the hands of Southern slavocrats, who used counterrevolutionary guerrilla bands like the Ku Klux Klan, Knights of the White Camelia, Pale Faces, to drive blacks out of the statehouses, out of the legislatures and the Congress, to drive them out of politics and to destroy Reconstruction, plunging the Afro-American people back into near slavery—now disguised as sharecropping and the peonage system, and enforced with items like the Black Codes and Jim Crow, which raised up segregation/discrimination.

It was during this period of deep reaction that Richard Wright was born in the very heart of the black-belt South, the Afro-American nation which was born with the death of Reconstruction. The end of Reconstruction meant that there would never be a democratic integration of blacks into the United States, because in the South, the lands the blacks had grown to nationhood on, ownership of the land could be the only basis of democracy, and democratic or equal rights. With that, the reality of those Thirteenth, Fourteenth, and Fifteenth Amendments thereafter became only so much fiction and disguise for the real national oppression that replaced slavery.

Only now, blacks were no longer chattel slaves. They had, in the South, been together for hundreds of years, picking the cotton in the deep South. They had consolidated into "a historically constituted, stable community of people, formed on the basis of a common language, territory, economic life, and psychological make-up manifested in a common culture"—Joseph Stalin's historically accurate and scientific definition of a nation. Denied democratic rights as an integral part of the United States nation, in the black-belt South, an area stretching roughly from southern Delaware to east Texas, they had been consolidated into an oppressed nation, with the right of self-determination up to and including secession. It was a democratic right, to be sure, but one that could only be secured by revolution.

Mississippi is the heartland of the Afro-American nation in the black belt. In it are concentrated the real horrors of national oppression, and the particular terrors of such national oppression as it is

174

practiced in the United States with its attendant horrors of racism, discrimination, exploitation, and terror. In the early 1900's when Wright was born, the continuous fascist terror that was whipped on black people in the South was at one of its peaks, in a still-violent reaction against the movement for freedom and democratic rights that the Civil War and Reconstruction had meant for black people. The memory of that was still very clear and very recent, and the face of rising capitalism that had revealed itself to blacks as slavery: first of an older patriarchal, domestic slavery and later as a slavery tied to cotton as an international commodity, a system which actually saw capitalism imposed on top of the older slavery. Thus, in the deep South cotton-bearing states like Mississippi, the slavocrats had developed a system which placed the blacks' top use to the slave system at seven years. That is, they would work the male field slaves to the outer reaches of their capability for seven years, from eighteen years of age until twenty-five, and by age twenty-five, they should be dead from overwork. The slavemasters reasoned, and correctly, that it was better to get top productivity for those seven years and then get a new model, than it was to nurse the slaves along for years at lower productivity, having to feed, clothe, house, and supervise them.

The end of slavery and the coming of Reconstruction saw blacks move into political representation, and in some states, where they were in the majority, any kind of democracy meant that they would dominate the political life of those areas. Hence the necessity of the absolute suppression of all such rights. In South Carolina, after the Civil War, during Reconstruction, the South Carolina legislature had a black majority! But after this period there was not even one black in Congress at all from 1901 until 1929. There was only one black in Congress at any given time between 1891 and 1945. There have to this day been three black senators, two during Reconstruction and Mr. Brooke, elected in 1967, when Newark and Detroit went up like bombs.

The material reality of the black-belt South into which Richard Wright was born and where he struggled for his consciousness is that it was an oppressed black nation, oppressed by United States imperialism, just as it is today. No longer chattel slaves under the plantation system, no longer scattered peasants, small farmers isolated on the land after the Civil War; now there was an Afro-American nation in the black belt, oppressed by imperialism, just as any nation in the

Third World: Africa, Asia, Latin America, or other regions—the so-called developing countries, underdeveloped by imperialism.

The characterization of racism as a "moral" question, unrelated to the reality of the domination of an oppressed people on their own soil in order to make superprofits, has no meaning. What Wright faced was different from what Douglass, Walker, Brown, and the others faced—though in truth its essence, oppression, is the same. They faced chattel slavery, and by the time of the abolitionist movement with the appearance of people like David Walker, Henry Highland Garnet, Douglass, a chattel slavery that now had, as Marx observed in *Das Kapital*, "the civilized horrors of overwork . . . grafted on the barbaric horrors of slavery, serfdom, etc." But Wright faced national oppression, for in the early 1900's it had become an imperialist country, having initiated the first modern imperialist war, the Spanish-American War, so it could rip off Puerto Rico, Cuba, and the Philippines from the declining Spanish. By 1914, it was ready to get in the big time, to take on the major imperialist powers for a redivision of the world market: what they called making the world safe for democracy—World War I!

But the United States also had at least one oppressed nation within its own boundaries, and Richard Wright's story is a narrative of the development of the post-Reconstruction, twentieth-century, modern Afro-American sensibility in the face of this imperialism. *Black Boy* is about transition, the literal movement of the Afro-American people, and their ideas and whole spiritual life, from a peasant people grappling with the weight of the post-Reconstruction reaction to a people moving toward a new consciousness that would come from the cities, from nonfarm work, from travel, from growing involvement with industrial labor, from education. Wright represents the Afro-American consciousness broadening past mere reflex reaction to oppression—from reflex to reflects.

This is not to say that black people or black writers were unconscious before Richard Wright, quite the contrary. As you discover when you read the stirring prose of heroes like David Walker, or the pre–Civil War black nationalists like Henry Highland Garnet, C. H. Langston, Charles Lenox Remond, and others who were ultimately as revolutionary as Wright, their prose must be considered a strong part of the beginnings of a distinctive Afro-American prose style, focused directly and consistently on the slavery and oppression of black people. They were outstanding activists, organizers, and rousing speakers, whose speeches were openly, burningly antislavery, years before the Civil War; they cursed the slave masters and challenged black people to free themselves by their own strength and struggle.

But Wright is the reflection of a new era, an era in which slavery has ended, been defeated, black people have triumphed, only to be crushed by the new forces, which have grown out of the old forces. It is Wright who describes what the conditions are, and what the struggle will be, under imperialism. A close reading of Wright must prepare us more thoroughly for what we must fight and eventually defeat, but in *Black Boy* there are no real solutions. There is sensitivity to, recognition of, and partial understanding of the evil, national oppression. And there is even some penetration through its surfaces to the reality, which ultimately is private ownership of the means of producing wealth in society. But there is no real clarity on this; it is barely perceptual. But there is a long sustained outcry against national oppression, if only in the precision of Wright's descriptions of it.

Wright was born on a plantation of a sharecropper father, a black peasant rooted to the real past of black oppression and unable to surmount it to become articulate even to his son, but Wright for the most part is of the city: Natchez and Jackson, Mississippi, and even Memphis, the big city at the confluence of rivers, where Southern culture is raised up to its urban flowering, both negative and positive at the same time. He is divorced from the peasant—the small family on the land—reality. When a white woman offers him a job milking a cow, she has to show him how to do it. When he works as the writer and reader for a black insurance man, he is an object of some strangeness on the plantations because he is a city boy, and by now already grimly self-educated and cynical. In the city we see the classic exploitation and oppression that is modern capitalism, with the double yoke that national oppression provides. The black is a worker, but also an ex-slave, an oppressed nationality, and even worse, he has a racial difference which makes the national oppression even more thorough and fiendish. We see Wright's family torn apart, the father disappearing, in the same fashion as Engels and Marx described the destruction of the English family by capitalism. And the mother, who is triply oppressed by being a worker, a black, and a woman, is driven finally from city to city trying to provide for her children, and broken finally in health and spirit. Wright said that the condition of his mother, and her life of struggle, was a metaphor that summed up the entirety of modern existence, and he said that in her life was to be found a summation of his entire response to modern society. This suffering, he said,

> made me want to drive coldly to the heart of every question and lay it open to the core of suffering I knew I would find there. It made me love burrowing into psychology, into realistic and naturalistic fiction and art, into those whirlpools of politics that had the power to claim the whole of men's souls. It directed my loyalties to the side of men in rebellion; it made me love talk that sought answers to questions that could help nobody, that could only keep alive in me that enthralling sense of wonder and awe in the face of the drama of human feeling which is hidden by the external drama of life. [*Black Boy,* p. 112]

In short it brought him near to materialism, but certainly directly to realism and naturalism. His early influences in writing were the naturalist and realist writers of the American tradition; not only were they his earliest literary influences, but also his basic method of education. Mencken, Sinclair, Lewis, Sherwood Anderson, Edgar Lee Masters, and especially Theodore Dreiser, a great but predictably neglected American realist author, these were his early models.

In Wright's development, what accompanied his movement away from the old, traditional Afro-American life in the black belt was also an extreme sense of aloneness and finally individualism. It was this ability to analyze and separate himself from his environment that let Wright survive, he implies, but it also forged within his consciousness as strong a sense of individualism and concentration on the salvation of the individual self as has ever been seen in modern fiction.

Wright rejects the old, traditional Afro-American reaction to the black-belt environment as he sees it, and in part, his view is objective. He is isolated, fatherless, becomes spiritually independent at an early age. He dismisses the metaphysical outlets that oppression sometimes enforces, and which had possessed in varying degrees his whole family, especially his almost fanatical grandmother and aunt. He also rejects the traditional "humility" which the black South has been told is its only means of survival under the heel of national oppression. He describes how this oppression has destroyed blacks and warped some minds. His descriptions are no lighter than earlier slave narratives talking about chattel slavery, and they are worse in the sense that officially slavery was ended. During slavery the narratives spoke about the ending of slavery. The more revolutionary spoke about ending it through real action. But the story of people deprived of their democratic rights, deprived in essence of the right to self-determination, imprisoned upon their own land—a land of the free, which they were not, and a home of the brave, when they were being ravaged by cowards and killed if they were brave—this is what makes Wright's tale as sharp as tales of people under the heel of Nazi fascism. Wright's story repeats again and again the conflicts and confrontations with whites. He asks or has others in the story ask over and over, why are whites so mean? Why do they hate us? He shows the deep hatred blacks have for the way of life of national oppression, and even of whites, who are the perpetrators of this on the surface. But Wright rejects nationalism; he toys with but never embraces open hatred of whites and the need to destroy them as a black nationalist (p. 88). His frequent cries about the barrenness and unkindness, the lack of love, in black life, his aloneness, his isolation, and final individualism also keep him at arm's length from black people, in a sense. His portrait of Bigger Thomas in *Native Son* is his portrait of the black nationalist impulse in Afro-American life: the inarticulate rebel, doomed to failure and death, convulsed and made inarticulate in part by his absolute outrage and hatred of whites. But Wright rejects not only reactionary cultural nationalism, which he connects with rituals and folk religion and unreality, but also he finally rejects revolutionary nationalism, though his very power comes in part by providing a voice for such a stance as would cry out that black people will not passsively submit to oppression, they will resist, and they will liberate themselves. But Wright's individualism (at times, you are not sure that there is anyone else in the novel but him, his voice, his sensibility, his path) is such that all else is almost totally blotted out, except in the richness and exquisite language of his descriptions, which renders life larger and more vivid than it is.

His reading, his self-education in the midst of ignorance, he says again and again, saved him in the middle of agonizing pain. But in the end only flight seems real to him. He says, "I could calculate my chances for life in the South, as a Negro, fairly clearly now." (This is in Memphis, where he is preparing to head for Chicago, the capital for socially conscious writers at the time, like Dreiser & Co., but also the big stop heading up the Mississippi valley for all those blacks fleeing the South at that time, called up out of the black homeland, by the needs of imperialism, which was readying for the First World War, offering promises of a new life, jobs, freedom from the national oppression of the South.) He continues:

> I could fight the southern whites by organizing with other Negroes as my grandfather had done. But I knew that I could never win that way; there were many whites and there were but few blacks. They were strong and we were weak. Outright black rebellion would never win. If I fought openly I would die and I did not want to die. News of lynchings was frequent.
>
> I could submit and live the life of a genial slave, but that was impossible. All my life had shaped me to live by my own feelings and thoughts. I could make up to Bess [Wright's proverbial prototype name for the black woman], marry her, and inherit the house. But that, too, would be the life of a slave; if I did that, I would crush to death something within me, and I would hate myself as much as I knew the whites already hated those who had submitted. Neither could I ever willingly present myself to be kicked, as Shorty had done. I would rather have died than to do that.
>
> What, then was there? I held my life in my mind, in my consciousness each day, feeling at times that I would stumble and drop it, spill it forever. My reading had created a vast sense of distance between me and the world in which I lived and tried to make a living, and that sense of distance was increasing each day. My days and nights were one long, quiet continuously contained dream of terror, tension, and anxiety. I wondered how long I could bear it. [pp. 276–277]

Wright's flight is representative of the large-scale flight of the black masses from the South during these years, and the reasons for that flight are what give so much strong reality to Wright's book. They are the underlying material conditions that he has tapped and which he sometimes gives eloquent voice to. Jimmy Baldwin's early backwardness about Wright's "Protest Novel" simply aped the political line of the oppressors who think that the complaints of the oppressed can hardly be pretty enough to be art.

What Wright plumbs is the growing consciousness of the educated individual in the twentieth century, a particular Afro-American consciousness. At his most expressivve the creative strength of Wright's work lies in the fact of his birth, his struggle, his triumph over the aspect of national oppression intent on killing him or leaving him a cipher as an individual. But it is not in the individual that successful resistance to oppression lies but in the collective. When Wright gets to Chicago, there is another story. And another flight. The ending of *Black Boy* is the Afro-American sensibility of the 20's when the North represented promise and possibility. *American Hunger* is the second half of this book. After suppressing it for over thirty years, the publishers brought it out in 1977, at a time when the whole Marxist-Leninist movement was gaining some new momentum in working-class and black and other oppressed national communities, perhaps because they thought it would be anti-Communist. But actually what we see in *American Hunger* is that Wright not only rejects revolutionary black nationalism, but rejects Communism as well. And he does not condemn the Communists, even though at the time the CPUSA was moving past its revolutionary peak toward its final demise and death as a revolutionary instrument of the people. It was turning into a reformist's trick, which it is today, and this might in some way account for the conditions of Wright's rejection of it. But the principal basis of that rejection is inside Wright and rooted closer to his own overpowering individualism, which made him *the outsider, the man who lived underground,* a long time before Mr. Ellison's classic exercise in capitulation, *Invisible Man.* But Wright, when he left the CPUSA, also soon left this country entirely, another flight. He set the classic model for the black expatriate, followed by writers like Chester Himes and James Baldwin. In reaction against this model the leading voices of the next generation firmly committed themselves to struggle in this time and this place, though not always correctly.

"With ever watchful eyes and bearing scars, visible and invisible, I headed North, full of a hazy notion that life could be lived with dignity, that men should be able to confront other men without fear or shame, and that if men were lucky in their living on earth they might win some redeeming meaning for their having struggled and suffered here beneath the stars" (p. 285).

Nicolás Guillén

Nicolás Guillén, one of the greatest writers in Spanish in the New World, is still relatively unknown in the United States. Guillén is fully the equal of Pablo Neruda, Cesar Vallejo, and García Lorca, all of whom are much more celebrated. There are many more translations of these other poets' works than of Guillén's, and of quite a few other Latin writers. Yet Guillén is one of the most popular writers in Latin America, one of the best known. The reason he is so little known in the United States is simple: he is a poet of the people, he is an openly political poet, and lastly he is a communist.*

One other reason, of course, is that Guillén is an Afro-Cuban, "the major exponent of black poetry in the Spanish world." Although a black poet (as United States publications say, "a mulatto"—but one drop makes you whole), he is not a poet of Negritude, like Senghor and Césaire. Negritude was essentially a cultural nationalistic trend, the positive aspect of which was the resistance to cultural aggression (as far as it did that), the negative aspect of which was a narrow nationalism that finally collaborated with capitalism.

Guillén does not put down European culture; he puts down imperialism, racism, colonialism, and the slave cultures they have created. He is a true internationalist, fighting ultimately for the liberation of humanity. Guillén still lives today in Cuba, where he

---

*Neruda experienced resistance in the U.S. as well, and for the same reason.

was born in 1902. His father was a highly political newspaper editor who was a strong example for his son as well as an inspiration, being killed by government troops in 1917 as the Cuban people were already in the full swell of resistance to United States imperialism. The United States had acquired virtual control over Cuba from Spain, in the first modern imperialist war, a war in which the United States copped Puerto Rico and the Philippines as well, in its debut as an up-and-coming imperialist power.

Guillén tried several careers after his father's death, but gradually was drawn to literature. Writing in the 1920's, he came under the influence of the so-called modernist school: poets and writers, largely European and American petite bourgeoisie, reacting to the madness that the era of imperialism, the twentieth century, had brought into being. The openly anti-traditionalist schools, Dada, surrealism, vorticism, futurism, cubism, free verse, were all in revolt against the traditions of nineteenth-century "humanism" with its deep contradictions of colonialism based on the subjugation by European imperialism of the majority of the world's peoples. As this flawed humanism was exposed by the full-out emergence of antagonism and finally by the First World War between the great powers, it brought disillusion and various forms of reaction, especially among artists and intellectuals. The beginning of the twentieth century is marked by consciousness of imperialism, by destruction of the old forms, destruction of "the certain certainties." Human progress defined only as the progress of Europe riding on the backs of the rest of the world could now be seen as a gigantic hoax, as the so-called great powers entered into a gigantic holocaust dragging down millions of people to fight over the domination of the world: Germany and its allies versus Great Britain, France, and their allies (including the United States).

Guillén was influenced by the modernists, because in their departures from tradition there was some aspect of rebellion, although in the main this rebellion had more to do with form—the method of passage through the world—than with an absolute change of content. The nineteenth century had failed, even though it had heaped up the exploits of technological advance, the flashy upward surge of productive forces. But what was actually happening, materially, was movement from an earlier, more progressive capitalism (progressive because it had replaced feudalism) to its highest but most thoroughly decadent stage, imperialism.

Guillén's poems in this period are influenced by the modernist Rubén Darío—his first small book, *Cerebro y corazón (Head and Heart)*. The disillusionment of Euro-American intellectuals with the era of imperialism saw a "celebration of the primitive" in opposition to what they now perceived as the played-out bourgeois culture. The Harlem Renaissance is part of this cultural attention and "celebration of the primitive," as far as most bourgeois-influenced whites were concerned—as Hughes said, "The Negro was in vogue." The subjective attempt was to comprehend the phenomenon of the first full flowering of an industrial working-class, urban culture, through its dazzling arts—literature and musical intelligence of the likes of a Fletcher Henderson and Duke Ellington.

The peoples and nations of the Third World, Asia, Africa, and Latin America, were now also astir, caused also by imperialism. Where it penetrates, as it seeks to find new sources of raw materials, new markets, new places to invest capital, new spheres of influence, it also forces people to organize against it. As it tries to rip off people's resources it must also build processing plants, railroads, mines, bridges, and in so doing it creates a modern working class where before there were mostly peasants. It consolidates a group of revolutionary nationalist intellectuals, whose politics and art arise in opposition to imperialism, a native intelligentsia, hip to the "mother country" but determined to destroy its oppression. Imperialism creates great national movements bent on destroying it, because the era of imperialism is also the era of proletarian revolution.

Guillén's work had a similar thrust, developing on a rising national consciousness. Its content and hot songful energy replaced the calmer ironies of the *vanguardistas*. Guillén's work basically is concerned with blackness and revolution. The book *Motivos de son* shows the change from earlier, more literary preoccupations. It was greeted by many critics as an example of the roaring energies of the primitive. Published in 1930, *Son Motifs* is based on Afro-Cuban dance-song rhythms. Particularly Guillén chose the *son* because it is very clearly the merging of two cultures—the Spanish and the African. Before Guillén, Cuban poetry, like other Latin poetry, tended to identify with the Spanish (conqueror) forms rather than the African (slave) forms. This is political. It is an expression of the ideology of the conquerors continuing their conquest. But Guillén changed all that. The *son* poems speak not with "elegant" Spanish mannered rhythms but from the persona of the Habana slum dweller bursting with song, dance, irrepressible rhythms, bopping at us in street-hip Afro-Cuban lingo. He also pierces beneath the songful exterior of the Afro-Cuban ghetto to the grim realities.

After the urban Afro emphasis of *Son*, Guillén broadened his themes in *Songoro consongo* (1931). He deals with the whole Caribbean in *West Indies Ltd.* (1934). In *Cantos para soldados y sones para turistas* (1937) he has grown continental in scope. In *España*, the same year, his perspective has become international, focusing on the attacks on the Republic of Spain by fascists.

By 1947 *El son entero (The Entire Son)* is *ideologically* developed even further. His *The Dove of Popular Flight* and *Elegies* were written in exile (1958) and contain some of his fiercest and most joyous poems—poems of praise and condemnation. These poems were the most open and direct in speaking of social justice.

The books *Tengo* (which I would translate *I Got,* not *I Have)* and *The Great Zoo* reflect a celebration and consideration of struggle and triumph in Cuba. *Elegies* ("Emmett Till," "McCarthy,") was published just before Batista fled Cuba and the *barbudos* (bearded ones) entered Habana in triumph.

In his work Guillén has passed through several stages, always expanding and carrying the best part of the period forward with him. From the early immature, "modernist" so called, efforts, to the brash ghetto strutting of *Son*, to the heavily onomatopoetic (for example the use of *jitanjafora*—invented atmospheric words), self-consciously drum-rooted works of *Songoro consongo*, there is upward motion. Guillén wanted, even then, consciously to create a Creole, a *mestizo*, poetry, which he took to be the true spirit of Cuba (but voluntary union as opposed to imperialist imposition). *West Indies Ltd.* (1934) was published right after the deposing of the dictator Machado. It is a period of transition in Guillén's poetry. In *Motivos*, he dealt with the mainly perceptual—slices of life from the Afro-Cuban ghetto. In *Songoro consongo* (the *jitanjaforos* title) Guillén goes deeper into the lives of Afro-Cubans, but speaks to the Cuban people as a whole. In *West Indies Ltd.*, Guillén focused on the whole of Caribbean life, and for the first time elements of social protest come out very emphatically in the work. Where before just the images of the lives of the black Cuban masses *show* us things we cannot accept, now the poet begins to be more clearly opposed himself to them too. (See "Riddles" and "Guadeloupe W.I.") It begins to be clear that this is a poet concerned with the national liberation of the

185

Cuban people—singing and shouting from the gut level, beginning to create "an art of unambiguously militant convictions," although still not as ideologically clear as he would become after 1934.

The rise of fascism in the world marked the absolute nadir of bourgeois humanist consciousness. Faced with world economic crisis, and the rise of strong communist parties in advanced industrial countries, particularly in Germany, the bourgeoisie had no choice but to resort to fascism, which is the rule by terror of the most reactionary, chauvinist, and imperialist section of finance capital. The struggle against fascism was characterized by the formation of a world united front against it that brought together the most progressive elements in a life-or-death struggle against fascism. Some of the erstwhile "modernists" like Pound, Wyndham Lewis, etc., actually came out in support of fascism, demonstrating the final resting place of the narrow elitism of their work and its real stance in the actual world. Artists like Guillén, however, and Langston Hughes, joined such organizations as the antifascist Second International Congress of Writers for the Defense of Culture. In 1936, Guillén went to Spain to oppose fascism and support the Spanish Republic. It was there that he came into contact with the poet Langston Hughes, and they became very great friends. (Guillén was to ask me in 1960 with a face full of disbelief and quizzical irony what had happened to Hughes as far as his public stance and the poetry which used to embody it.) By 1937 Guillén had joined the Cuban Communist Party, of which he is still a member today. He wrote poems about the tragedy of Spain, as the Spanish fascists killed Garcia Lorca—just as in the seventies the Chilean fascist junta murdered the great Pablo Neruda.

One interesting aspect of Guillén's work has been his attention not only to the face of United States imperialism in the Caribbean and Latin America, but also to its vicious oppression of the Afro-American people in the U.S.A., particularly in the black-belt South. (See "Emmett Till" and his attacks on Eisenhower, Nixon, Faubus, etc.) In *El son entero (The Entire Son)* he combines the *son*, the mulatto poem, accusation and anger, and a sharp identification with the pain and struggle of black people wherever they are. (See "Sweat and the Lash" and the great litany for McCarthy during the heat of the McCarthy era.) And as the Cuban revolution intensified, Guillén also began to write more and more about figures from Cuba's revolutionary past and present like Antonio Maceo, José Martí, Fidel Castro, Che Guevara.

186

With the triumph of the Cuban Revolution in 1960, Guillén's poems celebrate that revolution, and works like *Tengo* show the heights of hot pride and still-revolutionary spirit with which he greets the defeat of United States imperialism through its lackey, Batista, and the promise of the Castro era. Guillén is still full of fight but now in defense of the Cuban Revolution, pointing out at the same time the injustice that is still going on inside the United States ("It Is All Well") and the rest of the world.

The Grand Zoo (1967), with the Cuban Revolution an accomplished fact, is written with great irony and humor. Guillén takes us to a zoo of capitalist prototypes where the various "animals can be studied." He used a short-line, unrhymed, and free-verse style, as if the poems were the actual plastic signs one reads next to the cages, and as such they are interrelated and organic.

> *Lynch*
> Lynch of Alabama.
> Tail in the form of a lash
> and tertiary hooves.
> Usually appears
> with a great flaming cross.
> Feeds on Negroes, ropes,
> fire, blood, nails,
> tar.
> > Captured
> at a hanging. Male.
> Castrated.

Guillén has won a great many honors in the socialist world, and among Third World countries, and among people fighting for liberation everywhere. His poetry still upholds humanity in struggle against imperialism, speaking with the voice of a liberated fighter, fighting till the world is free. (See "Lynch," "KKK," "Tonton Macoute" against the Haitian repression.)

Guillén is presently editor in chief of *La Gaceta de Cuba,* an official cultural publication of the Unión Nacional de Escritores y Artistas Cubanos (UNEAC), of which he is president.

Guillén at each turn has sought the expression of life in the real world and has attempted to shape a poetry of commitment to struggle and change using the voice of the people themselves. As Mao Tse Tung points out in *The Yenan Forum on Art and Literature,* the fundamental question about art is what is its class stand, its world view: what does it praise and what does it condemn; who is its audience—a key question, that is, for whom, ultimately, is it written—and what work and study does it show?

In Guillén's case, it has been clear over the years that his class stand is that of proletariat, the working people, the peasants and oppressed masses of prerevolutionary Cuba and the world. His world view is, for that reason, materialist, based on the real world, its constant development and change, not idealism or metaphysics. Over the years he has consistently condemned what oppresses the people and has praised and supported in deeds as well as with words what supports and liberates the great world majority. It is this great world majority of workers, peasants, and oppressed nationalities and people to whom his work is addressed. In its simplicity, anger, irony, directness—and its Afro-Cuban *son* funk rhythms. His study has been of society, and of the science of revolution so that he would not only understand the world, but contribute to changing it, and his work also has been toward the transformation of reality, revolution. His work shows this clearly. Nicolás Guillén, from Latin America, is one of the great writers of the world. His work is obscured only by the bourgeoisie in their attempts to keep Guillén's example and message and great works from the masses inside the capitalist countries. (The bourgeoisie would celebrate instead, with the Nobel Prize, an obscure surrealist like Aleixandre in Spain—who did not even have to leave Spain during Franco's time, he was so weird.)

Aimé Césaire

To study Aimé Césaire's work, especially his major work of poetry *Return to My Native Land*, it is necessary to look at the world the man and his work grow out of. Art is an attempt to describe the world, an ideological form, which also describes the mind of the describer. It is a projection of life; it is a projection of the particular life, of the artist, as well. Art can exist independently of the context of its creation only at the risk of obscurity.

Césaire was born in Martinique, a French colony in the West Indies, in 1913. His growing to consciousness at the beginning of the twentieth century happens within the framework of certain world-shaking, world-changing events (the culmination of certain processes, etc.) Early competitive capitalism was being transformed into imperialism, or the monopoly stage of capitalism. This transformation meant that capitalism had now to leap out of its national boundaries and pursue surplus value all over the world. It had inexorably to seek new markets, ever expanding, seek new sources of raw materials, new places to invest its surplus capital, and new spheres of influence. This transformation meant that the capitalists had to penetrate every land on the face of the planet searching for these things, its lifeblood for expansion. But wherever it penetrated, in order to suck its fill, rip out resources, steal with impunity, dialectically it had to (as a result of every process in the world being composed of contradictions, opposites, which give life itself its motion) also build railroads, mines, ports, factories, as Lenin pointed out in *Imperialism, the Highest Stage of Capitalism*. And because it had to build these means of production in order to steal, it had also to create a proletariat, workers, where before there were peasants—a working class, in fact, that one day would destroy imperialism. Imperialism also created a nationalist intelligentsia in these mainly Third World countries, where it practiced its superexploitation to extract superprofits. This nationalist intelligentsia finds itself inevitably in opposition to imperialism.

But if the twentieth century is the century of imperialism, it is also the century of proletarian revolution. Imperialism means war as well: wars between the imperialists themselves to divide the world. In 1884 the colonial powers had actually sat down in Berlin and divided up Africa like a cake, but by 1913, the same year as Césaire's birth, the First World War was about to break out as imperialist groups fought to redivide the world's spoils.

By 1917, socialist revolution was victorious in Russia, the most backward country in Europe, led by Lenin and the Bolshevik Party, and this set a concrete example not only for working people but also for colonial people all over the world. And as imperialism had intensified its rape of the colonial people, they had intensified their resistance. In 1919, led by Lenin, the Communist International, the Third International, a meeting and joining-together of communist parties all over the world, was effected, and the impact of this also shook the very foundations of the imperialist world. Lenin at this historic series of congresses also put forward a mighty slogan that summarizes the era of imperialism and the resistance of the people perfectly. Where Marx had laid out "Workers of all countries unite," Lenin now, reflecting the changed conditions of imperialism, said, "Workers of all countries and oppressed nations unite!," reflecting the mighty torrent of colonial peoples that was already in motion fighting against imperialism.

So the 1920's saw evidence of a continuously higher level of resistance. It also saw the widespread emergence of the nationalist intelligentsia in oppressed nations and colonies everywhere. As a reflection of world imperialism, there is world resistance, and the emergence of the native or colonial intelligentsia worldwide. We speak of the Harlem Renaissance as one flowering of such a native intelligentsia, focused directly around the arts. Langston Hughes and Claude McKay were its finest examples.

There were parallel movements in Haiti around the journal *La Revue Indigène*, associated with men like Jean Price Mars and Jacques

Romain. Haiti's renaissance at this period came somewhat earlier, spurred on by the United States occupation in 1915. A movement to study Haitian folklore, a new self-consciousness born of a need to defend oneself against the cultural aggression and the bourgeois assimilation that imperialism always brings with it arose in Haiti, and a fiercely outspoken intelligentsia arose with this self-consciousness. In Cuba, Brazil, Martinique, there were parallel movements, part of the same outswell. In Cuba, it was called Negrissmo.

Paris was one center of colonial intellectuals. The imperialist countries themselves always draw the colonial peoples into them as cheap labor, but also they have become the "mother country," the beacons of civilization; the students and intellectuals as well flock to these fortresses of exploitation, some seeking merely to assimilate completely themselves and so become imitations of the conquerors, others seeking to answer questions that have been posed in the conqueror's language, by the conqueror's culture—but ultimately they answer those questions with a language of their own, resistance.

So Paris was one center for those intellectuals from the various countries the French had despoiled; as was London, for those oppressed by British imperialism; New York, for those ripped off by the U.S.A. Just as Amilcar Cabral or Augustino Neto could be found studying in Lisbon, before they returned to Africa to help destroy Portuguese colonialism, you could also find in Paris, at the same time, both Ho Chi Minh and Chou En Lai. Paris was a center for colonialized intellectuals from Africa, Asia, Latin America, the West Indies.

One important development of this collection of colonialized intellectuals in Paris, by the 1930's, was the movement represented by a booklet-manifesto called *Légitime Défense*, which not only verbalized the anticolonial feelings of young black intellectuals living in Paris but also launched a heated attack on the assimilationist native bourgeoisie and petite bourgeoisie in the colonial countries. It was a manifesto striking out against "this capitalistic, Christian, bourgeois world." *LD* was a cultural movement as well as a political movement, led by a young West Indian in Paris named Etienne Lero, a poet (also by René Menil, Jules Monnerot). The manifesto was directly focused on the French West Indian colonization process. And as often happens, it was put together by members of the very class of blacks it condemns: bourgeois, assimilationist, mulatto. In fact all the signers of the manifesto were specifically mulattoes, except for

Lero. Ultimately the manifesto gave rise to an intensifying nationalism, a calling forth of a nationalist national bourgeoisie to replace the comprador assimilationist bourgeoisie, which helped to stabilize the earlier colonialism.

The manifesto begins with aspects of a Marxist analysis of island society and sees the West Indians as descendants of African slaves held three centuries. But it wants to use Marxism not only as a weapon of liberation but also surrealism! It lays out its intellectual leaders as Marx, but also Freud, Rimbaud, and Breton, and as such presents an intellectual pastiche not uncommon in the twenties and thirties. *LD* mentions for instance that "surrealism alone . . . could liberate" the West Indian from his taboos and allow complete expression.

The reason that this essentially bourgeois and European intellectual and arts movement could have so much influence on these young black intellectuals, aside from the fact that they were in Paris, was the fact that surrealism purported to attack bourgeois values. It reflected the extreme disillusionment of Western petit bourgeois intellectuals with the emergence of imperialism, World War I, and the obvious drowning of Western lip service to human rights under a torrent of blood, slavery, and money.

But essentially it is the bourgeois and petite bourgeois class base of the writers of the manifesto that allows them to confuse bourgeois rebellion with revolution. Surrealism calls for a disordering finally of the bourgeois world, but even that is momentary, and it does not really call for its destruction.

Surrealism could attack bourgeois academic writing and art, and black intellectuals who wanted to attack the assimilationist tendency in West Indian writing felt common ground. *LD* attacks what they call "tracing paper poetry . . . stuffed with white morality, white culture, white education, white prejudice," a poetry of advanced mediocrity. It says that the West Indian intellectual "will stifle his originality in order to be considered civilized." He is afraid to "make like a nigger . . . in the world . . . or in his poetry." (See my essay "The Myth of a Negro Literature" for a parallel even in the 1960's. See my poem "Black Dada Nihilismus" for a parallel legitimization of the Dada-surreal utilization idea.)

The manifesto also picked up on Claude McKay and Langston Hughes, saying that "these two revolutionary black poets have brought us . . . the African love of life, African joy, and the African dream of death." It goes on, "Our distinguished writers never touch these subjects." The manifesto scathingly denounced West Indian poets still imitating the antiquated French Parnassian school, having not even moved toward realism, naturalism, and symbolism.

As poets, they denounced the imitation French literature created by the ten percent of the population that was literate, the same ten percent that was literate in French and hated Creole (this is in Haiti), when the ninety-percent majority who were illiterate spoke Creole.

This manifesto had a deep influence on the young student Aimé Césaire, then studying in Paris on a scholarship, as well as on two other writers important to the movement that would later be called *Negritude*, Leopold Senghor and Leon Damas. Senghor said *LD* reflected the "new Negro movement in the arts," the same phrase used by Alain Locke in the United States to describe the Harlem Renaissance.

These young poets were looking for a mode of expression, a method of saying what was uniquely theirs to say, and at the same time denouncing all sterile imitations of the colonial masters. Césaire said: "We have had no art. No poetry. Rather a hideous leprosy of counterfeits." Instead of Phillis Wheatleys and Jupiter Hammons they wanted an expression linked with continuity yet rebirth, indigenous *and* revolutionary, just as the Harlem Renaissance continued the legacy of the slave narratives, the pre–Civil War revolutionary black nationalists, by way of DuBois's *Souls of Black Folk*, to sum up black America and America itself's entrance into the twentieth century.

But even the title of the manifesto is a title gotten from André Breton, and the *LD* mentions all the masters of surrealism, Breton, Aragon, Crevel, Dali, Eluard, Peret, Tristan Tzara. So that the contradictions in the manifesto should be evident on the surface. In a few years, many of the surrealists, who during this early period had joined the French Communist Party, left the party, and this seems obvious since communists see literature as primarily a functional weapon in making revolution, not as simply cunning artifacts in some salon rebellion, which will be celebrated, even housed, by the bourgeoisie itself once it understands the commercial value of shock and canned outrage. Duchamp's toilet seat supposedly intended to scandalize bourgeois art becomes itself quite soon a standard of bourgeois art, sitting calmly in the same museums it has declaimed it wanted to burn down!

The great influence of communist ideas on intellectuals throughout the world by the 1930's and the economic crisis should be noted again. The presence of Marxist ideas in *LD* can be thus accounted for. Lero, it should be added, saw himself as a political figure as much as a writer, and *LD* was clearly and openly political, although clearly flawed. There is mention of the Scottsboro Case in the United States in the manifesto, and it asks quite openly, "When will American blacks really understand that their only escape from the American hell lies in communism." Jacques Romain of Haiti was a communist, Hughes was writing his Marxist-inspired poems, Guillén of Cuba had become a communist.

The return of the primitive, and the exoticism and primitivism that leaped through the West as part of the disillusionment with Western humanism, was very evident in the surrealist movement. The raising of the word as magic, and the poet as magician, these ideas were picked up by people like Senghor, and these ideas when pursued become cultural nationalism and metaphysics. But the conflict between *socialist* realism and *sur*realism got clearly more obvious.

The blacks wanted to use surrealism a different way. For Césaire, it represented a destruction of French literary tradition, which he felt stifled by. "It was a weapon which exploded the French language. It shook up absolutely everything." Césaire even refused to write poetry and wrote the *Retour* as a prose-poem to get away from stifling form. He says: "Even tho I wanted to break with French literary traditions, I did not actually free myself from them until the moment I decided to turn my back on poetry. In fact, you could say that I became a poet by renouncing poetry." It was the only way to "break the stranglehold the accepted French form held on me."

The *LD* writers had declared themselves traitors to their class, openly breaking, at least on the surface, with the bourgeois assimilationist West Indian writers of the colonized mentality. The movement began as one of national (and racial—since blacks regardless of nationality are oppressed as a race worldwide) self-consciousness, and then self-affirmation. But at the same time it was a movement of social awareness and struggle, utilizing the language and forms of Marxism. The parallel in movements throughout the colonial world is striking. And the direct influence of the Harlem Renaissance on the writers of Negritude is readily acknowledged. The most important book of that renaissance to these writers was Claude McKay's

Banjo, not only because of McKay's West Indian background and because he used in this book both Europe, the Marseilles docks, and the West Indies as his setting, but also because in *Banjo* there are ideas of resistance to colonialism, and statements about black people's situation, that are presented with the clarity of fire.

Both Césaire and later Sembene Ousmane were influenced directly by *Banjo.* Leon Damas of Guiana, one of the most important Negritude poets, was influenced by Hughes. Senghor translated Hughes and Cullen and Toomer. It was the openness, vitality, humanity, reality, of black life and feelings, and the passionate embrace of black people and black life and the will to struggle to raise it to a higher level, that attracted Senghor and the others to the Harlem Renaissance. The emerging national consciousness of the Afro-American people was being taken up and turned to good account by a similar nationalist intelligentsia. The United States was the most advanced capitalist country, and the illusion called bourgeois democracy was being pushed to its furthest limits. Within state the Afro-American people in their struggle for development and exploded in self-consciousness and self-affirmation. Whether it was movement of the twenties or the bashing entrance of big-band jazz, the shots heard around the world.

Another important influence on black French-speaking intellectuals in Paris and around the world at the time was the novel by René Maran, which was awarded the Prix Goncourt, *Batouala.* Awarded the prize out of a determined hypocrisy—bourgeois colonialist society had to congratulate itself as humane, but this book was at the same time denounced by the most important French critics and its author generally hounded into silence. Maran was the first black in Paris to tell the truth about colonialism and the true mentality of blacks rather than the pseudoscientific racism of the colonialists. Maran was a black who lived in French Equatorial Africa as a French colonial administrator. He lived among the Ubangis; Batouala was their chief. Maran said: "I showed blacks as they were. I had no intention of writing a polemic." And as one critic said, it was as objective as a police report—so objective that French critics associated Maran's name with *hate,* which is a favorite trick.

By 1934, Senghor, a Senegalese (in fact he is now the president of Senegal), along with Césaire, Damas, and some other West Indians, began to put out a newspaper called *L'Étudiant Noir.* Where *LD* showed the prevalence of politics, *LEN* showed the prevalence of culture. Obviously this is because of Senghor's influence. Senghor's relationship to Marxism he described as being "nondogmatic." In fact his relationship to it was so thoroughly cavalier that he could propose an "African socialism" parallel to what Negritude (blackness, niggerness) seemed to propose in one aspect, but this "African socialism" is, in fact, just black capitalism and neocolonialism.

In contrast to *LD*, neither Senghor, Damas, Diop, nor Soce were communists. Senghor related to the mystical and the magic, saying that his poetry captured invisible forces, and that it utilized "analogy images." Césaire did not share these concerns; to Césaire humanity was the most vital force. But there is little doubt of the enormous influence that Senghor's concerns with black culture and this general cultural nationalism had on Césaire.

It is important that we realize how clearly one breaks into two, how the contradictions in the Negritude movement and its different tendencies break it apart. Césaire reflects to one degree or another most of these tendencies, but he is in the main reflective, in *Retours*, of the revolutionary nationalist aspect of what is called the Negritude movement, rather than the negative or cultural nationalist aspect.

Oppressed by imperialism, colonialism, racism, Zionism, the oppressed nations and peoples fight back. To the extent that nationalism represents resistance to oppression it is revolutionary. Even where it focuses on culture, when it refuses to be wiped out by the imposition of colonial culture, when it raises up the history and lives of the oppressed people as part of the struggle for their future, it is revolutionary. That is revolutionary culture. When it sees that culture as some static, unchangeable, mystical phenomenon with certain eternal, metaphysical, nonmaterial, and nonmaterially derived values, it is reactionary; it is bourgeois nationalism; and finally it serves to raise a new bourgeoisie, the national bourgeoisie, to power. Senghor's Senegal is proof in living color of the reactionary nature of such cultural nationalism. The "eternal mystical values" of black communalism, supposedly raised in a modern African socialism, are the excuse for the most shameless bootlicking of French imperialism, and for one of the most relentlessly class-stratified black societies in West Africa today.

For instance, Senghor's definition of Negritude (which is niggerness or blackness), "the total of black Africa's cultural values," proposes that there is a static cultural essence to blacks apart from the development of the specific material base of the culture itself. But culture reflects first and foremost the material, i.e., the economic and with that the political, framework of its being. Africa's cultural values when? During primitive communalism, slavery, feudalism, or capitalism? During ancient Egypt? In Songhai, enslaved by colonialism, or up under the well-polished fingernails of black neocolonialism?

Césaire, on the other hand, defines Negritude in 1959 as "the awareness of being black, the simple acknowledgment of a fact which implies the acceptance of it, a taking charge of one's destiny as a black man, of one's history and culture." Here there is self-knowledge, self-affirmation, and the move to liberation. Blackness is not a static, mystical, "eternal" cultural quality; it is concrete consciousness and with that, concrete struggle. It is not enough to understand the world; we must change it.

Sartre said, mistakenly I think, that the Negritude poets wanted a world without race, which is why they, dialectically, stressed race. But I think they want a world not without race but without racism (which is impossible without the destruction of its parent, imperialism).

The Negritude poets began publishing in 1934, with Leon Damas's work in the magazine *Esprit*, and his first book, *Pigments*. Césaire began publishing *Retours* in 1939 in the magazine *Volontés*. Senghor's first volume did not appear until 1945.

Césaire was born of barely lower petit bourgeois parents in Martinique, a "difficult childhood" sharing hard-earned bread, got to college as a scholarship student. Senghor was the son of a wealthy, African bourgeois family. Damas, who lived the life of a petit bourgeois *assimilado*, cried out against those values throughout his poetry.

In 1939 Césaire was still influenced enough by the struggle for liberation and examples like Guillén, Romain, Aragon, Lero, Hughes, McKay, to become a communist.

In 1945 Césaire went back to Martinique, under the banner of the Communist Party of France, became a communist deputy to the national assembly and the mayor of Fort-de-France. The position of the CPF at this point was that Martinique should be a department of France. There was no Martiniquais Communist Party; it was a department of the CPF, a wildly chauvinist position! Césaire supported these positions at first, but by 1956 he had totally denounced this policy of departmentalization for what it was, national chauvinism. In 1956, Césaire resigned from the CPF, not only charging the same chauvinism in the CPF relationship to the Martiniquais communists and the departmentalization, but also incensed over the CPF vote on the Algerian question, in which they upheld French colonialist policy in Algeria!

Césaire's letter to Maurice Thorez not only sums this all up but also reflects Césaire's own petit bourgeois vacillation between Marxism and class struggle led by the proletariat of all countries, and a comfortable petit bourgeois nationalism. His condemnation of Stalin, based on the traitor Khrushchev's opportunist denunciation of Stalin, shows this confusion, although Césaire says truthfully enough, "I think I have said enough to make it plain that it's neither Marxism nor Communism I repudiate; that the use certain people have made of Marxism and Communism is what I condemn. What I want is that Marxism and Communism by harnessed into the services of colored peoples, and not colored peoples into the service of Marxism and Communism . . . that the doctrine and the movement be tailored to fit men, not men to fit the movement. (See Mao, *On Practice*.)

Césaire condemns colonialism masquerading as communism, which is correct to do. The French Communist Party totally degenerated, as did many of the European parties and the American party in the fifties, swept away by revisionism. Ho Chi Minh, one of the founders of the French Communist Party, had also denounced it earlier for its chauvinism.

Césaire now looked to Africa to revitalize blacks and the Antilles, which carries the tendency of cultural nationalism and Pan-Africanism, both aspects of which can be found in *Retours*. The liberation of Africa will bring imperialism to its knees, but its many tentacles must be chopped off in each specific country by each specific people, based on their concrete conditions.

In the letter to Thorez, Césaire saw "two paths of doom: by segregation, by walling yourself up in the particular; or by dilution, by thinning off into emptiness of the [fake] 'universal.'" He says, "I have a different idea of a universal. It is of a universal rich with all that is particular, rich with all the particulars there are, the deepening of each particular, the coexistence of them all." (This sounds almost like Mao in *On Practice* and *On Contradiction*.)

Césaire's early poetry was influenced by the wild imagery of

Rimbaud *(A Season in Hell)* and Lautréamont, but *Retours* goes beyond the scope of that imagery. Senghor condemned European poetry for using abstract words to explain images, whereas it is the power of the image itself which should do the "explaining." But William Carlos Williams was also explaining this to American poets who would not listen: "not in words but in things," he said. Césaire's thrashing images dig into the surreal in the sense that they are sometimes wildly unrelated elements, but juxtaposed they make a new dissociation that calls forth new associations and new meaning.

Césaire's poetry grows more traditionally surrealist in the volumes which follow *Retours*, like *Les Armes Miraculeuses* (1946) or *Soleil Coup Coupé* (1948). Wild imagery can cause brilliant new meaning. The power is in the focus on real life that can fuse into a new dialectic seemingly dissimilar elements. *Retours* abounds with this, but quite a bit of the poetry in the later books grows into simple abstraction, where dissimilar elements unfused by some powerful focus of life remain disparate and diffuse and obscure.

The language in *Retours* is rich, deep, and rhythmical, full of ecstasy, pain, introspection, celebration, but it is connected by feeling and the power of its focus. The language *rushes,* and this is my basic sense of it, it rushes, it leaps, it is a whirlwind, it literally sweeps us in torrents.

Even during the forties when Césaire was a communist his work proceeded in directions quite different from other well-known communist poets such as Neruda, Guillén, Aragon; it became more obscure, more solitarily flamboyant, more and more burdened with obscurity. (Read "Knives at Noon" and "Tornado." In "Tornado" again, rush of, unleashing of, the wild untamable, wind and blacks, the surreal—a twisting out of shape, a sudden violence too. But it is like an unfocused torrent of heat, which must be focused to blast steel. It is not the rebuilding we long for, the just transformation.)

In Martinique, Césaire has been the mayor of Fort-de-France for twenty-seven years, except for a brief period when he resigned from the Communist Party. He participated in the First and Second World Congresses of Black Writers and Artists, and in the fifties began to focus on the question of decolonization. His *Discourse on Colonialism* (1955), and other essays with similar themes appearing in publications like *Présence Africaine*, are important.

He has written also *Toussaint Louverture* (1961), a biography which is as well a history of Haiti. In the sixties he began to write plays because, as he expressed it, the problems of decolonization and nation building, real problems for the liberation movements as formal independence began to come, needed to be widely understood. In 1963 he wrote *La Tragédie du Roi Christophe*, again focusing on Haiti and the black ruler who led Haiti after Toussaint and Dessalines. In 1967 he wrote *Un Saison au Congo*, about Patrice Lumumba's betrayal and assassination. Both plays were about decolonization and nation building. In 1969, Césaire's *A Tempest* appeared, which was an adaptation of Shakespeare's play, but dealing with blacks in the U.S.A.

Ironically, after Césaire went back to Martinique, he got deeper into surrealism poetically, coming more fully into the imperialist system as mayor of Fort-de-France, so that a "rearrangement of reality" seems more and more to suffice rather than the creation of a new reality after the destruction of the old. Politically he now advocates "autonomy" rather than departmentalization, i.e., a middle ground when talking about a people under imperialism. Césaire says there are too many benefits under French patronage to completely cut away with independence, and so he has come under increasing fire from the younger revolutionaries on the island.

Ngugi wa Thiongo

In Ngugi wa Thiongo we have modern African writing—i.e., writing that is and reflects the Africa in a real world of suffering and change. His book *Homecoming* is must reading. It is solid, politically sound, artistically valid criticism of modern African and Caribbean literature.

Like Ayi Kwei Armah's *The Beautiful Ones Are Not Yet Born*, Achebe's *A Man of the People*, Okot Bitek's *Song of Lawino*, Okello Oculi's *Prostitute and the Orphan*, Ngugi's *Grain*, has begun to turn the full light of artistic analysis on the post-colonial period, and what it means. In the colonial period, the writers had to affirm the value, the strength of the vanquished. The colonial intellectual, the anti-imperialist intelligentsia first, as Fanon lays out so clearly, affirms, must identify with the culture, the people affirm this in the face of the colonial enemies and their *cultural aggression*.

In *Things Fall Apart* Achebe is affirming African society, describing its real chaos and anxiety, in the face of the rising colonial order. But as Ngugi points out, Africans are not the European Robinson Crusoe's man Friday . . . their lives cannot be summed up in *The Pacification of the Primitive Tribes of Lower Niger;* in their humanity, they are more complex . . . and what is more they will survive. Despite the dying, the craziness, of the old which is passing in the onslaught of the new.

The political reality of colonialism is not limited in some alleyway or tower called "politics"; it is the basis for the very shaping and process of the people's lives.

The facts of the Christian doctrine, the Christian church, Christian missionaries, are a lingering undercurrent and overcurrent in everything in Ngugi's *A Grain of Wheat* from its title . . . to the fixations of the characters torn between these and Ngai, the God of Black People.

The novel deals with the depths and levels and response to guilt, the mark of colonialism, the mark of slavery, and how the people react.

African writers have no choice but to deal with neo-colonialism, "imperialism ruling through native agents," as Cabral and Nkrumah informed us, no more choice than they had in dealing with colonialism. It is the actual life of the people, the reality. Only the colonialists, the neo-colonialists, or their apologists would have us *not* deal with these real-life shapers of our perceptions. And that is because they want to cover up to hide the real so they can pretend their hypes and lies, or the subjectivism and solipsism of their elitist intellectuals, are reality.

Ngugi's writing, like the most important of African writers', deals with colonialism and neocolonialism, or more precisely, African people up under the weight of, shaped by, these devilish systems. In *Grain of Wheat* he spoke about the transition from the colonial to what the people then did not quite understand, but a post-colonial consciousness. In *Petals of Blood,* his most complete statement to date, Ngugi hands us neo-colonialism. Not as a political sloganizing or abstract cliché, but as it is to be understood through its effect on real life.

Mere bitterness at neo-colonialism is not enough though. Some of the earlier works by African writers, e.g., Achebe, were bitter, but calling in the Army to end neocolonial corruption—consider it in real-life terms—is hardly desirable, though it is also real, mostly real tragedy. And it abounds in Africa today, for the same reasons that Achebe has laid out. Ngugi, however, goes further. In *Grain,* he tried to deal with the general guilt that colonialism made, the weakness, the suffering. How all of African life was distorted and made ugly by it. The general theme is betrayal, as a result of weakness under colonialism. Domestic betrayal, political betrayal, and cultural betrayal. What Ngugi insists upon is that we learn to tell weeds from grain. That the grain's "death" is so it can bear fruit, but the weed will bear no fruit.

Ngugi tells us how the whole people are stained, broken, but some will survive, the many. He also implies that some of the biggest heroes to the people are their biggest betrayers or will be. In *Petals* the prophecy, the perception, has come into full and treacherous view.

Petals is the grand evocation of neo-colonialism, made so horrible that it could only be rendered as high art. Sembene Ousmane is another African writer/filmmaker impressive, profound, sharp in his continuous relating of African reality. Sembene also deals closeup with colonialism, and now neo-colonialism. Both also deal with the phenomenon of the multiple layers of culture that exist in African society, and their significance. Sembene, focusing on West Africa, and Senegal in particular, shows the original Wolof culture and its successive transformations under the Islamic invasion and then the Christian one. So that one can see the complex reality of contemporary African life where the animist African culture is overpainted with an Islamic coat, a Christian-colonial one, and these all spark and ignite in constant confrontation with the present neo-colonial regime, where black "Frenchmen" run the country for their own aggrandizement and profit, the complete exclusion of the people's needs. *Mandabi* is a classic teller of this sad contemporary tale. A man receives a 25,000-franc money order and cannot benefit by it because he does not understand the neo-colonial bureaucracy, i.e., he does not know the "magic words," he is still caught back in a Wolof version of Islam. In fact a neo-colonial black "Frenchman" slickly rips him off and sends him back home to sit on the steps with his head in his hands. Yet, in the end there is a note of defiance, as the postman tells the sad protagonist who cries that the whole world is turned upside down and corruption is worshiped, he says well then you and I will have to change this. It is not hopeless.

Ngugi goes further. But he also goes deeper. *Petals* is a kind of murder mystery in one aspect, and this adds spice to it, but is secondary. It is primarily a "morality" tale, the measure of which is the needs of the many, the collective will. Three men are burned up in a whorehouse. They are three prominent Kenyans, but they are also three notorious (we find out as we get further and further into the novel) neo-colonialists. The black pigs who personally shove African people's faces into the muck of imperialist exploitation.

Four people are accused of the crime. Munira, the confused son of a similar black pig, high up in the Christian church. (And in this Munira reminds one of Mugo in *A Grain of Wheat*, who was similarly

203

impaled psychologically on Christianity, as it was brought to Africa with colonialism.) Wanja, the granddaughter of a peasant patriot, who gave up his life struggling against European invasion. She is also the daughter of another African traitor.

Abdullah, a hero of the Mau Mau war, disillusioned and hurt by the rise of neo-colonialism, who flees into the countryside to lose himself. Karega, the young peasant who is thrown out of the university for leading a strike. These four cross each other's paths in a boondock peasant village of Ilmorog. Their reasons for coming to Ilmorog, which Ngugi raises again and again, and how their lives are intertwined, even unknown

The three black traitors, Kimeria, Mzigo, and Chui, are also connected to the four accused. These connections spell out the suffering of modern Kenya under the black "Englishmen" and "nationalists" who run it now for imperialism. It is well known that Ngugi was taken off to jail for a year by Kenyatta's goons. They even arrested his library! And no charges were ever made, in what *The New York Times* refers to as "Kenya's liberal regime." Kenya is one of the most despicable of neo-colonial tragedies because it raised so much hope when the Mau Mau uprising took place and the British colonialists called an "Emergency." The retreat from all pretenses of independence and African popular government, not to mention socialism, by Kenyatta and company has been complete and ugly. Ngugi has recorded that retreat and the horrors it has wrought, so faithfully, and with such power, that you can see once you read this book why the nigger establishment went out to lunch and had Ngugi jailed. He portrays these neo-colonial functionaries, these government, church, business "leaders," for what they are, human carrion, feeding on African lives. He lets us see for once and for all that these are *monsters . . .* monsters.

Ngugi does not bite his tongue, he lays it out. He has upheld his responsibility so breathtakingly that one is given to putting the book down as one reads, standing up exclaiming, shouting out loud, that yes, yes, this is exact. A powerful book.

Munira is a confused petit bourgeois whose instincts have been ripped out by Christian gibberish. He comes to Ilmorog because he feels guilty that he has done nothing during the Emergency to bring about Uhuru. He goes to Ilmorog to head up the non-existent school. In this character, Ngugi shows a personality stunted by imperialism, a colored Hamlet who cannot get beyond stereotypes and emotional isolation from the masses because of his pathological up-bringing. His father, whom he hates and wishes to impress, is a man who first denounces his parents and African culture to take up with Jesus and the colonial Christianity, outspokenly courting success. He is also a man who denounces the Mau Mau during the Emergency and has his ear cut off in payment. But he still comes up on his feet after the war, an amazing and successful landowner capitalist who can now even deny jobs to the patriots that fought in the liberation struggle. The power of Jesus still runs the land, just as Barclays Bank and Exxon do. This is a man who denies his daughter the freedom to marry Karega because Karega's family was "mixed up" with the Mau Mau! (And they were peasants.) The daughter commits suicide.

Kimeria is another Christianity-quoting fraud who while married seduces Wanja when she is very young and then refuses to marry her, leaving her pregnant and horrified. She disposes of the baby and becomes a barmaid. She comes to Ilmorog seeking her grandmother, and perhaps a new start.

Kimeria also betrays two Mau Mau freedom fighters to the British. One is Karega's brother N'ding'uri, who is hanged. The other is Abdullah. Kimeria becomes a well-known rich businessman; Abdullah, the hero, a seller of fruits and sheepskins at the side of the highway.

Chui is the colonial hero who, once "independence" comes, betrays the people by becoming an instrument for the continuation of the same imperialist rule. The students strike to end British rule and cultural aggression at the university. They beg for Chui, the hero, to come and give them control of their own education in their own land, e.g., African studies, an end to the prefect system. But Chui mouths the imperialist clichés that education knows no nationality, while continuing to make them subservient to European history and culture. He also becomes a successful businessman, and board member for Theng'eta Breweries.

Mzigo is a government bureaucrat in charge of district education in the area where Ilmorog lies. He cares nothing for Ilmorog or the people themselves. Finally he comes to Ilmorog when it becomes a boomtown, to get a piece of the action, becoming a board member of Theng'eta as well.

Ilmorog becomes a boomtown first because Karega, ultimately the most politically advanced of the four who come to Ilmorog to live, convinces the people that they must go to Nairobi to see their MP to force him to help them in the face of a prolonged drought. A procession does go to Nairobi, in a really marvelous section of the book where the harassed peasants and the four travel to Nairobi, and for a time build a great solidarity amongst them because of their mutual participation in collective struggle. But they also come face to face with the grimest of neo-colonial horrors. They are refused help by the quoting Christian churchman Jerrod Brown. They are intimidatcd from even entering the partying Chui's house. Kimeria makes Wanja accept his rape again, otherwise he will have all of the people jailed as robbers. And the MP, Nderi wa Riera, is a conniving slickster who has found that "Cultural Nationalism" will trick a few people and allow him to get over at the same time. He calls for changes of names of banches in foreign companies to African names, advocates "Africanization" Mobutu style, but opposes socialism as "sloganizing" and pushes for an African capitalism that will permit of the emergence of African Fords, Krupps, Rockefellers, etc.

Ilmorog also gets suddenly big because Wanja brings the Theng'eta beverage, a kind of African absinthe, into commercial use and with Abdullah's help builds a big restaurant and bar and hotel which is a center of the new Ilmorog, until the Kimeria's, Chui's, etc., rip it off, just as they rip Ilmorog off and just as the native agents ruling for imperialism are ripping African people off. Ilmorog is one microcosm of the new Africa. A new, i.e., neo-colonial, Africa, where the white folks have been run off from the top spots, at least cosmetically, (though in Kenya there's still a bunch taking money right on the soil), and the African domestic bourgeoisie and reactionary sector of the petite bourgeoisie do the managing of the rip-off.

The four accused of murder are the main focus of Ngugi's analysis of how this last stage of imperialism affects African people, but there are many, many other examples and personalities in this rich and agonizing portrait. Munira loses his mind; Abdullah becomes a whipped alcoholic and fruit peddler; Wanja becomes a prostitute and then Ilmorog's most successful madam, proprietor of The Sunshine Lodge, complete with red wig and miniskirt. Her main clients, Chui, Kimeria, and Mzigo. (She lets Munira christen her in her new undertaking because he has also helped ruin her life by forcing Karega out of his job.) Karega leaves Ilmorog, and drifts from job to job. He is a dockworker, works in a sugar refinery, sells fruits and sheepskins by the side of the road, and finally becomes a radical union leader. At the end of the book, even though he has been cleared of the murders, the officials keep him in detention because he is "a communist at heart." But Karega's evolution to this is one of the aspects of the whole of political developments in Kenya, and among African people, that Ngugi brings us face to face with, as the growth of a single personality by means of that character's exposure to Ngugi's thorough and cathartic revelation of reality.

Petals of Blood is a novel of grim reality for sure, but it is, at the same time, a novel of hope because it is a novel of struggle. At the end of the book, Karega, though imprisoned, is visited by a young woman worker, who tells him of the further radicalization of the workers' movement, and assures him he will be back. Karega's detention and Ngugi's, essentially for the same reasons, only shows us proof in the real world of the truth of Ngugi's staggering portrait.

Stylistically, Ngugi's prose is thick with portent, implication, irony, and battlefield humor. The novel uses flashback and flashback within flashback. It is circular, coming round to where it started, but actually it is a spiral motion, since its "circularity" is motion to a higher level of revelation and perception. Ngugi lays out with great clarity exactly what class struggle is in Africa today; only the dangerously naïve (or perhaps it is youthful idealism) or upholders of the status quo would even shape their mouths to deny the reality of Ngugi's blistering art.

He gives us Africa old and Africa new and Africa in transition, and the hope of Africa future. The book is also rooted deeply in East African life and culture; its telling is itself like the griot high up in his gig, with a social and political concreteness and again *clarity* that constantly astonishes. The book is a chronicle, an analysis steeped in sharply wrought dialectic; it is also an admonition, that we must choose sides, that perhaps we have already chosen sides, and that there remain only two sides, regardless of our subjectivism or lies or evasions and copouts, only two sides—one that of the people, the other that of the enemies of the people. Ngugi demands that we choose and his demand, as *Petals of Blood*, is high revolutionary art.

BIBLIOGRAPHY: JAMES NGUGI

1. Herdeck, Donald E. *African Authors*. Washington, D.C.: eus Press, 1973. Ref./PL8010/H47
2. Jahn, Janheinz. *Who's Who in African Literature*. Tub H. Erdmann, 1972. Ref./PL8010/J345
3. Ngugi, James. *The Black Hermit*. Nairobi: Heinemann Educational Books, 1968. Cross Campus, PR/9381.9/N465
4. Ngugi, James. *A Grain of Wheat*. London: Heinemann, 1967.
5. Ngugi, James. *Homecoming: Essays on African and Caribbean Literature, Culture, and Politics*. London: Heinemann, 1972. Cross Campus, PR9340/N4
6. Ngugi, James. *The River Between*. London: Heinemann, 1965. Cross Campus, PR/9381.9/N465/R5
7. Ngugi, James. *Secret Lives and Other Stories*. New York: L. Hill, 1975. PR9381.9/N465/S4
8. Ngugi, James. *This Time Tomorrow*. Nairobi: East African Literature Bureau, 1970. PR9381.9/N465/T4
9. Ngugi, James. *Weep Not, Child*. London: Heinemann, 1966. Ir/N499/W4/1967
10. wa Thiongo, Ngugi. *Petals of Blood*. London: Heinemann, 1977.
11. wa Thiongo, Ngugi. *Devil on the Cross*. London: Heinemann, 1982.
12. wa Thiongo, Ngugi. *Detained: A Writer's Prison Diary*. London: Heinemann, 1981.
13. wa Thiongo, Ngugi and Ngugi wa Mirii. *Ngaahika Ndeenda: I Will Marry When I Want*. London: Heinemann, 1982.
14. wa Thiongo, Ngugi and Micere Mugo. *The Trial of Dedan Kimathi*. London: Heinemann, 1977.

Notes on the History of African/Afro-American Culture

Part I

African culture, which is to say African life, begins with the form of economic (and therefore ideological, social, political, and aesthetic) organization known as primitive communalism. But civilization all over the world begins with this basic form of economic and social organization. It is common to all continents and peoples. The idea that primitive communalism arises only in Africa is unscientific, and most likely that idea is due to some cultural-nationalist bias.

Culture, at one point, is simply the totality of how people live, its various aspects and products. It is based essentially on the economic and political structure of society. In dealing with black culture in any balanced sense, we must look at its antecedents and its parallels. Obviously to study Afro-American culture we must study African culture, the connections and variations. And we should see how one has developed from the other, connected yet singular.

Unlike the claims of cultural-nationalist cant, culture is in a form of constant development, a constant evolution, thrown forward even harder and faster by periodic revolution. African culture went through several important developments prior to the European slave trade or the general trade with Europeans that preceded that. It went through still more after this confrontation, as African culture, as well as Afro-American and Afro-wherever-else-blacks-were-brought-in-the-New-World-or-somehow-got-to culture. Culture develops anew, and with it ideology, however the people develop newly. It is not static and metaphysical but developing, given to

constant change and materialistically derived. Culture is life, life derived.

Ideology or worldview derives basically from material life as well;
it is a part of culture. But except for the earliest origins of humanity,
and the method of economic organization known as primitive communalism, groups of people have not had one ideology; there have
always been two operating: one of the rulers and one of the ruled.
That is, since the inception of class society, society divided according to classes, the rulers have had one worldview or ideology, the
ruled another.

Primitive communalism (or old communism) was characterized,
first, by an absence of classes, classes being groups of people defined
according to their relationship to the means of production. That is,
do they own it, or are they controlled by the owners of it? By the
means of production, we mean the means of producing wealth for
society—the land, mineral wealth, tools, waterways, factories, machines—the tools and what the work is done upon. In primitive
communalism, there was no private ownership of the means of
production. Production was characterized largely by hunting and
gathering. The land was not privately owned, and the earliest stone
and wood tools required that the hunting be done collectively. The
means of production were socially owned. "Stone tools and later, the
bow and arrow, precluded the possibility of men individually combating the forces of nature and beasts of prey. In order to gather
the fruits of the forest, to catch fish, to build some sort of habitation,
men were obliged to work in common if they did not want to die of
starvation, or fall victims to beasts of prey or to neighboring societies" *(History of the Communist Party of the Soviet Union [Bol-
shevik])*.

The society of the Pygmies was one of the earliest, if not the
earliest—as some historians posit—society in existence. Yale art historian Robert Thompson characterizes their yodeling and whistling
as an egalitarian music, which is true, since that form of music goes
back directly to the period of primitive communalism. Albert
Churchward, in a brilliant work still held in obscurity called *The Origin and Evolution of the Human Race*, said, "The Pygmy was the first
Homo sapiens—the little red man of the earth. Evolved in the Nile
Valley and around the lakes at the head of the Nile from the an-
thropoid ape. From Africa these little men spread all over the world,
North, East, South and West, until not only Africa but Europe,

Asia, North and South America were populated by them." We can think of them as everybody's ancestors. Pygmy skulls, and those of the later Nilotic Africans that followed them, have been found in Kent, England, and in Russian Asia. Woodward characterizes the Heidelberg man as a Nilotic Negro, as well as the Neanderthal and Piltdown *(The Origin of the Human Race).*

During primitive communalism, the level of productive forces was low. Friedrich Engels, using the American anthropologist Edwin Morgan's pioneer studies of the American Indian, laid out three basic stages of humanity: savagery, barbarism, and civilization. In the lower stage of savagery is represented the infancy of humanity. These categories were formed based on "the progress made in the production of the means of subsistence." Humanity lived in tropical forests of Africa, even lived partially in trees to escape wild animals, ate fruit, nuts, roots. The main progress during this period was the development of articulate speech.

In the middle stage of savagery, human diet is widened to include fish, and with this the use of fire. This new food enabled humans to be more independent of climate and locality. They followed the waters all over the world. This is the so-called Stone Age or Paleolithic period. Club and spear are also invented.

The upper stage of savagery begins with the invention of the bow and arrow, which was the key transitional weapon during the period of savagery. The bow and arrow was to this period as the iron sword was to the later period of barbarism, and firearms were to civilization, namely the *decisive* weapon. The bow and arrow made hunting a much more productive process. Engels characterizes savagery as "the period in which the appropriation of natural products, ready for use, predominated; the things produced by man were, in the main, instruments that facilitated this appropriation" *(Origin of the Family, Private Property, and the State).*

The transition into barbarism is characterized by Morgan and Engels, and repeated by John Jackson in his book *Introduction to African Civilizations,* as beginning with the introduction of pottery. The middle stage of barbarism in the East is characterized by the beginning of the domestication of animals, and in the West by the cultivation of edible plants by irrigation and the use of adobe and stone for building. The upper stage of barbarism is delineated mainly by the smelting of iron ore, a process discovered in Africa and carried by Nilotic Negroes to other parts of the world, and through Asia to

Europe. By the time Europeans penetrated the interior kingdoms of Africa, blacksmiths complete with their bellows and smelting process were ubiquitous.

Humanity passes through the upper stage of barbarism into civilization through the invention of alphabet writing and its use for literary records. (This was the stage of the Greeks of the so-called Heroic Age, also the pre-Roman Italians, similar to the Normans and Vikings.)

We now estimate that the Pygmies appeared in the lower Nile Valley of East Africa 2,000,000 years ago. Africans were at the iron-smelting level of development, and that of alphabet writing by at least 5000 B.C. An iron-smelting furnace was discovered in what is now northern Zimbabwe of an antiquity of 5,000 to 6,000 years. And of course, the founders of the magnificent, ancient Egyptian society were Nilotic blacks similar to the Masai, Suk, Ethiopians, and Turkana. The Nilotic Negroes, who first used the boomerang as a weapon, worked in iron and copper. So that metals were introduced into Egypt in very ancient times. A whole blacksmith cult grew up in Egypt associated with the god Horus.

The development of iron smelting, which we have placed at the upper stage of barbarism, just before the transition to civilization, is also the point around which primitive communalism, old communism, is changing to slavery as a mode of production. The production of iron ore, the domestication of animals, characterize some of the advances that are part of the transition to slavery. The period of barbarism, Engels summed up in *The Origin of the Family* as "the period in which knowledge of cattle breeding and land cultivation were acquired. And methods of increasing the productivity of nature through human activity were learnt." Just as primitive communalism covered most of the earth, so too eventually slavery as a mode of production would characterize the most advanced societies. Although some groups would still remain in primitive communalism. Amilcar Cabral in his essay "The Weapon of Theory" speaks of the Balantes of Guinea, the Coaniamas of Angola, and the Macondes of Mozambique, still existing today in societies which are for the most part primitive communal societies.

The line that says that modern society can approach socialism by returning to primitive communalism is, however, eminently idealist. It was the very low level of the productive forces, the constant migration of the nomadic hunter-gatherer society, that was surpassed by slave society. The increased productivity of the instruments of production made private ownership of the means of production possible, where before there had been collective ownership.

During primitive communalism, even the sense of "property" was not clear, or largely undeveloped. Possessions were prized for their mobility and ease of transportation. (Contemporary observers of groups still at the primitive communal stage grow frustrated trying to inculcate a regard for "things" in these people.) Their tools could be easily made. When they had reached a good spot where there was abundance, where game could be easily caught, and fruit and vegetables easily got at, this was good and not much else mattered. Of course getting to these areas of abundance required constant movement, since after a short period any one area would be picked and hunted clean. The nomadic character of the primitive communal life made impossible the development of permanency in housing, villages, etc. Civilization is characterized by the building of cities and the keeping of records.

The earliest form of family organization was the method by which humanity evolved past the anthropoids. Weaponless individual humans could not survive, so the "horde" or large group evolved, which practiced group marriage, where all the men and all the women in the group belong sexually to each other. Women had a great deal of influence in this kind of society, since for obvious reasons the individual woman was the only traceable parent. *Mother-right,* so called, the tracing of the lineage through the woman, exists for the most part throughout primitive communalism. As Engels showed the development of the family is tied to the development of the society in general, and its form changes as the society's form or content changes.

As the size of the initial family group grew larger, it had to break up into smaller subgroups; later on even the smaller groups had to subdivide. From group sex involving all members of the family, the family unit evolved to the Punaluan family, which excluded the mother and father and children from mutual sexual experience and later excluded the brothers and sisters as well. This kind of family changed to the pairing model, in which the man had a principal mate among the other mates in a group marriage. But this was not monogamy. Even though women had much more authority and status in the earlier forms of marriage, they pushed for monogamy. But ultimately the monogamous structure served men and oppressed women!

"The domestication of animals and the breeding of herds had

developed hitherto unsuspected sources of wealth and created entirely new social relationships." Fixed wealth, previous to the lower stage of barbarism, was sparse indeed: clothing, ornaments, boat, weapons, house, utensils. Everyday food had to be gotten. "Now there were herds of horses, camels, donkeys, oxen, sheep, goats and pigs," which only needed supervision to propagate in every increasing numbers and to yield the richest nutriment in milk and meat. "All previous means of procuring food now sank into the background. Hunting, once a necessity, now became a luxury' (Engels, p. 230). Originally this wealth belonged to the gens or clan, but private property in the herds developed early and became the separate property of the family chiefs, "in exactly the same way as were the artistic products of barbarism, metal utensils, articles of luxury and finally—human cattle, the slaves."

Slavery comes into being with the emergence of private property. Slavery was useless to "barbarians of a lower stage." They might take captives, and either kill them or adopt them as brothers; the women were either married or also adopted. "With the introduction of cattle breeding, of the working up of metals, of weaving and finally of field cultivation" there was now also a surplus produced. And there were a great many changes that occured. "Just as the once so easily obtainable wives had now acquired an exchange value and were bought, so it happened with labor power, especially after the herds had finally been converted into family possessions. The family did not increase as rapidly as the cattle. More people were required to tend them; the captives taken in war were useful for just this purpose, and, furthermore, they could be bred like the cattle themselves" (Engels).

Another great change was in the status of women. The emergence of wealth, surplus, related to the most important fact, that this wealth was now privately owned, meant that old communism, primitive communalism, was gone. Private ownership meant, as it means today, many might starve, but a few would not. It also meant that more and more of the many would actually work for the few. The two main jobs of early slaves were tending the newly domesticated herds and tending the larger, irrigated fields, which were now cultivated in a more advanced way. It was the *man* who owned the cattle and herds and iron-tipped tools. Earlier women had control over the primitive agriculture near the house (which was a more constant provider than pre-iron-tipped-weapon hunting). They controlled the house, especially in group marriages where all the women were together in the house. And all wealth and kinship, which was the most important bond of early humans, was passed through the females (matrilineally). This meant that the owner's own children were disinherited at his death because they belonged to the mother's clan (gens). Property, insignificant during earlier times, now with herds and slaves became very significant indeed. This marked the beginning of the end for mother-right and the emergence of father-right (patrilineal) inheritance. Engels says: "The overthrow of mother-right was the world-historic defeat of the female sex. The man seized the reins in the house also, the woman was degraded, enthralled, the slave of the man's lust, a mere instrument for breeding children."

There were other forms of family that followed. Shaped by father-right. One was the incorporation of the slaves and bondsmen into the family. In fact the Latin word *familia* means the slaves living with the family. It is at the point of the patriarchal family that we enter the stage of written history.

Directly preceding the monogamous family, which signifies the absolute rule of the men since only women are really monogamous (when they are), polygamy and polyandry occur, but both are specialized. Polygamy—one man, many wives—was always the province of the rich, usually only the patriarch himself. The slaves, and most times not even the sons of the patriarch, could live polygamously. Polyandry—many men, one woman—was in effect only when ravaged societies left few females.

Monogamy arises at the approach of civilization. Its chief function is the ascertaining of paternity for the inheritance of property. It is the form of family that arises with the emergence of class society, i.e., slavery, accompanied by the debasement and enslavement of women. Greece and Egypt and Rome are examples of the slave society at its most developed. The later enslaving of Africans by Europeans is part of another mode of production, which comes with the rise of capitalism. But all over Africa slave societies sprang up, as more advanced societies than earlier primitive communalism.

It was Karl Marx who discovered that the most important basis of all life is how material existence, subsistence, is sustained. That is, how we get food, clothing, and shelter—called the mode of production. Primitive communalism was succeeded by slavery, slavery by feudalism, feudalism by capitalism, and capitalism by socialism, socialism being the primitive form of communism.

Changes from one mode of production to another are brought about by revolution. Slaves did not walk willingly into the yokes. Women did not willingly submit to the double slavery of chattel bondage and monogamy.

The power of the loose clan (gens) councils now focused more consistently around the families that became richer and richer under the changed production relations. The punishment for almost any offense became slavery. (Wage labor existed alongside slavery, but slavery was the main mode of production of these early societies.) The ancient world is resplendent with African and proto-African slave civilizations—the ancient Ethiopian, Egyptian, Meroë, Sumerian. The first civilization in Europe, using the definition iron implements and alphabet writing, was Minos, on the island of Crete, created by eastern Ethiopians. Minos, of the fabled castle at Knossos with running water and baths unparalleled in Europe till the nineteenth century, was destroyed by northern barbarians called Greeks, who were the first Europeans to mount an actual civilization. Later the Greeks under Alexander pushed out to the edges of the civilized world in conquest, including Egypt. But even after Alexander died and his successor Ptolemy ruled over Egypt, it remained the light of the world. Later the Romans would destroy Alexandria with its world-famous library and universities that housed scholars from all over the known world, just as they went on to destroy Carthage, another slave-system North African kingdom. But when Imperial Rome and its slave empire was laid to waste by German barbarians, it sent Europe into a decline known as the Dark Ages, which lasted over 500 years (from the fifth to the tenth centuries).

It was during the period of slavery and because of slavery that the form of social organization changed. Earlier the extended family or gens had been the basic social unit. These grew larger and not only were subdivided but also incorporated into larger units called clans or phratries.

Many clans were brought together to form tribes. Tribes brought together would be the basis for nations, which began to rise later with the development of capitalism. A nation is not just a social unit, it is a historical category. It consists, in Joseph Stalin's scientific and revolutionary definition, of a historically constituted stable community of people, based on a common territory, common language, common economic life, common psychological development, manifest as a common culture.

However, in the epoch of slavery, another distinct and world-changing aspect of social organization arose, the *state*. In Africa, as in America, a great many peoples never got beyond the stage of tribal integration, with numerically small tribes separated from one another by wide border lands, enfeebled by perpetual warfare, occupying enormous territory with few people. The basic organization of extended family or gens and institutions related to it existed in the Americas until the time of European appearance. And these extended families, as in Africa, existed without soldiers or police, without nobles, kings, governors, prefects, or judges, without prisons, without trials. All quarrels and disputes were settled by the whole body of those concerned. The Zulus and Nubians, and Nilotic tribes (founders of Egypt) were among the highest examples of old-communist, extended-family social organizations. And when English infantry found them with advanced weapons and military formations, the English lost many battles faced with old socially organized tribes with great capacity and endurance. As one English writer said, "They can move faster and over a larger distance in twenty-four hours than a horse—their smallest muscle stands out, hard and steely, like whip cord." "This is what mankind and society were like before class divisions arose" (Engels).

But tribal society had to be bypassed. It presupposed an extremely undeveloped form of production, extremely sparse population spread over wide territory, and, therefore, almost complete domination of humans by external nature. And even though it seems that the lowest interests have been served by going beyond primitive communalism—theft, rape, deceit, treachery, and for 2,600 years the development of a small minority at the expense of an exploited majority—the power of these ancient communal societies had to be broken for humanity to progress, paradoxical as that seems.

The foundation of the state means that instead of the *armed people* as the ultimate form of authority there arises a special power, separate and distinct from the whole people. The state arises as an institution to undermine and destroy the old communistic traditions of the clan and tribe and to sanctify the accumulation of wealth by the indidual and the individual family as opposed to the clan or tribe. The state justified private property, created the earliest forms of "nobility" and monarchy, and opened up slavery to more than just prisoners of war. It laid out methods of enslaving other members of the tribe and even of the extended family itself.

The old ties of kinship, the most important in primitive communistic society, were superseded by ties of locality and of classes. That is, irrespective of their clan, the people were divided into classes, e.g., nobles, tillers of land, artisans. The democracy of the communal clans also disappeared, as *political rights began to be graded according to the amount of property one owned.* Soon there were more slaves than free citizens, and the state, a public power distinct from the whole people, controlled by a particular class, rose to full power. The police, the state force (along with its prisons, bureaucracy, courts, other agents), consisted of slaves but serving the slavemasters. In fact the word for civilized in French is *police!*

> The basis of the relations of production under the slave system is that the slave owner owns the means of production—the slave, whom he can sell, purchase, or kill as though he were an animal. Such relations of production in the main correspond to the state of the productive forces of that period. Instead of stone tools, men now have metal tools at their command; instead of the wretched and primitive husbandry of the hunter, who knew neither pasturage nor tillage, there now appear pasturage, tillage, handicrafts and a division of labor between these branches of production. There appears the possibility of the exchange of products between individuals and between societies, of the accumulation of wealth in the hands of a few, the actual accumulation of the means of production in the hands of a minority, and the possibility of subjugation of the majority by a minority and their conversion into slaves. Here we no longer find the common and free labor of all members of society in the production process—here there prevails the forced labor of slaves, who are exploited by nonlaboring slave owners. Here therefore, there is no common ownership of the means of production or of the fruits of production. It is replaced by private ownership. Here the slave owner appears as the prime and principal property owner in the full sense of the term.
>
> Rich and poor, exploiters and exploited, people with full rights and people with no rights, and a fierce class struggle between them—such is the picture of the slave system. *[History of the Communist Party of the Soviet Union]*

The rise of the kings begins in slavery but continues and is more solidified in the next period, feudalism. As we will point out, even though these changes in the mode of production occurred throughout the world, development was always *uneven.* The static absolute is metaphysics! For the African peoples when the Europeans penetrated and began the slave trade and set up colonies and settler colonies, in the main, development was wildly distorted. Commodity production and some early forms of capitalism had begun inside Africa, but it was mostly swept away by the slave traders and colonists. This made for one kind of development, but ultimately halted another. The disparities in Africa today between tribes still in primitive communalism and the modern proletariat, in areas which imperialism has transformed, are tremendous.

But to go back to the transition to feudalism: many of the larger states and empires that emerged in the interior of Africa were feudal empires. A few were slave kingdoms, but even some of the major feudal states maintained slaves, although slavery was not necessarily the dominant mode of production.

> The basis of the relations of production under the feudal system is that the feudal lord owns the means of production and does not fully own the worker in production—the serf, whom the feudal lord can no longer kill but whom he can buy and sell. Alongside of feudal ownership there exists individual ownership by the peasant and the handicraftsmen of his implements of production and his private enterprise based on his personal labor. Such relations of production in the main correspond to the state of the productive forces of that period. Further improvements in smelting and working of iron; the spread of the iron plough and the loom; the further development of agriculture, horticulture, viniculture, and dairying; the appearance of manufactories alongside of the handicraft workshops.
>
> The new productive forces demand that the laborer shall display some kind of initiative in production and inclination for work, an interest in work. The feudal lord therefore discards the slave, as a laborer who has no interest in work and is entirely without initiative, and prefers to deal with the serf, who has his own husbandry, implements of production, and a certain interest in work essential for the cultivation of the land and for the payment in kind of a part of his harvest to the feudal lord.
>
> Here private ownership is further developed. Exploitation is nearly as severe as it was under slavery—it is only slightly mitigated. A class struggle between exploiters and exploited is the principal feature of the feudal system. *[History of the Communist Party]*

The feudal system existed, and still exists to some extent, all over Africa, as it once existed all over the world. The Dark Ages in

Europe were the height of its feudal period. Although, ultimately, the new mode of production represents a distinct progress for humanity, a raising of the level of productive forces, at each turn there are also, dialectically, to be seen losses and sacrifice and a new kind of degradation. In Europe, Italy was the first capitalist country. "The close of the feudal Middle Ages and the dawn of the modern capitalist era was marked by a colossal figure. It was an Italian, Dante, who was at one and the same time the last poet of the Middle Ages and the first poet of modern times. That was 1300" (Engels).

In the year 1000 Europe was still in a state of barbarism, and the Moors had been ruling Spain for 300 years. Toledo and Cordoba producing steel swords of world renown. This was hundreds of years before there was a street light in London or paved streets in Paris. The city of Cordoba had a population of 1,000,000, paved streets and lamps, 70 public libraries and 500,000 books, 800 public schools, and 900 baths, at a time when throughout the rest of Europe, bathing was considered as extremely wicked. No city elsewhere in Europe had a population over 30,000.

Islam had risen as a force during the sixth century, with the birth of the Prophet Muhammad. It rose with the Arab civilization itself, and spread itself by the sword in all directions, from Spain to North Africa, across Asia to China. Islamic penetration of Europe was stopped in France. It was not until the thirteenth century that the Moorish power began to fade in Europe, and by this time, the Europeans had absorbed the science and culture of the Moors, and factionalism both religious and political had begun to split the Muslims. But the last Moor was not driven from Spain until 1492, the year Columbus begins the Western expansion of rising capitalism!

In the eighth century begins what has been called the Golden Age of Africa, though the great slave civilizations go back thousands of years before. But from the eighth century until the eighteenth, four enormous trading empires should be noted: Ghana (700–1200), which John Jackson calls "the first great empire" of the medieval Sudan; Mali (1200–1500), which absorbed the empire of Ghana and expanded it westward; Songhay (1350–1600), which took over the empire of Mali; and Kanem-Bornu, which evolved further eastward in the Sudan. Ancient Ghana covered a territory that now includes parts of the modern nations of Guinea, Senegal, Mali, and Mauritania. This empire began as a group of tribes and clans claiming a common totemic ancestor, the Soninke. Beginning about A.D. 300, they were working with iron and began to subdue their neighbors. They also had a seemingly inexhaustible supply of gold. Their social organization was matrilineal, and was essentially feudalistic, although slaves were still held. By the tenth and eleventh centuries Ghana reached its pinnacle of prosperity. Its ruler, called the patriarch or father, was commander in chief of the army, head of the state religion, chief dispenser of justice, and supreme overseer of the nation. On the death of the monarch, his successor was not his own son but the son of his sister. They raised a huge standing army not only to keep peace internally and discourage invaders, but also to annex territory. Their most important source of wealth however was in trade, primarily salt and gold. The rise of the traders, the merchants, is particular to the Middle Ages. Engels says of this phenomenon that "civilization strengthened and increased all the established divisions of labor, particularly by intensifying the contrast between town and country (with the cities in the middle ages now coming to dominate the country more), and added a third division of labor peculiar to itself and of decisive importance; it created a class that took no part in production, but engaged exclusively in exchanging products—*the merchants.*" A class appears for the first time which can manage production without taking part in it. A class that makes itself supposedly the indispensable intermediary between any two producers, and exploits them both. "A class of social sycophants, actually parasites who as a reward for very insignificant real services, skim the cream off production at home and abroad, rapidly amass enormous wealth and corresponding social influence, and for this very reason are destined to reap ever new honors and gain increasing control over production during the period of civilization, until they at last create a product of their own—periodic commercial crises."

With the rise of the merchants not only in Africa but in Europe and Asia and parts of the Americas, *metal money* is soon minted, the universal commodity. Since the time of slavery, hence class society, from private ownership, the making of products to be sold, has arisen. It is the smallest aspect of capitalism itself, its economic atom.

With the creation of money, a means is created by which the nonproducer can rule the producer and his products! The commodity that can be exchanged for all commodities, everything, that can transform itself into anything desirable. Whoever possessed it ruled the world of production; and who would have it above all others, *the merchant*.

Ghana was invaded by Muslims in the middle of the eleventh century; the people were forced to submit to Islam, and to pay tribute and taxes. Those who resisted were massacred.

Mali next. Its most famous ruler was Sundiata. It took over the salt and gold of the Ghanians. Mali was the first Muslim state in the Sudan or Guinea Coast. Another ruler, Mansa Musa, made a famous pilgrimage to Mecca; with an entourage of 60,000 he arrived in 1324. He brought with him 80 camels each loaded with 300 pounds of gold dust. The North African gold market was depressed for twelve years, so much gold was put into circulation! Mali went into decline in the early fourteenth century. In the fifteenth century, 1475, the Songhay empire rose as Mali continued to decline. By the end of the fourteenth century, Portuguese sailors had landed on the Atlantic coast of Mali, and the Mali governments tried to use them as mercenaries to fight the rising Songhay. (Mali lasted as a somewhat powerful state for two more centuries.)

In power after 1464, Sunni Ali and Askia Muhammad, the most famous rulers of the Songhay, represent the golden age of Songhay. The Songhay empire took Timbuktu from Mali, and Jenné from the Soninkes of Ghana. Timbuktu was the seat of the great university at Sankore. This great power lasted until the end of the sixteenth century, when invading Moors, equipped with firearms imported from England, invaded Songhay, and occupied it for a century and a half. By the beginning of the seventeenth century the Golden Age of African feudalism and merchant empires had reached its nadir. The Kanem-Bornu empire, located where the Hausa peoples of Nigeria now make their home, was another Islamic African state, which even in the early nineteenth century greeted English explorers with palaces and expansive courts. The city of Kano during the fifteenth century had been even more developed than Timbuktu and Gao. It was a city that actually began to manufacture cotton goods for the entire western Sudan, so that it had a relationship to the western Sudan somewhat like Manchester had to England, and as such was actually a seat of developing capitalism. And there were such centers in other parts of Africa, West and East, before the colonial invasions, which halted these developments and warped them.

W.E.B. DuBois, quoting Leo Hansberry, the eminent Africanist and Lorraine Hansberry's uncle, lists some kingdoms and empires in West Africa in the Middle Ages: (1) the kingdom of Ghana, (2) the kingdom of Melle (Mali), (3) the Mellestine empire, (4) the kingdom of Songhay, (5) the empire of Songhay, (6) the kingdom of Bornu, (7) the kingdom of Mossi, (8) the kingdom of Nupe, (9) the kingdom of Yoruba, (10) the kingdom of Benin.

The fourteenth century saw Europe beginning to stir itself at the beginnings of capitalism, which served a revolutionary purpose challenging and finally eliminating feudalism, which had once been revolutionary in moving humanity past slavery. DuBois's *The World and Africa* should be read by anyone wishing to understand the dynamics of the rise of capitalism in Europe and its effects on Africa, and to understand the decline of the African Golden Age, the very beginnings of handicraft and manufacturing capitalism in Africa, and to understand the subsequent interrelationship of these continents, which begins with trade, then colonization, then trade in black flesh.

Islam perpetuated itself in black Africa with the sword in the fourteenth century, and it continued into the nineteenth century, when the Arab slave trade was replaced by the overall domination of Western imperialism. The Bantu tribes, as DuBois points out, moved south when faced with the Muslim expansion, which is actually early capitalism, since the slaves were used on plantations on the east coast, the product of which was traded to foreign markets. The Bantu tribes

which probably had originally moved north from the great lakes toward the Mediterranean began a countermovement perhaps long before the eleventh century. They moved toward the west coast and the Kingdom of the Congo, which dominated the valley and forests of the great Congo system; they pressed upon the great lakes, threatening the Negroids and mulattoes of the east coast; and they fell upon the civilization the Monomotapa centering at Zimbabwe. They overthrew and changed the culture while at the same time continuing it. They marched on in a series of stops and forays until they reached South Africa at the beginning of the nineteenth century.

In the west came greater disaster to black Africa. The city-state coast culture, withdrawing from the Sudanese expansionism, met expanding Europe. And that Europe, beginning with trade in gold and pepper, turned to a trade in human flesh on the greatest scale the world has ever seen. The gain from American black labor together with the loot of India changed the face of world industry. Built on a miraculous union of science and technique, the capitalistic system was founded on African slavery and degradation. The very name of Songhay was forgotten and Europe came to rule the world. [DuBois, *The World and Africa*]

The most important fact that DuBois presents is that the colonization and slave trade are rooted in the development of capitalism. There is no so-called primitive accumulation without the African slave trade and the conquest of India.

The basis of the relations of production under the capitalist system is that the capitalist owns the means of production but not the workers in production—the wage laborers, whom the capitalist can neither kill nor sell because they are personally free, but who are deprived of means of production and, in order not to die of hunger, are obliged to sell their labor power to the capitalist and to bear the yoke of exploitation. Alongside of capitalist property in the means of production, we find, at first on a wide scale, private property of the peasants and handicraftsmen in the means of production, these peasants and handicraftsmen no longer being serfs, and their private property based on personal labor. In the place of the handicraft workshops and manufactories there appear huge mills and factories equipped with machinery. In place of the manorial estates tilled by the primitive implements of production of the peasants, there now appear large capitalist farms run on scientific lines and supplied with agricultural machinery.

The new productive forces require that the workers in production shall be better educated and more intelligent than the downtrodden and ignorant serfs, that they be able to understand machinery and operate it properly. Therefore, the capitalists prefer to deal with wage workers who are free from the bonds of serfdom and who are educated enough to be able properly to operate the machinery. [*History of the Communist Party*]

The so-called Industrial Revolution that transformed Renaissance Europe into modern Europe, and created the United States, is unthinkable without the trade in African slaves. The Portuguese were the first to initiate this trade. In 1441 the first cargo of slaves and gold was brought to Lisbon. Spain and Portugal were looking for a shorter route to the Indies in the fifteenth century. From this the Spanish discovered silver in the New World and set about destroying Native American civilizations. And the Portuguese found gold and slaves in Africa. If the Europeans had asked the traders of Mali and Ghana about the Americas, they could have told them about their existence, because they had been exploring and trading with Mayans, Mexicans, and Aztecs in the early fourteenth century. (See *African Explorers of the New World,* Lawrence, and the *Lost Cities of Africa,* Davidson, or *America Before Columbus,* DeRoo.)

For some years the Portuguese had the slave trade and gold trade to themselves. But we must remember that this trade was impossible at first without the assistance of Africans themselves. The Senegambia area for instance, the first area involved with the slave trade, was also a coastal base for interior European operations. The Wolofs, who were divided internally into four classes, the ruler lineage, freeman, artisans and griots, and slaves (who were also divided into strata), became great slave traders with the Portuguese and their later successors. In the sixteenth century the Senegambia region was one of two or three of the most important sources for the Atlantic slave trade. The trade was state controlled, and the profit was controlled by the Wolof ruling class. They made war and took prisoners, many from the more southern and central regions. They attacked neighboring villages. And also the general sentence for most crimes was to be sold into slavery.

The collaboration by African rulers in the European slave trade limited other forms of development because they were exporting labor and depleting the same in Africa!

The triangular trade that DuBois talks about brought the Africans themselves into capitalism. In 1738 the Wolof practice was described thusly by an English observer: "Whenever the King of Barsally wants Goods or Brandy, he sends a messenger to our Governor, at James Fort, to desire he would send a sloop there with a Cargo. . . . against the arrival of the said Sloop, the King goes and ransacks one of his enemies Towns, seizing the people and selling them for such Commodities as he is in want of, which commonly is Brandy or Rum, Gunpowder, Ball, Guns, Pistols, and Cutlasses for his attendants and soldiers, and Coral and Silver for his Wives and Concubines. In case he is not at war with any neighboring King, he then falls upon one of his towns, which are numberous, and uses them in the very same manner" *(Slavery in Africa: The Wolof and Sereer,* by Miers and Kopytoff). The Wolofs had three classes of slaves: (a) trade slaves got by war, kidnapping, or purchase; (b) domestic, who could become members of the family unit, in the same fashion as in Roman society; (c) *tyeddo,* state bureaucrat slaves, who fought the wars, collected the taxes, administered the government (just like the Athenian Greeks in the rise of their state).

The ruling classes of several African states became involved as suppliers of the slaves to European slavers. In the Senegambia area, as late as 1892, one-third of the people were still slaves domestically. In the Mandinka, at the beginning of the nineteenth century three-quarters were slaves. In Gambia by 1894, three-quarters were slaves. In Senegal in the same year fifteen to twenty percent were slaves. Domestic African slavery was not the same as the slavery that resulted from the European slave trade, but the idyllic version of the African masses being happy and passive under domestic slavery is as much a black cultural nationalist lie as the European imperialist and racist lie that the European slave trade turned Africans into passive, happy-go-lucky animals.

A century later, the slave trade in Portugal had turned a good portion of the Portuguese population into "brothers and sisters," with the vast majority of the southern province more black than white. Even the royal family became more black than white! John IV and VI, DuBois points out, were bloods. This new strain of black blood, by intermingling, reached into Italy, where even the Medici had colored descendants; it reached even to Albania and Austria.

Another factor that contributed to the trade was the internal dissension going on inside Africa itself. The Africans fleeing southward from the Islamic invasions as they fled, migration and native wars were the result, and the cheap labor of captives on the West Coast opened the way for the beginning of the American slave trade.

After the Portuguese, by the sixteenth century the French bogarted their way into the trade, by the later part of the sixteenth century the English had got into it as part of the expansion of Elizabethan England. John Hawkins, who threatened to serve God daily and his queen, sailing the good ship *Jesus,* was the first of the English traders. His coat of arms was a black slave bound and captive. A fitting symbol for a ship with such a heavy name. The Portuguese, Spanish, English, French, Dutch, all struggled intensely for control of the Guinea Coast and the trade in slaves. Spain annexed Portugal, and England defeated both of them with the defeat of the Spanish Armada in 1588. (It would be hard to lose with Betty Davis as Elizabeth and Errol Flynn as John Hawkins!)

DuBois sums it up like this: "With the seventeenth century the battle of commerce was on. The Dutch and the British fought to a finish in the Atlantic to dominate the Atlantic trade. The Portuguese, British, and Dutch fought in India. Between them they killed the trade of the German Hanseatic League and overthrew the economic dominance of Spain. Cromwell (signifying the ending of all but the superficial presence of the feudalistic sovereigns in England) seized Jamaica as the center of British slavery and the slave trade. In Africa, the kingdoms of the black Sudan moved east and displaced the 'Nilotic Negroes.'"

In Europe, slavery was so profitable because on the one hand the labor situation was limited by the devastation of the Thirty Years' War and the demand for labor and service on the feudal estates, and "on the other hand, sugar, cotton, and tobacco were suitable to mass production on the plantations with conventional standards of work, simple tools, and comparatively small outlay for clothing and food. The organized slave gang was more profitable on the land than the peasant proprietor." The Civil War and Interregnum in England came to an end in 1660, the war that saw the rise of the bourgeoisie to dominance over the feudal lords and their "divine rights." The bourgeoisie's ascension was not peaceful—they cut off the king's head—but it is appropriately glamorized in their tales of it. The triangular trade now sharpened in earnest: industrial goods to Africa; slaves to the Americas; cotton, sugar cane, and tobacco to England. Marx said this was the basis of world trade, and it is based on the trade in African slaves.

Part II

The establishment of world trade is based on the expansion of capitalism itself, based on the chattel slavery of Africans, Africans by the tens of millions.

Europe and Africa were moving apart like trains in the night. The Golden Age of West Africa, of Songhay, old Ghana, Mali, and Kanem-Bornu, was flowering and sinking into decline. Europe was going through the beginnings of its capitalist expansion, having passed from feudalism. Africa, whose feudalism saw the unfolding of its mightiest empires, had also begun to develop capitalism, but such development was frozen as a result of the interrelationship. The European slave trade, DuBois has called the rape of Africa, but it is key that we remember the participation of African feudal ruling classes in that rape.

Modern slavery is created, nevertheless, in the main, by newly capitalist European Christians. The English Civil War sealed the fate of the feudal ruling class. The bourgeoisie, the merchants, were now the true kings, and Charles I's head rolled in the dust to prove it. From the beginning, however, it should be carefully emphasized that the slave trade was accompanied stride for stride by slave revolts and rebellions. In the sixteenth century there were revolts by black slaves in America, and the organized rebellions by slaves called Maroons had already begun in Cuba, Jamaica, Haiti, Mexico, and Brazil. DuBois points out, as the trade increased, so too did the rebellions. Throughout the seventeenth century actual wars went on against slavery. There were nine major revolts in Jamaica, Barbados, Haiti, and the forming of an independent state, Palmares, in Brazil. This state was founded by Afro-Brazilians fighting against the Portuguese slavers—they were called *Zombis!* The name has been used as a negative and metaphysical term to characterize these warriors as rising from the dead and being unkillable, because of the ferocity with which these Afro-Brazilians fought against slavery.

Ultimately, the British dominated the slave trade taking it away from the Portuguese/Spanish, Dutch, and French. The Royal African Company, so called, with its dukes, earls, lords, and members of the royal family itself, plus after the Civil War, loads of merchants, was a direct profiter from the trade. By the eighteenth century, DuBois shows, the English had made the trade in black flesh the "greatest single body of trade in the world."

When we say that the very development of modern Europe is based on the slave trade, we mean that the primitive accumulation of wealth necessary to build capitalism as a world system was amassed then. Marx says in *Capital* that "the discovery of gold and silver in America, the extirpation, enslavement, and entombment in mines of the aboriginal population, the beginning of the conquest and looting of the East Indies, the turning of Africa into a warren for the ceremonial hunting of black skins, signalled the rosy dawn of the era of capitalist production. These idyllic proceedings are the chief moments of primitive accumulation" (Vol. I). Capital comes into the world, to further paraphrase Marx, dripping with blood from head to foot, from every pore, blood and dirt. Liverpool, a center in England of the Industrial Revolution, was made that by slavery. In 1730, fifteen ships left there dealing in slaves, in 1751, fifty-three; in 1760, seventy-four; in 1770, ninety-six; in 1792, one hundred and thirty-two, and that was just the increase in the eighteenth century.

We can only approximate how many slaves were taken from Africa. From 1680 to 1688 the English company alone sent 249 ships to Africa, took 60,783 slaves, out of which 14,387 died in middle passage and 46,396 became nigger slaves (see DuBois, *The Negro).* DuBois estimates that 25,000 a year *arrived* in North America from about 1698 to 1707, and that after the English monopoly was established and the treaty of the Asiento signed, the number rose to about 30,000. By the time of the U.S. Revolutionary War it reached 40,000 a year—perhaps even 100,000. The eighteenth century seems the high point of the trade. Philip Curtin in *The Atlantic Slave Trade* says that eighty percent of slaves brought to the New World came between 1701 and 1850. This is of course because the economic demand reached its highest point in the latter part of the eighteenth century and the beginning of the nineteenth century, and because of the development of bigger, faster ships. The trade went on however for *four centuries.* And when the anti-slavery-trade laws began in Europe it was not because of morality so much as it was that slave gang labor was proving too expensive, i.e., not yielding the maximum profit, which is the main theme of capitalism.

DuBois estimates that 5,000,000 slaves were imported and that his figure represents the survivors of at least five times as many who perished in Africa and on the high seas. Combine this with the Islamic slave trade, which went on until the early twentieth century, and we begin to see the numbers we are dealing with. DuBois ends by saying the total of blacks eliminated from Africa must approach 100,000,000. Sékou Touré of Guinea says it was twice that. Philip Curtin makes a conservative estimate that between fifteen and thirty-three percent of the slave cargo perished before reaching the New World, although DuBois says it was fifty percent. But also, and you should think about this, crew mortality was usually around twenty percent as well. In other words, the death and disease of the slave ship were not limited to blacks but also wiped out the whites who were crew for the slave ships. Clearly the billions made off black flesh did not go to these wretches. Employment aboard a slave ship is hardly the healthiest or safest work, and the rising class that profited ultimately from the trade were not on these ships, just as they are not actually in the streets of the ghettos today—they do not work in the agencies and inferior markets and jails, but they profit immensely from them.

The result of the four centuries of slave trade was ghastly: whole tribes disappeared, villages withered, regions depopulated; the magnificent culture in many instances became stunted and backward, raped into catatonia by emerging European capitalism.

The decline of feudal African civilizations, the incessant wars between the expanding African states in the west and the city-states on the coast, the impact of migrating peoples from northeast to south central who were fleeing the incursions of Islam, the culpability and collaboration of the African ruling classes with the European traders, all these things contributed to the success of the trade.

There were 50,000,000 dead, 50,000,000 "chained to each other hand and foot, and stacked so close that they were not allowed over a foot and a half for each in breadth. Thus crammed together like herrings in a barrel, they contracted putrid and fatal diseases, so that they who came to inspect this in a morning had occasionally to pick dead slaves out of their rows and to unchain their carcasses from the bodies of their wretched fellow-sufferers to whom they had been fastened."

The high cultures of Africa were stopped in their tracks by the slave trade. The Africans who had led the world toward civilization were now themselves subjected to decivilization.

Slaves were brought from the length and breadth of Africa, from many different cultures and tribes and nations and states.

We have talked before about the high level of civilization, at one time more advanced than anywhere in the world, which existed in Africa. This was a civilization and culture which varied throughout Africa. In each case the culture, basically the totality of life, is determined primarily by the economic base. As this base is changed, so too changes the superstructure, i.e., the worldview, ideology, ideas, customs, religion, art—the entire culture.

Alan Merriam, in Bascom and Herskovits's *Continuity and Change in African Cultures*, lays out eight or nine basic areas of cultural distinction in Africa: (1) Bushman-Hottentot area in Southwest Africa, (2) East Africa, (3) East Horn (Somalia, Ethiopia), (4) Central Africa, (5) West Coast, (6) Sudan A, Sudan B, (7) Desert, (8) North Coast.

Afro-American people, in the main, came from Areas 4, 5, and 6A, going to North America, as well as the black slaves going to the Caribbean, Latin America, and Europe. In the eastern areas, the Islamic slave trade took priority.

In each of these areas a charactcristic culture had emerged based on the mode of production dominating that area, plus other influences. The material base is principal, but not to recognize the influence of superstructural or ideological influence, even on the base itself, is mechanical and not dialectical—which recognizes the economic-base influence on ideas and also the influence of ideas on the base, but holds that the influence of the economic base is principal.

For instance, the music of the Babazele Pygmies, as Robert Thompson pointed out, consisted, and still largely consists, of the yodeling, hocketing style which requires no instruments at all. It is a basic communal collective style reflecting the communal character of the economic base as well as the extremely low level of the productive forces, i.e., the tools, instruments, etc.

The Pygmies are still found spread throughout Central Africa. The reason Pygmy music cannot be assigned to a specific cultural area, with the "structures" of the others, is because of the essentially nomadic hunting and gathering character of the Pygmy economy itself. The building of cities was the first stage of civilization.

The presence of drums in a consistent and endemic fashion must be ascribed to the peoples who went further in their development. The use of hides for drums implies the domestication of animals, the upper stages of barbarism, at least. Nilotic tribes first used drums, and in the tribes that followed in Kongo, West Coast, Sudan, the drums signified first of all political power and, because of this, manifest strength and domination—divine power.

The first owners of the drums were the owners of the cattle and the lands, the first amassers of private wealth in Africa, and the first ruling class.

The appearances of the *mbisi* or *sanza* can show the economic, hence cultural, development. The first *sanzas* were made completely of wood, with bamboo strips as the plucked "keys." Later these are replaced with metal strips—this could only be done by metal-making people of a still more advanced culture. Just as today in the U.S.A. we have a *sanza* attached to an electronic speaker, which tells of a still further developed society and a different economic base.

The songs which praised the chiefs for instance cannot be Pygmy songs, because the Pygmies had no chiefs. They could not be songs stemming from primitive communal societies; they had to emerge from slave and feudal society—or perhaps capitalist society, like John Philip Sousa's version of James Sanderson's "Hail to the Chief."

231

But the whole of African music is approached as functional to the whole of African society. The extreme specialization of late, more developed capitalism is only recently reaching Africa; such specialization, for instance, allows only a relatively small number of persons to be musicians or artists, whereas in earlier African society there was no division between "high" art and commercial art, or artist and audience. These are specializations which take their form from more highly developed commodity production in which "art" becomes primarily a commodity, something created to be sold, rather than the expression of one aspect of social life: birth, holiday, festival, hunting, an accompaniment for collective works, death, etc.

In preliterate cultures the songs were used to keep historic records. Influences on African culture can be seen to come from other Africans. There are some Indian influences, and, of course, the coming of the West and Islamic interventions make these influences the most obvious.

The European slave trade took on different aspects depending on who was the agent of it. Much of the very early trade brought blacks into Europe, particularly Spain, Portugal, and Italy as I mentioned before. The New World Portuguese and Spanish trade went to Central America and Latin America, Mexico, Cuba, Puerto Rico, Dominican Republic, even to places like Venezuela, Bolivia, Chile, Colombia, Panama, Equador, and Brazil, the huge Portuguese colony. The Dutch and Danish went to the Caribbean. The French went to the Caribbean, mainly Martinique, Guadeloupe, French Guiana, Haiti (Saint-Domingue), Louisiana. The English, American, and Canadian trade went to the many Caribbean islands, but focused mainly on Jamaica. One important fact is that the United States was only a marginal recipient of slaves directly from Africa. The real center of the trade was tropical America, with ninety percent going to the Atlantic fringe from Brazil through the Guianas to the Caribbean coast and islands.

This is one of the main reasons why throughout Latin America, Central America, and the Caribbean there are more openly mixed cultures, since in these places Africans outnumbered their European masters. The indigenous Indians added another aspect to the mixture. This is easily seen in places like Puerto Rico, Cuba, Brazil, etc. In the United States, Africans were a minority, and in many places of captivity there were only two or three slaves on the smaller farms, with the plantations being generally smaller in the U.S. than in the rest of the Americas. That is why segregation could be stricter in the U.S. than in the rest of the Americas. Although even with the heavier intermingling in the rest of the Americas, the class system was still indelibly indicated by a caste system which ran from darkest-lowest to lighter-higher to whitest-highest.

The emergence of racism is linked directly to the rise of the slave trade and the development of capitalism. Racism is not only an ideology, a system of justification for the slave trade, it is also an all-round method of inferiorization and a method of social organization, based on physical characteristics. It added an even more hellish twist to slavery, colonialism, national oppression.

So that Africans, who first founded civilization, who were the first *Homo sapiens,* the parents of the human race, as the slave trade progressed, and grew ever more profitable, were relentlessly down-graded ideologically as a people and culture by the need the Christian and Islamic capitalists had to explain and legitimatize their stinking business. The idea that Europeans are *a priori* racists is metaphysical. On the contrary, it is a particular mode of production, a specific economic base, creating a superstructure—philosophies, institutions, customs, etc.—that creates, strengthens, and supports racism. At first it was said that the slave trade was a method of conversion to Christianity. But by the middle seventeenth century even some of the Christian churches themselves could not stomach the lie. The reason so many blacks are Baptists is that they had taken on more democracy than the other sects, a feature which appealed to workers and even slaves.

Black Bolshevik: Autobiography of an Afro-American Communist by Harry Haywood *

The extreme importance of this book is that in one longish volume Haywood has given us an indispensable history, as reference and sum-up of practical struggles, of not only his particular thirty-six years in the Communist Party USA, including his road into and out of it, but equally has given us a good portion of political history (which is the struggle of various classes for power) of one period of capitalist North America itself.

For these reasons alone, this book is not only an invaluable document but a critical "link," connecting up the militant struggles that went down earlier in this century to transform American society, with those of recent years. For American political activists the book is required reading, and for Afro-American militants and revolutionaries it is the *missing link* explaining exactly what that relationship between the Black Liberation Movement and the multinational workers' struggle led by the Communist Party was at its most positive and revolutionary. It lays out as well how that relationship turned negative, what were the forces involved, and what this means to the struggle in the sixties and the meaning it holds for the future.

In addition to this, even more importantly, the book takes a consistently correct ideological and political line regarding the Afro-American national question. Haywood upholds the "Leninist line" on the nature of the black struggle in the U.S.A.: that black people make up an oppressed nation in the black-belt South—the old cot-

*A book review commissioned by *The New York Times*, but never printed. The book was published by the Liberator Press of Chicago.

ton-raising zone—and have the right of self-determination, that is, the right to decide what their relationship as a nation will be with any other country including, and most importantly, the U.S.A. Of course this right of self-determination can only be won in revolutionary struggle against United States imperialism, which is the oppressor of the Afro-American nation, and the struggle to achieve this right of self-determination, i.e., black political control of the lower South, is part and parcel of the movement of the entire multinational working class for socialist revolution. Haywood not only supports this line but gives us the entire history of the development of this revolutionary line in the Communist International in the late twenties and of the struggle to get the Communist Party USA to uphold and carry out this line.

The chronicle of Haywood's life, from his birth in South Omaha and his continuous traveling throughout this country and internationally, searching, struggling, organizing, the interwoven lives of his family, comrades, and the endless stream of personalities he encounters, Haywood makes a powerful political journal. We better understand the Civil War, Reconstruction—the high-water mark of American democracy and its betrayal. We are made lucid about the Garvey movement and the dialectics of black nationalism, its positive and negative aspects. We understand more clearly the social and ideological dynamism of the Communist Party USA, and are placed in the midst of its major line struggles. We march through the militant revolutionary thirties, and travel with Haywood to Moscow and the Lenin School for International Cadres. We are partisan observers closeup on the historic Trotsky-Stalin debates, and watch the mighty Communist International deal with the struggle against the bourgeoisie all over the world as well as take a hand in straightening out the factionalism that had turned the CPUSA against itself.

The strength of Haywood's narrative is that he was an actual participant (and still is) in the struggle to smash capitalism and build socialism, and the events and confrontations he speaks of, as well as the world view he brings to those descriptions, are instructive and inspiring. It was Haywood who actually helped draft for the Comintern the Leninist position on the Afro-American national question, and Haywood who was a key figure within the now hopelessly reformist CPUSA, who fought for the revolutionary position on that question and fought against the finally inundating tide of revisionism (using Marxist-Leninist terminology to cover reformism and collaboration with the bourgeoisie) in the CPUSA.

But the sweep of history and event contained in this book will fascinate any serious reader. The movement to build the Sharecroppers' Union in the South, to unionize nonunion workers, the mass struggles against national oppression (particularly the historic Scottsboro case and the frame-up of Angelo Herndon), the strike-support work, the constant attacks by the bourgeoisie, including some hidden agents within the party, make this book boil with excitement and political relevance.

Of particular interest to me was Haywood's description of the three major crises within the CPUSA: the first associated with the renegade Lovestone, the second with the renegade Browder, and the third and final crisis which saw the CP consolidate around the thoroughly revisionist line of "peaceful transition to socialism" (as if Rocky and Co. would let us vote them out of power and vote socialism in!). In each case where the right-opportunist (reformist) tendency gained the upper hand, white chauvinism emerged to underestimate and denigrate the revolutionary character of the Black Liberation Movement and to oppose the revolutionary slogan "Self-determination for the Afro-American nation in the black belt!" In each of these negative moves, the BLM was distortedly characterized as merely a moral struggle against racism, rather than as the struggle of a people, a nation, for political power, but as Haywood points out, and as the Leninist line on the Afro-American national question affirms, political power is the only guarantee of equality!

The events of the 1960's, after the CPUSA had turned completely revisionist in 1957 (sixteenth National Convention), and the Black Liberation Movement not only reached a high point of rebellion but stirred the entire workers' movement in a national revolutionary motion that moved almost wholly around nationalism, proved out the truth of Haywood's advocacy of the Leninist line, and the correctness of that line. It also demonstrated that without a genuine communist party to guide the struggle of the multinational working class and oppressed nationalities, those struggles, as in the sixties, remain spontaneous and rebellion cannot be turned into revolution. Haywood points out that once the CPUSA became a revisionist party in 1957, the central task of all revolutionaries and progressive people became the rebuilding of a new communist party, which is where we are now. *Black Bolshevik* is a stunning contribution to that anti-revisionist, party-building movement.

Your Future and America's Future*

Your future, you graduates, and all you others really, your future is bound up tight with this country's future. Just as the lives of your parents, your people, working people generally, and all your ancestors have been bound up and tied to the history of this country. But what we all need to find out is exactly how it is tied up, your life and this country's life, because if you do not understand this basic truth, this fundamental reality, your ignorance will doom you to flap around meaninglessly and tragically in the big toilet bowl that America is for working people, poor people, and oppressed nationalities and minorities. A big toilet bowl where they are constantly trying to flush you away forever.

First of all you must understand that the United States of America is a capitalist country. A capitalist country in which racism is used to make superprofits and to separate the working people according to nationalities so they will not rise up together and make revolution! By capitalism, we mean a society in which the land, the factories, the mineral wealth—oil wells, coal mines—the communication and transportation systems, the machines of industry, where all these means of producing wealth in a society are owned privately, that is, owned by a handful of vampires, the superbillionaires, who control the United States, the Rockefellers, Morgans, Du Ponts, Mellons, and the like. These buccaneers make up six-tenths of one percent of

---

*Graduation speech, Camden (New Jersey) High School, June 13, 1977.

the population. Only six-tenths of one percent, *less than* one percent of the population, yet they control the entire wealth of the country. This is what capitalism is, where a few members of the capitalist, ruling-class elite own everything, and the masses of us, the majority of us, are forced to work for them for little or nothing, while they live in luxury. These capitalists force us to live in places like Camden, or Newark, where I come from. To live in dangerous housing projects, jammed together like sardines, while they live in mansions with huge estates. They condemn us to disease-infested ghettos, where half of the people are unemployed, and because there are no jobs for many people under capitalism, and never will be, crime rates are sky high. Crime is caused by economic conditions. People steal because they don't have anything, and no prospects for getting anything; maybe if they're lucky, a lifetime of chumpchange. So that many of you graduates will not find jobs, and those who do, a great many of you will never be satisfied because a capitalist society is not interested in benefiting the people, but getting great amounts of work out of them at exploitation wages. Unemployment, bad housing, second-rate education, high crime rate, these things do not drop out of the sky; there are causes for them. And the causes for them are part of capitalism. Because a few people exploit the work of the majority and then take all the wealth for themselves and live fabulous lives, most of us must struggle and suffer and barely get to taste life.

But clear your mind and hear this: you never will experience life as it should be lived, nor will the great majority of us, until the system of monopoly capitalism is smashed, until capitalism itself is eliminated, by means of a socialist revolution led by a revolutionary Marxist-Leninist party, and until socialism is put in its place. To make change it takes struggle. Even Harold Melvin and the Blue Notes pointed that out in "Wake Up Everybody"; things will not change if we just let them be. Very true, there is no change without struggle. "Fight the Powers That Be" is what the Eisely Brothers said, and those powers are the bourgeois rulers of this country, the tiny class of capitalists that control our lives because they control this country's wealth. When the Ojays talked about the sixteen families that rule everything, in their song "The Rich Get Richer" (before the bourgeoisie cooled them out and got them singing about midnight trains, and such stuff), they were talking about this narrow class of vampire pirates that own the means of production in the

U.S.A., and against whom revolution must be made—revolution that will transform private ownership of those factories and lands into public, collective ownership, under the absolute domination of working people themselves. The workers themselves must own and manage the means of production; then and only then will exploitation cease. Standard Oil, the telephone company, the gas and electric company, railroads, factories, all must be owned collectively and publicly by the people. But this can only be accomplished by socialist revolution. Armed struggle, guided by a revolutionary Marxist-Leninist communist party based on Marxism–Leninism–Mao Tse Tung thought, the science of revolution. Socialist revolution cannot be made spontaneously; it does not just happen magically. Revolution is a science, and in order to make revolution we must study that science. In the sixties, the Black Liberation Movement leaped forward largely through the spontaneous outbursts of the masses, but that is why people now ask what happened to the BLM. Simply because it was spontaneous it rises and falls in waves. There were rebellions set off in over 100 major cities, but without science, rebellion could not be turned into revolution. Also, in the United States we have no genuine revolution Marxist-Leninist communist party. The so-called Communist Party of the USA sold out to the bourgeoisie in the late fifties and is now a reformist social club telling us that somehow the ruling class will let us vote in socialism. In other words, one day Rocky and Co. are going to give up their billions voluntarily by letting us vote them out of power. If you go for that you go for anything! These lies are called revisionism, people calling themselves communists and revolutionaries but in reality being about as revolutionary as backward Governor Byrne and the rest of the bourgeois parties. That is why we have to build a revolutionary Marxist-Leninist party today; it is why our central task is the building of such a party, because it is only by means of such a party that revolution, socialist revolution, can be made. The only progressive means by which this society can be totally transformed.

For working people, and oppressed nationalities, our whole history is one of struggle to make change. For blacks, we came here in chains, slaves, because slavery was the means by which capitalism made its first huge amounts of wealth, its early accumulation of wealth, which enabled the young capitalist societies to have their industrial revolutions. The industrial revolution in Europe and the U.S.A would have been impossible without the African slave trade.

239

In fact it was the trade in African slaves that initiated world trade in the first place, with a triangular trade in slaves, raw materials, and manufactured goods. Black people fought to liberate themselves and the rest of the country in the American Revolutionary War when this country freed itself from Great Britain and colonialism, but blacks did not achieve their freedom when the rest of the United States did. Black people fought in the Civil War to help destroy slavery and were supposed to receive land and equal rights after the war, but we were sold out by the federal government and thrown down into almost the same slavery with the coming of segregation, discrimination, Jim Crow black codes, sharecropping, and lynching and the rest of it to beat us back down. Black people fought again in the 1950's and 1960's in the civil-rights movement, and in the great rebellions, again for our democratic rights, and some gains were made. But by the seventies the bourgeoisie under Nixon, Ford, and now Carter took most of these gains away. But the struggle continues, and now we are in a period when advanced forces among us are struggling to grasp the correct ideology and political line, learning that the only solution is revolution and that capitalism must be eliminated and socialism built in its place. And we are learning that the science of revolution is Marxism–Leninism–Mao Tse Tung thought!

The United States is a capitalist country, and internationally this means it is an imperialist country. Its capitalist vultures are not confined to the boundaries of this country but search the world for new sources of raw materials, new markets to sell their goods, new spheres of influence, and new places to export capital. The United States has made Puerto Rico a colony, robbed its wealth, and forced Puerto Ricans to come to the United States mainland seeking employment because *yanqui* capitalists rob the wealth of the enchanted isle. The Puerto Rican people in the U.S.A. are now part of the multinational working class, a working class that is brown, red, black, yellow, white. A working class whose principal enemy is the six-tenths of one percent of the population that own all the wealth and that has condemned us to poverty and slums. And the Puerto Rican people like the Afro-American people are part of the heroic proletariat, the growing working class in this country who will be the principal force to smash capitalism and build socialism. It is this great working class which will make revolution.

Puerto Rico itself, like Africa, is part of the Third World: Africa,

Asia, Latin America, the peoples and nations whose struggles make revolution the main trend in the world today. The people of the Third World are the chief strugglers against imperialism, racism, and the contention of the two superpowers U.S.A. and U.S.S.R. Revolution is raging in Africa and moving forward rapidly in Puerto Rico, and the African and Puerto Rican people will smash imperialism, both United States imperialism and Russian social imperialism, and free themselves, and eventually build socialism. But those of us in the U.S., while supporting these struggles of the Third World, must understand that our struggle is here, in these streets, where *we* are the exploited and oppressed.

The main thing that you graduates must remember tonight is that without struggle nothing will be accomplished, and that the society itself must be changed. Do not become cynical or pessimistic; do not let yourself be used or tricked. Understand that the majority of your frustration and the reason for the dead-end streets you face, few jobs, few chances for higher education, is the fault of the society. And to change that society it takes struggle, first to build a revolutionary Marxist-Leninist communist party based on Marxism–Leninism–Mao Tse Tung thought, and then socialist revolution, to lay capitalism, the private ownership of the means of producing wealth, away forever. And build socialism, and a new society for the benefit of the majority of us.

Unity and struggle.

Students, fight for socialism.

Marxist-Leninist unite—win the advanced to communism.

Build a revolutionary Marxist-Leninist communist party based on M-L-M.

Speech at Wesleyan University, in Support of Student Movement to Force Wesleyan to Divest Itself of South African Holdings

It was Chairman Mao who devised the contemporary analysis of three worlds as a wholly accurate summing-up of the position of class forces in the world today. Chairman Mao's analysis drew on examples of such analysis made in previous situations by Marx and Lenin and Stalin, but brought these Marxist teachings into a contemporary setting. The three-world thesis holds that the U.S.A and U.S.S.R., the two superpowers, constitute the First World. The Second World nations are those developed and revisionist countries mainly of Europe, and the Third World countries are the so-called undeveloped countries of Asia, Africa, and Latin America. With this analysis it is possible for the people to see who is the main enemy, the superpowers, and to see who are the middle forces, who are vacillating but nevertheless can be united with against the superpower hegemony and the danger of World War III, i.e., the Second World countries. But also we can see what is the principal force making revolution in the world today and who can be united with closely by the proletariat of all countries in destroying the superpowers and carrying the revolutionary struggles through to the end, namely the peoples of Asia, Africa, and Latin America, who are the most oppressed and who therefore put up the most resistance to imperialism.

It is in the Third World that imperialism is being blown up, burned, shot, and driven out. In the First and Second World countries opportunism is a real factor in slowing the motion to make revolution. But the economic base of opportunism is not present in the Third World to the same extent, because it is by scooping super-profits out of the Third World that the imperialist countries can bribe small sectors of "their" working class and petite bourgeoisie and use these bribed elements to mislead and confuse large groups of people, slowing to some degree the process of revolution. It is one reason, for instance, that we have no genuine communist party in the U.S.A., only the sham Marxists of the so-called CPUSA, a clique of middle-class reformists whose principal work is confusing the people, talking nonsense like there is a peaceful road to social-ism—yeah, we know, in the bourgeoisie's head.

A few years ago in the Third World the hottest fires burning up imperialism were in Southeast Asia; Vietnam, Cambodia, and Laos freed themselves from United States imperialism, and the intensity of those struggles unleashed rebellion even inside the United States, as working people, oppressed nationalities, students, and anti-impe-rialist intellectuals opposed the imperialists' colonial war.

Today however the world struggle against imperialism is at its most intense on the continent of Africa. Throughout the world, the United States is on the defensive; it is fighting to hold on to its ill-gotten gains—the resources and lands of others—but not only has it suffered losses in Southeast Asia, but also in Africa its domination through its client states like Portugal was smashed as the African people smashed Portuguese colonialism in Mozambique and Guinea-Bissau. And to show how critical to imperialism are its Third World colonies, once Mozambique fell, a revolution jumped off in-side Portugal itself against its domestic fascism, because the cutting-off of Third World superprofits had actually undermined the metro-politan government itself!

In Angola, a tragedy befell the African people, because even though they had struggled for seventeen years to defeat Portuguese colonialism, and did, the contention of the two superpowers and in this case the intervention of the Soviet social imperialists has blocked any real independence from coming to Angola. Today, the Soviet Union has over 14,000 of its Cuban puppet troops inside An-gola, making the Soviet social imperialists the de facto rulers of An-gola. Under the cover of being "the natural ally of the liberation movements," as the Soviets crow to hide their real intentions, they labeled two of the Angolan liberation movements reactionary, brought in heavy arms and troops in support of the third movement (when for seventeen years their aid had been weak and perfunctory), created a civil war in Angola, and took control. In one year the Soviet social imperialists killed over 150,000 Africans, more than died in the entire seventeen-year struggle with straight-out Portuguese colonialism. The Soviets and their apologists babble they have killed reactionaries. But the African people ultimately will liberate themselves despite the armaments and lies of Soviet social imperialism and its puppets.

All over Africa, and beyond, struggle against imperialism, colonialism, racism, zionism, and superpower hegemonism is going on, whether it is armed people opposing the settler colony of Israel, or the struggle in Ethiopia and Somalia, where the true face of Soviet social imperialism is being shown as they support the bloody Ethiopian military junta in their attempts to suppress the Ethiopian people and smash the Eritrean people's fight for self-determination (and invade Somalia). And the struggle goes on in Rhodesia, real name, Zimbabwe; South-West Africa, real name Namibia; and in South Africa, real name, Azania—where the final showdown with imperialism in its colonial form is about to go down!

However, in the present situation of the world struggle against imperialism, one key to those struggles must be the anticolonial struggles in southern Africa. In Zimbabwe, the racist colonial government of Ian Smith is backed flat against the wall. Two years ago they talked much shit about how they would always rule, that the 450,000 white settlers would always rule the 5 million blacks through racist violence, and that any attempt to change that would be futile. But since then, faced with the unified armed struggle of the people of Zimbabwe, they have talked negotiations. They have said that majority rule could come through negotiations, and at the same time that they pretended to negotiate they continued their repression, even invading neighboring countries like Zambia, Botswana, and Mozambique, trying to no avail to stop the people's forces. They practice counterrevolutionary dual tactics, talking negotiation but going on with their killing, all at the same time.

Recently Smith has been able to isolate three traitors, Stepin Fetchit, Birmingham, and Sleep 'n Eat, who go under the names of Chirau, Sithole, and Muzorewa, to pretend that negotiations have been completed for majority rule. But this is an out-and-out hoax, and the agreement is so funky and neocolonial on the face of it, that even *The New York Times* came out and put it down.

The purpose of this sham negotiation is to set up a neocolonial government of Ian Smith–controlled minstrels, and then continue the war against the Patriotic Front, which is the legitimate revolutionary united front of the Zimbabwean people. This way the colonialists can continue their war, with black pawns fronting off as a majority government, when in reality it is spelled out very plainly in the Smith document that there is no way the blacks who are the overwhelming majority in Zimbabwe will see any change at all. The United States and Great Britain criticize Smith's sham negotiations because they know they will not stop the guerrilla warfare at all. The first two points of Smith's sham documents call for stopping the guerrilla war and recognizing his illegal racist settler government as the legal government of Zimbabwe. Smith maintains control over the police, army, and security forces, and a numbers game is laid out that makes it impossible for the black majority to do anything without the racists sanctioning it.

The United States and Great Britain also know that the frontline states of Tanzania, Zambia, Botswana, Mozambique, will not sanction such a bogus agreement. They also know the Soviet Union will capitalize on such a fiasco and use it in their hegemonistic sneaking-through-the-backdoor policy.

But the Patriotic Front, composed of ZANU, led by Robert Mugabe, and Joshua Nkomo's ZAPU, will not be cowed or fooled by such minstrel antics. They will persist in strengthening their unity, continuing the armed struggle through to the end, and they will depend principally on self-reliance, for these are the methods of making successful revolution, unity, self-reliance, and revolutionary armed struggle.

In Namibia, the racist South Africans have refused to leave this land, even though the UN year after year has demanded that South Africa leave Namibia and has charged them time and again with being in Namibia illegally. But the white racists in South Africa are attempting tactics in Namibia similar to Ian Smith's in Zimbabwe. In fact these tactics probably originated with South Africa—and possibly with Henry Kissinger. Vorster is propping up various tribal chiefs and black reactionaries as the leadership in Namibia, getting them to oppose the genuine revolutionary leadership of SWAPO. The South African attempt to parcel off small reservations the way the United States racists did to the American Indians, calling this the black people's homeland and setting up various tribal chiefs as the "government" of these sham nations, is the way the South African racists attempt to confuse and diffuse the people's struggle in Azania. But overwhelmingly the people are rejecting these Uncle Tom chiefs and Bantustan homelands. Two such chiefs in Namibia have met with sudden violent deaths, proving their behinds are as endangered as their philosophies.

In Azania itself, which the racists call South Africa, Vorster has had to urge Ian Smith in Zimbabwe to at least take on the front of compromise with majority rule. This has been the basic difference between United States foreign policy and the colonial settler colonies. The United States has demanded that Smith/Vorster change their style and update their oppression. They have tried to point out that colonialism is dead, and that a new wrinkle, neocolonialism, must be permitted to function. And that it is impossible for 4.5 million whites in South Africa to continue to rule 19 million blacks, and Vorster, etc., must find them some good little boys and girls—Andrew Young–Kenneth Gibson–Barbara Jordan style—to play government, so that imperialism can continue to function as it does in neocolonial states where imperialism rules, as Cabral and Nkrumah pointed out, through native agents. Vorster sees the need for Smith to do this in Zimbabwe. Smith has no choice, yet his sham negotiations are doomed to failure because he has moved too late. The United States imperialists realize that to be intransigent and fail to find some good nigger to front off for imperialism is to risk carrying the revolutionary struggle all the way through to its completion, which would be the expulsion of imperialism and the setting up of people's democracies in order to do away completely with capitalism and build socialism.

But South Africa is a key situation internationally. The fall of South Africa to revolutionary people's forces would probably result in the toppling of the British government in the same way that the Portuguese imperialists fell. Great Britain is a second-rate imperialist power, and the slender margin of superprofit still controlled by its capitalists is the slim margin of bribe reform and compromise characterizing the opportunism obstructing revolution in Great Britain. Without the support of the South Africa piece, Great Britain must then throw the entire weight of its failing system onto the backs of its own working people, and they will rise up and smash capitalism there. The attempt to stir up national chauvinism and use blacks and Indians and Pakistanis in Great Britain as the scapegoats is the classic tactic of the bourgeoisie trying to keep the people from uniting and crushing them forever.

The United States commitment, despite any grunts and groans to the contrary, is total. The South African settler colony could not last more than a few months without the support and protection of United States imperialism. The fact that the United States tries to run a smokescreen, much of it pumped out of the opportunistic mouth of Andrew Young, pretending it is for change in South Africa, changes nothing. The only change the United States supports is a cosmetic, neocolonial stunt, black faces in high places, but no real change. The masses of the Azanian people would still be crushed down and exploited and oppressed. The United States government's emphasis on ending apartheid, and bringing South Africa to heel about "civil rights" and "human rights," means they wish Vorster and company would grow more sophisticated and learn how to utilize neocolonialism, but that is all. United States business and foreign policy is responsible for South Africa continuing to function. Their cries, as if South Africa were some wholly independent bandit state which affronts their morality, are simple bullshit. Ninety-two percent of the blacks in South Africa live below the poverty level (in the U.S.A. it is only 25 percent). The 19 million blacks live on only 13 percent of the land and share less than 20 percent of the national income even though there are 5 times as many blacks as whites. When Vorster created the Bantustans he said that there would be jobs created in the homelands to offset the fact that black unemployment is at 1.5 million and with workers now being laid off at a rate of 1,000 a day. But they send 60,000 people to the Bantustans each year and create only 10,000 jobs!

United States corporate involvement with the South African racist settler colony is not casual. The United States corporations aggressively uphold and support the South African government. The Caterpillar Corporations conducts one-half of its South African business with the government. General Electric supplies electronic equipment to the government and machinery to the South African railways. IBM supplies electronic goods and computers to South African Prison and Defense. It is IBM computers that enforce the oppressive passbook system. GM and Ford supply all the police trucks and military vans. Newmount Mining is a co-investor in South African mining with the government. They are also owners of the largest copper mine in South Africa. Standard Oil of California and

Texaco are striving every day to make South Africa independent of oil imports. And the huge taxes paid to South Africa, by these companies are used to strengthen the racist military might of South Africa, and that part of those revenues used for so-called "black development" is used mostly for removing black families to the Bantustans and building grim barracks there for the people to live in.

To say that the American corporations are bringing progress to South Africa is a simple lie. No more than they are bringing progress to the United States! It is still illegal for blacks to unionize in South Africa (just as it is de facto in much of the U.S. South!)

Between 1960 and 1970 American investment in South Africa increased from $88 million to $284 million, but in the same period the wage differential between black and white workers increased from 17 to 1 to 20 to 1 in favor of the whites. In the mining industry wages are no higher and possibly lower today than they were in 1911!

United States imperialism will not give up South Africa, no matter how much lip service they give to human rights. In their reeling decline, the United States rulers (who are the corporate monoliths) will grow even more aggressively protective of South Africa. The struggle to smash South African colonialism affects us here in the U.S.A directly, since it is the superprofits gouged out of Third World countries like South Africa that allow the rulers of the United States to continue to bribe a small sector of the American working class and petite bourgeoisie and to use these elements to obstruct socialist revolution in the United States. United States imperialism is caught between the sharpening of revolutionary struggle in the Third World, which has already cut back large amounts of its superprofits, and the growing danger of world war resulting from its contention with the Soviet Union, because it must arm itself to the teeth, despite the babble of the Soviet Union about "detente" and of Carter about "human rights." Arming for this war—and the military industry is the only industry in the United States that still runs at full tilt—means that the American rulers must cut back on social services, lay more people off, make budget cuts, close and cut down community colleges, while inflation and unemployment run neck and neck.

The struggle of the American people against South African colonialism is a blow against United States imperialism and an important step toward revolutionary change coming here to this bastion of imperialism. African Liberation Day in 1972 saw some 60,000 people march throughout the United States in support of the African liberation struggles, and this people's movement against colonialism in Africa has never abated. The growing movement in American colleges to force the boards of trustees to divest themselves of the stock of corporations holding investments in South Africa is important. Yale, for instance, has an investment of $8 million in GM, which along with Ford and Chrysler control 50 percent of the South African auto industry. Yale invests $1,197,500 in Mobil Oil. Mobil has 13.5 percent of United States investment in South Africa. Yale invests $8.5 million in Caltex (Standard Oil of California), which represents 11.4 percent of total United States investment in Africa (Caltex, $103 million). Yale's investment in Ford is $6,855,000. Ford constitutes 11 percent of the total United States investment. Yale has $16 million worth of IBM. IBM employs over 95 percent whites and controls 50 percent of the South African market. Yale invests $947,000 in Caterpillar, which invests $6.8 million in South Africa. Yale also invests $6.855 million in GE, and about $2 million or $3 million in Namibia, through Newmount Mining and Amax.*

You should find out, you probably have, just how involved Wesleyan is in this bloody business of supporting racism and apartheid, propping up the settler colonies.

But you can be certain that the pressures brought to bear by students to force these universities finally to divest themselves of their bloody South African stock is worthwhile, because pressure must be applied from as many places as possible, and the level of United States support for these racists must be blocked to whatever extent is possible.

Obviously it will not be easy to get these colleges to pull out of South Africa. It's the best, most profitable investment they've got going, for obvious reasons! But by continuing to struggle with them to divest you become very consciously part of the world united front against imperialism (and you strike out against petit bourgeois vacillation, and the bourgeois ideology being taught at these universities).

The destruction of the apartheid-ridden racist settler colony of South Africa and the emergence of a liberated *Azania* will be one

---

*From a position paper of the Anti-apartheid Coalition at Yale University, October, 1977.

more step toward the eradication of imperialism from the planet. Ultimately our job is to eliminate monopoly capitalism here in the U.S.A itself, and to do that it takes socialist revolution. Just as in South Africa, there can be no transformation of that racist place without people's revolution; no coaxing, no wheedling, no peaceful transition, nothing save the unity, self-reliance, and revolutionary armed struggle of the people can force that change in South Africa. So in the United States ultimately only revolutionary armed struggle can eliminate capitalism and bring socialism. The building of a revolutionary Marxist-Leninist communist party now in the U.S.A. to lead such a struggle must be for this reason the central task of all revolutionaries. And then we will see clearly that revolution will be the main trend even inside the U.S.A.

The Significance
of Black History Month

February is Black History Month, and this should be a good thing, in that it should make us focus for a time on really getting a better understanding of the history of black people generally and especially of the history of the Afro-American people—descendants of the African slaves brought to the United States in the slave ships of rising capitalism. From the beginning we have known, unlike many immigrants to the United States, that the streets were not paved with gold, but with blood—much of it ours!

Black History Month should make us more than casually inquire into the dynamic and heroic history of the Afro-American people, and struggle to get a firmer grasp of it. Because if you can be lied to about your own history, you can certainly be lied to about the history of the world. And if you can be lied to about history, you can be lied to even about the nature of the present, and have a totally distorted picture of how the world itself functions.

The Afro-American people were sold into slavery by the feudalistic rulers of Africa. Because even in feudal Africa there were classes and class struggle. The European slave traders did not just run into Africa and run out *Roots* style, ripping off the helpless savages. In fact, black flesh was a highly priced commodity that a corrupt African ruling class profited by selling, until there was so much of the productive forces of Africa traded away that the great empires of the African coast began to decline, and finally they were humbled before the rising might of capitalist, industrial Europe.

The majority of whites in the United States also arrived here in bondage, as indentured servants, debtors, prisoners of the oppressive English and European society of the era. But very quickly the new American ruling class found out that to have black and white slaves is to have black and white rebellions. So the white servants were freed in the sixteenth and seventeenth centuries, and given a new title, the keepers of the slaves, and tricked by being told that even though they were suffering that somehow, since they were white like the ruling class, they were better than the blacks.

The U.S.A has a history of revolution. The Revolutionary War to end British colonialism was an anticolonial war, and blacks joined in that struggle after being promised freedom by G. Washington and Company, once the British were defeated. This was because the British had done the same thing and blacks and Indians early in that war fought on the side of the British.

After this war it was thought that slavery would disappear of its own accord, but the invention of the cotton gin transformed cotton from a domestic product which a small group of slaves could harvest into an internationally sought-after commodity. This meant that capitalism was now imposed upon black people as well as slavery. It meant that in the black belt, where the cotton was grown and harvested, the life expectancy for a mature black slave of eighteen was seven years.

If the nineteenth century saw the intensification of slavery because of rising economic expectancy associated with cotton, it also saw the intensification of slave resistance to slavery, slave revolts. Gabriel Prosser, Denmark Vesey, Nat Turner, all led rebellions. Turner's actually was so successful that for years an aura of fear and terror hung over the slave masters. This was the period when Harriet Tubman constructed her great underground railroad leading hundreds of slaves into Canada and freedom, and this period reaches its height with John Brown's rebellion composed of blacks and whites, and finally with the outbreak of the Civil War.

The Civil War was fought between two social systems: one based on slavery, controlled by the Southern planter-slavocrats; the other a rising industrial system of so-called free labor, actually wage slavery, controlled by the bankers of the Northeast. The South was winning the war until blacks came into the war in great numbers. At first the North tried to keep them out, because the Northern armies were led by many Southern sympathizers, the Copperheads, and because of the racism of the American ruling class, that always tried to keep blacks inert and carefully defined. But black people rose, burned plantations, fled wholesale from the plantations, and fought their way into the Civil War. At least 186,000 blacks joined the Union Army and one out of three black soldiers gave their lives for the defeat of slavery. Unlike *Roots*, where the blacks read about the Civil War and that they were being freed in a newspaper, and then stayed on the plantations, the black masses fought and died to destroy slavery, and Lincoln's Emancipation Proclamation was merely the legitimatizing of something that the black masses were already actively doing.

After the Civil War came the period called Reconstruction. This was perhaps the most democratic period in United States life. There are still not as many black congressmen and senators today as there were in the Reconstruction period. The Northern rulers, the industrial capitalists, needed the Reconstruction period to completely strip the Southern slavocrats of their political and economic power, and once they had, they sold the blacks out, to the infamous Hayes-Tilden Compromise of 1876–77, pulled out the federal troops, disarmed the black militia, bankrolled terrorist organizations like the Ku Klux Klan to rule by fear and bloodshed, drove blacks out of the state legislatures, passed Jim Crow laws like the black codes, and tried to crush the progress of Reconstruction and plunge black people back into slavery with peonage and sharecropping and poll taxes and lynching.

It is after the destruction of the Reconstruction governments that the Afro-American nation arises in the black-belt South—the area where the cotton was grown and harvested by generations of blacks, the area today where 53 to 60 percent of all the blacks in the U.S.A. still live, an area stretching from the bottom of Delaware to east Texas: 1,800 miles long, half-moon shaped, and 300 miles deep. The black belt is the location of the Afro-American nation—a nation risen out of slavery, forged through bloodshed and struggle, a nation that resulted from the fact that the black people by that time were a historically constituted, stable community of people with a common land, common language, common economic life, and common psychological development manifest as a common culture.

And since the late nineteenth century in this country, black people have been no longer disconnected African tribes bound in slavery, or scattered peasants, but a nation of people, a modern nation with all the classes of capitalist society, oppressed by United States imperialism in much the way that the nations of the Third World are (Africa, Asia, Latin America), a nation with the right of self-determination up to and including the right to secession. But this is a right that can only be realized through revolutionary struggle. I am saying that the land of the American South is black people's land. Look on the maps put out by the United States Department of Commerce, which show how the various nationalities are situated today, right now, and you will see a black half-moon where the Afro-American majority still lives today. And even though some of us have migrated North in search of a better life, eight out of ten blacks in the North were born in the South. The South is the black homeland, the black-belt nation, of the Afro-American people. But it can only be liberated through revolutionary struggle.

The twentieth century in this country for the Afro-American people has been marked by much migration out of the black belt, but the majority never left. Those of us in the North and West and Midwest came looking for jobs, fleeing the oppression of the Ku Klux Klan and black-codes South. As the United States imperialists readied to make war in the early part of the century, the First World War, they needed cheap labor and brought us North. The Garvey movement of the 1920's was a movement largely of black peasants fresh from the South following the impoverished middle-class idealism that characterized the Garvey Movement.

But there could be no back to Africa; the black people were already a nation in captivity, their land was where the majority of them lived. And those of us in the North had to fight for democratic rights, and ultimately join in the revolutionary struggle with the other exploited and oppressed people of this land in overthrowing the degenerate system of monopoly capitalism. In the 1930's after the Great Depression, the example and teachings of the Russian Marxists had great influence in the U.S.A. This example was carried out in the United States by the CPUSA, though even in their most influential period of the thirties they were plagued, as were other largely white socialist movements before them, by white chauvinism and the disease of white supremacy. But in the thirties, through the guidance of the great Lenin, the leader of the Russian Revolution, the United States Communist Party took up the correct political line on black people, proclaiming their recognition of the existence of the oppressed Afro-American nation in the black-belt South, and put out the stirring revolutionary slogan: "Liberation for the black nation. Self-determination for the Afro-American nation." These cries still raise fire in the black hearts today, because this is a true description of the Black Liberation Movement's real goals: "Liberation for the Afro-American nation in the black-belt South! Self-determination for the Afro-American nation."

In the 1940's, however, the CPUSA came under the total domination of a group of reactionaries, servants of the United States bourgeoisie, and sold the party over to the American rulers. In the thirties thousands of blacks had joined the communist party, because they came to realize that only revolution could make change in this country—not submission or turning the other check or waiting till after you die to be free in some never-never-land paradise. But in in the forties the CPUSA turned its back on the black struggle, and by the fifties the CPUSA had turned its back completely on revolution and socialism and began to babble stupidly that socialism— which is the collective ownership by the people of the means of producing wealth, the land, factories, mineral wealth, oil wells, transportation, communication—could be won by working people peacefully!

The 1950's and 1960's saw the rise of the Civil-Rights Movement, which had a mass following but was led essentially by the black bourgeosie and petite bourgeoisie. The bankrupt CPUSA began in the fifties to say that black people had already achieved self-determination under imperialism, and that the NAACP and Urban League and the black bourgeoisie were the leaders of the black freedom movement. And they said that this freedom could be accomplished peacefully just like socialism, and that integration was the key to socialism.

Dr. King was the greatest of the black bourgeois leaders, but his line of nonviolence, turn the other cheek, and metaphysical forbearance under the abuse of racists was not a political line most black people could believe in, in practice. This is why Malcolm X rose so forcefully during the same period to put forth the line of the black majority: self-determination, self-respect, and self-defense. Malcolm X's influence was wide. He changed the Black Liberation Movement from "civil rights" to self-defense and black nationalism. The student movement, SNCC, once influenced by King, hence the name Student Nonviolent Coordinating Committee, was transformed under Malcolm's influence, and Stokey Carmichael rose as leader of SNCC echoing Malcolm's line calling for *black power*. Rap

255

Brown rose in SNCC as its next leader calling for black rebellion, saying that if America did not come around it should be burned to the ground! The message was not submission and nonviolence, but struggle and self-defense and finally rebellion. The Black Panthers rose, coming from Malcolm's line of armed self-defense. The cultural nationalists rose, coming from Malcolm's line on the black nation and the importance of our African heritage, though they distorted it and made it metaphysical, myself included. Malcolm was murdered because he broke with cultural nationalism and religious nationalism and began to talk about a black united front of all classes and strata of black people in struggle against imperialism, because he was becoming an internationalist, because he began to talk about how the Black Liberation Movement was linked up with the struggle of oppressed peoples everywhere and about how capitalism and racism go always hand in hand.

In the late 1970's the bourgeoisie tried to tell us the movement was dead. Can 30 million people be dead?? True, they killed and locked up and bought out some leaders, but the people themselves persist, and where there is oppression there will be resistance. It has become clearer and clearer to more and more of us that it is capitalism itself, the system of private ownership of the means of producing wealth by six-tenths of one percent, that is the enemy. That the Rockefellers, Morgans, Du Ponts, Mellons, the sixteen families the Ojays used to sing about before they were cooled out, are the enemies not only of the oppressed black nation but of the majority of people, black, white, Puerto Rican, Asian, Indian, Chicano, in this country. Our history is continuously distorted to make us think that black people, and all people, always enjoyed capitalist rule, slavery, lynching, union-busting, indentured servitude, Appalachia, Wounded Knee, Indian genocide, the oppression of women. In many black history exhibits, for instance the one at the Newark Museum, or in the various schools, or official exhibitions, they make black history out to be about the black middle class or black entertainers. In one grammar school they had Sammy Davis and Diana Ross, but not Malcolm X. At the museum they did not have Harriet Tubman or Paul Robeson, and of course not Malcolm. In an exhibit at a Texas college they had all the blacks in Texas who fought on the side of the Confederacy as the black heroes! Yes, they will distort, they will raise up the weak or submissive and try to hide the people whose struggle makes history. As in the TV presentation

King, where the representation of Malcolm X was a hideous distortion.

So Black History Month is important for us to seek out the real history of black struggle, a history that will invariably see us joining the struggle of the majority of people in this country to build a new communist party, based on Marxism–Leninism–Mao Tse Tung thought, and to carry out a socialist revolution to put the wealth and resources of this society into the hands of the working masses, and at the same time to liberate the black nation and bring freedom, liberty, and prosperity to all the people of this land.

African
Liberation Day
1977

The struggle to liberate Africa is a component part of proletarian revolution throughout the world. In the national liberation struggles of the Third World peoples (Africa, Asia, Latin America) are to be found the fiercest struggles against imperialism, colonialism, racism, Zionism, and particularly against the hegemonist designs of the two superpower imperialists, the U.S.A. and the social imperialist U.S.S.R. It is these struggles that are the motor driving revolution around the world. And our presence here today, not only to demonstrate our support of African Liberation struggles, but also to intensify our own struggle against the hated bourgeoisie of our own country, attests inspiringly to the fact that although the factors for both war and revolution are rising, "the world situation continues to develop in a direction favorable to the people of all countries," as our Chinese comrades have stated, which means that indeed revolution is still the main trend in the world today. Countries want independence, nations want liberation, and the people want revolution—this historical trend is moving forward irresistibly.

Fighting against five main enemies, imperialism, colonialism, racism, Zionism, and superpower hegemonism, as expressed recently in a meeting of the OAU African summit, it is important that the people of the world see that the most ferocious enemy the African people or people of the Third World, or the Second World, have is the superpower hegemonists, and the most dangerous of all are the superpower hegemonists of the U.S.S.R. because they are not yet fully exposed as the social imperialists they truly are, and still creep around disguised as "socialist" and "natural allies" of the liberation movements, giving economic and military "aid" that has not only strings attached but huge chains which are the symbol of the Soviet Union's new colonial designs on Africa, and the world!

The contention between the two superpowers, the U.S.A. long exposed as a bloody-beast imperialist, and now in clear decline, and the U.S.S.R., the new lean-and-hungry imperialist, wildly ambitious and daring, and on the openly proclaimed offensive—the contention between these two monsters is sure to lead to war. A war which can only be stopped by revolution, and such a war, should it happen, would simply give rise to further revolution, and move the people of all countries closer to the time when they will snatch the world from the imperialists.

The superpower contention, which has increased sharply, has seen one superpower, the U.S.A., go into its bag of tricks and come out with one of the black bourgeoisie's political cadres, Andrew Young. It has made him a full-fledged member of the Jimmy Carter/ Howdy Doody Clown and Snake-Oil Liberal/Fascist Revival Hour to try to trick the people of Africa particularly and of the Third World generally, as well as the masses inside this country, about continued United States support of the panic-stricken and besieged racist regimes. While the Soviet Union, to counter this bit of slicksterism, has sent two of its top badwill ambassadors, Fidel Castro and President Podgorny (before he got busted), to try to cover up the open butchery of their social imperialist, colonial designs on Africa. The gravest menace African people face today is Soviet expansion. And let whoever doubts that explain the slaughter of 150,000 Africans in Angola by the Cuban mercenaries and Soviet overlords—more blacks than were killed by Portuguese colonialism in the 17 years of colonial war! And who has heard yet of *one* South African shot, or even cursed at, by the Soviets and their mercenaries in Angola? The Angolan people have not yet got their independence, and a fierce liberation struggle and civil war rages still.

In Zaire the Soviet social imperialists have again bared their fangs, resurrecting the same Kantanganese gendarmes who helped in the assassination of Patrice Lumumba to do their dirty work for them. And the bourgeois Pan-Africanists, such as AAPRP, who support the Soviet Union, are doing for the Soviet Union exactly what Andrew Young is doing for United States imperialism! With much less pay!

The heightening struggles in southern Africa have brought African people more and more to the realization that the two superpowers are their deadly enemies, and that only by strengthening their unity, practicing self-reliance, being clear on and using dual revolutionary tactics against dual counterrevolutionary tactics (as in Zimbabwe), and always basing their action on armed struggle will victory be attained. It is only by means of armed struggle that Africa can be swept clean of imperialism, colonialism, racism, Zionism; and superpower hegemonism can be opposed.

It is important that revolutionaires in the U.S.A. continuously point out the unbreakable connection between the national liberation struggles in the Third World and our efforts to make revolution here in the United States. The national liberation struggles against imperialism and the Third World's victories are victories for the United States proletariat and working people and for oppressed nationalities worldwide. The internal economic crisis in the United States, which is linked to an international economic crisis of imperialism, is heightened and intensified by the unstoppable victories of Third World liberation struggles, which force the imperialists to intensify their exploitation and oppression of the people here in the U.S.A., and bring all of us to more revolutionary positions!

The ALSC has long been at the forefront of struggle not only to support the revolutions that surge through Africa and the Third World, but also to show the linkage of these struggles to our own struggles in the U.S.A. The fact that there are three ALD demonstrations attests to the great disorder in the world today and to the fact that the people, and the world, advance amidst turmoil. However, it is critical that we understand that even mass organizations like the African Liberation Support Committee, if they are to go forward to meet the demands of the people, need the guidance of a revolutionary Marxist-Leninist communist party, based on Marxism–Leninism–Mao Tse Tung thought. But in the U.S.A. we have no such party, since the tragic betrayal of the people by the infamous revision of the so-called CPUSA, in 1957. The bourgeois social club led by Gus Hall and Angela Davis has practiced collaboration with the bourgeoisie and mouthed it as well. Thus, the central task of all revolutionaries has been building a party of the new type, as Lenin called it, a proletarian vanguard party, a revolutionary Marxist-Leninist communist party based on Marxism–Leninism–Mao Tse Tung thought.

At the present stage of party building, political line is the key link, i.e., the application of the theories of Marxism–Leninism–Mao Tse Tung thought to the concrete task of making revolution in the U.S.A. And the ideological struggle over this application, over the correct political line, in the midst of struggle and work within the mass workers' movement, is the method by which our struggle to build the party moves forward, and by means of which we can put together a party program, which is the maximum and minimum goals of such a party and the strategy and tactics for achieving them. It is only through the construction of such a party program that a party congress can be called and Marxist-Leninists and advanced forces come forward to build the revolutionary Marxist-Leninist communist party based on M-L-M that we must have to wage armed struggle in this country to destroy capitalism, institute the dictatorship of the proletariat, and build socialism.

Part of the great disorder in the world today, through which the people move to make revolution, is the fact that there are many sham party-building sideshows going on to delude and sidetrack the people, against which all genuine Marxist-Leninist and advanced forces must struggle unceasingly. Sham forces like the revisionists of the so-called "RCP," * petit bourgeois, ruling-class pets, or the misguided child prodigies from the OL,† who try to disorient the ranks of the revolutionaries with their shamming that they are the party or will be in a minute. And though right opportunism and revision are the main danger in the communist and workers' movement, we should also oppose the "left" neo-Trot ravings of the dangerous duo, PRRWO‡ and RWL,§ who keep threatening us with a non-party of non-Bolsheviks in some fantasy land known only to them. We must resist all petit bourgeois hysteria and profiling that the party will spring full blown from some one organization's brow like Athena from Zeus (who were also mythical) or that one organization

---

* RCP—Revolutionary Communist Party, formerly Revolutionary Union. Erroneously declared themselves the vanguard M-L party.

†OL—October League, now called Communist Party (Marxist-Leninist). They also erroneously called themselves *the* new Communist party.

‡PRRWO—Puerto Rican Revolutionary Workers Organization. Developed from the sixties Young Lords. Later joined with several organizations to call themselves the "Revolutionary Wing," all other M-L's being "opportunist."

§RWL—Revolutionary Workers League. Developed from YOBU, Youth Organization for Black Unity. Later joined with PRRWO in the Wing.

is the core around which the party will be built. In this wild country with hundreds of Marxist-Leninist organizations, collectives, study circles, and revolutionary mass organizations, and millions of advanced workers all struggling around correct political lines, the only correct line is "Marxist-Leninists unite, win the advanced to communism," in an effort to build the party that will finally destroy the bloody-beast United States imperialism and contribute to the progress of humanity the world over.

The southern African people will surely win victory through self-reliance and armed struggle!

Kick the two superpowers, U.S. imperialism and U.S.S.R. social imperialism, out of Africa!

Down with the fascist white minority regimes, reject all sham independence schemes!

U.S. people, oppose the superpower war preparation, defeat U.S. imperialism!

Workers and oppressed nations and peoples of the world, unite!

In the U.S.A., Marxist-Leninists unite, win the advanced to communism, build a revolutionary Marxist-Leninist communist party based on M-L-M!

Malcolm X and
Paul Robeson

Malcolm X killed, February 21, 1965/Robeson died, January 27, 1976.

Two black men killed in the struggle for democratic rights and self-determination for black people, and for liberation of all oppressed people!!

Malcolm was outright assassinated, murdered in front of our eyes. But Paul Robeson was also assassinated: character assassinated, economically assassinated, politically assassinated, and finally assigned to *domestic exile.*

Their lives can be joined together because they were both fighters. Both were part of the same struggle, and in a sense one picked up and took over where the other left off. Paul Robeson was not only an internationally known singer and actor but also a leader and activist in black people's struggles. He was a black man who at any time could have entered into the mainstream of bourgeois-sanctioned American society. He had won a scholarship to Rutgers in 1915. He received the Phi Beta Kappa key at Rutgers, and at the same time won thirteen varsity letters in four sports and was named the first All-American athlete at Rutgers and the first black All-American ever. He was hailed as the best all-around athlete in the United States in 1917 and 1918. He later went on and got a law degree from Columbia. When he got out he began a career as a singer and an actor, being acclaimed as one of the greatest baritone voices in the world and one of the finest actors of his time. Robeson acted in both contemporary works such as those by Eugene O'Neill as well as in Shakespeare, and Robeson's Othello is still considered the classic American portrayal, Olivier notwithstanding. But because of the high level of racism and national oppression, discrimination, Jim Crow segregation—all the survivals of slavery and the effects of the oppression of the black nation in the U.S.A—Robeson had to travel a great deal throughout the world in order to gain full recognition of his talents as an artist. He was always very outspoken about the discrimination that haunted the black artist and performer, which was related directly to the national oppression of black people by United States imperialism.

Robeson considered himself a "people's artist" and made many trips to the Soviet Union during the period when the U.S.S.R. was a socialist country and was free from racism and prejudice. In the late 1930's he performed around the world for the "International Brigades" that were fighting against racism and the rise of Hitler. Back in the U.S.A he performed for trade unions, on picket lines and in factories. He led delegations to protest discrimination, lynchings, segregation of black people in the North and in the black-belt nation, at work, and in the armed forces.

The Soviet Union, at this time, was the greatest single influence in the world for the struggle of the working people against capitalism and the struggle of oppressed peoples against imperialism. The victorious socialist revolution of the Russian people in 1917 had made them the popular leader of the world's oppressed masses, and the Soviet Union guided by Lenin, Joseph Stalin, and the heroic CPSU(B), and the science of Marxism-Leninism, was the foremost supporter of the struggles of oppressed peoples. So progressive and revolutionary a consciousness as Robeson's could not fail to be directly influenced by the development and progress of the Soviet Union during the thirties and forties, when they were a beacon of socialism that guided the entire world. We must keep in mind when we talk about the heroic Socialist Revolution of 1917 and the party and land of Lenin and Stalin, and the powerful and correct influence it had on Paul Robeson, that this all took place before the death of Stalin and the rise of the revisionist traitor Nikita Khrushchev, who, by means of a political coup, led a new bourgeoisie to arise in the Soviet Union, restoring capitalism. The Soviet Union, tragically, is now a capitalist country and a social imperialist country. They are in fact at this time the most dangerous source of war in the world. But during the period of which we speak, the Soviet Union was a leader of the world's peoples led by a great leader and a heroic party,

CPSU(B), and by the science of revolution and socialism, Marxism-Leninism. The fact that Nikita Khruschev and his gang were *revisionists*—who cut proletarian revolution and the dictatorship of the proletariat out of Marxism, talking about the "peaceful transition to socialism" and about peaceful competition and coexistence with imperialism—is the reason also that capitalism could be restored in Russian and a new bureaucrat-monopoly bourgeoisie formed.

During the Second World War the United States had an alliance with the Soviet Union against Nazi, Italian, and Japanese facism, but after the war the U.S.A., because all of Europe and Asia had been destroyed, rose to the top of imperialism because it received less direct blows from that war. The United States naturally, because it is a monopoly capitalist country ruled by a tiny handful of imperialists, began to oppose the Soviet Union directly as it did before the Second World War, and began to persecute any of its own citizens who could be associated with the Soviet Union and its anti-imperialist line or who admired its then progressive social system. Communists in the United States, until the total decline of the party in the late forties, had been outstanding fighters against black national oppression and racism, and their correct Leninist line as put forward by the Communist International in 1928, that black people in the United States, in the black-belt South, constituted a nation, an oppressed nation with the right of self-determination, which could only be liberated by revolution in unity with the whole multinational working class, was so progressive that it mobilized thousands of blacks during the thirties and forties with an intensity that frightened the United States bourgeoisie.

And in the 1950's, even though the CPUSA was moving rapidly toward becoming a completely revisionist organization, the United States bourgeoisie began their McCarthy witch-hunts and anticommunist crusade, trying to destroy completely any real communist militancy and program left in the United States. It was during this period that Robeson had his passport revoked by Harry "Give-'em-Hell" Truman. And the next time you see some advertisement or TV or movie telling what a great democrat "Give-'em-Hell" Harry was, you should raise the question of his foul attack on Robeson: keeping Paul Robeson, one of the greatest artists in the world, imprisoned in the great fortress of the free world and world democracy. Truman reacted to Robeson making the statement that "the Soviet Union has demonstrated how it is possible to wipe out colonialism and all the word connotes within a single generation. No wonder this imperialism cries stop Russia." This and other pro-Soviet statements during the McCarthy era, and before the Soviet Union's fall to revisionism and social imperialism, convinced the United States bourgeoisie that they had to shut him up. Asked by a Congressional committee why he did not go to Russia to stay if he loved it so much, Robeson replied: "Because my father was a slave, and my people died to build this country just like you. And no fascist minded people like you will drive me from it. Is that clear?" Robeson was questioned by senators, who if it were not for the national oppression of blacks in the black belt would not even be sitting in Congress, since any democracy would see a black or someone favorable to black people's needs sitting in the seats representing the black belt, the deepest concentration of blacks in the U.S.A. For thirty years, from World War I until after World War II, Robeson's extraordinary achievements kept him in the spotlight. But then the bourgeoisie saw that that spotlight was switched off, a smokescreen set up, a blackout and boycott. All doors to stage, screen, concert hall, radio, TV, and recording studio were locked to him, and by taking his passport they thought then they could totally deprive him of a living. He could not even leave the country to go to countries that do not require a passport for entry like Canada and the West Indies. He published a book that was reviewed by no major publication in the country. *The New York Times* did not even record its being published! It was not until 1958 that he received his passport back. He went abroad for a five-year world concert tour and returned in 1963 to retirement, making very few appearances due to his poor health up until his death.

Robeson had spoken out all of his life against black national oppression, racism, segregation, when lesser artists rolled their eyes, had their heads and behinds patted, and yes-sired their way to lackeydom. And for this he was exiled in his own land, sealed off from the masses, and slowly killed. Robeson was always a "partisan of scientific socialism" and a defender of communism, and this, in a era when the bourgeoisie did not even want to extend democratic rights to black people, was taken as a dangerous precedent the bourgeoisie could not allow! The fact that a black artist, of great talent and genius, who reached not only the black masses but the whole of the American people, would direct that talent and genius to fight against the exploitation and oppression of the people was dangerous, dangerous. And whenever this happens the response has been the same. When Miriam Makeba married Stokely Carmichael she still had records on the hit parade, "The Click Song" and "Pata Pata," but the bourgeoisie made her name quickly disappear. Even Nina Simone when she came out with her "Four Women" and "Young, Gifted, and Black" was whisked away into obscurity, and the Ojays and Eisely Brothers better watch out if they get too much more conscious. But what made Robeson so great is that he became completely conscious, a complete fighter, a developed revolutionary. And though he was never a significant figure within the communist party, still he brought socialist ideas, anti-imperialist ideas, to a broad range of people around the world.

Almost at the time of Robeson's retirement, Malcolm rose on the scene, a voice of the black working class, spokesman for the cultural- and religious-nationalist "Nation of Islam," but more than that Malcolm put forward the line and was himself a representative of revolutionary black nationalism. He said that black people were an oppressed nation with the right of "self-determination, self-respect, and self-defense." And throughout his public life Malcolm again and again put forward lines that demonstrated the anti-imperialist character of the Black Liberation Movement. Malcolm talked about revolution and said if you talked about revolution you talked about bloodshed—real revolution. He said that there was no such thing as a "nonviolent revolution." Malcolm condemned capitalism over and again, saying that if you found a capitalist you found a bloodsucker, a creature living off somebody else's blood. Malcolm talked about the liberation of the black nation, alliance with Third World peoples. He raised Africa in a revolutionary way, and went to the continent and met the African and Asian leaders and made us understand that black people's struggles were part of the international struggle against imperialism and its oppression of nations, particularly the Third World nations and peoples. Malcolm signified how the mass movement in the U.S.A among black people had changed from the civil-rights movement to the Black Liberation Movement! Malcolm criticized nonviolent struggle, saying that the black masses thought Dr. King should first get the white people to be nonviolent, then black people would take it up!

The significance of Malcolm's being fired from Muslim Temple Number Seven by Elijah Muhammad is that it showed the split in the movement between those who understood it would take a political solution to liberate black people, the revolutionary nationalists, and the wing which followed the cultural and religious nationalism associated with the Nation of Islam.

The CPUSA had turned revisionist and had degenerated so much that they now followed the comprador assimilationist wing of the black bourgeoisie e.g., Roy Wilkins and the NAACP, having liquidated the call for black self-determination, eliminated organizations like the militant Sharecroppers' Union in the South, and for a time the CPUSA itself, turning into the "Communist Political Association" under the "American Exceptionalist" line of revisionist Earl Browder.

Malcolm X's emergence signified that the Black Liberation Movement would still be led by the working class, by the black masses, and, despite the temporary control by the black bourgeoisie and petite bourgeoisie of the civil-rights movement and the disillusionment of the working class movement by the defection of the CPUSA to revisionism, that the working class would still put forward the still correct call for *liberation of the black nation, self-determination in the black belt!* And that the liberation of the black nation could only be brought about by revolution! And it is clear today that only by the black nation and oppressed nationality struggling and waging war against the bourgeoisie, ultimately uniting with the whole working class led by a revolutionary vanguard party, a Marxist-Leninist communist party guided by the science of Marxism–Leninism–Mao Tse Tung thought, can that revolution be carried through to the end.

Malcolm X was killed because he was still developing ideologically and politically. And his break with the Nation of Islam suggested a clear political development that was already anti-imperialist and whose further development the bourgeoisie did not dare to take chances on.

Both these leaders we must consistently remember and learn from, study their growth and development. Malcolm X was truly a revolutionary nationalist and reflecting the truth of his message the movement was transformed from nonviolence and civil rights to self-defense, black nationalism, black power, urban rebellions, the Panthers' introduction of Marxism and the *Red Book*, and a heightening of anti-imperialist struggle, as well as cultural nationalism and Pan-Africanism.

Out of the turbulent 1960's and the "neocolonialism" that developed by the 1970's with the Black Liberation Movement more and more animated by sharpening class struggles within and the sharpening of the class struggle between the oppressed black nation and United States imperialism and between the multinational working class and the United States bourgeoisie, more and more people in the Black Liberation Movement have grown aware that if there is to be black liberation in reality it can only be accomplished by a union of the Black Liberation Movement and its revolutionary struggle for self-determination with the struggle of the whole working class in the U.S.A. for socialist revolution. Not only the BLM but many of the other oppressed nationalities in the United States are also developing Marxist-Leninist organizations that grew to maturity struggling in the Chicano liberation movement or the Puerto Rican liberation movement or the Asian struggle for democratic rights. All these groups and others from the student and antiwar movements have also determined that monopoly capitalism is our enemy and revolution is our weapon to smash it. But we have also learned that socialist revolution can only be brought about by the science of revolution, by studying and understanding and practicing Marxism–Leninism–Mao Tse Tung thought, and uniting universal principles with the day-to-day struggle of the U.S. working class and oppressed nationalities!

Jazz: Speech at Black Film Festival (on the films *Jazz on a Summer's Day* and *The Cry of Jazz*)

Of these two films, one is very widely circulated, the first, and the latter is circulated hardly at all. The reason is because *Summer's Day* is more related to the uses the American ruling class wants to put the music to (a cheerful soporific), while *Cry* is trying to say some basic truths about the music and the society and the people who make it. Since America is a capitalist society and capitalists oppose truth because lies allow them to dupe people and continue to rule, *Cry* is of no use them.

Summer's Day looks at jazz as rootless entertainment—the flash of teeth, roll of eyes, and rumble of happy rhythms unconnected with the lives and histories of the people who create it. As the film maker said in an interview, "We wanted to make a happy jazz film, a film showing musicians and audiences enjoying the wonderful experience of jazz." Jazz for jazz' sake (really strictly for the entertainment of the largely white middle class) is as mindless as art for art's sake, a meaningless abstraction.

Jazz is an American music with distinct Afro-American origins. It is the offspring of the Afro-American parent form, blues, and other Afro-American musical forms, spirituals, hollers, shouts, gospel. Jazz is a more instrumentalized, harmonically richer extension and development of basic blues. Jazz, however, has absorbed many other elements, social and musical tendencies, many other people and forms. It is an international tongue now, but it still gains its fundamental strength by its reflection of what was essentially the life experience of the Afro-American people, the working masses of those people.

And the further jazz moves away from the stark blue reality of the blues continuum and the collective realities of Afro-American and American life, the more it moves into academic, concert-hall lifelessness, which can be replicated by any middle class showing off its music lessons.

Jazz on a Summer's Day is the basic USIA type film, great to show around the world to demonstrate the happy-go-lucky progress all of us am making. It actually creates a mood like Jimmy Carter's invitational propaganda session at the White House last week, which also showed us how well informed those White House researchers keep Carter, using our tax monies. He not only quoted one factual hypothesis stated in *Cry*, viz., that the music is a dialectical construct of freedom and restraint, but Carter also said that it might be that jazz has not been more recognized because of an element of racism! Heavy Shat! The overall reality, however, is that as the Baake decision is crushing affirmative action, Carter is bs'n the people by rubbin' up against some jazz musicians—see how happy and together and hip we are?

Cry states some of the socio-cultural and historical features of the music clearly and at a time when it definitely was not something people wanted to hear—the late fifties: that jazz was black art! That the music black and white musicians made is different (usually) based on the sociocultural background of the players. The harshness of black worker and peasant life—exploited as workers oppressed as a nationality, an oppressed nation—the harshness of such a life in capitalist, racist America contrasted with the relatively less harsh and jagged, the softer, cooler sounds of white musicians, because ideas as Mao Tse Tung said come from social life, how we live. Therefore our music is produced by our lives. *Cry* also speaks of white musicians imitating blacks, but this is only natural since the blacks were the creators and innovators of Afro-American music; it began there. Imitation is not negative *per se* but is how all cultures are enriched. By adopting aspects of other cultures, the collective international life of humanity is responsible for all human progress. Only racists believe truth comes from one nationality! Imitation takes on a negative implication because in capitalist America blacks are not only exploited workers but an oppressed nation in the black-belt South, and an oppressed nationality everywhere else in the U.S.A—a double yoke—so that black people never benefit by their energies and innovations in the main, because of this oppression, this racism, although

271

the innovators' contributions will be used readily once they are appropriated by white players. White rock groups don't even have to be able to play, just be well advertised, witness Kiss, etc. Like the Beatles saying they learned everything from some blood running an elevator in Philly or Memphis—well then, how come he running an elevator and you-all running around gettin' rich bein' him in whiteface?

It is the inequality of the system itself that creates the tension around black innovations and white co-optation (really, monopoly co-optation, as it is the recording companies who run the business, based on capitalist exploitation and racism).

Cry also predicts the rising tide of cultural nationalism that appeared in the 1960's, really taking off after Malcolm's murder and for a time almost overshadowing the revolutionary nationalism Malcolm was assassinated for articulating so clearly even though he at first came from a cultural and religious nationalist and black capitalist organization. His split signified the emerging differences between black revolutionary nationalism, which is to free the black nation, and bourgeois nationalism and cultural naturalism, which merely want to give the black bourgeoisie a chance to exploit its black market more fully.

Cry's line that black folks must teach whites how to be human sounds like the cultural nationalism of several years later, both emanating originally from the Nation of Islam. What is true is that the BLM and its battle cry, self-determination for the Afro-American nation in the black belt, and liberation for the black nation—self-determination and democratic rights, carried by the revolutionary black nation—will be responsible in part for turning this whole society upside down. But this transformation is more than likely to be the result of a full-scale socialist revolution in this country, and the BLM and the multinational workers' movement and the struggles of the other oppressed nationalities will have come together, first forming a revolutionary Marxist-Leninist party and then smashing capitalism, thereby setting the conditions for the eventual disappearance of both black national oppression, the oppression of women as well as the general exploitation of working people.

Plus jazz is not dead. Its body is the people; its spirit is theirs. It is alive and well and going through changes, as usual, growing and developing. At the time *Cry* was made what was happening is that one form of the music was giving way to another. After the revolution of Bebop, which restored the jazz fire from the commercial debilitation visited upon it by the monopolies who put out corny "Swing," there was another period of reaction called "Cool," which again tried to regulate and cool out the African rhythms and voice of jazz. But then Hard Bop—Rollins, Horace Silver, Monk, Messengers—the return of the hard sounds and funky rhythms, prepared the way for the new thing, Avant-garde, the Tranes, Ornette Colemans, Sun Ras (who was in *Cry*), the Cecil Taylors and Albert Aylers, and so many others to restore the life and beat to the music and take it to yet higher levels of expression which accurately reflect the contemporary socio-cultural and aesthetic matrix. Jazz is a people's music and it is alive as long as the black masses live. And some people these days are saying even the Black Liberation Movement is dead. But this is only the wishful thinking of the bourgeoisie. Where there is oppression, there is resistance. And this resistance will ultimately help transform this society from a capitalist and racist society. The movement of the sixties was largely spontaneous and without the scientific leadership of a revolutionary party. That is why today the central task of revolutionaries is to build such a party to make revolution. Meanwhile the music keeps evolving and when the sixties Avant-garde reached stagnation, the blues came to its rescue, from the Ojays to Isley Brothers to Marvin Gaye to Earth, Wind, and Fire. And then the new voices of David Murray, Steve McCall, World Saxophone Quartet, Art Esembles, Lester Bowie, etc., arrived to carry the music to new levels.

But, as usual, there are commercial diversions. Disco takes the blues impulse and turns it into dope. As Max Roach said, somebody is trying to "choreograph our ideology." Fusion is a ripoff of the concept of *unity music*, a combining openly of all the strains and strands of Afro-American music, blues and jazz and Caribbean, to make something newer and stronger; instead we get the "cool" corporate white-out of the fifties over a "funk" memory. But the actual new music will use all the elements of Afro-American music and anything else it needs to, to create an expression which is blues, black, American, and international—an expression of a people ready for revolution!

The "Me" Generation: What It Is?*

A few people have come up with the term the "Me" Generation for the present wave of youth, focusing I suppose on student types. But also on the general tone of young folks today, especially in contrast to the young people of the 1960's. The Me Generation would probably be described as at least self-absorbed, more interested in doing their ("my") thing, as opposed to everybody else's thing. They are disco soaked and *shake their booties* at the drop of a d.j. It is said that they are less casual, more dressed up (sometimes all the way up to bizarre, if we check out the punk rockers), and the thing that they are most serious about is *making it,* some way, some sweet day. They are the post-Watergate cynical naïfs, who apparently back away from the promise of America by merely settling for it.

Some of these generalizations are true, or seem true. But what we ought to check out as well are the causes, the reasons for this cooled-out, booty-wiggling generation (excuse me, the term is *laid back*). By obvious contrast we raise up the youth of the sixties or at least the dominant *image* of what they were—rebellious and militant. Whether we mention black youth spearheaded by organizations like SNCC (Student Nonviolent Coordinating Committee) or SOBU (Students for Black Unity), which came after it, on the campuses, or the Black Panther Party or "US" organization or Congress of African People, which were all filled with college-age, noncollege, and some

---

*Address at George Washington University, 1978.

college students in the street, the image for black youth was militant, rebellious, even revolutionary. And on white campuses the SDS moved with the same kind of identification, erupting at Berkeley and Columbia and hundreds of other campuses—bringing the Vietnam War home, clawing at the jugular of bourgeois America with the "Days of Rage" in Chicago, helping actually to drive Lyndon Johnson into the mass-murders' retirement home. But not only black and white, all the movements of the oppressed nationalities had the same image, based on real struggle. The young Chicanos identified with groups like the Brown Berets and La Raza Unida. The Puerto Rican youth with the Young Lords. There were militant Asian and Indian organizations, like I Wor Kuen and AIM.

But the entire workers' and oppressed peoples' movement without real revolutionary guidance remains, as Lenin pointed out in *What Is to Be Done,* spontaneous. It rises and falls in waves. The sixties was a perfect example of this process. The so-called revolutionary party, the Communist Party USA, by 1957, had completely succumbed to reformism, officially becoming *revisionist,* saying that socialism did not have to come through revolution, but could be brought via the ballot. As if Rocky's mob would give up the ownership and control of the means of production and the collective social wealth generated therefrom simply because the people *need* to control it, and we could do this by merely voting the rascals out!— bourgeois mythology.

Without a genuine revolutionary Marxist-Leninist communist party, the entire movement remained spontaneous and gradually flattened out. This was aided by continuous attacks from the bourgeois state (police, courts, FBI, etc.), which murdered, jailed, harassed, and bought out or sent into exile as many of the leaders as they could. Reflect on this, between 1963 and 1968 in the "Land of the Free, etc.," John Kennedy, Malcolm X, Robert Kennedy, and Martin Luther King were murdered, by that same state!

From the fevered peak in the late sixties when there were rebellions in hundreds of cities across the country, and sit-ins, take-overs, struggles of one kind or another on hundreds of campuses in this country, by the mid-seventies the movement had subsided.

It is interesting also that many of the youth-oriented organizations had become Marxist-Leninist. For instance the SDS split into many parts: Weather Underground, October League (now Communist Party [Marxist-Leninist]), Revolutionary Union (now the so-called Revolutionary Communist Party) and some others. The Young Lords became the Puerto Rican Revolutionary Workers Organization. The SOBU, which became YOBU, now become part of the Revolutionary Workers League. Some of the Brown Berets became part of the August Twenty-ninth Movement (Marxist-Leninist). IWK remains IWK but is now a Marxist-Leninist organization. The Congress of African People became the Revolutionary Communist League (Marxist–Leninist–Mao Tse Tung thought). And all these organizations today are struggling, with much obstructive sectarianism and state-added confusion, to create a real communist party, but they have not yet discovered how to harness the massive forces unleashed in the sixties, though they will.

By the late 1970's, when the movement had reached a valley as opposed to its 1960's peaks, several things began to be evident. First, the bourgeoisie inundated us with propaganda that the sixties were dead and all the uncoolness was gone forever. They said, "But things are so much better now, we don't need that unpleasantness. We can all settle down and be reasonable," after they had assassinated our leaders and destroyed our organizations. The few gains that were made in the sixties the bourgeoisie pointed to and said, "Look how well you're doing, look how we're integrating, look how equitably we're distributing the wealth, look at the proportional representation you're getting" (pointing at a few antipoverty programs and black mayors, a couple of affirmative-action programs, and the end of South Africa–type segregation in the U.S.A.).

And so a generation emerged postrebellions, post–street fighting and marching and sitting in and taking over and raging, and they were the beneficiaries of what few actual gains had been made. The Me Generation has emerged in relatively calm surroundings, though for certain the movement is not dead but is steadily rebuilding. The Me Generation was brought up without the same struggle and so their ideas reflect this and their goals. Like the Princeton student whose parents tell him, when we were young they did not let Jews and blacks in Princeton; that was a real struggle. Now, the only struggle this student has is to stay awake in class.

Ironically, at the same time the bourgeoisie was saying that the old struggle times were gone forever, because things were so much better that the millennium had been reached, they began to try to take back all of the gains of the sixties. While misguiding people that the ERA would end women's oppression (yet opposing it), they systematically took back all the gains women made in the sixties. While trumpeting about the gains in equal rights in the United States, they crushed affirmative action with the Baake Decision. While they fed us the "okeydoke" about the Freedom of Information Act and "tsk-tsked" about bad ol' Homo Hoover and bad ol' CIA who caused everybody so much trouble, they tried to pass the neo-fascist S-1 bill, and failing that have already got its replica S-1432 through the senate under the "liberal" mumbling of Ted Kennedy.

And at the same time, in the media, they pushed nostalgia, metaphysics, pornography, love your heroic police, but decadence *über Alles! Burn, Baby, Burn* was transmuted from the heroic cry of the Watts Rebellion to a Disco Inferno. Martha and the Vandellas' "Dancin' in the Street" was changed to "Shake Your Booty." The Impressions' "Keep on Pushin," the Temptations' "You Can't Stop Me Now," James Brown's "Black and Proud," Marvin Gaye's "What's Goin' On," were switched off and Backward Bootsie and the Mindless Funkadelics are hoisted into view. And simply compare Dylan's sixties songs or the Stones with Kiss or the freaked-out caricature of the working class done by the likes of the Dead Boys or Sid Vicious—punk rock for sho! The climate of compromise, copout, laidbackness (read, coolout), has been actively encouraged by the bourgeoisie. Television consists mainly of the-police-are-our-heroes shows—*Baretta, Starsky and Hutch, Kojak, Barney Miller, Police Woman, Police Story*. In films, a cocaine-snorting pimp (Superfly) replaces and intimidates the militant. Blacula passes for equal opportunity or the Werewolf from Watts. Robert Redford gives us cynical establishment heroes, and the symbol of rebellion is the Mafia (vide *The Godfather*)! And now we are allowd to hear dirty words in films, so that this passes for the truth—wow, they said *shit;* they must be telling us the whole truth. But nothing could be further from the truth.

The Me Generation is a product of a demilitanizing program being mashed on all of us by the rulers of this capitalist society. They try to drench us in their philosophy and worldview, so that we will want to support the status quo. They have even stopped working-class youth from getting into college, as in the sixties, building inner-city community colleges which only go two years. The workers' children caused too much trouble in the sixties, being at the heart of the sit-ins and campus takeovers!

As the bourgeoisie sees college students, their role is to become part of the loyalist petit bourgeois supporters of capitalism, racism, and women's oppression. But students must make a choice; there is no doubt they are part of the middle class, which vacillates because of its economic position between loyalty to the rulers and commitment to the people. But they *can* choose to serve the people rather than the rulers, to be part of the struggle to transform society, rather than part of what is being struggled against.

Most of the youth of the so-called Me Generation are, of course, not college students, and never will be. Despite this, they too are being all but drowned in the negative "Me-Me" philosophy the bourgeoisie floods us with. Ultimately reality will give the lie to those lies, and working-class youth will be forced to fight merely to survive.

The U.S.A. is a declining world power locked in a death struggle with the equally imperialist Soviet Union to see who will control the world. The U.S.A. has it; the U.S.S.R. wants it. This will lead to World War III. But revolution is the main trend in the world today. Mao said: "Countries want independence, nations want liberation, people want revolution." The Me Generation must make a choice; they must come to understand that all these me's make a big we, and that it is we who must struggle not only to understand the world, to paraphrase Karl Marx, but to change it!

A Reply to
Saunders Redding's
"The Black Revolution
in American Studies"

Saunders Redding's writing has, in the main, consistently upheld views that this author feels are not only "conservative," but are basically supportive of the oppression of the Afro-American nation and white chauvinism in general. Though, to be sure, Redding, like everyone else, is not perfect, and sometimes contradictory fragments ease through which speak of confusion more than consolidated white chauvinism (or great-nation chauvinism). The fact that Redding is black means this white chauvinism is even more effective within the circles in which Redding is adept at spreading it.

His article "The Black Revolution in American Studies" is classic in this sense. It begins, predictably enough, like the subtle "nigger calling" of one of the Southern Agrarians, babbling: "The concept 'Black Studies' conceived in frustration and bitterness by an articulate and highly emotional minority, is of questionable validity as a scholarly discipline." This little sentence is the core dictum of the racism and national oppression that grew out of the European slave trade: that the Afro-American people do not exist as a people at all, but in some servile nonperson relationship to their white masters. The first understanding we must come to to oppose this imperialist philosophy is that the Afro-American people in the United States not only exist but are an *oppressed nation*. They have a history, culture, literature, music, art, related to but at the same time distinct from these categories of Anglo-America, though without focus on these Afro-American life dimensions, no real description of the United States as an actual entity can be offered.

Redding says of Black Studies that "it encompasses too much," that it seeks to go back to "pre-Islamic times" (not very far back really, the seventh century, only the eleventh century if one is talking about the beginning of deep penetration into sub-Saharan [Black] Africa). But could one take up American Studies without studying the people who came to be Americans, their history and development? Why would anyone want to? The Afro-American people are connected to Africa, as the Euro-American people are connected to Europe. To understand the present we have to look at history; obviously Redding knows this when it comes to any other people. The detail of this concerning Afro-American people is white chauvinism.

Redding also resents that Black Studies is "action oriented," and therefore "anti-intellectual." It *is* action oriented since its appearance in the curricula of American universities came as a result of recent struggle, part of the struggle of the Black Liberation Movement. The inclusion of Black Studies on these campuses is only as a result of the attacks Afro-Americans made on the capitalist and racist America system in the 1960's. (And already the bourgeoisie is trying to cut away even these few gains, e.g., the Baake Decision.)

Redding has the classic bourgeois world view, that intellectual activity must be the antithesis of action, but as Marx said, any professor can understand the world, the struggle is to change it! Black Studies, at its most lucid, seeks to expand the very nature of intellectual activity, by including a whole area of human life and endeavor, artificially excluded by slavery and racism. It *is* anti-intellectual to say Black Studies is of "questionable validity"—why less valid that English or Germanic Studies, etc.?—except to justify the superexploitation and oppression of a whole nation of people (who do not exist for the white-racist American bourgeoisie, except as laboring automatons).

Redding reacts negatively to the bourgeois nationalist "mystique" called Negritude, and so do I. But we have to make a distinction between resistance to imperialism and colonialism, which black people all over the world have done and still have to do, and the cultural nationalism of one segment of the black petite bourgeoisie that "pimps" its existence off the legitimate revolutionary struggle of the black masses! The Negritude of a Senghor is laughable, until we remember the people of Senegal reeling under Senghor's neo-colonialism. We see then that this Negritude does not serve the majority of Senegalese. They are still exploited and oppressed, and revolution must still be made even against this wizard of Negritude who is also a wizard of continuing the (indirect) rule of imperialism.

But Redding is so steeped in a defensive antiblack consciousness in trying to be "a scholar," not a black scholar, "a critic," not a black critic, and, one would suppose, "a man," not a black man (all of which are impossible in a racist society), that he has long ago succumbed to the succubus of *compradorism*. Compradorism among the black petit bourgeois intellectuals takes form by denying the particular historical and cultural experience of the Afro-American nation and "integrating" them into America, a process which has never taken place in reality. And this, objectively, is in the service of United States imperialism, which has always reduced us to zero. The separateness of black life in America was the one constant that served to show off and develop black life in relief, though it could always be defined by the official ruling-class definers as not existing at all.

Redding confuses *black nationalism*, which has legitimate reasons for existing (though only its revolutionary form, which is resistance to national oppression, should be upheld), with the fact of the existence of the Afro-American people and their lives in a way different from that of the slavemasters or whites or others in general, though there are similarities between all working-class people and oppressed nationalities as far as the conditions under which they are forced to live.

Redding also sees racism as merely a *moral lapse*, rather than as a tool of capitalism to superexploit one group of people even more so than the "average" worker in the U.S.A. He seems not to understand that racism is a description of one aspect of the social relations under capitalism, and that unless the economic base of this sick oppressive ideology is destroyed, it will continue. Redding's line reminds one of the official line of the NAACP national leadership who, because their salaries are paid by the absolutely questionable "largesse" of the corporations, think that the U.S.A. can be "integrated." But this denies the real nature of this society which is *based on* the systematic super exploitation and exclusion of the Afro-American people from slavery forward. Racism is not a lamentable moral lapse or simply, as Redding has it, "the ignorance of whites"; it is the basic social organization of this society.

But Redding's confusion is obvious as well. Although he has a basic comprador-like view, he does mention some scattered works by blacks that "document the development and the operation of race prejudice," as if this could partially legitimatize or "make respectable" the demand for Black Studies. Redding also mentions the exclusion of Afro-Americans from American history and says, "The tradition of studying Negro history and literature is more than a half century old." This sounds like the racist history we were brought up on which would say things like "the first Negro architect," as if blacks throughout the world knew nothing about architecture before white racists allowed one to get a U.S. architect's license (the Great Pyramid notwithstanding). Redding treats racism as if *it* were legitimate, as if it really is a case of a backward people being allowed to come forward to see the light of civilization rather than the bloody saga of black resistance to the slave trade, slavery, and national oppression. He also uses DuBois questionably by quoting an early statement of DuBois that the solution to the "Negro problem was a matter of systematic investigation." DuBois meant, then, that racism could be solved by shedding light on misconceptions and "white ignorance." But DuBois, certainly by the time of *Black Reconstruction* (1935) or even *The Negro* (1915), saw the international nature of imperialism and capitalism as the material base of racism. Redding ignores these later perceptions of DuBois, since, I would imagine, DuBois's evolution from petit bourgeois scholar, to apologist for black capitalism, through Pan-Africanism, until he arrived at his Marxist position, distresses Redding, so he chooses to ignore it.

Redding also does not clearly understand the role of the black students in the struggle for Black Studies. He charges them, and certain writers, with emotionally blurring "the content that Black Studies must have if it is to attain respectability as a scholarly discipline." But if it were not for the black students fighting on the campuses for Black Studies, in reflection of what the black masses were doing in the streets of America, there would be no black Studies in the first place! The inclusion of Black Studies on these campuses came only as a result of student struggles, and if some of the rhetoric which accompanied these struggles was overblown, even metaphysical and idealistic, the revolutionary core of those struggles was correct. Black Studies would not yet be on these campuses, nor will it remain, if it had to depend solely on the efforts of Redding-type intellectuals and their pleas for "moral uplift" among the bourgeoisie. Black Studies came only as a result of struggle and confrontation, as usual.

Redding wants Afro-American Studies to "attain that respectability" and indeed this is probably his cry concerning everything in black life. But it is racism that makes black life *not respectable*, the social organization and ideology of capitalism! Redding thinks that if he says, "Hey, some of this black stuff is actually well done and scholarly," that the powers that be will say, "Oh, yes, now that you mention it there are some real scholars here . . . black studies is hereby respectable!" But this is simply house-servant fantasy, which serves as neat propaganda for a corrupt and unworkable system which cannot be fundamentally changed except through revolutionary means.

Redding's final shot that "Afro-American Studies is basically American Studies" is the burden of the thinking that lurks throughout his entire essay. Of course Afro-American Studies can be seen as part of American Studies, but as Bruce Franklin has pointed out (*The Victim as Artist and Criminal*), American literature, for instance, as taught in these universities ought really be called Anglo-American or White American literature, or actually White Man American literature. It is no more than a reflection of the racist society itself. (And we need more, and more independent, Afro-American Studies Programs, not "inclusion" in American Studies, which would simply justify the removal of Afro-American Studies, its weakening through some fake "integration.") Also, American Studies itself is having no picnic breaking through the barrier of English Department colonialism that still does not understand that "George Washington and them" won that war that started in 1776. But this approach of Redding's eliminates the national character of the Afro-American people, the fact that there is an Afro-American nation in the U.S.A with a history and culture of its own. In a revolutionary country this national development would be supported, documented, and given the presence it needs to reflect upon and improve itself. This national character would be encouraged and given a certain amount of autonomy (certainly regional political autonomy in those areas where that nationality was concentrated, e.g., in the United States, the black South, the homeland of the Afro-American nation). And this approach would finally encourage the Afro-American people to make a voluntary union with the overall multinational American state, but such a union, such "integration," can only be based on the control of the American economy and state by the people, and the control of the black nation by the black masses. But in the United States today, the world center of capitalism and racism, the cry must continue to go up of *self-determination for the Afro-American nation in the black-belt South/liberation for the black nation!!*

Redding sees the inclusion of black materials in American Studies programs as "the educational revolution that must take place in American Studies" and that "the adversaries of the revolution . . . will scarcely prevail," still talking about the integration of America under imperialism. Sure, American Studies will be revolutionized by the progress of the American revolution itself, but Afro-American Studies will also continue to develop as a summation of the lives of the Afro-American people on the one hand, and one catalyst for further struggle to transform those lives on the other. And in the best of those programs of Afro-American Studies will be seen the clear and irreducible motion of the black masses for self-determination and democratic rights.

Bibliography to
A Reply to Saunders Reddings' . . .

General and Key

Chan, Shih. *A Brief History of the United States*, Peking, Foreign Languages Press, 1976. Objective political-economic overview of U.S. history, so *real* development of U.S. and Afro-Americans can begin to be understood.

DuBois, W.E.B. *Black Reconstruction* . . . , New York, Harcourt Brace, 1935 (reprinted New York, Meridian, 1969). Indispensable to understanding the development of Afro-Americans in this country.

DuBois, W.E.B. *The Negro*, New York, H. Holt, 1915. No real understanding of black studies can be had without a correct historical overview of the Afro-American nationality.

Franklin, Bruce. *The Victim as Artist and Criminal*, New York, Oxford, 1978. Establishes the essentially racist character of academic views of "American literature" and culture and their relationship to academic views of "black studies."

Haywood, Harry. *Black Bolshevik*, Chicago, Liberator Press, 1978. Lays out the scientific and historical emergence of the view that there is an Afro-American nation inside the U.S.

Haywood, Harry. *For a Revolutionary Position on the Negro Question*, Chicago, Liberator Press, 1975. Same as above.

Lenin, V.I. *Sociology and Statistics, Collected Works*, Moscow, Progress Pub. Scientific basis for Afro-American nation thesis.

Marx, K., and F. Engels. *The Civil War in the U. S.*, New York, International Pub., 1961. In-depth analysis of Civil War and effect on blacks and U.S. future.

McAdoo, B. *Pre–Civil War Black Nationalism*, reprinted Newark, N.J., People's War (Box 663), 1977. An analysis of basic ideological tendencies within Afro-American nation historically.

RCL, Afro-American Comm. *The Black Nation*, Newark, N.J., People's War, 1977. Treatise on history of Afro-American people.

Stalin, J.V. *Foundations of Leninism*, Peking, Foreign Languages Press, 1975. (See especially "The National Question.") Includes basic scientific analysis of "National Question."

Stalin, J.V. *Marxism and the National-Colonial Question*, San Francisco, Proletarian Pub., 1975. A classic work on the rise of nations and national oppression.

Representative Afro-American Literature (Chronological Order)

The works included in this are all part of what I feel constitute the "Revolutionary Tradition in Afro-American Literature" (this in contrast to the "liberal" or conservative or assimilationist or capitulationist trend, which also exists, obviously, in Afro-American literature as well).

Douglass, Frederick. *Narrative of the Life of Frederick Douglass, The Life and Writings of Frederick Douglass*, ed. Philip Foner, New York, International Pub., 1950–55.

Garnet, Henry Highland. *An Address to the Slaves*, 1843.

Turner, Nat. *The Confessions of Nat Turner*, New York, Hamilton, 1861.

Walker, David. *Appeal . . .*, Boston, Walker, 1892.

Douglass and the slave narratives are the real beginnings of an Afro-American literature as a *genre*. Turner, Walker, Garnet, all are part of the pre–Civil War revolutionary nationalist tradition, which runs parallel to and extends beyond the slave narratives.

Brown, William Welles. *Clotel*, 1853 (reprinted New York, Arno, 1961).

The beginnings of Afro-American belles lettres tradition, as the genuine ideological reflection of the black masses (as are the works cited above).

DuBois, W.E.B. *The Souls of Black Folk*, Chicago, A. C. McClurg, 1903 (reprinted New York, Fawcett, 1961).

DuBois, W.E.B. *Darkwater,* Washington, D.C., Austin Jenkins, 1920.

DuBois is the indispensable historian and man of letters who forms the link between the 19th century and the Harlem Renaissance.

Hughes, Langston. "The Artist and the Racial Mountain," *The Nation,* Vol. 122, No. 31, June 1926.
Hughes, Langston. *Scottsboro Ltd,* New York, Golden Stair, 1932.
Hughes, Langston. *The Big Sea,* New York, Knopf, 1940.
Hughes, Langston. *Selected Poetry,* New York, Knopf, 1959.
Hughes, Langston. *Good Morning, Revolution,* ed. Faith Berry, New York, Hill, 1973.

Hughes, as part of the urban revolutionary nationalist intelligentsia that formed in the early part of the 20th century, is one of the most influential of all Afro-American writers.

McKay, Claude. *Home to Harlem,* New York and London, Harper, 1928.
McKay, Claude. *Selected Poems,* New York, Bookman Associates, 1953.

Obviously, there are many other fine writers out of the Harlem Renaissance but Hughes and McKay, to this author, are the most important.

Wright, Richard. *Uncle Tom's Children,* New York, Harper, 1938.
Wright, Richard. *Black Boy,* Cleveland, World Pub., 1945.
Wright, Richard. *American Hunger* (originally part of *Black Boy,* suppressed by publishers), New York, Harper and Row, 1977.
Wright, Richard. "Blueprint for Negro Literature," *Richard Wright Reader.*

Richard Wright was the voice of the 30's and remains one of the most important fiction writers in Afro-American literature.

Ward, Theodore. *Big White Fog, Black Theater U.S.A.,* ed. J.V. Hatch and T. Shine, New York, Free Press, 1974.

Ward is a giant of a dramatist, hidden and obscured by racist America. His *Big White Fog* remains the most striking ideological portrait of an Afro-American family.

Walker, Margaret. *For My People,* New Haven, Conn., Yale, 1942.
Walker, Margaret. *Jubilee,* Boston, Houghton Mifflin, 1966.

Margaret Walker has written the classic Afro-American poem, *For My People,* and her poetry makes exemplary uses of the oral and folk tradition of Afro-American life.

Baldwin, James. *The Fire Next Time*, New York, Dial, 1963.
Baldwin, James. *Blues for Mr. Charlie*, New York, Dial, 1964.

Baldwin's works often fit into the tradition I have outlined and *Blues for Mr. Charlie* was truly an important and prophetic work.

Jones, LeRoi. *Blues People*, New York, Morrow, 1962.
Jones, LeRoi. *Dutchman*, New York, Morrow, 1964.
Baraka, Amiri. *The Motion of History*, New York, Morrow, 1978.

Jones/Baraka's best works represent an attempt to continue the revolutionary tradition.

Malcolm X (with Alex Haley). *The Autobiography of Malcolm X*, New York, Doubleday, 1964.

Malcolm X's autobiography, like the slave narratives or *Black Boy* or even *Black Bolshevik*, is a classic Afro-American autobiography, and crucial for understanding the present period.

Anthologies and Collections

Locke, Alain. *The New Negro*, 1925 (reprinted New York, Atheneum, 1968).
Brown, Sterling. *Negro Caravan*, 1941 (reprinted New York, Arno, 1969).
Bontemps, Arna, and Langston Hughes. *Negro Poetry*, New York, Doubleday, 1949.
Baraka, Amiri, and Larry Neal. *Black Fire*, New York, Morrow, 1969.
Miller, Ruth. *Black American Literature*, Beverly Hills, Calif., Glencoe/Macmillan, 1971.
Barksdale, R. & K. Kinnamon. *Black Writers of America*, New York, Macmillan, 1972.
Hatch, J.V. and T. Shine. *Black Theater U.S.A.*, New York, Free Press, 1974.

Locke's *New Negro* opens the door to the Harlem Renaissance. Brown chronicled further development. Bontemps/Hughes's work is a general survey of Afro-American poetry. Baraka/Neal's work presents the 60's Black Arts Movement. Both the Barksdale/Kinnamon and Miller works are useful anthologies in studying Afro-American literature. But the Miller work is just adequate; the Barksdale/Kinnamon book is *outstanding*. The Hatch/Shine anthology is the classic anthology of Afro-American drama, a really well-done work, with a critical introduction to each play.

Black Solidarity*

The essence of black solidarity is black unity. And black unity is the key to what we used to call black power. Nothing wrong with that term, or that direction: black power. But at the same time we must understand that when we talk about black unity, we must be talking about a unity based on struggle. Open and above-board political struggle among ourselves to reach a closer, higher, more militant form of unity, and also struggle against our common enemies. Unless black unity is based on struggle, and revolutionary principles, then it cannot really unite the majority of the Afro-American people because it will not serve their needs.

Two things that always make revolutionary black unity difficult to attain are, first, the state, i.e., the police, CIA, FBI, red squads, plus National Guard, courts, prisons, government bureaucracy. The state is the instrument the white racist bourgeoisie who run this country use to maintain their power. They comprise six-tenths of one percent of this population yet they own the means of producing wealth, the land, factories, mineral wealth, machines, transportation, communication. For the Du Ponts, Mellons, Rockefellers, Morgans, and the like, the state is their tool to suppress us. Lenin said, the state is an instrument used by one class to suppress other classes. So that in our organizations the bourgeoisie will always try to slip some representatives of the state mechanism, spies, informers,

*Address at Rutgers University, in 1979.

288

provocateurs, to make such revolutionary black unity as we are talking about very difficult. That is their job.

Second, if these organized attempts at black unity really represent the whole spectrum of the black nation, then all the classes in the nation will be represented, and each of these classes will be struggling for its own interests, which is natural, and the ensuing class struggle will also make such all-class unity more difficult. But such struggle is absolutely necessary if we are to base our unity on revolutionary principles.

In the Afro-American nation we have all the classes found in a modern nation. The working class is the overwhelming majority in the black nation. They form some ninety-five to ninety-six percent of the Afro-American people. Machine and equipment operators, workers on assembly lines, construction workers, truck drivers, coal miners, steel workers, service workers, and on and on. This is the black majority. And any black unity that is truly revolutionary must be based on the needs of this black majority. It is important that we understand this.

In the Afro-American nation and among the black oppressed nationality there is also a small class of the petite bourgeoisie, the middle class, the doctors, lawyers, teachers, preachers, social workers, office workers, who comprise no more than four percent of the black nation. They must be involved in our attempts at black solidarity as well, but obviously this minority cannot lead such a front. Such a black unity must be led by the black majority, by the working class, because not only are they the majority, but also they are the most militant and ultimately the most revolutionary. The rebellions of the 1960's were spearheaded by black workers. Young black workers who knew that, as Rap Brown said, America wouldn't come around, so it had to be burnt to the ground!

The bourgeoisie tried to imply, even some petit bourgeois Negroes, that those rebellions were merely examples of the Lumpen, another class that exists in the black nation. They tried to say the rebellions were just the Lumpen acting wild. The Lumpen are the tiny class of pimps, prostitutes, dope addicts, muggers, who have already been broken by capitalism, which is what their name means, and who live as parasites on the working people. This is a dangerous class, the Lumpen, although the Panthers mistakenly, under the traiterous misleadership of Eldridge Cleaver, sought to romanticize the Lumpen as the "brothers and sisters on the block."

When if we were doing any real study of revolution we would know that most black folks are not on the block, they are at work! And if we want to make revolution, those are the people we must involve. There is also a small class of small farmers who are part of the class structure of the black nation. Once this class of peasants was the largest class in the black nation, but that was transformed by the mass black migrations out of the South at the beginning of the twentieth century, right up into the 1940's.

And when we talk about the black nation, the Afro-American nation, we mean the nation formed in the last part of the nineteenth century, whose land base is the black-belt South, the lower South, where the majority of black people in this country have lived for centuries, where blacks form a historically constituted stable community of people, with common language, territory, economic life— meaning that all the classes found in a modern nation exist—and also a common psychological development manifest as a common culture. This is the land we have fertilized with the blood of our slavery and national oppression; the land where at this moment the majority of us, some fifty-two percent of us, still live, and where eight out of ten of us were born. This is the land base of the Afro-American nation, a nation oppressed by United States imperialism in much the same way that the countries and nations and peoples of the Third World, Africa, Asia, and Latin America, are exploited and oppressed. This is a land whose liberation is to be made by revolution, just as those other nations and peoples in the Third World are making revolution to liberate their lands.

Throughout the rest of the United States we exist in significant numbers in about twenty-six cities, and in those places we are an oppressed nationality, a national minority tied to an oppressed nation, oppressed because that whole nation is oppressed. And because we are a different race from the white racist rulers of this society, we also suffer from racism, which makes the black national oppression even more hellish and thorough. So that wherever black people are they are doubly oppressed, not only as workers under monopoly capitalism, exploited to make surplus value for the capitalists, but also as an oppressed nation—double trouble. And black working women, like all Third World women in this society, are triply oppressed, by class, nationality, and sex.

When we speak of black power, we mean the self-determination of the Afro-American nation in the black-belt South. Our slogan, "liberation for the black nation," is the essence of black power. Because it is only political control over the south by the black masses that is the *guarantee* of equality. There is no such thing as equality without power. To talk such is to talk nonsense. The bottom line is that the black masses must determine what their political relationship will be to say America, even the socialist America we will build after the revolutionary destruction of monopoly capitalism in this country.

In the ghetto reflections of the black-belt South we live in outside of the actual land base of the black nation, political control of those areas is simply the people's democratic right, since they are the majority in those places as well. But these democratic rights can only be based on the liberation of the Afro-American nation in the black belt, because that alone is the guarantee of political power!

So that first and foremost our black solidarity ought to be based on a unity that demands self-determination for the Afro-American nation in the black-belt South, and democratic rights, equal rights for black people wherever else in the country they are. But we know that such demands as these, even though they are just, democratic demands, cannot be achieved without struggle. Malcolm X told us that; Frederick Douglass told us that; Nat Turner, Denmark Vesey, John Brown, showed us that. Our black solidarity must be based on the struggle completely to transform this society and that means revolution. Make no mistake. To change this society meaningfully, it means revolution, socialist revolution.

At this time we cannot all unite around socialist revolution, but we must unite around struggle. We surely must unite against police brutality, unemployment and layoffs, racism in public institutions such as Rutgers University. We can certainly unite to oppose the tenth-rate education our children are getting in the ignorance factories they try to tell us are public schools. And now here in Newark, the foolish-ass puppet who manages this town for Prudential tells us that they are thinking about closing those schools early and laying off all kinds of city workers because they do not have any money. We must unite against such garbage, and break the backs of those who support it. We must be able to unite in support of our democratic rights and against such outrages as the Baake Decision, the S-1 neofascist bill now called S-1432, which continues the bourgeoisie's determined strides to the right. We can unite to free political prisoners like our sister Assata Shakur, who is being kept locked up in an all-male prison under constant torture, while the bourgeoisie cries, "Free Patty Hearst." We must unite to support the strike strugglers of the multinational working class, whether it's the coal miners, the railroad workers, the postal workers. Strike struggles are a continually rising form of resistance to monopoly capitalism. And certainly you students must unite to support these workers' struggles because your turn will come to demonstrate, especially to fight against the school layoffs which will come, where they will tell you there is no more money to have niggers and Puerto Ricans in college! And then you will need support, you will need not only black unity but multinational unity.

But in the rising strike struggles don't make the mistake of thinking the police are workers and so their strikes need to be supported. The police, as I pointed out, are the *hitmen* for the bourgeoisie. I wish all they asses would get laid off, and if they want to tear up some more police cars, right on! Blow up police headquarters if they want to, right on! But they are part of the capitalist state, the enemy of working people and oppressed people. Now they gonna come on like workers, but when you strike, or when you demonstrate, watch who comes to suppress you, beat your head, and cart you off to jail. And their pay raises help suppress us, make them more efficient at killing us. The police are not workers, but hired killers for the bourgeoisie!

Our unity must be based on the needs of the black masses because otherwise we will halfstep or settle for partial reforms. Just as in the civil-rights movement, which was led by the black bourgeoisie and petite bourgeoisie, they could settle for access to public facilities (which allows those of us who can afford it to go to high priced white hotels, or if we got $60,000 we can buy a home somewhere where we could not before). Voting rights means that some of the illegally elected white politicians representing black majorities could be put out and the black middle class could replace them. And even if this does represent some positive motion and some progress, obviously equal access and voting rights alone cannot solve the problems of the black majority. The consistent fight for the democratic rights of the black majority is a revolutionary struggle, and ultimately will lead to revolution. That is why Malcolm X, when he appeared as spokesman for the black masses, talking not "turn the other cheek," or "we shall overcome" someday, probably after we die, but self-determination, self-respect, and self-defense—that is why he was so dangerous to the bourgeoisie, and that is why he had to be killed when he was, because he was the spokesman for the black working masses, and he told us that revolution was bloody, revolution was violent, revolution was about land!

There are sections of the middle class and even others who think that our problems can be solved through the courts or by the ballot. This is not true. The so-called laws of this country are simply the legitimatization of monopoly capitalism in legal language; the courts are part of the state mechanism. We can use the courts only as a tactic, and we should use them as a tactic, but that is all. Electoral politics must be seen in the same way, as a tactic, but a tactic that must serve our real goal, revolution. We should support politicians who actually represent the black masses, who use the elected office as a vantage point to tell people how corrupt and unworkable this system is, as a place to make propaganda for the struggle for democratic rights and for revolution. And such a tactic is best utilized under the leadership of an M-L party. But no ultimate change can come through the ballot. I don't care that Angela Davis and the reformist CPUSA say that socialism will come peacefully, via the ballot, and that Prudential (part of the Prudential–Manufacturers Hanover financial group), for instance, which owns New Jersey through its control and profits over Manufacturers Hanover Trust, First National State Bank of New Jersey, Fidelity Union Trust, First Jersey National Bank, Mutual Benefit, Continental, Howard Savings, Public Service Gas and Electric, F. W. Woolworth, National Airlines, Sperry Rand, Scott Paper, Warner-Lambert, Raytheon, United Fruit, Gillette, TWA, Cities Services, Campbell Soup, Philip Morris, Bristol-Myers, GE, Boeing, Chrysler, Union Carbide, RCA, Engelhard, and Ken Gibson, will give up their power to the people just because you ask for it, or because you pull down the election lever saying Prudential must go. They tell us that Rocky and Mellon will give up control of Standard Oil, Gulf, and the rest of it peacefully, but we had to get beat up just to integrate Dreamland Skating Rink. It is absolute nonsense.

No, only mass movement, the revolutionary movement of the masses of people, can make real change. And the 1960's should have taught us one clear thing about such mass movements, that they must be led by a revolutionary party, a party of the working class, a party guided by the science of revolution, Marxism–Leninism–Mao Tse Tung thought, otherwise they will remain spontaneous as they did in the sixties and rise and subside in waves. In the sixties we went on "guts, emotion, and love," and even hate, but little science. And to defeat this monster we must have science. We must be able to analyze this society and find out who are our friends and who are our enemies, who will oppose and struggle against racist monopoly capitalism (the private ownership of the means of producing wealth) and who will fight for socialism. We must be able to create not only black solidarity but multinational working-class solidarity, because the only thing scarier to the bourgeoisie than black unity is multinational working-class unity. Because that means their divide-and-conquer strategy to defeat revolution has been understood and rendered inoperable.

The creation of such a revolutionary Marxist-Leninist party is the central task of all revolutionaries of whatever nationality, because without such a party, rebellion cannot be turned into revolution!

We live in a imperialist superpower whose great wealth has been guided first by exploiting the people inside it, and second by the exploitation and oppression of people all over the world, especially in the Third World, Asia, Africa, Latin America. In the last few years, however, this superpower has been in a dramatic decline, getting its ass kicked spectacularly by small nations in Southeast Asia and Africa and Latin America. The Vietnam War marked the beginning of the rapid deterioration of this superpower, and also the intensification of its contention with the other superpower, the U.S.S.R., which is social imperialist, socialism in words and imperialism in deeds. These two superpowers are struggling to see who will control the world. The U.S.A. is trying to hold on to its ill-gotten gains; the U.S.S.R., the lean hungry new imperialist, is trying to come in the back door, after the United States has been kicked out the front door. Capitalism was restored in the Soviet Union in the early sixties led by the traitor Nikita Khrushchev. The resurgence to power of an old and new bourgeoisie has turned the U.S.S.R. into a fascist country domestically and a social imperialist country internationally. It is from this superpower, which is willing to take more chances because it is hurting economically, and whose economy is much less developed than the U.S.A. that there comes the main danger of world war. A war fought like World War I and II to redivide the world between imperialists.

The United States must constantly produce new weapons in its contention with the Soviet Union, even though both talk about SALT and the Russians' mouth "detente," while producing "Backfire" bombers and neutron bombs. The finance for these weapons must come from the funds that would be used for social programs, for health, education, housing, the raising of the quality of life. The United States could use much of its wealth to cool out the American people from the superprofits it got from superexploiting the nations and peoples of the Third World. But each time a Vietnam or Cambodia occurs, or a Mozambique or Guinea-Bissau, those superprofits dry up. Just as in so-called Rhodesia and South Africa—real names, Zimbabwe and Azania—the United States talks about supporting majority rule, but at the same time the United States capitalists are the chief reason those racist settler-colony regimes can continue to exist. They would disappear in a few months without United States imperialism.

So that the layoffs, the cutbacks, the elimination of minority hiring and university admission programs are all linked to the fact that the United States bourgeoisie is getting its ass kicked all over the world and struggling to keep the Soviet Union from sneaking in the back door. And it is obvious from the Soviet Union's hegemonistic activities in Africa, like Angola, Ethiopia, Somalia, Sudan, Egypt, that they are exploiters of the people with a new jargon but representing the same old bullshit of imperialism.

The United States bourgeoisie meanwhile moves continuously to the right, because that is the only way it can cope with the rising tide of people's struggles, as it tries to shift the weight for its international losses onto the backs of the American working class and oppressed nationalities. The Baake Decision is a means of cutting back and ultimately trying to eliminate affirmative action not only in these schools but in factories and construction sites as well, and it will affect not only oppressed nationalities but women as well. Here at racist Rutgers, the Rhodesia of the northeastern colleges, the recent move to include white lower-income students, meaning the sons and daughters of white workers, in the minority admissions program is double poison. While coming on like they are favoring some egalitarian process, they are actually diminishing the opportunities of blacks and Puerto Ricans on the one hand and causing friction between the nationalities on the other, right in tune with divide and conquer, their basic strategy against the workers' movement.

The reappearance of the Nazis and Klan out of mothballs is the work of the bourgeoisie, just as they are trying to unearth assbreath Imperiale here in Newark, who even the Italians refused to vote for. Meanwhile Rutgers could admit only seventeen blacks to its freshmen class last year, and then you find out thirteen of them are from Africa and the West Indies. It's the bourgeois lying with figures. They keep their English department faculty almost lily-white, and when the lone sister on the English department faculty broke her leg last year, they canceled her classes because they could not find any qualified nigras. They did not dare mouth such racism in the militant sixties because they felt somebody would drag they moth-eaten asses out of their offices, dump them in the trash can, and take over the buildings.

Yes, this bourgeois society is moving toward the right, and if necessary they would replace this bourgeois democracy, in which they rule by both carrot and stick, with the straight-out stick of fascism; if that was the only way to stop socialism! That is what they did in Germany. Hitler was bought and paid for by the big German and American industrialists.

But a militant black unity based on struggle will oppose those moves to the right. And this revolutionary black unity joined ultimately with other united fronts of oppressed nationalities, and finally with the whole of the multinational working class, will smash such rightward motion, as it will finally smash capitalism itself. On these campuses, you students also have a responsibility to build black unity, to build multinational unity, and to struggle to defeat racism and women's oppression and their source, monopoly capitalism. But you must remember that each day you are in this institution you are being taught bourgoise ideology, the stand, viewpoint, and method of the bourgeoisie, the rulers. And you must look at your education dialectically, using what is positive for the people and rejecting what is useful to the people's enemies. You must divide it in two. You must also remember that your struggles on this campus must be linked up to the struggles of the black nation and oppressed nationality, and also to the whole working class. If you isolate yourself from the workers and the oppressed nationalities, you are in danger of becoming their enemies or the tools of their enemies. You must resist this. Your life depends on it! You have a choice, unlike the majority, you have a choice; make it a positive and revolutionary one!

Unity and struggle.

Self-determination for the Afro-American nation in the black-belt South.

Socialist revolution!!!

Howdy Doody and the Mind Bandits!

So now we come to the story of Howdy Doody and the Mind Bandits. It is dedicated, in this humble rendering, to Clarence "Penny" Pendleton (the nickname refers to his Fee for Mindless Tomming), Howard alumnus and civil rights commissioner, who is a model of advanced social punkery and pootbootyism). Jazz and Newark and petit bourgeois bureaucrat Nigras also fits in dis, Jo-Jo, so keep your fingers off de dials!!

First: Imperialism, worldwide, is in crisis. At root is an economic crisis caused by contracting markets. Revolution is the main trend in the world today. "Countries want independence, nations want liberation, people want revolution," says Mao Tse Tung, and it coincides with objective reality. This is the basis of the contracting markets of all imperialism, including United States imperialism. (By imperialism we mean capitalism driving out beyond its own borders, as it has monopolized markets and resources there, and with a surplus of capital it begins to search for surplus value . . . profit . . . around the world—overthrowing governments, imposing colonialism or neo-colonialism, propping up Shah-like bloody dictators, e.g., Pinochet in Chile or Park Chung Hee in South Korea.)

Even when the United States imperialists were at the top of their powers Mao made the statement they were sitting on a volcano. The Korean War was a turning point downward for the brief "American century"; Vietnam was the crusher. Since the humiliating defeat of United States imperialism in Vietnam and Kampuchea, it has been in open decline. A retreating tiger trying to hold on to its ill-gotten gains, but being shot and driven out all over the Third World. And each time it does get driven out, a vicious wolf tries to slink in the back door, yodeling nonsense about itself being the "natural ally of the liberation movements"—the U.S.S.R. social imperialists, who are socialist in word, but imperialist in deed.

Each time the United States gets driven out of its markets, spheres of influence, its sources of raw materials and places to invest capital, it loses some of the superprofits gained by superexploitation, usually in the ex-colonies of the Third World (Asia, Africa, and Latin America). Since the fundamental drive on monopoly capitalism is *maximum* profit (not just to profit but to max out!), it means that if superprofit is lost in Southeast Asia or Africa or the Middle East or Latin America, then the people inside the imperialists' "own" country must be bled even more—to keep that maximum profit. (For instance, in 1970 the oil bandits, Rocky and the Seven Sisters—Exxon, Texaco, Royal Dutch Shell, Mobil, British Petroleum, Gulf, Standard of California—"paid" only $1.80 for a barrel of oil. A barrel is 0.137 metric tons or about 55 gallons. But since the liberation of oil nations from straight-out colonialism and with the growing independence of these countries, OPEC demands to be paid actual money for its oilooo, or something approaching it, about $18.00 per 55 gallons at last count. But the oilies, with Jimmy Doody's permission, jack up the prices here so they can still make more profit than they were making in 1970—maximum profit, to max out at our expense!)

So extensive is this crisis of contracting markets and sources of pillage caused by the world revolution against world imperialism that cutbacks, layoffs, unemployment, have reached stunning proportions. Despite the rulers' babbling about "new upturns," the United States economy, as the economies of the capitalist countries the world over, steadily worsens. And the frenzy in the face of this rising tide is wilder, and the extent to which they try to dump the weight of their losses onto our backs grows everyday more intense. It is this trend that will eventually transform even the U.S.A itself, the most formidable bastion of imperialism, into a steaming cauldron of socialist revolution!

The cutbacks, layoffs, unemployment, are always heaviest among the oppressed nationalities, even though they are very visible everywhere the working class is concentrated. But the blacks, browns, reds, yellows, are the easiest marks for this because of the national oppression and racism that always accompany imperialism. The Afro-Americans, Puerto Ricans, Chicanos, Asian-Americans, Indians, can be hit hardest: "last hired, first fired." And the racism which is both *a method of social organization as well as an ideology* can make it seem "natural." "Them niggers don't want nuthin' no way—them pordaricans'll work for nuthin'," etc. Working women also figure in this superexploited group—oppressed by class and sex, and for Third World women the triple oppression of class, sex, and nationality!

So that now we have the Baake case, attacking affirmative action—not only for oppressed nationalities, but for women—which has been followed very quickly by the Weber case challenging such programs in industry, and the Sears Roebuck challenge in the Supreme Court to all affirmative action as unconstitutional.

While Howdy Carter grins his humble Christian Draculaic grin, his bosses move the entire society further and further to the right. With revolution in the Third World cutting back the superprofits, it means that the material base of opportunism is also contracting, that there will be less money for the United States bourgeoisie to cool out "its own" working class. Since these superprofits are used to bribe a small sector of the working class (the labor aristocrats, and the petite bourgeoisie, who are then touted as leaders of the working class, e.g., trade-union bureaucrats, well-funded reformists, petit bourgeois politicians, and now even some figures in the arts, entertainment, and sports, etc.). This bribed sector, along with programs used to create the illusion of democracy, are financed by the superprofits gouged out of the Third World. As the superprofits dry up so do the programs, and more and more, objective conditions for revolution are created, strengthening the subjective factor—the understanding by the people that revolution is the only solution—better enabling the revolutionaries to create, in the very near future, a genuine Marxist-Leninist communist party based on Marxism–Leninism–Mao Tse Tung thought.

Carter is in charge of eliminating the gains of the 1960's with a giggle. So that the Baake Decision is made the same day that Howdy has a buncha music woogies down at his pad (the Caucasian crib) so he can rub up against them while icing the rest of us. Sun Tze called this "make a noise in the east, and strike in the west."

But not only are the United States imperialists harassed by revolution in the Third World, they are now in a deadly and escalating contention with the other superpower, the Soviet Union, for control of the world. It is a contention between an old and dying imperialism and a new and aggressive imperialism, Soviet social imperialism—socialism in words, imperialism in deeds. But the U.S.A. is still economically superior to the U.S.S.R., and the U.S.S.R. to contend—it spends as much now in weapons as the U.S.A, with one-half the gross national product!—is in a veritable frenzy for colonies, new sources of raw materials, new places to invest capital, new spheres of interest, new markets, and so it has become even more aggressive than declining United States imperialism, and *the most dangerous source of world war!!*

"Between a rock and a hard place" is the neo-folk wisdom. That is where United States imperialism is. It means for us here that we must combat the rightward motion the bourgeoisie is pointing society toward. (Suddenly, the Klan and Nazis are back! The leadership, probably, has F.B.I. ID's!) It means we see grim spectacles such as in Newark where the result of this international crisis of imperialism and motion toward the right is the announcement and implementation of "Program Modifications" in the Newark school system where, get this, *art, music, physical education, industrial arts, home economics, are removed from the elementary schools,* along with truant officers, school aides, security guards (a dog walked into my five-year-old son's kindergarten class and had to be 86ed by the teacher), and cafeteria workers.

On the face of it this is a clear move to make the Newark school system *a separate and unequal system.* It definitely is not the "thorough and efficient" criterion the New Jersey state constitution lays out. But by turning the inner cities into Bantustans, maximum profit can better be maintained.

How strange to contemplate this now, in a city with wall-to-wall black bureaucrats—the elected sector of them mostly elected by a black and Puerto Rican united front fighting for their democratic rights, inspired by the rebellions of the 1967!

You see the three-piece-suit-wearing bloods, excuse me, ladies and gents, no, rather, petit bourgeois bureaucrats, pontificating and bullshitting and selling out the very people whose blood spilled in the streets and who provided them with entrance into the establishment! So that "black power," transformed, is hipper than gasoline to fuel the white-racist, capitalist system.

(The Program Modifications, as well, are a test, a tentative exploration by the rulers to see if the people will go for it, and if so, they will run it out in all the ghettos and working-class areas in this country.)

It shows you the sterility and fantasy of a cultural and reactionary nationalism that sees skin color as the determinant of political line. These are cold-blooded niggers with stripy navel cords hooked up to imperialism running this! My wife, Amina, was recently convicted of assault and battery on a public official—a Negro named Carl Dawson Sharif. Sharif, when he was Dawson, had a rep as "a white boy," in his younger days. He so aspired and was so attired that he finally got hired, as a colored version of bad stuff. It was he who as President of the Board of Education (all appointed by Gibson— Sharif is a $21,000-a-year Gibson aide) pronounced the Program Modifications, the delivery of Newark into Bantustan status.

Sharif* is typical of the petit bourgeois black bureaucrats who Amos-'n'-Andy it up in Newark's City Hall and other administrative dens. They are "capitalism's cute coons"!—pimps off black struggle, the coolout agents brought in after any of the partial victories the people make in the struggle for their democratic rights, to turn things around and restore the *status quo* of capitalism at "a higher level." Negations to be negated in the upward spiral of evolutionary motion to revolution!

Sharif is a Wallace Muhammad Muslim, a relatively recent convert who could only belong to the Nation of Islam, now called the World Community of Islam, post-Malcolm and even post–Elijah Muhammad, when the priorities of that organization are Islamic orthodoxy, government grants, and black capitalism. When the revolutionary nationalism that once animated "the nation" is in the main liquidated, with no sign of the Muslim demands on the black page, and an American flag on the front page of their newspaper.

Sharif and the rest of Gibson's dwarfs initially hatched the PM's in a semiclosed session of the Board, but the people fought back, forcing the courts to rule that Sharif and Co. had violated the "Sunshine Law," which says such matters must be done before the public, with adequate public notice. The Board seemingly complied, but held the key meeting at a high-school auditorium with only about 1,500 seats, rather than the largest hall in town, and so took

*Since this writing Sharif has opted for more independence from Gibson and has been railroaded out of office by the K.G.B. (Ken Gibson's Buffoons).

pleasure in turning away about 300–500 people outside who they claim would be in violation of fire laws.

Even so, as speaker after speaker rose to oppose the PM's, Sharif refused to answer questions and sat haughtily, having brought the elitist and exclusivist quality that rewarded him with his youthful nickname into full view. But the people raged and cursed him, some even mentioning that Sharif had his own children driven by city car to West Orange, a half-slick suburb, to go to school, while he led attacks on ours and tried to condemn them to a lifetime of ignorance and disco thinking. Finally Sharif called a recess, ostensibly to cool the people out, but in reality to take the Board vote on the issue as clandestinely as the previous illegal vote.

When we returned from the recess a rumor shot around the hall that the vote had already been taken and that the PM's had been passed seven to one. (The one dissenting voter, Charles Bell, actually had a child in the Newark school system!) My wife and many others demanded that Sharif tell the people what he'd done—was he just going to chump us all off like this? As she repeated her question, advancing toward the stage, the mostly white police these Negroes keep stashed out in the empty classrooms leaped through the doors. Plus the unidentified karate creeps Sharif has milling around him passing as "security" rushed forward. But Amina walked around them up the stairs, confronted Sharif directly at the microphone, and then tried to left-hand-swat him right across his chops! She missed (the testimony says), hitting the microphone, and Sharif, bug-eyed, pushed back away from the table and ballet-danced back among his black belts. (One such Hollywood caricature told an outraged citizen that he, the HC, was "a fifth-degree black belt." Said citizen wanted to know, did this enable this nigger to stop .357 Magnum bullets with his teeth?)

The now clearly illegal meeting broke up, and the PM's were put in motion. Your correspondent got a slight hicky on his forehead after being tackled by a pride of policemens. And the three-piece-suit-wearing Negroes and Negresses who are the bureaucratic pimps that run this Bantustan had demonstrated how fiercely they will fight to defend monopoly capitalism, national oppression, and racism.

The people's struggle against the PM's has continued, and in the face of this popular opposition and the obvious chaos created by this reactionary program the administration has had to rescind some of the stupider sections of it. (Three hundred aides have been rehired, and about thirty security guards; also twenty-five recreation centers will be opened this summer. But this is all temporary. The bulk of this repression still remains and the people still oppose it.)

Sharif told many people, with characteristic dishonesty, that he would not press charges against Amina Baraka, but of course he did. The judge was a Gibson apointee, just as were the lying Board members who testified. For pointing this out, from the witness stand, your correspondent was threatened with a contempt charge.

At the end of the one-day trial, after many postponements, the judge found Amina Baraka guilty of assault and battery on a bureaucrat and find her $25 (suspended) and $25 court costs. As one blood said, however: "Shit, I'd pay $25 just to hit one of them mf's!"

Prudential (Manufacturers Hanover) runs New Jersey. Rockefeller runs Prudential–Manufacturers Hanover. And Rocky and Morgan still contend over CBS!

In a related bit of doodoo—which smell is monopoly's breath in our faces as it tightens the chains around our already injured brains—I was asked by Woody Shaw, who was raised in Newark, to do liner notes for his forthcoming Columbia album, *Woody III.* Woody Shaw is among the premiere trumpet players of the improvised Afro-American music called jazz. The fact that he also comes out of Newark, like a whole host of other artists, especially black jazz and R&B performers, made him think that I might be able to add something of what the Newark experience was to the liner notes.

But in trying to do this, talking about Newark past and present, the musicians and other artists both black and white to come out of there (e.g., Sarah Vaughan, Scott LaFaro, Dionne Warwick, Gloria Gaynor, Wayne and Allen Shorter, Grachan Moncur, Willie "The Lion" Smith, Melba Moore, Tyrone Washington, Larry Young, Jr., Charli Persip, Eddie Gladden, Walter Davis—Betty Carter lived there for a time, ditto James Moody and Hank Mobley, plus folks like Allen Ginsberg, Philip Roth—hey, even Eva Marie Saint and Jerry Lewis, etc.), a horrible irony gripped me. Woody S. learned to play trumpet in public school. He had a few teachers of great skill and sensitivity who laid what they could on Woody and he took it the rest of the way. I pointed out that even that basic and traditional transfer of information and inspiration were being eliminated in "The New Newark" as the Chamber of Commerce describes this

Bantustan—talking no doubt about some new bus shelters, a few cardboard public matchboxes, and the Gateway hotel–office building uncomplex, plus new sites for Rutgers, New Jersey Institute of Technology, and Essex County College, a two-year educational illusion built especially for the oppressed nationalities to keep them out of Rutgers, etc. *There are no longer music teachers in Newark elementary schools!* Woody Shaw was saved from the "delinquency" rap put on the wilder youth in their mad reaction against enforced mediocrity, boredom, and frustration, who strike out wildly and many times incorrectly against the real "delinquency" of the way of death of United States monopoly capitalism. Woody was saved, very literally, by music, as are a significant number of other poor and oppressed people. It often is music vs. the penitentiary—art vs. junkiedom (sometimes, tragically, they are even combined and their carriers scramble promisingly "out of the ghetto" only to get shot down in flight!).

The liner notes put the heat of Shaw's music in the hot center of people's real lives, as they are really lived in all the Newarks of this land, up under the hammer of the bloody corporate class. So naturally, CBS objected.

I got word from Shaw's agent's office that CBS had pulled everything they thought of as objectionable out of the notes. But I was still not prepared for what they actually did. They simply *rewrote* them—not only eliminating all the dirty parts but even changing the shape and style of the writing itself. They turned the notes into simply biography and then wanted my permission to use them this way.

My "no" to their censorship would probably have been "overed" the way these biggies usually do. Just get someone else. There are lines of scabs, professional and amateur, to do just such tasks as these. But CBS made one big mistake; in their rush to get the product out, they printed the cover of the album with my name on it. Going their usual "over that crazy nigger" route would cost money, more than they wanted to spend. Do all the covers over—at this time—plus add more delay to the product's appearance? What to do?

But before we get to that, what could be these dirty, obscene (to be kept off the scene) words CBS objected to? Let's look at a few of them. In talking about the chancy nature of American society for the majority, I said, it is "a lottery for most of us. I mean we don't even know if we gonna make it, in the totality of everything that means, like the survivors of a catastrophe. . . . Woody hails from Catastrophe City where the wicked witch of the west has located her largish urban commode."

All information relating to the Program Modifications in Newark schools, of course, was removed. I had footnoted the extent of the PM's attack on art, music, physical education, etc., particularly relating to Woody Shaw's experience, and that he was lucky to have gone through the Newark school system "when music was still part of the elementary school curriculum."

When I mentioned that Newark was the worst city in America, according to *Harper's* magazine—that was gone, also the class and nationality breakdown of the city, including the fact that many Puerto Ricans were "jobless refugees from America's colonial prison, Puerto Rico," and that the Italian-Americans were mainly "working-class Italians at the lower rung of 'well it was sposed to be better than this for white people–ism'" or that the Afro-Americans were "black immigrants from the Afro-American nation in the black-belt South"! Also lifted was the fact that inside that city, "the pressure to be broken by incredible odds, by the poverty, ignorance, violence, indifference, that is one's day-to-day environment . . . is immense." That was gone. And even gone was "One thing is clear, that within these stagnant graveyards the rich lock us in to make their maximum profit, the will and fire of life burns and throbs anyway."

Also removed was mention of the fact that not only were music teachers removed from the school Woody went to, but a couple weeks before I had been at a meeting where parents complained that that school is about to fall down on their children's heads. That was gone too. A characterization of the black Newark bureaucrats as "capitalism's cute coons" was also excised, as well as mention of the "sham democracy pipsqueaked" by these CCC. These things and more were liquidated by the Mind Bandits at CBS.

Wild! Prudential Insurance Co. squats over downtown Newark like the demented white knight, the clearest representative of the exploitive and oppressive system of monopoly capitalism and its chief attendant evils—national oppression, racism, and the oppression of women. Prudential–Manufacturers Hanover is part of the Rockefeller financial group. They control most of the major banks and utilities in New Jersey. (A random survey of some their holdings looks like Howard Savings, First Jersey, Gillette, Public Service, Johnson and Johnson, etc., etc.)

As for CBS, Rocky's mob does not have a big say in the goings-on. The two giant financial groups, Rocky and Morgan, have locked ass for several years over CBS, but it is bitter or delicious irony, perfect, depending on your class stand, for Prudential to be in charge of actually kicking our ass (though it is the hand of our "brother" Coonish Kenneth Gibson, or Coonish Ken, or CoonKen for short, by which the actual laying on of hands is performed). And CBS, like all the bourgeois media, is responsible for seeing that absolutely no word of the people's struggle gets disseminated, only distortion and misrepresentation. (*The New York Times*, another Rocky-influenced sheet, does not even deliver in Newark!) So they attempted to throw a blanket of silence over so humble an attempt at mass communication as liner notes! Freedom of speech means you can babble in Washington Square, provided nobody listens, or you can fight ABC, NBC, and CBS with a mimeograph machine! Freedom of the press is cool if you own one! But liner notes got to be free of social controversy. There is a school of commerce that says no liner notes, just list personnel and tunes and a couple of flicks. So that any *reflection* on the music whatsoever is iced, like the fusion station WRVR (NYC) playing tune after tune with no announcement of tunes, players, and certainly no knowledgeable socio-aesthetic commentary—they do it disco style without a pause. But any commentary on that station at all might expose the fact that Chuck Mangione, Phoebe Snow, John Klemmer, George Benson, etc., do not constitute the jazz greats.

So the CBS blackout is to smash and prevent consciousness, to repress consciousness with and for the sake of commerce and monopoly rule. This is the reason that they feel it all right to remove culture from our schools.

On the liner-note question, CBS finally requested a meeting. It was held on the twelfth floor of their Fifty-second Street castle. In the meeting were three CBS lawyers (white guys) and one (colored) director of black music there, George Butler. And the ironies still do not cease. This is the same George Butler I went to Howard University with—who used to play like Erroll Garner at campus sets, who had a wonderful-looking sister, Jackie, who was the campus everything. Wild[20]! It was Butler who had called me about the threatened impasse and suggested the meeting. He sounded like he was *trying* to be positive. I had been told he was up at Columbia awhile before I had received the assignation. Butler's voice was cool and precise, but his CBS-executive-of-no-known-nationality accent threw me off.

At any rate we came together a few days later for a meeting along with the chosen three. One, the "bad cop," did all the talking. He was supposed to be the aggressive, hell-for-leather type. He right away pointed out in a loud voice that "moderation" was the only way into the land of milk and honey (Beverly Hills?) and began to go down the list of CBS no-no's. When I told them that their whole proposal was bullshit, that their version of the liner notes could not under any circumstances be printed, reason partially descended. We went page for page, and I offered a compromise—that of the stuff they were uncomfortable with (which included some discussion about dope addiction among jazz musicians), all the strictly factual material must remain, but any gratuitous insults could be cooled out. This said, "capitalism's cute coons" came out, as well as a sardonic reflection on whether the state's trying mostly black and Hispanic youth "as adults" would end the people's problems. But, impasse faced, most of the "no-no" material stayed in, and the conference had barely lasted an hour. But all this for liner notes? With three of CBS's finest and bona fide HNIC? What they wanted to keep out was any mention of Newark in reality, how black power was transformed to black bureaucracy, what Bantustans U.S.A.-style look like, and any other attack on capitalism or its byproducts. I could not call Down Beat "a lottery" because they might sue. One mention of a Newark jazz club, now long gone, as "a cutting joint" brought close scrutiny. They thought it had to do with drugs rather than music. But it was attacks on capitalism that most unfriendlied them.

And for deconstructionists, anticontext chumps, art-for-art's-sake fakers, who want to know what all that has to do with the music—it is the specific context of the music's creation, the flesh and blood of its form and content. The music is a reflection of the Afro-American people—their history, their lives and their struggle, their culture. It is the music of an oppressed nation struggling to liberate itself from imperialism. And their enemies, whether the Prudential–Manufacturers Hanover branch or the CBS branch, stem from the same class—the corporate class, the bourgeoisie, who are only six-tenths of one percent of the United States population, but who control the means of production, the means of producing social wealth in this society—the land, factories, machines, mineral wealth, communication, transportation. While Howdy Doody, a really unusual-looking vampire, runs the state for them with lower-level bureaucrats like the CoonKens or the Kochs or Rizzos or Browns keeping it tight all

the way down the line to the bloody killer cops. And in the superstructure (which is the ideology—philosophy, arts, literature, etc—
and the institutions created by the economic base) more Mind Bandits in the service of the same capitalist class make certain that
pro-capitalist ideas dominate this society, that pro-imperialist art is
most celebrated or at least that which is only minimally anti-imperialist, because there is a core of anti-imperialist sentiment even for
the majority of petit bourgeois artists and intellectuals which must
be continuously combated by the Mind Bandits. For instance, the
hatchet job done on *Zoot Suit*, smashing it for its millitance, was
classic. Mao said that literary and art criticism is the key method of
class struggle in the arts. So that Richard Eder–Walter Kerr one-two
punch coupled with backshooting like the *Village Voice*'s critic, whose
world view prepared him to be much more interested in a play about
a homosexual school teacher's lust for one of his students, airily dismissed *ZS* for some "art" reasons, like Eder, who for some other
"art" reasons found the scene where the white liberal is accepted by
the wild Chicano Pachucos as the best scene (!?!) and for other "art"
reasons really disliked the scene where the Chicano hero chooses a
Chicana over the white woman activist (!?!). The bureaucrats at CBS
are just more of the same Mind Bandits, like those at station
WRVR, playing Phoebe Snow more times than Sarah Vaughan,
Betty Carter, Ella Fitzgerald, put together, or Chuck Mangione
more times than all of the great trumpeters of jazz put together:
Mind Bandits pushing imperialism in the superstructure. Consider
anthologists of literature who include few blacks, Latinos, Asians,
Native Americans, or women in their anthologies, who push Henry
James, the Southern Agrarians, Eliot, etc., and dead academic poets
over Melville, the slave narratives, DuBois, Twain, Dreiser, Richard
Wright, Langston Hughes, Margaret Walker, Michael Gold, etc.
Look at the theater people, who produce garbage nondrama dead-
plays by Mr. or Mrs. White Anyface and a few black or Latino
neocolonial faces, but look for anything live and real and its suppressed!, whether it is contemporary American or Brecht, Gorky,
O'Casey, Theodore Ward, George Sklar. There are Mind Bandits
ensconced in the city halls and boards of educations, in the universities, museums, and repertory theaters, on Broadway, in Hollywood
(Hollywood means Mind Bandit in Gibberish), on the radio and TV
networks, giving us Huggy Bear and Rooster and George Jefferson,
or the soaps and quiz shows, and the bullshit sophomore head-in-

asshole-ism of education TV, Channel 13, all of which, like their detergent commercials, is very very white.

It is a small army of bureaucrats, vampires, and Frankensteins, upholding the *status quo,* usually the bribed sector of the petite bourgeoisie and working class. And in our struggle to smash capitalism and build socialism, we cannot fail to expose and isolate these Mind Bandits who help the bourgeoisie rule by deception (since this is a bourgeois democracy), but they also help them rule by "stick" when that's called for, because ultimately *the gun* is the essential means of bourgeois rule.

Howdy and the Mind Bandits are part of a team. On their jerseys could be written "People's Enemies." Check the oil ripoffs pronounced from Howdy's buck fangs, "explained" by Mind Bandits at all levels of government and media. Or the nuclear ripoff pronounced and explained and implemented by the same team.

We need a team too—the majority of us! Such a team would be a genuine Marxist-Leninist communist party, based on Marxism–Leninism–Mao Tse Tung thought. Building a party of the working class is the central task of revolutionaries today, because without it we remain at the mercy of the monopolists and their lackeys. Society can only be changed fundamentally by socialist revolution, led by a revolutionary party which can guide the whole of the masses to smash capitalism forever and build socialism under the revolutionary dictatorship of the proletariat (that is, the absolute control of the majority, who are the working class).

Howdy and the Mind Bandits advise against it!

Afro-American Literature and Class Struggle *

In an essay published in a prose and drama reader by William Morrow and Company in 1979, I put forward the idea that there is a revolutionary tradition in Afro-American literature. I also implied, and to a certain extent discussed, the obvious capitulationist tradition in that literature as well. Obvious, because the dialectic would automatically suggest that if there was a revolutionary tradition, then its opposite would also be present. I think it should also be added that probably the majority of Afro-American writers fall somewhere between those two poles, as "middle forces" that are swayed, guided, directed, or influenced, given their peculiar individual experience, by one of those stances or the other. But the genuine, major Afro-American writers have been part of the revolutionary tradition, and there is a preponderance of patriots as opposed to copouts among black writers.

It occurred to me that these traditions existed, very clearly, when I went to teach at Yale, and witnessed the teaching of Afro-American literature, how the positive and negative could be shoveled together under the national rubric, yet given the bias of the American superstructure, very little would get to the students about what these writers and their writing actually represented in the living, breathing real world. It was Charles Davis, the head of the Afro-American Studies Department at Yale, who pointed out that Jupiter Hammon

---

* Published first in *Black American Literature Forum*.

310

and Phillis Wheatley were not really representative of the beginnings of Afro-American literature as a *genre*, that black literature as a body of work precisely reflecting a particular people must begin with the slave narratives. My recognition of this fact was positive enough, but it was also accompanied by the further understanding that here was an obvious case of two *ideologically opposite* reflections of society, both emanating from the same people, or national group.

There are other circumstances here that should be noted. Wheatley and Hammon are eighteenth-century blacks, and privileged house slaves. Writing by blacks and reading was outlawed in the general society, so for these two to have written meant they were pets of the slave society, and their generally favorable accounts of that society were reflective of pet-nigger house servants isolated from the masses of black people.

The nineteenth century was a century of struggle in this country which led to the end of slavery. There was an intensification of slavery in the early part of that century (which was the result of cotton becoming an international commodity, and the black slaves' condition being transformed so that they were not only tied to the land for life as patriarchal slaves but now had the "civilized horrors" of capitalism added to their humps, since they now had to produce cotton not just for a domestic market but an international one); this intensification of slavery led to an intensification of resistance, which culminated in the Civil War.

The slave narratives are an ideological and emotional reflection of the great majority of the Afro-American people as well as a stunningly incisive portrait of slave America. They are the voice of the *majority* of black people, as literally as that can be taken. They are also a *genre*, a distinctive *body* of work, that indicate a way of living and thinking in the society. They are antislavery, fierce indictments of American slave society, the exact opposite of Wheatley-Hammon. When the various teachers of Afro-American literature scramble the narratives and Wheatley-Hammon together, they scramble the history and the idcology (i.e., perception of realty) contained in each. So that what is hidden is just where these writers are coming from *seen in the context of real life*—who and what they really are and their *use*, finally, to the Afro-American people and to American society as a whole (and to the entire world!).

I know when I mention historical (and with that social, political, economic, etc.) context the structuralist and neo-new-critical types get their dander up. Good! This essay is meant to jump all over them. "New Critics," as Bruce Franklin points out in *The Victim as Artist and Criminal*, or one branch of "new critics," the Southern Agrarians (John Crowe Ransom, Allen Tate, Robert Penn Warren, etc.), actually upheld slavery, which they euphemized as a necessary "defect," in order to create the great Southern culture (as Allen Tate said, "a fine, elegant and lasting culture"). Ironically, when onc looks for that GSC, especially for what is "lasting," one finds it is largely Afro-American, whether it is food, music, or literature! Compare Frederick Douglass with Stephen Longstreet and William Gilmore Simms, or compare slave authors H. Box Brown, Linda Brent, the Krafts, Henry Bibb, with Hugh Legaré, George Fitzhugh (author of *Cannibals All!*), or the other hopeless justifiers and sentimentalizers of the slavemaster class.

The "new criticism" with its stress on literature as self-contained artifact removed from real life was actually part of the McCarthyism and reaction of the 1950's. These reactionary writers—Tate's first book of criticism was called *Reactionary Essays*—wrote some of these backward ideas in the 1930's, but the period was too progressive, so that they could not get much attention until the fifties. The fifties upsurge of reaction was aimed at removing all traces of thirties-forties radicalism. It accompanied the overall Cold War United States imperialism was waging to try to take over a world market after World War II (during which it was forced to make a united front with the U.S.S.R. against fascism). The emphasis, necessarily, was on technique, on *how* was it said, not *what* was it saying. But the bourgeoisie must always emphasize formalism, form over content, because if people check out what they are saying they will not give too much of a shit how, or they will at least reject what and try to learn from how, but not suck it in wholesale.

The most important personalities and trends of the revolutionary tradition (which is antislavery, anticapitulationist, anti-imperialist, etc., given the particular epoch and conditions of its existence) begin with the slave narratives (e.g., Douglass, H. Box Brown, Bibb, Moses Roper, Brent, Austin Steward, among many others), though these differ individually as to the degree of their consciousness, obviously Frederick Douglass's remaining perhaps the most moving, poignant, and revolutionary. These are the beginnings of Afro-American literature, as genre.

Then there are the pre–Civil War nationalists, David Walker,

Henry Highland Garnet, C. H. Langston, Charles Lenox Remond, among the best, and I would also include Nat Turner's confessions, as classic black autobiography and also pychological and mystical reportage of the matrix of the times. Also there is William Wells Brown as the "transitional figure," or at least the figure showing the transition to come from purely "functional literature" to "art," but, of course, it is all art, and all functional, and its functionalism is anti-oppression and the art is in how it lays it out. Mrs. Francis Watkins Harper should also be mentioned as a strong antislavery poet.

DuBois is the great link between the ninetecth and twentieth centuries. His *Souls of Black Folk,* and indeed DuBois's constant *forward movement* ideologically, from isolated democrat to black capitalist and yeasayer for the "talented tenth" and the emerging black bourgeoisie (its militant national wing as opposed to the comprador wing of Booker T. Washington) to Pan-Africanist and socialist and finally to Marxist communist, is the underlying dynamic of all of our intellectual and political journey. But *SOBF* is the connection to the Harlem Rcnaissance. Its multiple forms and omnisensitivity, from music and cultural history and criticism to polemic ("Of Mr. Booker T. Washington and Others") to short fiction, prepares a whole artistic and ideological pallet for the young urban intelligentsia of the Harlem Renaissance. Langston Hughes's seminal "The Negro Artist and the Racial Mountain" is impossible without *SOBF;* it not only defends the black artist but identifies his truest sources, the black masses, the souls of black folk. And Hughes audaciously sets the lines for the attack on the antiblack, intellectual reactionaries and compradors who deny the heauty and strength of the black experiencc and thereby try to limit life itself.

(Interestingly enough, even today, cause that's where it all leads, and on past to tomorrow, there is a sector of the black artist-intelligentsia that continues to identify with the objects of the ire of DuBois and Hughes's righteous patriotic national consciousness, i.e., BTW and shrimps like George Schuyler, but we will come back to them, as the objects of our own ire—update on de struggle!)

To continue the historical perspective, the Harlem Renaissance is the maturation of an urban, Afro-American intelligentsia, symbolizing the movement of large numbers of the black masses out of the Afro-American nation in the old black-belt South into the rest of the United States, as an oppressed national minority, transforming from a largely Southern, rural and agricultural, peasant people, to the present day: almost half of the black masses live in the North, Midwest, and West, in urban centers, as part of an industrial working class; ninety-six percent of the black masses are part of that multinational working class in the United States. The development of this intelligentsia identified with the Harlem Renaissance replicates parallel developments all over the Third World (the colonial world), but the Harlem Renaissance was a leading and influential force on black artists and intellectuals all over the world, whether it was the *"indigisme"* of Haiti, the "Negrissmo" of Puerto Rico and Cuba, or the "Negritude" of the African and West Indian intellectuals living in Paris, like Aimé Césaire, Leopold Senghor, and Leon Damas; they all claimed the Harlem Renaissance as their chief influence, especially Langston Hughes and Claude McKay.

Hughes and McKay stand out in my mind as the chief forces of that period, though for sure there were many others. (Technical innovators like Toomer, with *Cane,* fall off into mysticism, even repudiation of blackness, and Zora Neale Hurston ends up writing articles against voting rights for blacks, the FEPC, and integration of schools, among other things.) Hughes's early work is classic "Black Is Beautiful—We Are an African People" writing, which is the revolutionary nationalism of the oppressed people whose first utterances are defense against the cultural aggression of imperialism, which says those it oppresses are stupid, ugly, and have no history! The two McKay novels I have read, *Home to Harlem* and *Banjo,* are classics of a muscular, graphically descriptive, beautiful prose. His poetry, probably because of the irrelevant stiff sonnet form he was wont to impose on himself, is much less interesting, though for sure its content makes it so strong it still fights through.

The 1930's and 1940's brought changes to Langston Hughes's work, and perhaps the strongest work is collected in the volume *Good Morning, Revolution.* There we see a distinctive move into a militant internationalism, embracing the struggle of the majority of the world's peoples for liberation with a stirring and conscious anti-imperialism. Richard Wright, of course, is one of the most impressive Afro-American writers, one of the most important American writers of the period. *Uncle Tom's Children* is for me Wright's most powerful work. There is nothing of his as sustained in its description of the national oppression of the Afro-American nation in the black-belt South as *Uncle Tom's Children.* His *Black Boy* and *American Hunger,* taken together, as they were written, before the repression of

American Hunger (by Harper's for thirty years), is a powerful work, a novel of ideology in the strongest sense of the term, an accomplishment of tremendous dimensions. I am only touching highlights to make a case for these writers in the Afro-American tradition. (For further discussion of this, see my essay "The Revolutionary Tradition in Afro-American Literature" in the prose reader I mentioned.) Obviously, there is no monolithic anything; everything splits in two parts to be looked at dialectically; separated into its positive and negative aspects it can be understood and learned from. So we can pick up the good in it, discarding the negative.

Richard Wright was a creature of contradiction. It is obvious in his work that he never quite integrated himself with reality; his depictions of black women are, frankly, usually demeaning or absent. Wright, except in *American Hunger*, lived in the unreal bookworld too much and never "got down" with black people. But the hot sensitivity and resistance to evil are clear in the books I mention, and generally, to various degrees in much of his work.

Wright's break with the Communist Party is wonderfully documented and honestly so. The petit Bourgeois individualism he acquired with his aspirant intellectualism is his own undoing, though, for the reconstituted CPUSA was committing grave errors as well, and they passed each other like trains in the night.

Another important writer of the late 1930's and 1940's is Theodore Ward, whose *Big White Fog* is one of the finest plays written in this country, with an ideological scope and precision that forced the powers that be to block the performances of *Fog* in the Federal Theater and to heap mountains of obscurity on Ward ever since. His later works like *Our Lan'* and *John Brown* have been equally neglected, but Ward is a giant!

Margaret Walker is another giant, abused by the vagaries of white-racist "scholarship," white-racist "criticism," and white-racist paternalism and self-esteem. (Yale University Press has even let *For My people* go out of print!) Margaret Walker's form and content come straight out of the genuine roots of Afro-American life and speech. And as for her great work *Jubilee*, there is as much basis for her plagiarism suit against Alex Haley (*Roots*) as Harold Courtlander's, but his publisher, Crown, joined in the suit; Walker's, Houghton Mifflin, would not, so it was only her lawyer-son vs. ABC and Doubleday.

As I pointed out, the 1950's was a period of reaction, not only in

the sense of the Cold War, the Korean War, McCarthyism, new criticism, but also the once-revolutionary Communist Party U.S.A. began to come apart at the seams and by 1957 declared that socialism
could be gained through the ballots rather than by revolution, which
is revisionist nonsense. For blacks, the defection was visible earlier,
as the white-chauvinist, opportunist element of the party emerged
more clearly as its leadership. So that by the fifties the CPUSA had
renounced its correct line of self-determination for the Afro-American nation in the black-belt South, and declared that black people
had already achieved self-determination under imperialism, which is
a racist insult! If we have already achieved self-determination, it
means that we are in charge of these slums and deathholes we are
forced to live in, and that we are responsible for unemployment,
substandard education, hospital closings, police brutality, which is a
flat-out lie! Certain Negro intellectuals began to talk about how the
national aspect of Afro-American writing had to be cooled out,
lessened, that black writers wrote too much about black people,
which sounds like the straight-out bourgeoisie. Did anyone ever run
that on O'Casey or Joyce that they leaned on Irishmens too much, or
get to Dostoevski and his Russian self??

Ralph Ellison and James Baldwin arrive on the scene now,
putting down Richard Wright ("Richard's Blues," "Alas, Poor Richard," "Everybody's Protest Novel"), which was part of the McCar-
thy-type cleanup of all radical ideas and persons left from the
turbulent thirties. Richard Wright had left the United States in
1947, just after the Communist Party U.S.A had declared itself a
"Political Association" dedicated to "twentieth-century Americanism," like Paine, Jefferson, etc. In France, Wright caught up with
Stein and Sartre and existentialism. (The whole of Wright's life can
be summed up in the metaphor of flight—from the South, from
whites, from blacks, from the Communist Party, and from the
U.S.A., finally from reality, though obviously this latter was mitigated by his ability to record his experience accurately.)

Fortunately for us all, Baldwin grew much wiser than those early
essays and got involved with the civil-rights movement. *The Fire Next
Time* is eloquent reflection of this involvement, but even more,
when he wrote *Blues for Mr. Charlie*, he openly questioned nonviolence. Once *Charlie* appeared, Baldwin was removed as *the* black
writer vis-à-vis the white bourgeois press, and Ellison was pumped
up. A difficult job, since Bro. Ralph only has that one book, but it is

touted up a storm by the academies and officialdom because of its content. Ellison puts down both nationalism and Marxism, and opts for individualism. Which is, like they say, right on the money!

The Black Arts Movement of the 1960's was certainly a rebellion against the bourgeoisie's and revisionists' fifties liquidation of the Afro-American national question, and the rise of conservative, reformist, capitulationist, as well as comprador, writing as "Negro writing." Just as Malcolm X emerged to forcefully oppose the black bourgeoisie's domination of the Black Liberation Movement, as well as the reformist and even outright comprador (agents of the oppressor nation) lines that dominated the movement in the fifties. The "blackness" of the Black Arts Movement was the attempt to restore the national priorities of the Afro-American nation and oppressed nationality to the art of black artists. Art had to be an extension of the people themselves, involved with them, expressing their lives and minds with the collective fire of actual life committed to the necessary struggle and revolutionary transformation that we need in the real world!

Our writing actually accompanied and reflected and exhorted rebellion. When the chump judge that sentenced me to three years without parole for alleged gun carrying during the Newark rebellion read that sentence he quoted my poetry (!) as one of the reasons he knew I was guilty. Askia M. Toure (Roland Snellings), Larry Neal, Clarence Reed, Charles and William Patterson, Harold Cruse, Marvin X, Ed Bullins, Sonia Sanchez, Welton Smith, Mari Evans, David Henderson, Sun Ra, Carolyn Rogers, Clarence Franklin, Carol Freeman, Don L. Lee, Ted Wilson, Reginald Lockett, Ron Milner, Ben Caldwell (and Trane and Albert!), and so many more put out strong black art in the turbulent sixties, as part of the breadth and scope of that movement, not just in literature but in all the arts, as part of the sweeping upsurge of the Black Liberation Movement itself! It was a broad united front of creativity and struggle.

The Black Arts Movement had an impact similar to the Harlem Renaissance: it influenced a whole generation of artists around the world, and not just black and Third World artists, but also artists in Europe and among the Euro-Americans. The emphasis was on a people-shaped, high-oral, intensely direct statement, in whatever medium. The BAM said, the function of art is to reach and educate and move and unify and organize people, not to mystify them or offer dazzling support of the *status quo*! The mainstream of the Black Arts Movement was rooted in the revolutionary tradition of Afro-American literature and in the revolutionary traditions of the Afro-American people. It spoke to the Afro-American people because it was consciously aimed at them. As Mao Tse Tung in *The Yenan Forum on Art and Literature* pointed out, the artist's audience is one key shaper of the artist's work, i.e., who it is *for* helps make it what it is.

But, of course, at the same time that the Black Arts Movement emerged nationally, its opposite already existed and was developed to a certain extent as an answer to the BAM. In the sixties the literature of the capitulationists and the compradors was left in the dust by the roaring surge of what life itself was, and the struggle and unity of the BLM itself. The various capitulationists and compradors could only sit in the dust and bide their time (like the Southern Agrarians in the 1930's), occasionally pipsqueaking something supportive of the people's enemies. Rocky and the Fords began to toss around some bux, as they had in the early part of the twentieth century, when they saw a generation rise up to oppose Booker T.'s capitulationist and finally comprador philosophies. When DuBois and Trotter organized the Niagara Movement, Carnegie co-opted it with the NAACP, to urge system-stifled legal reform. It was the imperialist bourgeoisie consciously blocking struggle with treadmill reforms and turning potential strugglers into reform freaks rather than radicals, or into outright agents.

But the sixties upsurge drew many of the middle forces and even some "conservatives" into positive motion. Artists, even black ones, still predominantly come from the petite bourgeoisie. The intellectuals are, in the main, a sector of the petite bourgeoisie. The petite bourgeoisie ("middle class") is a vacillating flip-flopping class because that is where it is in capitalist society's production process— neither absolutely flattened (underfoot by the bourgeoisie) nor are they, despite the sickies who serve them and big-wish-it, the big B's themselves. The petite bourgeoisie attach themselves to one class or the other, either the rulers or the ruled. They either serve the people or serve the owners.

In the rebellion-1960's most of the black artists and intellectuals aligned themselves with the people, drawn by the revolutionary upsurge. Even a writer like Calvin Hernton, who is often identified with the "conservative" sector of Afro-American literature and with people like Ishmael Reed, in the sixties could write violently anti-imperialist essays like "Dynamite Growing out of Their Skulls" (*Black Fire*, William Morrow, 1969). Yes, the tide was so strong that even some of the conservatives wrote work that took the people's side. The metaphysical slide of the later BAM even allowed Reed to adopt a rebellious tone with his "Black Power Poem" and "Sermonette" (*Catechism of NeoAmerican Hoodoo Church*, Heritage Series, London, 1979), where he saw the struggle of blacks against national oppression as a struggle between two churches: "May the best church win. Shake hands now and come out conjuring."

But even then Reed, during the heat and heart of the BAM, would say things like calling that very upsurge itself and the BAM "a goon squad aesthetic" and that the revolutionary writers were "fascists," or that taking up African culture by black artists indicated such artists were "tribalists." (*Propaganda and Aesthetics*, Johnson and Johnson, p. 185).

The bourgeoisie opened Negro ensembles as defense against black arts and opened up assorted colored coolout canteens which would lessen the fire and divert the attack. They funded a Negro theater, a skin thing, so that what was hot and revolutionary would be overshadowed—an NAACP theater as opposed to a revolutionary nationalist theater. And even some of the folks who were associated with the BAM legitimately got caught up in a bogus "professionalism" which put Broadway *modus operandi* and a minute's worth of prosperity over the need of the black masses for revolution!

By the time the heat had cooled in the middle seventies (not because the source of the oppression or the resistance had disappeared, but only because of the very spontaneity of *any* mass people's movement unguided by a revolutionary party and a scientific ideology) the bourgeoisie had not only set up a whole series of counters to the heat of the BAM, but later on could even begin to dismiss and close down these counters because the heat was off for a minute! But there were still enough middle-class blacks who had gained from the sixties upsurge of the people, some with small gains, some outright bribed, so that there appeared to be a pimple of socio-economic "vertically" (to paraphrase Cabral in "The Weapon of Theory"), which could be continuously praised as the result of the reforms that the sixties had brought about. A Gibson in Newark now functions as a straight-out comprador, agent, of the imperialists, whose twofold task is to fake democracy, since he got into office in the rush of black motion for political rights, and at the same time carry out the grim bullshit white faces would cause immediate rebellions by doing.

This is also manifest in the arts, and for the same *political* reasons. The brief flurry of black publishing by the major bourgeois presses in the 1960's cooled right out once the fire cooled. Like the Harlem Renaissance (its exotic and commercial aspect created by the bourgeoisie, in contradistinction to the genuine emergence of an urban and national black intelligentsia in the 1920's) it was simply *turned off*. This writer must struggle intensely to get the large presses to publish anything, after they had blanked out for almost eight years between 1971 and 1978. Major magazines simply refuse to publish my work, and even pseudo-controversial sheets like *The Village Voice* try to edit and delay publishing my letters to the editor.

What is being done in the late seventies is to emphasize now the conservatives, capitulationists, and outright compradors who lurked around the edges of the sixties pipsqueaking opposition to the Black Liberation Movement's mass upsurge as reflected in the arts (just like they attack sixties-gained affirmative action with the Baake Decision!). People like Ishmael Reed and the rhythmless Michael Harper are at the one point of this. They also raise up new voices whose content is not advanced or is confused, like Michele Wallace (the former) and Ntozake Shange (the latter). What is so grim is that they can push this group and others under the rubric of *feminism*, and even distort the real questions. Question: What is the cause of women's oppression? Answer: Class society, and in this epoch, that means monopoly capitalism. Question: What will end it? Answer: Socialist revolution, which destroys the material base of women's oppression, i.e., no one can then make money off it, which is why it is around now, and thus the conditions will be set for eventually eradicating it. What is cool about the bourgeoisie is that they can push misinformation, division and confusion as *radicalism*, obscuring the real nature of problems and the real solution, which is revolution, but still get over pretending to deal with mass questions like women's oppression and black national oppression (in the sixties).

The bourgeoisie makes Ralph Ellison the patron saint of these folk for obvious reasons. They can always use individualism and need a model of the "kept" intellectual individualizing off the mass pain. Once Jimmy Baldwin came out with *Blues for Mr. Charlie*, which questioned nonviolence, he was finished with the *New York*

Times and *New York Review of Books* crowd, the bourgeoisie's intellectuals.

Another outpost of this late-seventies *odeur* is the Ivy structuralists, as I mentioned, who with publications like *Chant of Saints* (*Massachusetts Review*, ed. M. Harper and R. B. Stepto, Vol. XVIII, Nos. 3 and 4) want to distort Afro-American literary history and Mandrake up a tradition of elegant (?) copout as the heavy mainstream of A-A Lit! Their group runs from Ellison with his embarrassingly corny "story" "Backwacking" and his interview continuing to patronize Richard Wright, plus folks like James Allan McPherson, the recent Pulitzer Prize winner—a Constitutional Democrat who believes, so he said in an interview in *The Washington Post,* that all the bourgeoisie need do is implement the constitution, goddamit, implement the constitution!—Robert Hayden, who has always been disturbed by the loudness and blood of conflict, and Derek Walcott, whose play *Rememberance* will send the hair on the most back of your neck straight up as his hero mourns the passing of the white woman from his life and warns his son not to make the same mistake, as his backward black wife lolls around being West Indian in the background! Ellison and Stepto talk about the "black aesthetic crowd," though they are both comfortable enough apparently with the "white aesthetic" crowd. (Ellison quotes Burke, James, Hawthorne, who are among the most backward writers extant.)

The chains of critics like Stanley Crouch and Clifford Mason are rattled and they dance fantastically for a few pennies. Crouch in *The Village Voice* makes a specialty of rendering Afro-American art as primitive posturing for the general delectation of the "white aesthetic" crowd, who thought that all the time. Mason raises Joe Papp, Shange and Walcott's mentor, as the founder of a new black theater (*The New York Times Magazine,* July 22, 1979) to do Shakespeare with the darks—which Papp needs in order that he receive the government grants that used to be reserved for black folks, under the guise that he is the white officer for the charging black volunteers. Papp keeps folk like Bullins around as "in residence," and does most black and Latino plays as workshop presentations, but the big stuff, the regular productions, are reserved for the good-stuff white folks (you guessed it?)!

The "white aesthetic" is bourgeois art, like the "national interests" of the United States at this late date when the United States is an imperialist superpower. Ellison says that the "black aesthetic crowd" "buys the idea of total cultural separation between blacks and whites, suggesting that we've been left out of the mainstream. But when we examine American music and literature in terms of its themes, symbolism, rhythms, tonalities, idioms and images it is obvious that those reject 'Negroes' have been a vital part of the mainstream and were from the beginning." This is the NAACP's argument. We know we have been exploited, Mr. Ralph, sir, what we's arguing about is that we's been exploited! To *use* us is the term of our stay in this joint, but being left out of the mainstream means that Bird died scag, Jelly Roll had to play in a whorehouse, Duke played one-night stands till he died, the Beatles make millions and cite some blood running an elevator in Jackson.

In terms of separation, there *is* an Afro-American culture, impossible without the American experience, but it is a *specific* culture, used like the black people themselves, to make superprofits, mainly for the white bourgeoisie, but there are some blacks who do get some big-sized crumbs, chairs, grants, fame, etc., some of whom think they are actually in that mainstream, and some of whom actually are (in the sense that they will defend what this means and is, for their bribe). It is the question of this use, the exploitation, the oppression, that we take issue with, and from the first batch of slaves, have sworn to annihilate. We take issue with the comfortable commentator, used with his own permission, who seeks no connection with the mass pain except to get rich and famous off it.

In the *Massachusetts Review* interview Ellison defends the book *Time on the Cross*, which implied that, ahhh, slavery wasn' as bad as y'all say. And he even pipes up his own little mitigator (a constant tone from the backward sector of the black petite bourgeoisie) that it wasn't that bad, it's just you niggers that think so, you poor niggers, you working-class niggers, you dark niggers, you majority of niggers. When Ellison says (defending *Time on the Cross*) that "perhaps we have too damn much of a wound-worshipping investment in the notion that the slaves were brutalized beyond the point of exercising their human will to survive." And further, he says that the authors "held that the slaves were not reduced to a gas-oven state of docility, a view that would see each and every slavemaster as a Hitler and American slavery as a preview of the Holocaust." Wow, we'll analyze that, Bro. But even further Ellison says, "After all I did see my grandaddy and he was no beaten-down Sambo. Rather he was a courageous, ingenious old guy who *owned property* [my emphasis,

AB], engaged in Reconstruction politics of South Carolina and who stood up to a mob after they had lynched his best friend. . . . I also knew one of his friends who, after years of operating a printing business for a white man, came north and set up his own printing shop in Harlem."

Does this mean that everybody who did not own property or become a small politician was "a beaten-down Sambo"? Ishmael Reed and Stanley Crouch both make the same kind of rah-rah speeches for the black middle class. Reed, in fact, says that those of us who uphold black working people are backward (see *Shrovetide in Old New Orleans*, pp. 136–137), or, as he says, "The field nigger got all the play in the sixties." Focus on the middle class, the property owners, and music teachers, not the black masses, Ellison tells us. This is the *Roots* crowd giving us a history of the BLM as a rags-to-riches, Horatio Alger tale in brownface, going off into the sunset and straight for Carter's cabinet or the National Book Award. No, slavery was not as bad for house negroes, nor is national oppression as grim for the petite bourgeoisie, and especially not bad at all for the tiny bribed element among us. But for most of us it is hell, and we want it destroyed! We even want to use our poetry and song as yet another means to the destruction of this national oppression and its material base, monopoly capitalism. The bourgeoisie, and the intellectual sector that serves them, tell us we cannot—we say, Fuck You!

And, get to this, we do not think that slavery made black people "beaten-down Sambos." It is the "white aesthetic crowd" that thinks that. There has been resistance ever since there was oppression. Ellison and the capitulationist wing of Afro-American literature are the ones who try to reduce the methods by which we can oppose it, and they usually get paid well for opposing our resistance, albeit *aesthetically*! The slavemasters *were* our Hitlers. You think slavery is different in its essence from fascism? And even after slavery, after the destruction of the Reconstruction governments, fascism was resumed, with peonage, sharecropping, the black codes, segregation, discrimination, Jim Crow, lynching, etc. (Check out Wright's *Uncle Tom's Children*, which is a far more accurate and powerful version of black life in the South than Ellison has produced.)

Ellison's line repeatedly is, we are a part of this, we are a part of it and it ain't half bad! (Reed says, and I am not making this up, "Did you know that the woman who runs the computer controlling five or so missile carriers is black?" *Shrovetide*, p. 136.) This is the cry of the NAACP leadership.

Where I differ with the bourgeois nationalists who are identified with the "black aesthetic" is illuminated by a statement by Addison Gayle: "An aesthetic based upon economic and class determination is one which has minimal value for black people. For black writers and critics the starting point must be the proposition that the history of black people in America is the history of the struggle against racism" ("Blueprint for Black Criticism," *First World*, Jan./Feb. 1977, p. 43). But what is the basis for racism, i.e., exploitation because of one's physical characteristics? Does it drop out of the sky? Is it, as Welsing and others suggest, some metaphysical racial archetype, the same way the white racists claim that "black inferiority" is? Black people suffer from national oppression—we are an oppressed nation, a nation oppressed by United States imperialism. Racism is an even more demonic aspect of this national oppression, since the oppressed nationality is identifiable anywhere as that, *regardless* of their class. But we know even racism is mitigated, cooled out somewhat, if someone is living in a Chicago condominium, or in some exclusive suburb, than say it is for a black worker, or small farmer, or migrant worker, or unemployed worker.

The material base of racism, what allows it to exist as other than a "bad idea," is monopoly capitalism. Its material base before the Civil War was the slave system and developing capitalism. The destruction of monopoly capitalism will allow the conditions to exist in which we can begin to destroy racism and chauvinism, but no such conditions can ever exist under capitalism.

Our struggle against racism must be our struggle against national oppression, and the fundamental answer to that is the revolutionary struggle for self-determination! But against whom and what must that struggle be waged? Who and what now has the power to keep us powerless? We must see that ultimately it is monopoly capitalism, the private ownership of the land, mineral wealth, machines, factories, transportation, communication—the means of production—by a white-racist corporate class, itself comprising only six-tenths of one percent of the population, that must be destroyed if black people or the other people in this society are to be totally liberated!

I understand that Afro-American culture has absorbed all the elements it came in contact with, but it is still a specific entity in itself. It is particular, yet interrelated with the whole of American culture.

It is impossible without the overall U.S. culture, and likewise the overall culture, as it is, and has been for 300 years, is impossible without Afro-American culture. The "black aesthetic" is the form, content, style, history, psychological development, of a particular nationality, the Afro-American. There is, in the United States, however, an Afro-American nation, in the black-belt South, what Ellison mentioned Richard Wright as upholding at one point. A historically constituted, stable community of people based on a common language, land, economic life, and common psychological development manifest as a common culture. This is a paraphrase of Stalin's scientific definition of nation. The Afro-American nation is an oppressed nation, born in the South after the destruction of the Reconstruction governments by the resurgent planter class in the South, but paid for and made possible by the big bourgeoisie on Wall Street, who after the Civil War completely dominated United States politics and economy, controlled the ex-planters, and turned them into their compradors.

It is a complicated picture—a nation within a nation—whose landbase is the whole lower South, where even today fifty-two percent of the Afro-American people live, and where eight out of ten of us were born. (Get a Department of Commerce map and look at the concentration. Outside of the black belt we exist in significant numbers in only about twenty cities!) But the point is that our basic demand must always be self-determination for the Afro-American nation in the black belt, and equal rights—democratic rights for the black oppressed nationality wherever else they be!

We are not denying that we are linked together with the overall U.S. political state (up under it is more precise) and U.S. life in general, but black people want *self-determination,* not just to be told that everything in the U.S.A. bears their mark. We know that. We know we helped build it, *free.* But in order to get self-determination, there is a revolutionary process that must be followed, and a tiny minority of blacks living in kept elegance will not dissuade us from carrying this process out to the end.

I am focusing on Ellison's most recent interview because he is the godfather of the "antistruggle crowd" that the bourgeoisie has tried to re-prop up as Afro-American literature. Ellison says, in the same interview, "After all, given a decade of emphasis upon 'blackness' and 'militancy' how many writers of Wright's stature are there to conjure with." One of the basic weapons imperialism uses is absorption, to absorb sections of the oppressed, usually backward sections of the petite bourgeoisie and the right wing of the black bourgeoisie, so that they uphold the oppressor culture, and therefore the ideas of the oppressor, the central one of which is that the oppressed *need* to be oppressed! The cries of "blackness" were opposition to this absorption and agentry, at their most revolutionary. The metaphysics and narrowness of some of these cries (some of my own included) were lamentable, but the essence of them was resistance. (Shit, Ralph, Hawthorne was pro-slavery!)

Ellison says, "How many writers of Wright's stature are there to conjure with?" Well, let us begin with Frederick Douglass, William Wells Brown, David Walker, Henry Highland Garnet, W.E.B. DuBois, Langston Hughes, Claude McKay, Margaret Walker, Theodore Ward, to drop a few names. One task that confronts us is that we must go beyond the stale "histories" and anthological chauvinism, especially that the would-be educated blacks have been shaped by, and investigate Afro-American literature with a fresh eye, with an eye to discovering the hidden riches that are there. In an early and somewhat confused essay I wrote called "The Myth of a Negro Literature," I dismissed Afro-American literature because I was put off by the whited-out Negro literature that was merely a brown imitation of the dull parts of Euro-American literature. Because even white literature is distorted in this terrible capitalist land to hold up the conservatives, the backward, to trumpet the Henry Jameses and Hawthornes over the Melvilles and Mark Twains and Jack Londons and Theodore Dreisers and Mike Golds! And certainly in official U.S. literary history, they usually raise the most conservative, the backward, or so mix them with the progressives that the radical or revolutionary trend is obscured. And the blacks, Latinos, Native Americans, Asians, and women are in distorted minority if they are represented at all.

Recently, the bourgeoisie has been pushing Ishmael Reed very hard, and to see why let's look at his most recent book, *Shrovetide in Old New Orleans*. In essay after essay Reed stumps for individualism, and asserts ubiquitously that the leadership of black folks is the black middle class, rather than the working class, but it gets even further out than that. Reed actually resurrects the old whited-out "conservative" George Schuyler. The man who once wrote an essay (which Hughes blasted) called "The Negro Art Hokum," in which, of course, he asserted that there was no such thing. There's Irish literature, Spanish literature, Russian literature, French literature ... but no, no Afro-American literature or painting. Schuyler, the man who supported Portuguese colonialism, and agreed that the Portuguese were doing a civilizing job over in Africa. Schuyler, the man who makes even some of the straight-out agents of the NAACP leadership look rational. Dig this conversation between Reed and Schuyler:

"Reed: Why do you think the people who are more into the collectivist type of poetry and 'for the people' have a bigger reputation than those who are independent? [Obviously he was talking about the sixties—AB.]

"Schuyler: Because they've been played up and built up.

"Reed: Who builds them up?

"Schuyler: Well, people who are interested in building them up. It's a clique. Who would ever think of Malcolm X as a leader?

"Cannon: Really.

"Schuyler: Lead what?

"Cannon: Every time we talk about that, we get shouted down.

"Reed: You can't say that. He's a holiday now" (pp. 203–204).

This is straight-out agentry, and in certain circumstances could easily get these dudes iced. But this is the level of antiblack the straight-out agents of the oppressor run with. In the sixties obviously neither Reed nor Cannon would make such a statement. But in the recent climate of celebration of capitulation and upholding of the compradors, the real garbage in the brains of these traitors comes out. And this is what their aesthetic is built on.

Reed also upholds the feudal-capitalist dictatorship of "Baby Doc" Duvalier in Haiti, which he and a woman painter acquaintance describe as "clean poverty," unlike the rest of the Third World.

Like Nikki Giovanni, poet Michael Harper went to racist South Africa and even wrote a poem about it, so disconnected is he with the international black power struggle. (Reed says in *Shrovetide,* "'Black power' might have begun from talk circulating at cocktail parties in Paris in the 1940's. Brian Gysin wrote a book about it called *The Process.*" I would suggest this arsehole read C. H. Langston during the Negro Convention Movement of the 1840's and 50's. This is from the minutes of the Cleveland Negro Convention, 1854: "Man cannot be independent without *possessing* the land on which he resides." And further, "That under no circumstances, let the consequences be as they may, will we ever submit to enslavement, let the power that attempt it, emanate from whatever source it will.") But Harper, in his poem, seemed most to lament that the white supremacist South African authorities who arrested him momentarily did not differentiate him from the general run-of-the-mill blood in Azania-to-be.

Michele Wallace attacks the Black Liberation Movement with bourgeois feminism. Her fundamental problem is that she was not here and does not know. She has some genuine frustration and the issue of women's oppression is real, and for Third World women in this country there is triple oppression if they are working women, as workers under capitalism—class oppression, national oppression, and oppression because of their sex. But because Ms. Wallace does not have a scientific method of analysis she can be used by the bourgeois feminists at *Ms.* magazine, who just want to get in on the oppression, not to smash the system that fosters it, and she is also used by the bourgeoisie not only to suggest that there was nothing of value in the rebellion-sixties but also that bourgeois feminism can accurately sum up history, which it can't. She also drops the same chauvinist line on black women, while at it, suggesting that black women were too backward to struggle against the male chauvinism of myself and others in the BLM, some of whom even made a *doctrine* of it. But to say that "the riots, during the Black Movement days, were spontaneous and largely ineffective outbursts of rage that were directed inward and hurt the ghetto dweller most," or to see Malcolm X as merely "partiarchal black macho," or to say that the BLM was merely "a big Afro, a rifle, and a penis in good working order" is to take the side of our oppressors.

Shange deals in effects but not causes, in *Colored Girls*, which is only one-sideness and lack of information. But obviously if she raised the *cause* of women's oppression—class society and, in this epoch, monopoly capitalism–imperialism—no such a play would get on the Great White Way. They hurried up and bashed *Zoot Suit* because of its militancy, and even put the badmouth on the movie *Wiz*, cause it was much too hip. But Shange must go deeper into her material and get to the root causes of things in the real world, if she is truly to be honored by the masses in the long run. Removing parts of her plays offensive to white-racist critics and producers, as she did with the "anti–white woman" sequence in *Spell No. 7*, is a motion toward the ocean, as a drownee sponsored by Imp Productions, not toward communion with the people.

But have no fear, the fire is still bubbling and hot and ready to raise up another 'gin. Poets like Askia M. Toure, Jayne Cortez, are at the top of their number right now! I am sure Toure's "John Wayne Poem" helped that worthy "book." Jayne Cortez's *Mouth on Paper* is dynamite, connecting up as Mao indicated in the *Yenan Forum,* so that our works will be aesthetically powerful and politically revolutionary! That is the combination we seek, the dialectical matrix that includes both form and content. We cannot be one-sided, though it must be obvious that *content is principal*! *What* you are saying. We must learn to say that content which unifies the people, identifies the enemy, that content that is in itself a form of struggle and is an aspect of victory as it tells us about the need for unity, struggle, victory. We must shape the content so powerfully, so beautifully, that its message, like our struggle itself, like the people themselves, is invincible!

The endless acrobatic "avant-gardists" many times go through such rigamarole because they have *nothing* to say. Except that they have nothing to say. Some of the *concrete* boredom makers, various minuscule-content typewriter freaks, and even more generally the various *formalists,* for whom form is principal or form is everything, generally uphold bourgeois aesthetics. We get offered nothing, really, except subjectivism, elitism, solipsism—the world-erasing super "I" over everything. Bourgeois aesthetics are a reflection of bourgeois ideology or world view generally. A small class rules everything, benefits absolutely, while the rest of us go through horrible changes. So art is only for the sanctified few—who are so great because they are so hip because they are so sensitive—so sensitive, in fact, that they can bang out meaningless bullshit on typewriters while most of humanity is in pain.

Obviously we are not putting down legitimate scientific experiment. Scientific experiment plus the struggle for production and class struggle are the three fundamental struggles that push history forward, though ultimately the people are the makers of history! But we want higher levels of understanding from higher levels of communication. We want more information, more development—mass development—not less. And our scientific experiments should be so aimed.

Poets like Toure need new books. Their in-person work is very hot, like the music. Also, there are new poets about, like Pili (Michael L. Humphrey), whose new yet unpublished work *Black Blood*

Runs Red is a major contribution to the new wave of anti-imperialist poetry coming back clearly into view. Ditto, *Songs for the Masses* by Sylvia Jones, grounded in the black working class, and focused on revolution. These poets are carriers of the tradition of struggle of the BLM, though they will probably never be run up the flagpole of bourgeois celebration. They started talking bad about the capitalist hell too young, so the rulers and their colored and white henchpersons see them coming. So we must celebrate them and publish them, as we must shore up and put back into the field with 1,000 times more strength older, proven warrior poets and writers and artists, and rebuild a network of struggle-oriented art institutions—theater companies, magazines, mass organizations focused on arts and culture—because the more intense the struggle gets the less likely the bourgeoisie is to publish us. But we must always try to win those middle forces which are not opposed to art based on struggle.

Sonia Sanchez's new book *I Been a Woman* is a very solid, and a welcome event, because it demonstrates the genuinely strong and beautiful poetry poets like Sonia were making in the sixties and have continued to make, and it puts the lie to the brainwashed line that thinks that the poetry of the sixties was somehow "technically deficient." The masses dug it, I suppose, because they were backward? Also, we need new works from Lance Jeffers, David Henderson, Lorenzo Thomas, Larry Neal (whose play *The Glorious monster in the Bell of the Horn* is, I hope, an announcement that he is back on the scene), Welton Smith. Dig Marvin X's beautiful and moving "Palestine" (*Black Scholar*, Nov./Dec. 1978). For all his weird Cleaver-related preaching activities, Marvin X remains a dynamite poet. He needs a book.

The people we published in the anthology *Black Fire* are all due new works—Lindsay Barrett, James T. Stewart, Dingane (Joe Goncalves), Keorapsetse Kgositsile, and so many others, Reggie Lockett, Sam Anderson, Clarence Franklin, Clarence Reed (one of the most lyrical singers and one of the most unsung of the BAM!). Some of these have never even had a first book, yet they are beautiful and strong, and we must see that they get into print to help struggle against imperialism and its intellectual lackeys. Where is Yusef Rahman? Has Norman Jordan recovered? Poets like Gaston Neal have needed books for the last decade and Ahmed Alhamisi and Rudy Bee Graham. What about Bad Bobb Hamilton and Charles Patterson or Ronald Drayton or Carol Freeman? What is Julia Fields doing or

Jacques Wakefield? Yusef Iman's poetry is now at a much higher level, able to do so many more of the things that he could always do in person. And why no new poetry from Ted Wilson or Richard Thomas (who was focused on the working class even back in *BF*). Are Al Haynes and Jimmy Garrett still ready to get in print on the heavy side? And Charlie Cobb and Charlie Fuller and Joe White or Jay Wright? What's their new work look like?

We know that poets like Mari Evans are still producing good work, and Carolyn Rodgers, although she has gone heavy into the church, and the obscurity that promotes, is still capable of stunning poetry. She was one of the truly underpublicized doers of the sixties. The whole generation of fighting black artists did not disappear, were not assassinated or bought off. Most of us have not turned into Eldridge Cleaver or Nikki Giovanni (another South African traveler). June Jordan's work has gotten progressively stronger since the earliest volumes. Kalamu ya Salaam shows signs of broadening past our sixties narrowness; if he can only drag his man Haki Madhabuti a little further out in the open, it would help us all. Certainly Haki's works were among the most popular of the BAM works among the masses. Likewise *The Last Poets* (Kain, Luciano, Nelson)!

Younger poets like Sekou Sundiata and B.J. Ashanti are new forces tuned in the right direction. Aishah Rahman's play *Transcendental Blues* signaled she could write works of the necessary clarity. Let's hope Joe Papp don't do her too much damage in the meantime. Vertamae Grosvenor's poetry and prose will be a real surprise to some—she has some valuable insights on the black woman's struggle. Quincy Troupe has a couple strong poems in *Snake Bash*, the "Up Sun" and "Neruda." And of course Margaret Walker is very much with us, working away down in Jackson. Theodore Ward, another old master, remains in Chicago, until we can get ourselves together enough to produce his masterworks. James Baldwin's recent statements (in *The New York Times* and at San Diego State University) could be a portent of a new breakthrough, in the pattern of *The Fire Next Time* or *Blues for Mr. Charlie,* as opposed to the other less mass-oriented side of his works.

Nathan Heard's new prison novel will reveal a much more developed ideological stance. And there are strong playwrights like Oyamo, Ben Caldwell, Clay Goss, (Ron Milner's still doin' it), Martie Charles, Richard Wesley, Paul Carter Harrison. All this work is generally focused against black national oppression, to varying degrees depending on the consciousness and skill of the writers, but the resistance is there, and so is the art.

Henry Dumas is one name many of the capitulationists try to conjure with because his work is so highly stylized and myth-conscious, as if, because of these things, Dumas was a capitulationist. But Dumas's works generally, and in the main openly, opposed national oppression. Great works like *Fon* and *Will the Circle Remain Unbroken* are not only beautiful, but *fighting* works aimed squarely into the sour hearts of our enemies. Dumas's book of poetry was called *Poetry for My People*. Toni Morrison is also hooked up with these capitulationists, they try to mislead us into believing, but *Sula* and especially *The Bluest Eye* give the lie to such b.s.

It is obvious that the bourgeoisie will push antistruggle art over art based on and focused on the need of the struggle. But straight-out racism will trim even a few of those antistruggle people out of the select few and may even make their jaws tight enough to understand that the entire system must be destroyed, and that being kept literary whatnots under the bell jar of some capitulationist aesthetic will only make them enemies of the majority (not only of blacks but of everybody else). In the early seventies, to try to turn the tide of the BAM around, the bourgeoisie pushed projects like the Negro Ensemble Company and even gave out its big prizes, theretofore reserved strictly for white folks, to its select because of its content; that way the bourgeoisie could say, "Hey y'all, later for that black stuff, here's what we want." And saying thus, gave a Pulitzer Prize in drama to Flash Gordone, who has trouble even writing a recognizable play much less one of any merit. But because Gordone would openly kill off black militancy once a night on the stage, and come out in drag to drag us back to outright gay minstrelsy, he could cop.

In the sixties Clifford Mason had to hide his capitulationist rap under the cover of a play about Gabriel Prosser, militant cover but capitulationist essence. In the recent seventies he can come out and openly proclaim from the pages of *The New York Times* that Joe Papp and Shakespeare are *the* new black theater. In the sixties we spoke up loud and clear about the need for independent black institutions of every imaginable kind, a clear thrust for self-determination and democracy. In the seventies people flock around Joe Papp, the downtown New York Lincoln Center, or do the Broadway minstrelsy, or don't work too regularly. And the Black Theater Alliance squashes criticism of Lincoln Center for not appointing any black director in its new junta of directors, in exchange for $300,000 or $400,000 to put on a "Black theater festival" that was patently and openly antistruggle.

The late seventies, the bourgeoisie has tried to turn into open sellout time. Economism is trying to rule the airwaves. Militant poets of the sixties show up really funny-ha-ha in the seventies. Flip and cute and slightly dadaistic, all for the bux and to pump up the careers. Or they are just "influenced" by this trend instead of the militant one. This has affected not only black artists but every other kind of artist as well. Strong poets like Pedro Pietri and Jose Angel Figueroa for instance (see *Puerto Rican Obituary* and *East 110th Street*) wrote hot books aimed dead at setting imperialism's ass ablaze. But their recent works give the imps more slack by not being as focused on it. However, Miguel Algarin's translation of Neruda's *Song of Protest* is dynamite, and Louis Reyes Rivera is really someone to watch, ditto Raul Santiago, Sandra Esteves, Amina Munoz, Tato Laviera, Miguel Loparena, and Lucky Cienfuegos. Miguel Pinero, who is one of the most impressive of the Latin writers, is in Hollywood, so we must wait to see how this affects his work, though one *Baretta* story, in which he also played a lead, was *no bueno*.

We could go on and on, but the main line is that class struggle is as much a part of the arts as it is in anything else. (And criticism especially, as Mao instructed us in *Yenan Forum*, is one place where open class struggle always rages.) The struggle-oriented artists, the artists who consciously or in practice see their works as "for the people," as weapons to help in transforming society, must regroup, and given the bloody experiences of the sixties and early seventies raise the level of struggle even higher. We must try to get even clearer on the meaning of class stand, attitude, audience, and study, and their relationship to our work. What is our class stand, i.e., whose side are we on? What is our attitude to various things (from one's attitude—whether we condemn a thing or praise it—can be told what our class stand is)? Despite middle-class vacillation, one *cannot* be in the middle. Whether we say it or not, our practice, our acts, objectively place us on one side or the other.

Who is our audience, for whom do we write? That is the key. Whom do we want to reach or impress? Are we educating or titillating? Audience is one large shaper of content, and content is principal. Finally, what is it we are saying?

Study, also, is a shaper of content. What we study and what we do shows very clearly in our work. We must study society carefully and with passionate interest, and study history. As Mao said, we must study "the various classes in society, their mutual relations and respective conditions, their physiognomy and their psychology." But we must represent the working class, even as members of an oppressed nationality; ninety-six percent of the Afro-American people are members of the working class. And they are the most advanced force of the nation. We are members of an oppressed nationality representing not only the working class of that nationality but also the whole multinational working class. Because at the same time we struggle for an alliance of the multinational working class and the black nation, for the alliance of the multinational working class and all of the oppressed nationalities, because their mutual freedom can only be gained by the destruction of monopoly capitalism—the same enemy!

Our art—literature—must embody this. It must be as hot as fire and as relentless as history. People always say, "Well, what's Baraka doing now? He keep on changing." I am a Marxist-Leninist, because that is the most scientific approach to making revolution. But for a long time most of y'all knew I wanted to be a revolutionary—I'm still committed to that. Most of us, regardless of what we call ourselves, are still committed to change, complete social change. We just got to get back on it!

5057